Listen and Sing

Listen and Sing

Lessons in
Ear-Training
and Sight-Singing

David Damschroder

The University of Minnesota

SCHIRMER BOOKS
Simon & Schuster Macmillan
New York

Prentice Hall International
London   Mexico City   New Delhi   Singapore   Sydney   Toronto

Schirmer Books
Simon & Schuster Macmillan
866 Third Avenue
New York, NY 10022

Library of Congress Catalog Card Number: 94-17168

Printed in the United States of America

printing number
1   2   3   4   5   6   7   8   9   10
Library of Congress Cataloging-in-Publication Data

Library of Congress Cataloging-in-Publication Data
Damschroder, David.
    Listen and sing : lessons in ear-training and sight-singing / David Damschroder.
        p.   cm.
    Includes index.
    1. Ear-training.   2. Sight-singing.   I. Title.
    MT35.D165   1995
    781.4'2—dc20   94-17168
                                                                        CIP
                                                                        MN

The paper used in this publication meets the minimum requirements of American National Standard for Information Sciences—Permanence of Paper for Printed Library Materials. ANSI Z39.48-1984. ∞™

Contents

Contents

Contents

Preface

Listen and Sing is designed for a course that is often called "Ear-Training and Sight-Singing." "Ear-Training" (learning to *Listen*) does not affect your ears. It focuses on your mind—on your capacity to process and make sense of the various sounds that enter your brain through your ears. "Sight-Singing" (learning to *Sing*) requires considerable practice. It focuses on strategies that develop your ability to read music notation accurately and with insight. These skills will enhance your enjoyment of music and your success in performing it.

The text has been designed to give your instructor considerable freedom in the choice of analytical notation and solmization (words for singing). Because instructors have strong opinions on these matters, I have made the text as ecumenical as possible. Your instructor will choose the analytical and solmization systems that you should use. To avoid confusion, do not read the instructions for the other systems.

A Cassette Program accompanies the text. You can practice in a dorm room, in a practice room, even outdoors at any hour of the day. I encourage you to use the cassettes in a private setting that permits you to respond by singing or by playing the piano or another instrument.

Listen and Sing is designed to coordinate with the tonal portion of an undergraduate music theory program. The arrangement of materials follows as closely as possible that of standard textbooks on tonal music theory. Although each chapter includes a summary of new concepts, analytical symbols, and music notation, I assume that you will also study these topics in a music theory course. Upon completing this text, you will be ready to proceed to a course on twentieth-century listening and singing strategies, for which other textbooks are available.

Listen and Sing

Chapter 1

PITCH

The **major triad** pervades Western music. You hear major triads whenever you listen to tonal music. You can learn to distinguish between major triads and other sounds through practice. Compare, for example, C-E-G (Ex. 1–1) and B-D-F. C-E-G, a major triad, is stable and harmonious. A composition could end with these pitches. B-D-F, in contrast, is unstable and would never be used at the end of a composition.[1]

EXAMPLE 1–1

Major third   G (Fifth)   Perfect fifth
E (Third)
C (Root)

A major triad contains three pitches, named **root**, **third**, and **fifth**. As Example 1–1 shows, the interval formed by the root and third of a major triad is a **major third**. That formed by the root and fifth is a **perfect fifth**. This chapter focuses on the **tonic** triad C-E-G in the **key of C major**.

Using the **treble clef**, the tonic triad in C major will usually appear in one of the two ranges shown in Example 1–2. These ranges may or may not coincide with your vocal range. If, for example, you are asked to **arpeggiate** the pitches of these triads (i.e., to sing in succession the root, then the third, and then the fifth), you may have no choice but to sing *both* triads starting on middle C or, especially men, to sing starting on the C below middle C. Throughout this text, perform all vocal exercises in a range appropriate for your voice. When completing dictation exercises, however, write the exact pitches that you hear.

EXAMPLE 1–2

---

1. Explore the differences between these triads by comparing at the keyboard the number of keys (both white and black) that come between C and E to the number of keys that come between B and D. Likewise, compare C-G to B-F. Then examine the triad A-C-E. Is it constructed like C-E-G? Like B-D-F? Or is it an example of yet another quality of triad?

The three pitches of a major triad form three ascending intervals and three descending intervals, shown in Example 1–3a. Example 1–3b shows how each interval can be filled in by one or more **passing notes**. **Scale degree** numbers $\hat{1}$, $\hat{2}$, $\hat{3}$, $\hat{4}$, and $\hat{5}$ are displayed above the pitches.

EXAMPLE 1–3

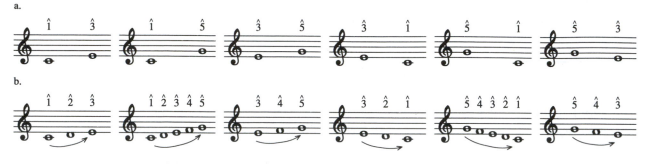

Keep the pitch C constantly in mind when singing these melodic progressions. For example, in singing E-G the mental reinforcement of C will prevent you from singing G♯ by mistake, as demonstrated in Example 1–4.

EXAMPLE 1–4

METER AND RHYTHM

In $\frac{4}{4}$ **meter**, also called **common time**, each measure contains four beats. Either "$\frac{4}{4}$" or the symbol " **C** " will appear to the right of the clef to indicate this meter. Three note values are employed in chapter 1: the **quarter note** (♩), which fills one beat; the **half note** (♪), which fills two beats; and the **whole note** (o), which fills four beats. To promote accurate performance and to prepare a framework for the more complicated rhythms of later chapters, practice by counting the four beats of each measure out loud, as shown in Example 1–5.

EXAMPLE 1–5

SOLO MELODIES

Note on Performance: *Singing melodies to develop one's internal ear is part of a tradition that goes back many centuries. Music teachers over the ages have devised various strategies to help students get the most out of their practice efforts. The choice of* **solmization** *system (i.e., the syllables that you pronounce while singing the pitches) influences how you think about the pitches of a melody. Several different solmization systems are common in colleges and conservatories today, and your instructor probably has a specific preference, which you should follow. Although this text provides instructions for all common solmization methods, you should read only those instructions that deal with the particular method you will employ in your coursework.*

The pedagogical differences among solmization systems will not be apparent in this chapter because these differences relate to the diversity of keys, the contrast between major and minor modes, the treatment of accidentals, and tonicization. As these concepts are introduced, you will learn how your solmization system responds to them. Follow the appropriate set of instructions and your instructor's guidance for the melodies of this and future chapters.

The instructions below provide enough information to sing the melodies of this chapter. A more comprehensive display of each solmization system appears in the appendix on p. 653.

SCALE DEGREES: *Sing the scale degree numbers $\hat{1}$, $\hat{2}$, $\hat{3}$, $\hat{4}$, and $\hat{5}$ for the pitches C, D, E, F, and G in C major. In this system, the relationship of each pitch to tonic ($\hat{1}$) is emphasized.*

MOVABLE DO: *Sing the syllables "do" for C, "re" for D, "mi" for E, "fa" for F, and "sol" for G in C major. In this system, the relationship of each pitch to tonic (sung as "do" in all major keys) is emphasized.*

FIXED DO: *Sing the syllables "do" for C, "re" for D, "mi" for E, "fa" for F, and "sol" for G. To speakers of Romance languages such as French and Italian, these syllables are their names for the corresponding pitches. A French musician might say that a symphony in C major is in "do majeur," while an Italian would say that it is in "do maggiore."*

LETTER NAMES: *Sing each pitch's letter name as its solmization syllable. In the absence of accidentals, this method is very straightforward for English-speaking musicians.*

SAMPLE SOLMIZATION

SCALE DEGREES:	$\hat{1}$	$\hat{2}$	$\hat{3}$	$\hat{4}$	$\hat{5}$	$\hat{3}$	$\hat{1}$
MOVABLE DO:	do	re	mi	fa	sol	mi	do
FIXED DO:	do	re	mi	fa	sol	mi	do
LETTER NAMES:	C	D	E	F	G	E	C

MELODIES STARTING ON 1̂

S1–1.

- Perform a C at the piano before you sing the melody. Use middle C if you intend to perform the melody as written, or the C below middle C if your vocal range requires that you sing the melody an octave lower.

- Even though this melody emphasizes stepwise motion, you should think beyond the individual steps and focus on what they combine to form: ascending thirds (C-E in measure 1, E-G in measure 2) and a descending fifth (G-C in measures 3 and 4). By keeping the pitches C, E, and G in mind (if necessary by performing all three pitches instead of only the starting pitch, C, at the piano before you begin), you will have less difficulty performing the passing notes and sensing how they connect the triadic pitches.

S1–2.

S1–3.

- The E that begins measure 6 recurs in measure 7. Think of the melody in multiple dimensions: while at one level there is a motion from E to C in measure 6, at another level the E is retained for continuation in measure 7. You will not have to think about ascending a third from C to E at the beginning of measure 7 if you retain the preceding E in your memory.

S1–4.

MELODIES STARTING ON 3̂

S1–5.

- When a melody starts on a pitch other than tonic, it is especially important that you hear the tonic pitch internally. Perform an E at the piano, then imagine C internally. (Sing C out loud at first if necessary.) Only when you know where you are heading in measure 2 can you begin measure 1 with confidence.

S1–6.

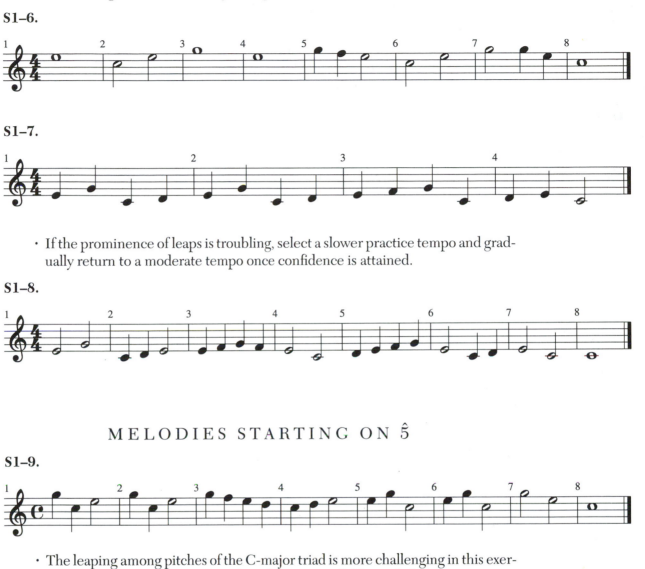

S1–7.

- If the prominence of leaps is troubling, select a slower practice tempo and gradually return to a moderate tempo once confidence is attained.

S1–8.

MELODIES STARTING ON $\hat{5}$

S1–9.

- The leaping among pitches of the C-major triad is more challenging in this exercise than in earlier ones. Allow the solmization syllables to help you. For example, if you are using Scale Degree numbers, every time you pronounce the word "three" you sing the same pitch (E). Or, if you are using Movable Do or Fixed Do, every time you pronounce the word "mi" you sing the same pitch.

- As a practice strategy, try singing only the pitches found on beats 1 and 3 of each measure. When security is attained, add the remaining pitches.

S1–10.

S1–11.

> • The rhythm establishes four two-measure groupings. In each of the first three groupings, the melody starts on G and ends on E. Practice each two-measure grouping separately, noting the similarities and differences among them.

S1–12.

DUETS

Note on Performance: *The relationship between the two parts should be maintained in all Duets. For example, a woman might sing the upper voice as written and a man the lower voice down an octave. But a man should not sing the upper voice down an octave while a woman sings the lower voice as written.*

D1–1.

D1–2.

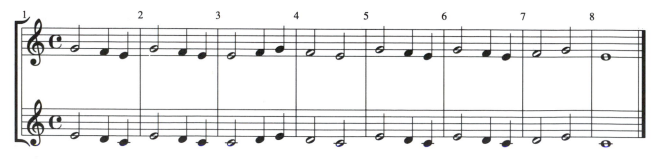

D1–3.

ACCOMPANIED SOLO MELODIES

Note on Performance: *If you lower the vocal line (always the upper line) one or two octaves to coincide with your vocal range, also lower the accompanying line by the same amount.*

AS1–1.

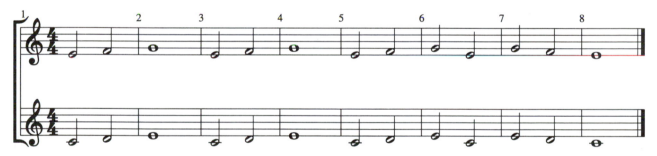

AS1–2.

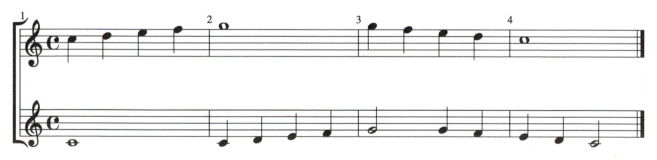

AS1–3.

RHYTHMS

Note on Performance: *As a practice strategy, count out loud when performing Rhythms. The solo rhythms (Exercises 1 through 3) may be clapped, sung, or played at a keyboard. You might want to position the numbers 1 through 4 underneath each measure, as demonstrated in Exercise 1. Rhythmic duets (Exercises 4 through 6) can be performed by two performers or groups of performers, or by a single performer using one finger of each hand at a keyboard. When practicing away from a keyboard, tap one part using a pencil and the other part using your palm.*

R1–1.

R1–2.

R1–3.

R1–4.

R1–5.

R1–6.

___

INTERVAL WORKSHOP

I1–1.   Play the lowest C in your vocal range at a keyboard. Sing it. Then sing E, a major third higher. Play E at the keyboard and confirm that it matches what you sang. Then sing ascending thirds starting on other pitches.

I1–2.   Play the lowest C in your vocal range at a keyboard. Sing it. Then sing G, a perfect fifth higher. Play G at the keyboard and confirm that it matches what you sang. Then sing ascending fifths starting on other pitches.

I1–3.   Play the highest E in your vocal range at a keyboard. Sing it. Then sing C, a major third lower. Play C at the keyboard and confirm that it matches what you sang. Then sing descending thirds starting on other pitches.

I1–4.   Play the highest G in your vocal range at a keyboard. Sing it. Then sing C, a perfect fifth lower. Play C at the keyboard and confirm that it matches what you sang. Then sing descending fifths starting on other pitches.

___

ARPEGGIATION WORKSHOP

A1–1.   Play the lowest C in your vocal range at a keyboard. Let this C be $\hat{1}$. Sing each of the following arpeggiations of the C-major triad, either in the order given or in random order. Whenever necessary, use the keyboard to confirm that you have sung the correct pitches.

    Note on Performance: *Sing the given numbers as your solmization syllables in all Arpeggiation Workshop exercises.*

a.	$\hat{1}$	$\hat{3}$	$\hat{1}$	$\hat{5}$		j.	$\hat{3}$	$\hat{5}$	$\hat{1}$	$\hat{3}$
b.	$\hat{1}$	$\hat{3}$	$\hat{5}$	$\hat{1}$		k.	$\hat{3}$	$\hat{5}$	$\hat{1}$	$\hat{5}$
c.	$\hat{1}$	$\hat{3}$	$\hat{5}$	$\hat{3}$		l.	$\hat{3}$	$\hat{5}$	$\hat{3}$	$\hat{1}$
d.	$\hat{1}$	$\hat{5}$	$\hat{1}$	$\hat{3}$		m.	$\hat{5}$	$\hat{1}$	$\hat{3}$	$\hat{1}$
e.	$\hat{1}$	$\hat{5}$	$\hat{3}$	$\hat{1}$		n.	$\hat{5}$	$\hat{1}$	$\hat{3}$	$\hat{5}$
f.	$\hat{1}$	$\hat{5}$	$\hat{3}$	$\hat{5}$		o.	$\hat{5}$	$\hat{1}$	$\hat{5}$	$\hat{3}$
g.	$\hat{3}$	$\hat{1}$	$\hat{3}$	$\hat{5}$		p.	$\hat{5}$	$\hat{3}$	$\hat{1}$	$\hat{3}$
h.	$\hat{3}$	$\hat{1}$	$\hat{5}$	$\hat{1}$		q.	$\hat{5}$	$\hat{3}$	$\hat{1}$	$\hat{5}$
i.	$\hat{3}$	$\hat{1}$	$\hat{5}$	$\hat{3}$		r.	$\hat{5}$	$\hat{3}$	$\hat{5}$	$\hat{1}$

A1–2.   Play the lowest C in your vocal range at a keyboard. Let this C be $\hat{1}$. Sing each of the following arpeggiations of the C major triad, either in the order given or in random order. The asterisks indicate the borders among versions of the basic arpeggiation shape. Whenever necessary, use the keyboard to confirm that you have sung the correct pitches.

Note on Performance: *Hold each pitch for one to two seconds. The asterisks have no time value. For example, you might perform Exercise 2.a. as follows:*

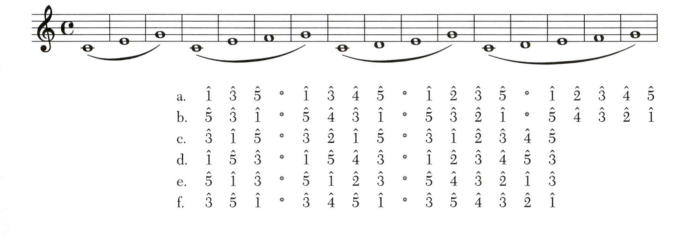

a.	$\hat{1}$	$\hat{3}$	$\hat{5}$	*	$\hat{1}$	$\hat{3}$	$\hat{4}$	$\hat{5}$	*	$\hat{1}$	$\hat{2}$	$\hat{3}$	$\hat{5}$	*	$\hat{1}$	$\hat{2}$	$\hat{3}$	$\hat{4}$	$\hat{5}$
b.	$\hat{5}$	$\hat{3}$	$\hat{1}$	*	$\hat{5}$	$\hat{4}$	$\hat{3}$	$\hat{1}$	*	$\hat{5}$	$\hat{3}$	$\hat{2}$	$\hat{1}$	*	$\hat{5}$	$\hat{4}$	$\hat{3}$	$\hat{2}$	$\hat{1}$
c.	$\hat{3}$	$\hat{1}$	$\hat{5}$	*	$\hat{3}$	$\hat{2}$	$\hat{1}$	$\hat{5}$	*	$\hat{3}$	$\hat{1}$	$\hat{2}$	$\hat{3}$	$\hat{4}$	$\hat{5}$
d.	$\hat{1}$	$\hat{5}$	$\hat{3}$	*	$\hat{1}$	$\hat{5}$	$\hat{4}$	$\hat{3}$	*	$\hat{1}$	$\hat{2}$	$\hat{3}$	$\hat{4}$	$\hat{5}$	$\hat{3}$
e.	$\hat{5}$	$\hat{1}$	$\hat{3}$	*	$\hat{5}$	$\hat{1}$	$\hat{2}$	$\hat{3}$	*	$\hat{5}$	$\hat{4}$	$\hat{3}$	$\hat{2}$	$\hat{1}$	$\hat{3}$
f.	$\hat{3}$	$\hat{5}$	$\hat{1}$	*	$\hat{3}$	$\hat{4}$	$\hat{5}$	$\hat{1}$	*	$\hat{3}$	$\hat{5}$	$\hat{4}$	$\hat{3}$	$\hat{2}$	$\hat{1}$

QUICK SWITCH

Note on Performance: *Repeat the contents of a single box within each group of four boxes (starting with the upper left box) until instructed to move to another box. Your instructor will use the words "Right," "Left," "Down," and "Up" to shift boxes. Also practice these exercises on your own, shifting boxes only when you have attained security within a given box. Sing Exercises 1 through 3; clap Exercise 4.*

Q1–1.

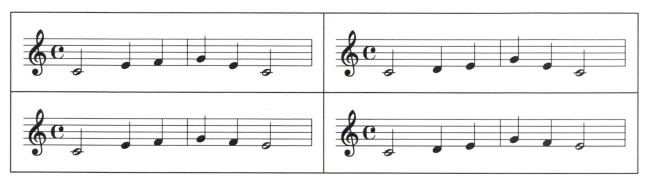

Q1–2.

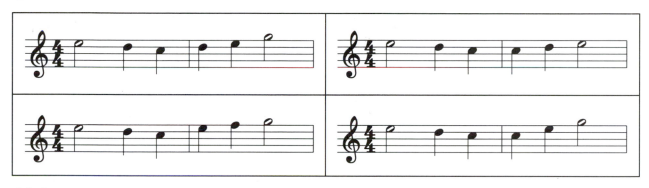

Q1–3.

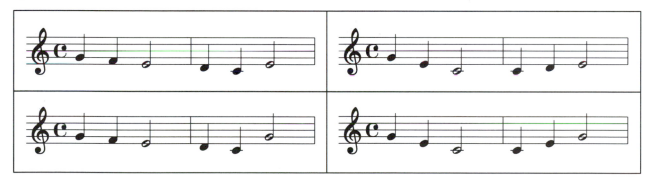

Q1–4.

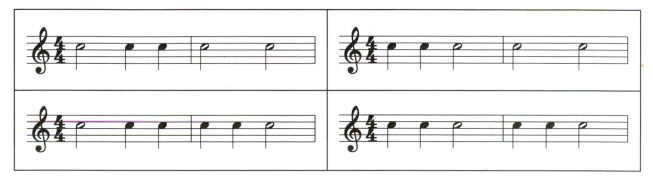

IDENTIFICATIONS

ID1–1.   A triad is performed. Is it a major triad?
Sample triads for performance:

ID1–2.   A melody is performed. Identify the correct score notation.

ID1–3. A C-major triad is performed. Then two of its three pitches are performed melodically: root-third, root-fifth, third-root, third-fifth, fifth-root, or fifth-third. Identify which of these choices is performed.

ID1–4. An interval is performed melodically, either ascending or descending. Identify it as a major third, a perfect fifth, or neither.

RHYTHMIC DICTATIONS

Instruction: A rhythm will be performed several times. Write down the rhythm that you hear. The first note is provided.

RD1–1.

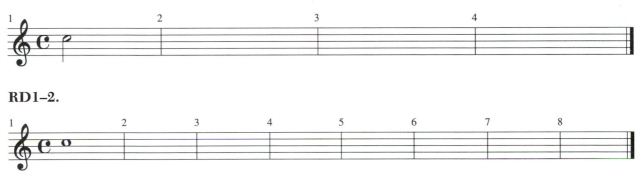

RD1–2.

MELODIC DICTATIONS

Instruction: A melody will be performed several times. Write down the melody that you hear. The first note is provided.

MD1–1.

- Because the collection of possible pitches is restricted to C, D, E, F, and G in this chapter, you may concentrate your listening on two considerations: the contrast between stepwise motion and leaps (thirds or a fifth); and whether a pitch is part of the C-major triad or connects pitches that are. In this melody, assess how many pitches are involved in the ascent to the summit versus how many are involved in the return to $\hat{1}$.

MD1–2.

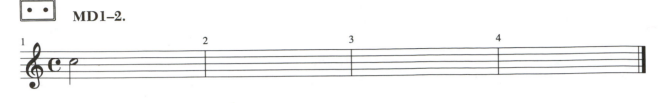

- C serves as a springboard for ascents in the first two measures. Compare the pitch on beat 3 of measure 1 to that on beat 3 of measure 2. Which is higher? Are both pitches members of the C-major triad?

MD1–3.

- How would you describe the relationship between measures 1 through 4 and measures 5 through 8 in this melody? Which group of measures *increases* the tension? Which group of measures *releases* that tension?

MD1–4.

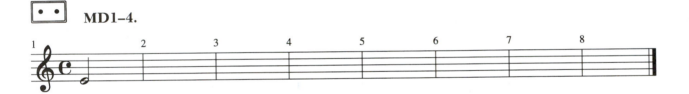

- Often an eight-measure melody will divide into two groups of four measures. Composers sometimes use variation techniques to unify these two halves. For example, compare measures 1 and 5. Though not identical, they share the same contour. The passage from measure 2 through measure 4 involves an increase of tension as the melody ascends. Observe how measures 6 through 8 follow this model until the end, when the stability of $\hat{1}$ substitutes for the upward surge to $\hat{5}$.

MD1–5.

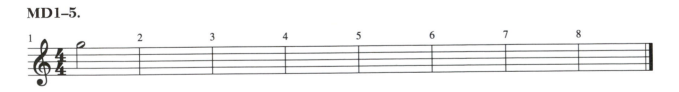

- Consider how measures 3 and 4 relate to measures 1 and 2. Also, how does measure 7 relate to measure 6?

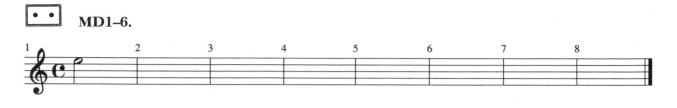

MD1–6.

- Each of the first three measures involves the space between E and G. How does measure 3 differ from measures 1 and 2? How is the strategy of measures 1 through 3 modified in measures 5 through 7?

CASSETTE PROGRAM (TAPE 1, SIDE A)

C1–1.   Twelve melodies are performed, twice each. During the silence after each playing, respond in one of the following ways: (1) Sing the melody, using solmization syllables; (2) Play the melody on the piano; (3) Play the melody on your primary instrument; (4) Write the melody on staff paper.

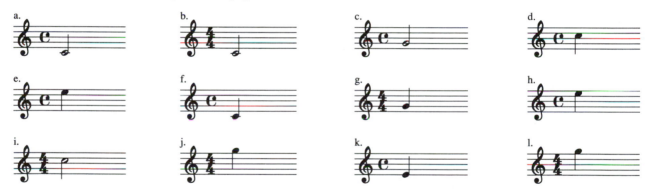

Chapter 2

PITCH

Few interesting melodies could be written within the limited span of the major triad's perfect fifth. More intervals become available as the range increases. For example, when a melody surges upward beyond the triad's fifth to the octave, as shown in Example 2–1, the interval of a fourth is outlined. To reach C in measure 3, two consecutive passing notes (A and B) are employed. When singing this melody, project the instability of the A and B leading to stability as C arrives.

EXAMPLE 2–1

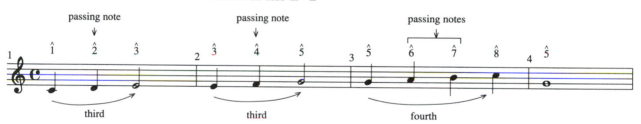

Tonic is prolonged throughout these four measures. The rhythmic placement of the pitches and the leap from C to G emphasize C, E, and G while subordinating D, F, A, and B. This hierarchy is upset in the revised melody shown in Example 2–2.

EXAMPLE 2–2

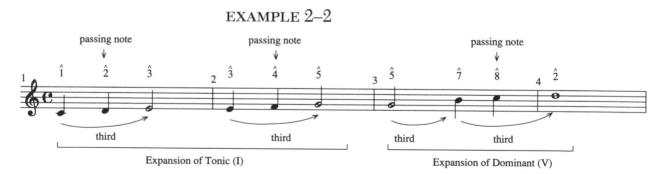

The G–B leap in measure 3 conflicts with the tonic prolongation of measures 1 and 2. B is no longer a passing note; C now *is* a passing note. The melodic outline of G, B, and D prolongs the **dominant** triad.

This melody demonstrates a fundamental principle: *A pitch may fulfill several different functions within a key.* Analysis of the musical context reveals which function applies. In Example 2–2, D is an unstable passing note in measure 1 but attains stability as the fifth of the dominant triad in measure 4. G is the fifth of the tonic triad in measure 2, but when repeated in measure 3 it becomes the root of the dominant triad.[1]

Example 2–1 is static. Tonic controls all four measures. Example 2–2 is active. After two measures of tonic, the dominant takes charge. Examples 2–3a and 2–3b display these analytical observations using **Roman numerals** as shorthand for "tonic" and "dominant." (Each numeral specifies which scale degree serves as root.) Such analyses are useful guides for your internal ear when you sing melodies.

EXAMPLE 2–3

a. Analysis of Example 2-1   b. Analysis of Example 2-2

The dominant (V) is tonic's most important partner in harmonic progression. Its root may be positioned either a fifth higher than that of I (as in Ex. 2–2) or a fourth lower (as in Ex. 2–4). A descending fourth (C *down* to G) is the **inversion** of an ascending fifth (C *up* to G).

EXAMPLE 2–4

Just as the pitch G fulfills a variety of roles within the key of C major, the G-major triad fulfills a variety of roles within the tonal system. It may serve as V in the key of C major. It may also serve as I in the **key of G major**. The tonic and dominant triads in C major and G major are shown in Example 2–5. G major's **key signature** (one sharp, F♯) is employed.

EXAMPLE 2–5

C MAJOR   G MAJOR

_____

1. The new role for G might not be understood by a *listener* until the remaining pitches of measures 3 and 4 have been performed. As a *performer* you should look ahead to know that these two measures prolong the dominant in much the same way that measures 1 and 2 prolong tonic.

In the **key of F major**, one flat (B♭) appears in the key signature. Observe in Example 2–6 that I in C major is identical to V in F major.

EXAMPLE 2–6

METER AND RHYTHM

$^2_4$ **meter** and $^3_4$ **meter** are similar to $^4_4$ meter, but contain two and three beats per measure, respectively. A sample of each meter, with appropriate counting syllables, is shown in Example 2–7. Example 2–7b makes use of the **dotted half note** (𝅗𝅥.), which fills three beats.

EXAMPLE 2–7

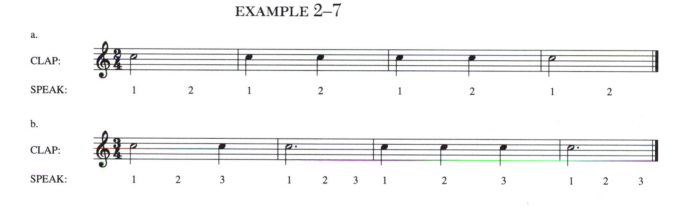

SOLO MELODIES

SCALE DEGREES: *The scale degree numbers* $\hat{1}$, $\hat{2}$, $\hat{3}$, $\hat{4}$, $\hat{5}$, $\hat{6}$, $\hat{7}$, *and* $\hat{8}$ *correspond to the pitches C, D, E, F, G, A, B, and C of C major. Sing "sev" in place of the awkward two-syllable "seven."*

$\hat{1}$ *corresponds to tonic regardless of the key. In F major, F is* $\hat{1}$, *G is* $\hat{2}$, *and so on. In G major, G is* $\hat{1}$.

The B♭ of F major is $\hat{4}$; *the F♯ of G major is* $\hat{7}$. *Because these pitches are diatonic (i.e., the flat and sharp appear within the key signatures rather than as insertions within the melody), no modification of the solmization syllables is warranted.*

In melodies that span more than an octave, you may choose to call the tonic pitch $\hat{1}$ *or* $\hat{8}$. *Numbers higher than* $\hat{8}$ *are not employed. (See the sample solmization below.)*

MOVABLE DO: *To the syllables "do," "re," "mi," "fa," and "sol," add "la" for A and "ti" for B in the key of C major.*

"Do" corresponds to tonic regardless of the key. In F major, F is "do," G is "re," and so on. In G major, G is "do."

The B♭ of F major is "fa"; the F♯ of G major is "ti." Because these pitches are <u>diatonic</u> (i.e., the flat and sharp appear within the key signatures rather than as insertions within the melody), no modification of the solmization syllables is warranted.

FIXED DO: *Sing "la" for A and "ti" for B. "Do" corresponds to C regardless of the key. In the sample solmization below, the syllable for F♯ has been* **inflected** *to acknowledge the sharp (from the key signature): because "fa" corresponds to F, "fi" is used for F♯. Similarly, because "ti" corresponds to B, "te" is used for B♭. Your instructor will indicate whether you should use these inflected syllables or instead use* **uninflected** *"fa" for any F and "ti" for any B, regardless of any accidental that may apply.*

LETTER NAMES: *Sing "C," "D," "E," "F," "G," "A," or "B" for pitches not modified by accidentals. If your instructor prefers* **inflected** *syllables to acknowledge accidentals (from the key signatures of G major and F major), sing "Fis" for F♯ and "Bes" for B♭. If your instructor prefers* **uninflected** *syllables, use "F" for both F and F♯ and "B" for both B and B♭.*[2]

SAMPLE SOLMIZATION

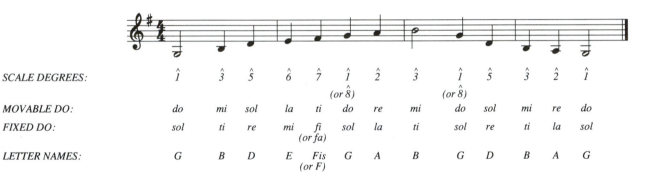

SCALE DEGREES:	1̂	3̂	5̂	6̂	7̂	1̂ (or 8̂)	2̂	3̂	1̂ (or 8̂)	5̂	3̂	2̂	1̂
MOVABLE DO:	do	mi	sol	la	ti	do	re	mi	do	sol	mi	re	do
FIXED DO:	sol	ti	re	mi	fi (or fa)	sol	la	ti	sol	re	ti	la	sol
LETTER NAMES:	G	B	D	E	Fis (or F)	G	A	B	G	D	B	A	G

M E L O D I E S   I N   C   M A J O R

S2–1.

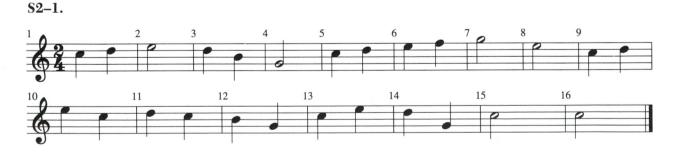

---

2. The Letter Names system combines elements of English and German note names. Germans use "H" for B and "B" for B♭, a practice incompatible with English terminology and thus modified for this text. "Fis" is the German name for F♯.

· Few melodies juxtapose tonic and dominant arpeggiations as clearly as does this one. Here, each triad's root (C or G) appears within its arpeggiation. That will not always be the case.

S2–2.

S2–3.

· Measures 5 through 8 match, in the context of V, the opening four measures. The G of measure 5 is no longer the fifth of I (as are the Gs in measures 3 and 4) but instead the root of V. By thinking of G–D in measure 5 as root–fifth, you will minimize the chances of singing C (instead of D) by mistake.

S2–4.

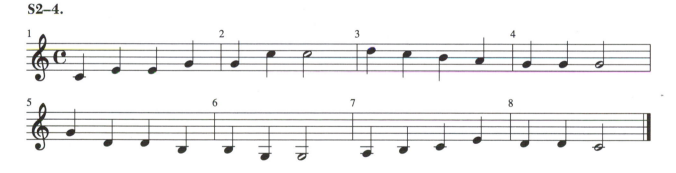

MELODIES IN F MAJOR

S2–5.

· Take advantage of the fact that C is a common tone of I and V in F major. Find the C of measure 5 not by thinking of a descending fifth from G but by association with the C of measure 3.

S2–6.

S2–7.

- The E in measure 5 bridges the Fs of measures 3 and 7. As you practice, listen for similar associations among nonadjacent pitches. For example, does the G of measure 7 connect the preceding A with C or with the F of measure 8?

S2–8.

MELODIES IN G MAJOR

S2–9.

- The B that ends measure 3 reinstates the B of measure 1. Likewise the A that ends measure 7 reinstates the A of measure 4. By thinking of the melody in this way, your performance can project the unifying force of a descending stepwise line (B-A-G) over these measures. Without this insight, your performance might sound like a meandering succession of descending and ascending gestures.

S2–10.

S2–11.

- A pitch can perform different functions at different times. The A that begins measure 6 might at first seem to function as a passing note, following the model of measure 2. The melody continues in a different way in measures 6 and 7, however, causing us to interpret A as the fifth of V.

S2–12.

DUETS

D2–1.

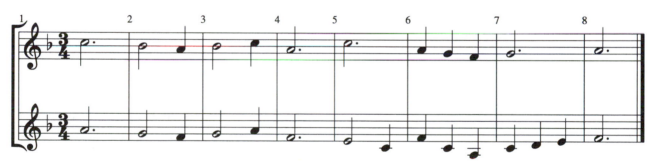

D2–2.

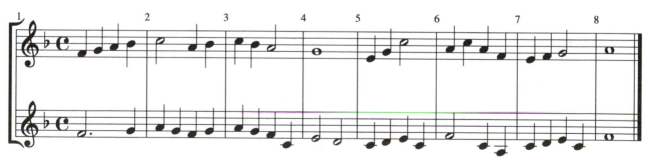

D2–3.

ACCOMPANIED SOLO MELODIES

AS2–1.

AS2–2.

AS2–3.

RHYTHMS

R2–1.

R2–2.

R2–3.

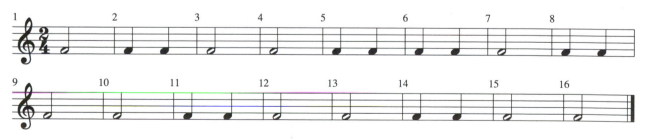

R2–4.

R2–5.

R2–6.

INTERVAL WORKSHOP

I2–1.   Play a pitch that is low in your vocal range at a keyboard. Sing it. Then sing the pitch a perfect octave higher. Use the keyboard to confirm your performance. Then sing ascending octaves starting on other pitches.

I2–2.   Play a pitch that is low in your vocal range at a keyboard. Sing it. Then sing the pitch a perfect fourth higher. Use the keyboard to confirm your performance. Then sing ascending fourths starting on other pitches.

I2–3.   Play a pitch that is high in your vocal range at a keyboard. Sing it. Then sing the pitch a perfect octave lower. Use the keyboard to confirm your performance. Then sing descending octaves starting on other pitches.

I2–4.   Play a pitch that is high in your vocal range at a keyboard. Sing it. Then sing the pitch a perfect fourth lower. Use the keyboard to confirm your performance. Then sing descending fourths starting on other pitches.

ARPEGGIATION WORKSHOP

A2–1.   Play a C, F, or G that is low in your vocal range at a keyboard. Let this pitch be $\hat{1}$ in a major key. Sing each of the following arpeggiations, either in the order given or in random order. Whenever necessary, use the keyboard to confirm that you have sung the correct pitches.

a.	$\hat{1}$	$\hat{3}$	$\hat{5}$	$\hat{8}$		j.	$\hat{5}$	$\hat{3}$	$\hat{1}$	$\hat{8}$
b.	$\hat{1}$	$\hat{5}$	$\hat{8}$	$\hat{1}$		k.	$\hat{5}$	$\hat{8}$	$\hat{1}$	$\hat{3}$
c.	$\hat{1}$	$\hat{8}$	$\hat{5}$	$\hat{1}$		l.	$\hat{5}$	$\hat{8}$	$\hat{1}$	$\hat{5}$
d.	$\hat{1}$	$\hat{8}$	$\hat{5}$	$\hat{3}$		m.	$\hat{8}$	$\hat{1}$	$\hat{3}$	$\hat{5}$
e.	$\hat{3}$	$\hat{1}$	$\hat{5}$	$\hat{8}$		n.	$\hat{8}$	$\hat{1}$	$\hat{5}$	$\hat{3}$
f.	$\hat{3}$	$\hat{1}$	$\hat{8}$	$\hat{5}$		o.	$\hat{8}$	$\hat{1}$	$\hat{5}$	$\hat{8}$
g.	$\hat{3}$	$\hat{5}$	$\hat{1}$	$\hat{8}$		p.	$\hat{8}$	$\hat{5}$	$\hat{1}$	$\hat{3}$
h.	$\hat{3}$	$\hat{5}$	$\hat{8}$	$\hat{1}$		q.	$\hat{8}$	$\hat{5}$	$\hat{1}$	$\hat{8}$
i.	$\hat{5}$	$\hat{1}$	$\hat{8}$	$\hat{5}$		r.	$\hat{8}$	$\hat{5}$	$\hat{3}$	$\hat{1}$

A2–2.   Play a C, F, or G that is low in your vocal range at a keyboard. Let this pitch be $\hat{1}$ in a major key. Sing each of the following arpeggiations of I–V, either in the order given or in random order. The asterisks indicate where the arpeggiation of I ends and that of V begins. Whenever necessary, use the keyboard to confirm that you have sung the correct pitches.

Note on Performance: *In all Arpeggiation Workshop exercises pitches within a central octave are displayed as* $\hat{1}$, $\hat{2}$, $\hat{3}$, $\hat{4}$, $\hat{5}$, $\hat{6}$, $\hat{7}$, *and* $\hat{8}$. *A pitch higher than the central octave will be displayed in* <u>superscript</u> *(e.g., the* $\hat{2}$ *in* $\hat{5}$ $\hat{7}$ $\hat{2}$*). A pitch lower than the central octave will be displayed in* <u>subscript</u> *(e.g., the* $\hat{5}$ *and* $\hat{7}$ *in* $\hat{5}$ $\hat{7}$ $\hat{2}$*). You might perform Exercises 2.a. and 3.a. as follows:*

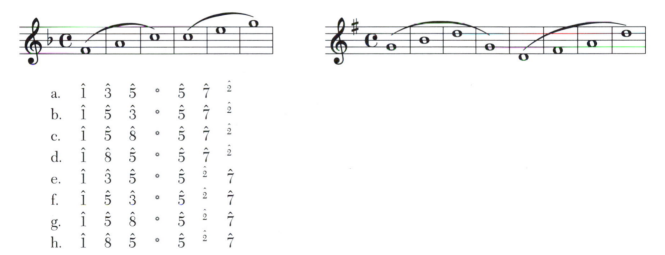

a.	$\hat{1}$	$\hat{3}$	$\hat{5}$	✲	$\hat{5}$	$\hat{7}$	$\hat{2}$
b.	$\hat{1}$	$\hat{5}$	$\hat{3}$	✲	$\hat{5}$	$\hat{7}$	$\hat{2}$
c.	$\hat{1}$	$\hat{5}$	$\hat{8}$	✲	$\hat{5}$	$\hat{7}$	$\hat{2}$
d.	$\hat{1}$	$\hat{8}$	$\hat{5}$	✲	$\hat{5}$	$\hat{7}$	$\hat{2}$
e.	$\hat{1}$	$\hat{3}$	$\hat{5}$	✲	$\hat{5}$	$\hat{2}$	$\hat{7}$
f.	$\hat{1}$	$\hat{5}$	$\hat{3}$	✲	$\hat{5}$	$\hat{2}$	$\hat{7}$
g.	$\hat{1}$	$\hat{5}$	$\hat{8}$	✲	$\hat{5}$	$\hat{2}$	$\hat{7}$
h.	$\hat{1}$	$\hat{8}$	$\hat{5}$	✲	$\hat{5}$	$\hat{2}$	$\hat{7}$

A2–3.   Play a C, F, or G that is at least a perfect fourth above the lowest note of your vocal range at a keyboard. Let this pitch be $\hat{1}$ in a major key. Sing each of the following arpeggiations of I–V, either in the order given or in random order. The asterisks indicate where the arpeggiation of I ends and that of V begins. Whenever necessary, use the keyboard to confirm that you have sung the correct pitches.

a. 1̂ 3̂ 5̂ 1̂ ❋ ₅ ₇ 2̂ 5̂   i. 1̂ 3̂ 5̂ 1̂ ❋ ₅ 2̂ 5̂ ₅

b. 1̂ 5̂ 3̂ 1̂ ❋ ₅ ₇ 2̂ 5̂   j. 1̂ 5̂ 3̂ 1̂ ❋ ₅ 2̂ 5̂ ₅

c. 1̂ 5̂ 8̂ 1̂ ❋ ₅ ₇ 2̂ 5̂   k. 1̂ 5̂ 8̂ 1̂ ❋ ₅ 2̂ 5̂ ₅

d. 1̂ 8̂ 5̂ 1̂ ❋ ₅ ₇ 2̂ 5̂   l. 1̂ 8̂ 5̂ 1̂ ❋ ₅ 2̂ 5̂ ₅

e. 1̂ 3̂ 5̂ 1̂ ❋ ₅ 2̂ ₇ 5̂   m. 1̂ 3̂ 5̂ 1̂ ❋ ₅ 5̂ 2̂ ₅

f. 1̂ 5̂ 3̂ 1̂ ❋ ₅ 2̂ ₇ 5̂   n. 1̂ 5̂ 3̂ 1̂ ❋ ₅ 5̂ 2̂ ₅

g. 1̂ 5̂ 8̂ 1̂ ❋ ₅ 2̂ ₇ 5̂   o. 1̂ 5̂ 8̂ 1̂ ❋ ₅ 5̂ 2̂ ₅

h. 1̂ 8̂ 5̂ 1̂ ❋ ₅ 2̂ ₇ 5̂   p. 1̂ 8̂ 5̂ 1̂ ❋ ₅ 5̂ 2̂ ₅

QUICK SWITCH

Q2–1.

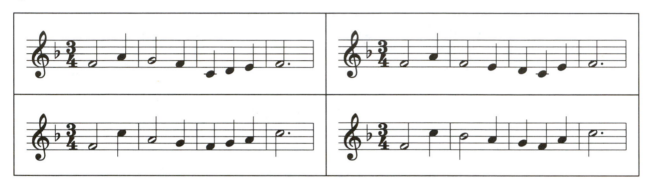

Q2–2.

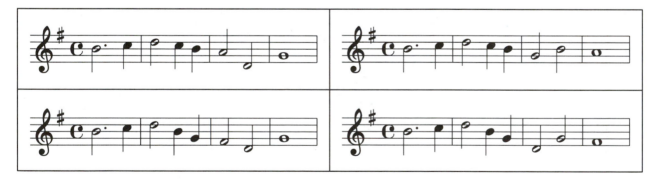

Q2–3.

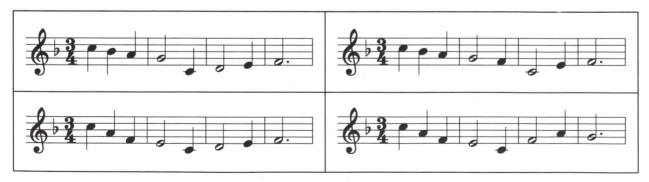

Q2–4.

IDENTIFICATIONS

ID2–1.   A major triad is performed. Then two of its three pitches are performed simultaneously: root and third, root and fifth, or third and fifth. Identify which of these choices is performed.

ID2–2. $\hat{1}$, $\hat{3}$, $\hat{5}$, and $\hat{8}$ in a major key are performed simultaneously. Then one of the following melodic successions is performed:

$$\hat{1}\text{-}\hat{3},\ \hat{1}\text{-}\hat{5},\ \hat{1}\text{-}\hat{8},\ \hat{3}\text{-}\hat{1},\ \hat{3}\text{-}\hat{5},\ \hat{5}\text{-}\hat{1},\ \hat{5}\text{-}\hat{3},\ \hat{5}\text{-}\hat{8},\ \hat{8}\text{-}\hat{1},\ \hat{8}\text{-}\hat{5}.$$

Identify the scale degrees performed.

ID2–3.   An interval is performed melodically, either ascending or descending. Identify it as a major third, perfect fourth, perfect fifth, or perfect octave.

ID2–4.   Two triads are performed, each preceded by its root alone. Interpret the first triad as tonic (I) in a major key. Does the second triad function as tonic (I) or as dominant (V)?
Sample triads for performance:

ID2–5.   A melody is performed. Identify the correct score notation.

a.   b.

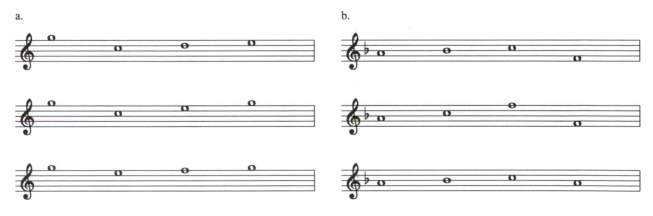

c.

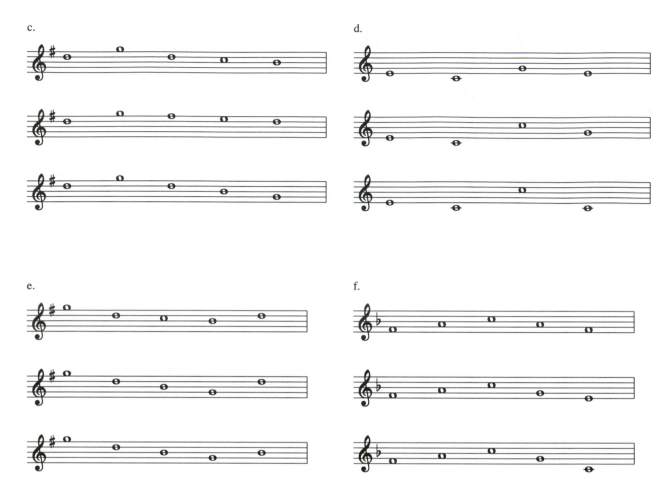

d.

RHYTHMIC DICTATIONS

RD2–1.

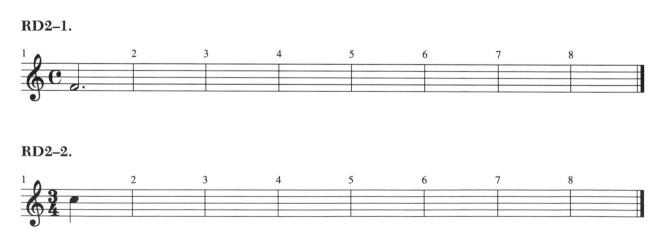

RD2–2.

MELODIC DICTATIONS

MD2–1.

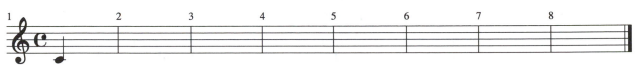

- The first four measures ascend mainly by step, while measures 5 and 6 contain many descending leaps. At what point do the ascending steps reach $\hat{8}$? At what point do the descending leaps reach $\hat{1}$?

MD2–2.

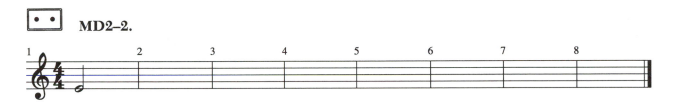

- Compare the last pitch of measure 1 and the last pitch of measure 2. Which is higher? Is one of them the tonic pitch, C?

MD2–3.

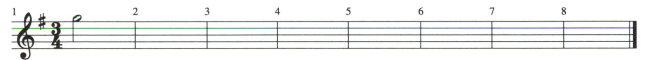

- Measures 4 through 6 contain several leaps. Write down the first pitch in each of these measures before turning your attention to the leap *within* measure 5.

MD2–4.

- Listen for stepwise relationships between nonadjacent pitches. How does the pitch of measure 4 relate to that of measure 1? How does the pitch of measure 8 relate to that of measure 4?

MD2–5.

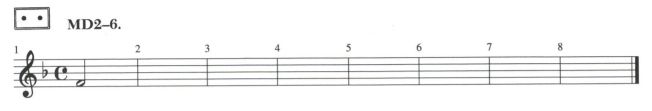

- The two halves of this melody are very similar. Beginning at measure 9 you hear, in the context of the *dominant* harmony, the same material that established *tonic* beginning in measure 1. At what point does this similarity end?

MD2–6.

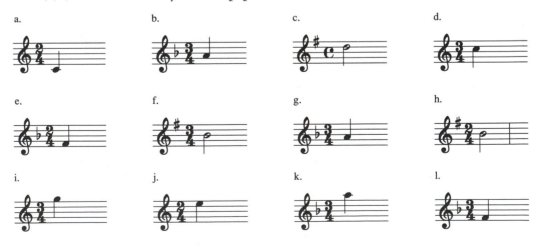

- How do measures 5 and 6 relate to measures 1 and 2? How do measure 3 and measure 7 compare?

▣ CASSETTE PROGRAM (TAPE 1, SIDE A)

C2–1.   Twelve melodies are performed, twice each. During the silence after each playing, respond in one of the following ways: (1) Sing the melody, using solmization syllables; (2) Play the melody on the piano; (3) Play the melody on your primary instrument; (4) Write the melody on staff paper.

Chapter 3

PITCH

Thirds, fourths, fifths, and octaves owe their prominence to the basic chordal architecture of Example 3–1a. These pitches and the passing notes that connect them can be arranged as a ***major scale***, shown in Example 3–1b. Though the presentation of all eight scale degrees lacks the harmonic emphasis of Example 3–1a, distinctions among these pitches still prevail: $\hat{1}$ and $\hat{8}$ hold the most authoritative positions, as tonic; $\hat{3}$ and $\hat{5}$ hold intermediate positions, as members of the tonic triad; $\hat{2}$, $\hat{4}$, $\hat{6}$, and $\hat{7}$ hold subordinate positions. The slurs underneath the scale clarify this hierarchy.

EXAMPLE 3–1

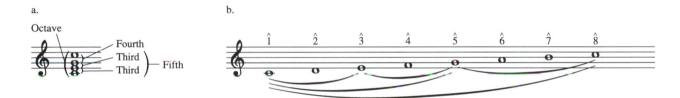

A pitch can fulfill several different functions within a key, as mentioned in chapter 2. B, sometimes a passing note (with A) connecting G and C of tonic (I) in C major, serves as the third of the dominant (V) triad when G is established as a root. Similarly, A serves as the third of the ***subdominant*** (IV) triad when F is established as a root.

The distinction between I-IV-I and I-V-I may not be easy to hear at first. IV and V are both major triads, and their roots are adjacent scale degrees. Focus especially on the bass, listening to distinguish between leaps of fourths and fifths. Also consider that I and IV share $\hat{1}$ (or $\hat{8}$) as a common tone, while I and V share $\hat{5}$ as a common tone. The resolution from leading tone ($\hat{7}$) to tonic ($\hat{8}$) is characteristic only of V-I.

IV often precedes V, with a distinctive stepwise ascent in the bass. I-IV-V-I, shown in Example 3–2, expands the basic I-V-I progression. Because IV and V are juxtaposed, this progression is comparatively easy to recognize (at least at present, given a chordal vocabulary of only I, IV, and V!).

EXAMPLE 3–2

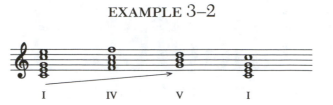

Any major key signature designates seven distinct pitches (in multiple oc-taves)—the **diatonic** pitches of a key. Each pitch will perform a variety of functions. In C major, F may serve as a passing note connecting the tonic triad's E and G, as the root of IV, or as a **neighboring note** to E. Unlike a passing note, which connects two different pitches, a neighboring note embellishes a single pitch, as shown in Example 3–3. F is particularly suitable for this role because only a **half step** (the smallest distance between two distinct pitches) separates E and F. The interval E-F is a **minor second**.

EXAMPLE 3–3

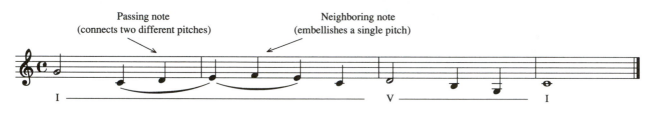

Only two pairs of scale degrees in the major scale are related by half step: $\hat{3}$-$\hat{4}$ and $\hat{7}$-$\hat{8}$. (Locate these positions in Ex. 3–1b.) All other adjacent scale degrees are separated by a **whole step** and form the interval of a **major second**. A neighboring note may relate to the pitch that it embellishes by either half step or whole step. Both upper neighbors (e.g., E-F-E) and lower neighbors (e.g., C-B-C) are common.

Example 3–4 displays two special types of neighboring notes. An **incomplete** neighboring note occurs when the note that is embellished appears on only one side of the neighbor (generally after the neighbor). **Double** neighboring notes are two pitches that surround the embellished note both above and below (in either order).

EXAMPLE 3–4

The **key of D major** and the **key of B♭ major** are introduced in this chapter. Their key signatures contain two sharps and two flats, respectively.

METER AND RHYTHM

When a pitch sounds for a duration longer than a measure, a **tie** (⌣ or ⌢) is required to bind noteheads that appear within adjacent measures, as shown in Example 3–5. Do not confuse the tie, a symbol of rhythmic notation, with the *slur*, a common performance mark. A tie will always bind two noteheads that represent the same pitch.

EXAMPLE 3–5

SING:

THINK: 1 2 3 1 2 3 1 2 3 1 2 3 1 2 3 1 2 3 1 2 3 1 2 3

Silence is indicated with the same precision as is sound. The **quarter rest** (𝄽) fills one beat in the meters introduced to this point. The **half rest** (▬) fills two beats (either beats 1 and 2 or beats 3 and 4) in $\frac{4}{4}$ meter. It does not occur in $\frac{2}{4}$ or $\frac{3}{4}$ meter. The **whole rest** (▬) fills an entire measure, regardless of how many beats the measure contains. These symbols appear in context in Example 3–6.

EXAMPLE 3–6

SING:

THINK: 1 2 3 4 1 2 3 4 1 2 3 4 1 2 3 4 1 2 3 4 1 2 3 4 1 2 3 4 1 2 3 4

SOLO MELODIES

FIXED DO: *Use "di" for C♯ and "me" for E♭ in the inflected Fixed Do system.*

D Major scale: re mi fi sol la ti di re.

B♭ Major scale: te do re me fa sol la te.

LETTER NAMES: *Use "Cis" for C♯ and "Es" for E♭ in the inflected Letter Names system.*

D Major scale: D E Fis G A B Cis D.

B♭ Major scale: Bes C D Es F G A Bes.

MELODIES THAT FEATURE THE MAJOR SCALE

S3–1.

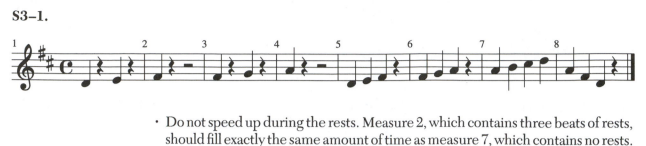

- Do not speed up during the rests. Measure 2, which contains three beats of rests, should fill exactly the same amount of time as measure 7, which contains no rests.

S3–2.

S3–3.

- The descending scale featured in measures 1 through 3 is followed by an ascent that, though more jagged, nevertheless contains all but one pitch of the scale: D (measure 3), E (measures 4 and 5), F♯ (measure 6), G (omitted), A (measure 6), B (measure 7), C♯ (measure 7), D (measure 8).

S3–4.

MELODIES THAT EMPHASIZE THE SUBDOMINANT CHORD

S3–5.

- Though twelve pitches appear within this melody, direct your attention to the four that function as roots: B♭, E♭, F, and B♭. If your internal ear holds these pitches for two measures each, the remaining pitches should give you little problem. As a practice strategy, sing those four pitches before attempting the melody.

S3–6.

S3–7.

- Take advantage of the fact that G is a common tone of I and IV. The G of measure 5 repeats, in the context of IV, the Gs of measures 1 and 3. By keeping this G alive in your mind during measures 5 through 8, the F♯ of measure 9 will seem more convincing as the initial pitch of the V arpeggiation.

S3–8.

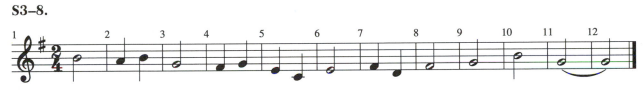

MELODIES THAT EMPLOY NEIGHBORING
NOTES

S3–9.

- Do not think of the first five pitches in a single dimension (as ascending fourth, descending second, ascending fourth, descending second). Instead, think in two dimensions. At a basic level, the tonic triad is arpeggiated (F-A-C). At the surface, two of these pitches (A and C) are embellished by incomplete upper neighbors.

S3–10.

S3–11.

- The first note of this melody functions as an incomplete upper neighbor to A. It is important that tonic D-F♯-A be firmly implanted within your mind before you begin.

S3–12.

DUETS

D3–1.

D3–2.

D3–3.

ACCOMPANIED SOLO MELODIES

AS3–1.

AS3–2.

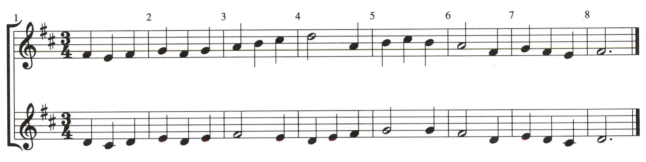

AS3–3.

RHYTHMS

R3–1.

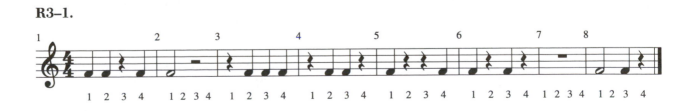

R3–2.

R3–3.

R3–4.

R3–5.

R3–6.

INTERVAL WORKSHOP

I3–1.   Play a pitch that is low in your vocal range at a keyboard. Sing it. Then sing the pitch a minor second higher. Use the keyboard to confirm your performance. Then sing ascending seconds starting on other pitches.

I3–2.   Play a pitch that is low in your vocal range at a keyboard. Sing it. Then sing the pitch a major second higher. Use the keyboard to confirm your performance. Then sing ascending seconds starting on other pitches.

I3–3.   Play a pitch that is high in your vocal range at a keyboard. Sing it. Then sing the pitch a minor second lower. Use the keyboard to confirm your performance. Then sing descending seconds starting on other pitches.

I3–4.   Play a pitch that is high in your vocal range at a keyboard. Sing it. Then sing the pitch a major second lower. Use the keyboard to confirm your performance. Then sing descending seconds starting on other pitches.

I3–5. At the keyboard, play a pitch that is low in your vocal range. Sing it. Then sing an ascending major scale from that pitch.

I3–6. At the keyboard, play a pitch that is high in your vocal range. Sing it. Then sing a descending major scale from that pitch.

I3–7. At the keyboard, select a pitch near the middle of your vocal range as the "starting pitch" (SP). Then sing the following groups of pitches on "la." Practice both in the order given and in random order.

a.	SP	m2 above SP	SP		
b.	SP	m2 below SP	SP		
c.	SP	M2 above SP	SP		
d.	SP	M2 below SP	SP		
e.	SP	m2 above SP	SP	M2 below SP	SP
f.	SP	m2 below SP	SP	M2 above SP	SP
g.	SP	M2 below SP	SP	m2 above SP	SP
h.	SP	M2 above SP	SP	m2 below SP	SP
i.	SP	M2 below SP	SP	M2 above SP	SP
j.	SP	M2 above SP	SP	M2 below SP	SP
k.	SP	m2 above SP	M2 below SP	SP	
l.	SP	m2 below SP	M2 above SP	SP	
m.	SP	M2 below SP	m2 above SP	SP	
n.	SP	M2 above SP	m2 below SP	SP	

ARPEGGIATION WORKSHOP

A3–1. Play a C, D, F, G, or B♭ that is low in your vocal range at a keyboard. Let this pitch be $\hat{1}$ in a major key. Sing each of the following arpeggiations, either in the order given or in random order.

a.	$\hat{1}$	$\hat{3}$	$\hat{5}$	∘	$\hat{4}$	$\hat{6}$	$\hat{8}$	∘	$\hat{8}$	$\hat{5}$	$\hat{1}$		
b.	$\hat{1}$	$\hat{3}$	$\hat{5}$	∘	$\hat{5}$	$\hat{7}$	$\hat{2}$	∘	$\hat{8}$	$\hat{5}$	$\hat{1}$		
c.	$\hat{1}$	$\hat{3}$	$\hat{5}$	∘	$\hat{4}$	$\hat{8}$	$\hat{6}$	∘	$\hat{8}$	$\hat{5}$	$\hat{1}$		
d.	$\hat{1}$	$\hat{3}$	$\hat{5}$	∘	$\hat{5}$	$\hat{2}$	$\hat{7}$	∘	$\hat{8}$	$\hat{5}$	$\hat{1}$		
e.	$\hat{1}$	$\hat{3}$	$\hat{5}$	∘	$\hat{4}$	$\hat{6}$	$\hat{8}$	∘	$\hat{5}$	$\hat{7}$	$\hat{2}$	∘	$\hat{8}$ $\hat{5}$ $\hat{1}$
f.	$\hat{1}$	$\hat{3}$	$\hat{5}$	∘	$\hat{4}$	$\hat{6}$	$\hat{8}$	∘	$\hat{5}$	$\hat{2}$	$\hat{7}$	∘	$\hat{8}$ $\hat{5}$ $\hat{1}$
g.	$\hat{1}$	$\hat{3}$	$\hat{5}$	∘	$\hat{4}$	$\hat{8}$	$\hat{6}$	∘	$\hat{5}$	$\hat{7}$	$\hat{2}$	∘	$\hat{8}$ $\hat{5}$ $\hat{1}$
h.	$\hat{1}$	$\hat{3}$	$\hat{5}$	∘	$\hat{4}$	$\hat{8}$	$\hat{6}$	∘	$\hat{5}$	$\hat{2}$	$\hat{7}$	∘	$\hat{8}$ $\hat{5}$ $\hat{1}$

A3–2. Play a C, D, F, G, or B♭ that is at least a perfect fifth above the lowest note of your vocal range at a keyboard. Let this pitch be $\hat{1}$ in a major key. Sing each of the following arpeggiations, either in the order given or in random order:

a. $\hat{1}$ $\hat{3}$ $\hat{5}$ $\hat{1}$ ✹ $\hat{4}$ $\hat{6}$ $\hat{1}$ ✹ $\hat{1}$ $\hat{3}$ $\hat{5}$

b. $\hat{1}$ $\hat{3}$ $\hat{5}$ $\hat{1}$ ✹ $\hat{5}$ $\hat{7}$ $\hat{2}$ ✹ $\hat{1}$ $\hat{3}$ $\hat{5}$

c. $\hat{1}$ $\hat{3}$ $\hat{5}$ $\hat{1}$ ✹ $\hat{6}$ $\hat{4}$ $\hat{1}$ ✹ $\hat{1}$ $\hat{3}$ $\hat{5}$

d. $\hat{1}$ $\hat{3}$ $\hat{5}$ $\hat{1}$ ✹ $\hat{7}$ $\hat{5}$ $\hat{2}$ ✹ $\hat{1}$ $\hat{3}$ $\hat{5}$

e. $\hat{1}$ $\hat{3}$ $\hat{5}$ $\hat{1}$ ✹ $\hat{4}$ $\hat{6}$ $\hat{1}$ ✹ $\hat{5}$ $\hat{7}$ $\hat{2}$ ✹ $\hat{1}$ $\hat{3}$ $\hat{5}$

f. $\hat{1}$ $\hat{3}$ $\hat{5}$ $\hat{1}$ ✹ $\hat{4}$ $\hat{6}$ $\hat{1}$ ✹ $\hat{5}$ $\hat{2}$ $\hat{7}$ ✹ $\hat{1}$ $\hat{3}$ $\hat{5}$

g. $\hat{1}$ $\hat{3}$ $\hat{5}$ $\hat{1}$ ✹ $\hat{4}$ $\hat{1}$ $\hat{6}$ ✹ $\hat{5}$ $\hat{7}$ $\hat{2}$ ✹ $\hat{1}$ $\hat{3}$ $\hat{5}$

h. $\hat{1}$ $\hat{3}$ $\hat{5}$ $\hat{1}$ ✹ $\hat{4}$ $\hat{1}$ $\hat{6}$ ✹ $\hat{5}$ $\hat{2}$ $\hat{7}$ ✹ $\hat{1}$ $\hat{3}$ $\hat{5}$

QUICK SWITCH

Q3–1.

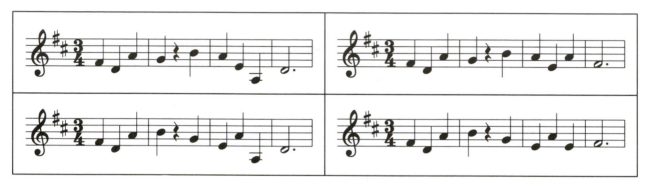

Q3–2.

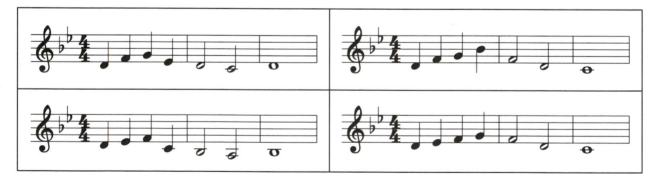

Q3–3.

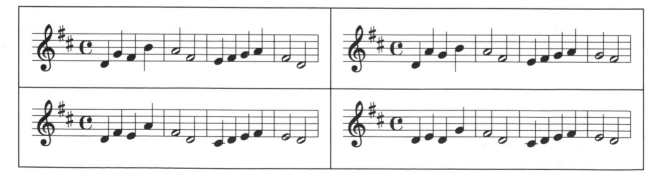

Q3–4.

IDENTIFICATIONS

ID3–1. An interval is performed melodically, either ascending or descending. Identify it as a minor second, major second, major third, perfect fourth, perfect fifth, or perfect octave.

ID3–2. Two triads are performed, each preceded by its root alone. Interpret the first triad as tonic (I) in a major key. Does the second triad function as tonic (I), as subdominant (IV), or as dominant (V)? (Also try this exercise performing just the triads, without the roots alone.)

ID3–3. Three triads are performed, each preceded by its root alone. Interpret the first triad as tonic (I) in a major key. Select the appropriate Roman numerals for the three triads, given the following choices:

$$I \quad - \quad IV \quad - \quad I$$
$$I \quad - \quad V \quad - \quad I$$
$$I \quad - \quad IV \quad - \quad V$$
$$I \quad - \quad I \quad - \quad V$$

(Also try this exercise performing just the triads, without the roots alone.)

ID3–4. A melody is performed. Identify the correct score notation.

a.   b.

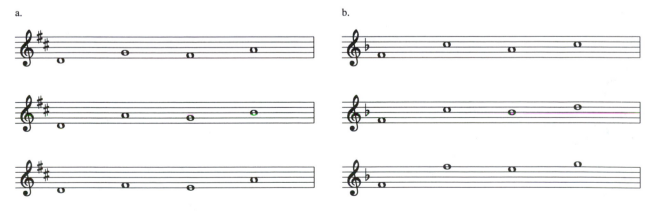

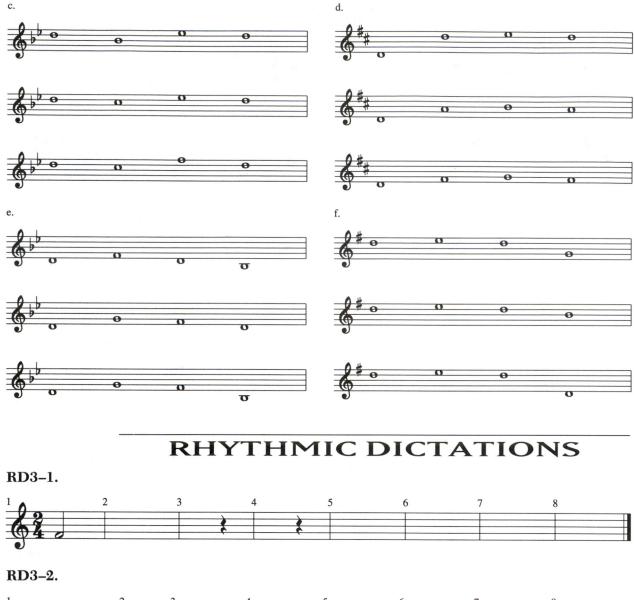

RHYTHMIC DICTATIONS

RD3–1.

RD3–2.

MELODIC DICTATIONS

MD3–1.

- The two halves of this melody are very similar, but not identical. Compare the underlying harmonic content of each half.

MOZART: STRING QUARTET NO. 14 IN G MAJOR, K. 387, MVMT. 4

 MD3–2.

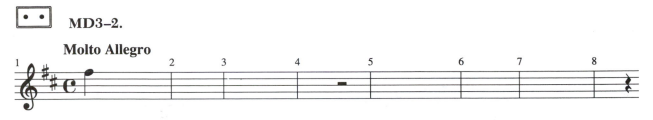

- Compare measures 4 and 8. Though both correspond to tonic harmony, measure 4 leaves open the opportunity for continuation while measure 8 concludes more definitively.

MD3–3.

- Though tonic is the most stable chord, its pitches can play a subordinate role in some contexts. For example, consider measures 5 and 6. What harmony serves as the foundation for these measures? What role do the pitches in the second half of measure 5 play? (Hint: Compare the structure of measures 5 and 6 with that of measures 1 and 2.)

MD3–4.

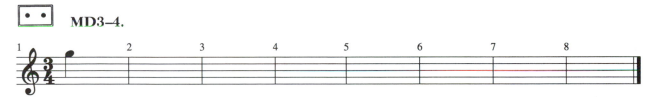

- Compare the descent in measure 1 and the ascent in measure 2. Do they aim at the same pitch? Then compare measures 3 and 4. Finally, compare measures 5 and 6.

MD3–5.

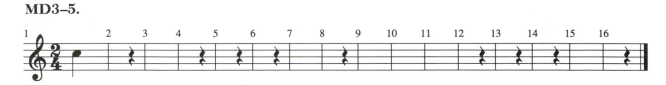

- Remember that a new symbol of rhythmic notation, the tie, has been introduced. This melody requires two ties.

MD3–6.

· Why does the first pitch of measure 6 attract so much attention?

··CASSETTE PROGRAM (TAPE 1, SIDE A)

C3–1.   Six melodies are performed, twice each. During the silence after each playing, respond in one of the following ways: (1) Sing the melody, using solmization syllables; (2) Play the melody on the piano; (3) Play the melody on your primary instrument; (4) Write the melody on staff paper.

C3–2.   Six chord progressions are performed, twice each. Each progression consists of three triads. During the silence after each playing, respond in one of the following ways: (1) Sing the roots of the three triads, using solmization syllables; (2) Play the three roots on the piano; (3) Play the three roots on your primary instrument; (4) Write the three triads on staff paper and provide an analysis.

Chapter 4

PITCH

The treble clef is convenient only for pitches in the upper half of music's range. The **bass clef** is used for lower pitches. In Example 4–1 a **system** (combination of treble and bass clefs) is employed to demonstrate how a triad can be expanded into four-voiced **chords**. A chord's **bass** (its *lowest* note) will always appear on the lower staff of a system.

EXAMPLE 4–1

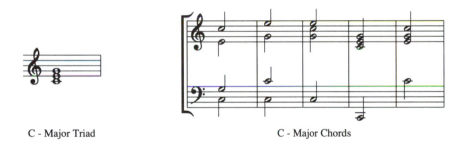

C - Major Triad   C - Major Chords

Pay special attention to the **outer voices** of a chord. Bass notes will give you important information regarding the harmonic progression, while **soprano** (the highest) notes shape the melody. The **inner voices** (the two remaining voices, the higher called **alto**, the lower called **tenor**) affect a chord's character but play a subsidiary role.

Chord members are evaluated in relation to the bass. Though the soprano E in Example 4–2 forms the visually prominent interval of a sixth with the alto G, musicians instead measure it in relation to the bass (as a **compound** major third).[1]

---

1. **Simple** intervals are those that fall within the span of an octave, while **compound** intervals are formed by spreading the pitches of a simple interval apart by one or more octaves.

EXAMPLE 4–2

Sixth above alto
(Incorrect)

Fifth and third above bass
(Correct)

The chords displayed in Examples 4–1 and 4–2 are in **root position,** a term employed when the *root* (the lowest pitch of the triad from which the chord is derived) also serves as the *bass* (the chord's lowest pitch). Another way of conveying this information is by taking an inventory of the intervals that appear above the bass, not counting any duplications or octave doublings. In the chords displayed in Examples 4–1 and 4–2, nothing but simple or compound fifths, simple or compound thirds, and octave doublings appear above the bass notes. These chords are in $^5_3$ **position.** The symbol $^5_3$ is an example of *figured bass,* figures (numbers) that designate the intervals formed with the bass.

The **key of A major** and the **key of E♭ major** are introduced in this chapter. Their key signatures contain three sharps and three flats, respectively.

METER AND RHYTHM

Two *eighth notes* (♫) occupy the same musical time as one quarter note. Example 4–3 shows a melody that emphasizes eighth notes, along with appropriate counting syllables (spoken as "one and two and . . .").

EXAMPLE 4–3

SING:

THINK: 1 + 2 + 3 +   1 + 2 + 3   +   1   +   2 + 3   +   1 + 2 + 3 +

Beginning in this chapter, all materials excerpted from actual compositions will include the performance indications that the composer provided. Many should be familiar to you from your experience in music performance: slurs, staccato dots, dynamic markings, and so on. The words used by composers—to indicate the tempo, to give special instructions for a passage—come in a variety of languages (often Italian, although since the early nineteenth century increasingly in the language the composer spoke). A glossary of the most common foreign terms used in music begins on page 655. You might also consult the appropriate foreign-language dictionary as the need arises.

SOLO MELODIES

FIXED DO: *Use "si" for G♯ and "le" for A♭ in the inflected Fixed Do system.*

A Major scale: la ti di re mi fi si la.

E♭ Major scale: me fa sol le te do re me.

LETTER NAMES: *Use "Gis" for G♯ and "As" for A♭ in the inflected Letter Names system.*

A Major scale: A B Cis D E Fis Gis A.

E♭ Major scale: Es F G As Bes C D Es.

MELODIES WRITTEN IN BASS CLEF

MOZART: *DON GIOVANNI,* **K.** 527, ACT 1

S4–1.

- Think of this melody as a scalar ascent from $\hat{3}$ to $\hat{8}$, with detours (the descending thirds) in measures 2 and 4.

S4–2.

S4–3.

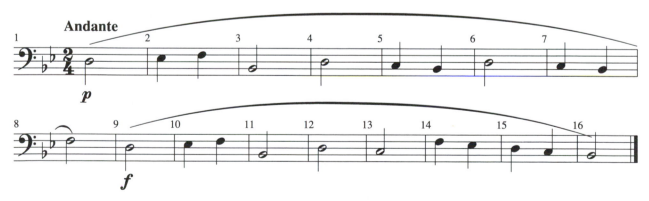

- This melody is constructed in two parts of eight measures each. Measures 9 through 12 are identical to measures 1 through 4. Measures 5 through 8 contain ascending gestures (B♭-D and B♭-F) that prevent a sense of closure during the first half. In contrast, measures 14 through 16 descend to $\hat{1}$, releasing the melody's energy in a sweeping downward gesture.

S4–4.

S4–5.

- Find the B of measure 5 through reference to the A of measure 3.

MELODIES THAT EMPLOY EIGHTH NOTES

S4–6.

BEETHOVEN: SYMPHONY NO. 9 IN D MINOR ("CHORAL"), OP. 125, MVMT. 2

S4–7.

- As a practice strategy, omit the B at the end of measure 4. Once the stepwise connection between D and E (measure 5) is secure, add the descending leap from D to B.

S4–8.

MELODIES THAT ARE WRITTEN IN BASS CLEF AND EMPLOY EIGHTH NOTES

S4–9.

- Think of the B in measure 2 as a passing note connecting A in measure 1 and C♯ in measure 3. Likewise, think of the D in measure 2 as a passing note connecting C♯ in measure 1 and E in measures 3 and 4.

MOZART: *DON GIOVANNI*, K. 527, ACT 1

S4–10.

S4–11.

- The A in measure 2 is part of a tonic arpeggiation, while the A in measure 6 is part of a dominant arpeggiation. Both As are embellished by B, a neighboring note.

S4–12.

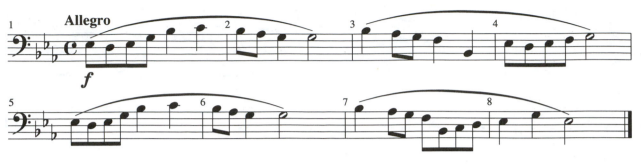

DUETS

D4–1.

D4–2.

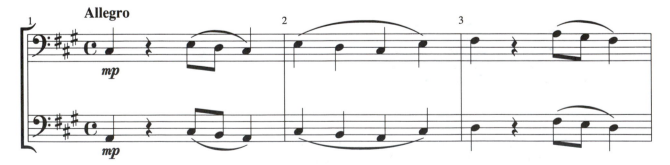

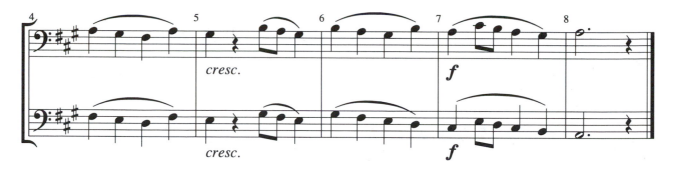

ACCOMPANIED SOLO MELODIES

AS4-1.

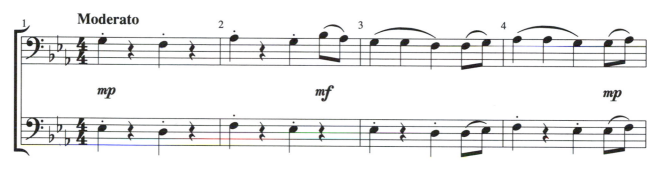

AS4–2.

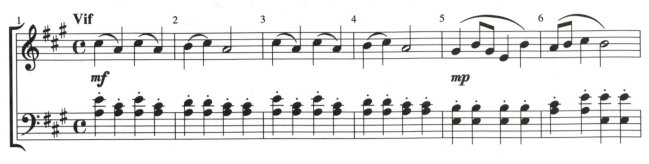

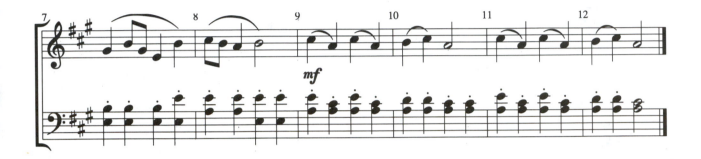

RHYTHMS

R4–1.

1 + 2 + 3 +   1 + 2 + 3 +   1 + 2 + 3 +   1+2+3+   1 + 2 + 3 +   1 + 2 + 3 +   1+2+3 +   1+2+3+

R4–2.

R4–3.

R4–4.

R4–5.

R4–6.

INTERVAL WORKSHOP

I4–1. Practice singing the intervals of a major third, perfect fourth, perfect fifth, and perfect octave higher than a sounding pitch. The sounding pitch should be at or beyond the lower limit of your vocal range, and could be sung by a classmate or your instructor or performed on the piano or another instrument such as the cello. Also practice singing compound versions of these intervals.

I4–2. Practice singing the intervals of a major third, perfect fourth, perfect fifth, and perfect octave lower than a sounding pitch. The sounding pitch should be at or beyond the upper limit of your vocal range, and could be sung by a classmate or your instructor or performed on the piano or another instrument such as the flute. Also practice singing compound versions of these intervals.

ARPEGGIATION WORKSHOP

A4–1.   Play a C, D, E♭, F, G, A, or B♭ that is low in your vocal range at a keyboard. Let this pitch be $\hat{1}$ in a major key. Sing each of the following arpeggiations, either in the order given or in random order.

a. $\hat{1}$ $\hat{3}$ $\hat{5}$ $\hat{3}$ ✽ $\hat{4}$ $\hat{6}$ $\hat{8}$ $\hat{6}$ ✽ $\hat{5}$ $\hat{7}$ $\hat{2}$ $\hat{7}$ ✽ $\hat{8}$ $\hat{5}$ $\hat{3}$ $\hat{1}$
b. $\hat{1}$ $\hat{3}$ $\hat{5}$ $\hat{3}$ ✽ $\hat{4}$ $\hat{6}$ $\hat{8}$ $\hat{6}$ ✽ $\hat{5}$ $\hat{3}$ $\hat{1}$ $\hat{3}$ ✽ $\hat{5}$ $\hat{7}$ $\hat{2}$ $\hat{5}$
c. $\hat{1}$ $\hat{3}$ $\hat{5}$ $\hat{3}$ ✽ $\hat{5}$ $\hat{7}$ $\hat{2}$ $\hat{7}$ ✽ $\hat{8}$ $\hat{5}$ $\hat{3}$ $\hat{1}$ ✽ $\hat{5}$ $\hat{7}$ $\hat{2}$ $\hat{5}$
d. $\hat{1}$ $\hat{5}$ $\hat{3}$ $\hat{1}$ ✽ $\hat{4}$ $\hat{8}$ $\hat{6}$ $\hat{4}$ ✽ $\hat{5}$ $\hat{2}$ $\hat{7}$ $\hat{5}$ ✽ $\hat{8}$ $\hat{5}$ $\hat{3}$ $\hat{1}$
e. $\hat{1}$ $\hat{5}$ $\hat{3}$ $\hat{1}$ ✽ $\hat{4}$ $\hat{8}$ $\hat{6}$ $\hat{4}$ ✽ $\hat{5}$ $\hat{1}$ $\hat{3}$ $\hat{5}$ ✽ $\hat{5}$ $\hat{2}$ $\hat{7}$ $\hat{5}$
f. $\hat{1}$ $\hat{5}$ $\hat{3}$ $\hat{1}$ ✽ $\hat{5}$ $\hat{2}$ $\hat{7}$ $\hat{5}$ ✽ $\hat{8}$ $\hat{5}$ $\hat{3}$ $\hat{1}$ ✽ $\hat{5}$ $\hat{2}$ $\hat{7}$ $\hat{5}$
g. $\hat{3}$ $\hat{1}$ $\hat{5}$ $\hat{3}$ ✽ $\hat{6}$ $\hat{4}$ $\hat{8}$ $\hat{6}$ ✽ $\hat{7}$ $\hat{5}$ $\hat{2}$ $\hat{7}$ ✽ $\hat{8}$ $\hat{5}$ $\hat{3}$ $\hat{1}$
h. $\hat{3}$ $\hat{1}$ $\hat{5}$ $\hat{3}$ ✽ $\hat{6}$ $\hat{4}$ $\hat{8}$ $\hat{6}$ ✽ $\hat{3}$ $\hat{5}$ $\hat{1}$ $\hat{3}$ ✽ $\hat{7}$ $\hat{5}$ $\hat{2}$ $\hat{5}$
i. $\hat{3}$ $\hat{1}$ $\hat{5}$ $\hat{3}$ ✽ $\hat{7}$ $\hat{5}$ $\hat{2}$ $\hat{7}$ ✽ $\hat{8}$ $\hat{5}$ $\hat{1}$ $\hat{5}$ ✽ $\hat{7}$ $\hat{5}$ $\hat{2}$ $\hat{5}$

A4–2.   Play a C, D, E♭, F, G, A, or B♭ that is at least a perfect fifth above the lowest note of your vocal range at a keyboard. Let this pitch be $\hat{1}$ in a major key. Sing each of the following arpeggiations, either in the order given or in random order.

a. $\hat{1}$ $\hat{3}$ $\hat{5}$ $\hat{1}$ ✽ $\hat{4}_{\text{low}}$ $\hat{6}_{\text{low}}$ $\hat{1}$ $\hat{4}_{\text{low}}$ ✽ $\hat{5}_{\text{low}}$ $\hat{7}_{\text{low}}$ $\hat{2}$ $\hat{5}_{\text{low}}$ ✽ $\hat{1}$ $\hat{3}$ $\hat{5}$ $\hat{1}$
b. $\hat{1}$ $\hat{3}$ $\hat{5}$ $\hat{1}$ ✽ $\hat{4}_{\text{low}}$ $\hat{6}_{\text{low}}$ $\hat{1}$ $\hat{4}_{\text{low}}$ ✽ $\hat{1}$ $\hat{3}$ $\hat{5}$ $\hat{1}$ ✽ $\hat{5}_{\text{low}}$ $\hat{7}_{\text{low}}$ $\hat{2}$ $\hat{5}_{\text{low}}$
c. $\hat{1}$ $\hat{3}$ $\hat{5}$ $\hat{1}$ ✽ $\hat{5}_{\text{low}}$ $\hat{7}_{\text{low}}$ $\hat{2}$ $\hat{5}_{\text{low}}$ ✽ $\hat{1}$ $\hat{3}$ $\hat{5}$ $\hat{1}$ ✽ $\hat{5}_{\text{low}}$ $\hat{7}_{\text{low}}$ $\hat{2}$ $\hat{5}$
d. $\hat{1}$ $\hat{5}$ $\hat{3}$ $\hat{1}$ ✽ $\hat{4}_{\text{low}}$ $\hat{1}$ $\hat{6}_{\text{low}}$ $\hat{4}_{\text{low}}$ ✽ $\hat{5}_{\text{low}}$ $\hat{2}$ $\hat{7}_{\text{low}}$ $\hat{5}_{\text{low}}$ ✽ $\hat{1}$ $\hat{5}$ $\hat{3}$ $\hat{1}$
e. $\hat{1}$ $\hat{5}$ $\hat{3}$ $\hat{1}$ ✽ $\hat{4}_{\text{low}}$ $\hat{1}$ $\hat{6}_{\text{low}}$ $\hat{4}_{\text{low}}$ ✽ $\hat{1}$ $\hat{5}$ $\hat{3}$ $\hat{1}$ ✽ $\hat{5}_{\text{low}}$ $\hat{2}$ $\hat{7}_{\text{low}}$ $\hat{5}_{\text{low}}$
f. $\hat{1}$ $\hat{5}$ $\hat{3}$ $\hat{1}$ ✽ $\hat{5}_{\text{low}}$ $\hat{2}$ $\hat{7}_{\text{low}}$ $\hat{5}_{\text{low}}$ ✽ $\hat{1}$ $\hat{5}$ $\hat{3}$ $\hat{1}$ ✽ $\hat{5}_{\text{low}}$ $\hat{2}$ $\hat{7}_{\text{low}}$ $\hat{2}$
g. $\hat{3}$ $\hat{1}$ $\hat{5}$ $\hat{3}$ ✽ $\hat{6}_{\text{low}}$ $\hat{4}_{\text{low}}$ $\hat{1}$ $\hat{6}_{\text{low}}$ ✽ $\hat{7}_{\text{low}}$ $\hat{5}_{\text{low}}$ $\hat{2}$ $\hat{7}_{\text{low}}$ ✽ $\hat{3}$ $\hat{1}$ $\hat{5}$ $\hat{1}$
h. $\hat{3}$ $\hat{1}$ $\hat{5}$ $\hat{3}$ ✽ $\hat{6}_{\text{low}}$ $\hat{4}_{\text{low}}$ $\hat{1}$ $\hat{6}_{\text{low}}$ ✽ $\hat{3}$ $\hat{1}$ $\hat{5}$ $\hat{3}$ ✽ $\hat{7}_{\text{low}}$ $\hat{5}_{\text{low}}$ $\hat{2}$ $\hat{5}$
i. $\hat{3}$ $\hat{1}$ $\hat{5}$ $\hat{3}$ ✽ $\hat{7}_{\text{low}}$ $\hat{5}_{\text{low}}$ $\hat{2}$ $\hat{7}_{\text{low}}$ ✽ $\hat{3}$ $\hat{1}$ $\hat{5}$ $\hat{3}$ ✽ $\hat{7}_{\text{low}}$ $\hat{5}_{\text{low}}$ $\hat{2}$ $\hat{5}$

QUICK SWITCH

Q4–1.

Q4–2.

Q4–3.

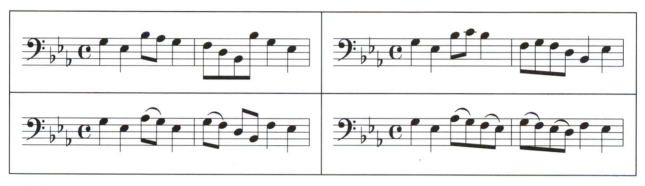

Q4–4.

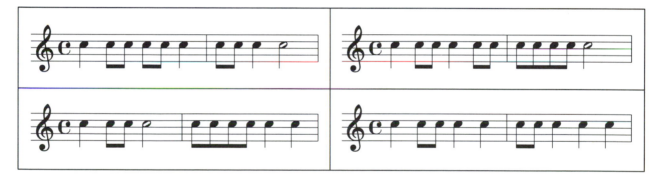

IDENTIFICATIONS

ID4–1. $\hat{1}$, $\hat{3}$, $\hat{5}$, and $\hat{8}$ in a major key are performed simultaneously. Then two of these four scale degrees are performed simultaneously. Identify the scale degrees performed from among the following choices: $\hat{1}$-$\hat{3}$, $\hat{1}$-$\hat{5}$, $\hat{1}$-$\hat{8}$, or $\hat{5}$-$\hat{8}$.

ID4–2.   An interval is performed as a simultaneity. Identify it as a major third, perfect fourth, perfect fifth, or perfect octave.

ID4–3.   A chord is performed. The root serves as the bass. Does the root, the third, or the fifth serve as the soprano?

ID4–4.   A melody is performed. Identify the correct score notation.

ID4–5.   A chord progression in the major mode is performed. Identify a suitable Roman-numeral analysis from among the following choices:

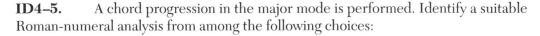

Group 1			
a.	I	IV	I
b.	I	IV	V
c.	I	V	I

Group 2				
a.	I	IV	I	V
b.	I	IV	V	I
c.	I	V	I	V

ID4–6. A chord progression is performed. Identify the correct score notation for the outer voices. If you wish, add Roman numerals.

a.

b.

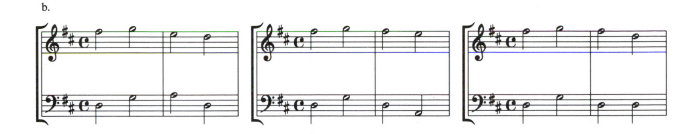

c.

d.

e.

f.

RHYTHMIC DICTATIONS

RD4–1.

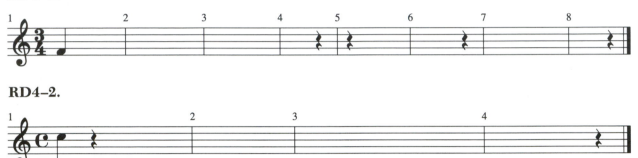

RD4–2.

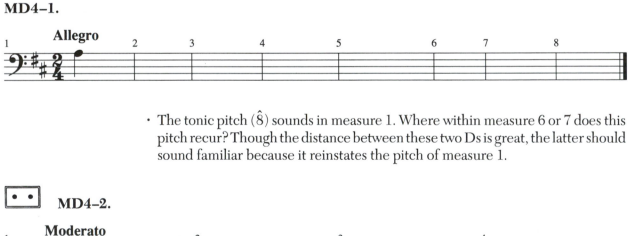

MELODIC DICTATIONS

MD4–1.

· The tonic pitch (8̂) sounds in measure 1. Where within measure 6 or 7 does this pitch recur? Though the distance between these two Ds is great, the latter should sound familiar because it reinstates the pitch of measure 1.

MD4–2.

Moderato

· How does measure 3 relate to the descending line initiated in measures 1 and 2?

MD4–3.

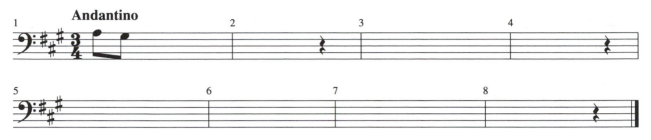

· How do measures 3 and 4 relate to measures 1 and 2? Do measures 5 and 6 relate somehow to the motivic idea of the earlier measures?

BEETHOVEN: SYMPHONY NO. 6 IN F MAJOR ("PASTORALE"), OP. 68, MVMT. 1

 **MD4–4.**

· Measures 1, 2, 5, and 6 emphasize dominant pitches, while measures 3, 4, 7, and 8 emphasize tonic pitches.

GLUCK: *IPHIGENIA IN TAURIS*, ACT 1

MD4–5.

· The pitches on beat 1 of measures 3, 4, and 5 form an ascending stepwise line.

BRAHMS: QUINTET FOR CLARINET AND STRINGS IN B MINOR, OP. 115, MVMT. 3

MD4–6.

· Observe how measures 3 and 4 retain the basic shape of measures 1 and 2.

HARMONIC DICTATIONS

Instruction: *Write down the outer voices (bass and soprano), paying attention to both pitch and rhythm. Underneath the bass, provide a Roman-numeral analysis.*

HD4–1.

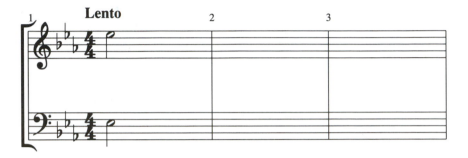

- Focus especially on the bass pitches because they uniquely identify the harmony when the choice of chords is limited to I, IV, and V. Vertically aligned soprano and bass pitches should not contradict one another. (Only a third, fifth, octave, or compound of one of these intervals will appear above a bass pitch in this chapter.) Do not assume that every successive chord represents a different harmony. In this progression, for example, the two chords of measure 1 share the same Roman numeral.

HD4–2.

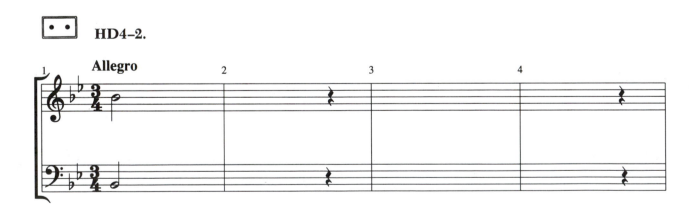

- Leaps in the soprano occur against common tones in the bass in measures 1 and 3. Because the bass does not move, you can limit your choices for the second soprano notes of these measures.

HD4–3.

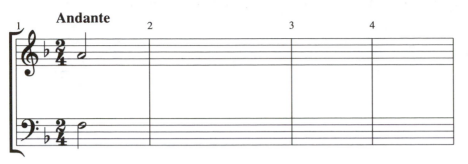

- The brief progressions used for Harmonic Dictation will not necessarily end on tonic. This progression, for example, ends on V.

 HD4–4.

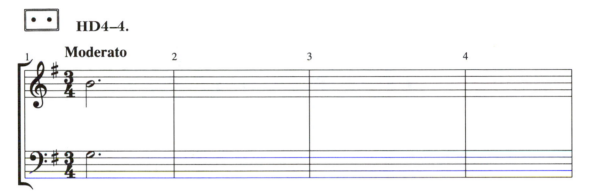

- Compare the bass pitches on beat 1 of measures 2 and 3. Are they the same, or is one lower than the other?

HD4–5.

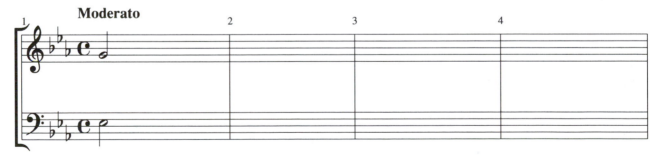

- Where do tonic chords appear within this progression? Although there are many leaps in the bass, you should sense when E♭ sounds simply because it is tonic, rather than by calculating the melodic interval from the preceding bass note. In this excerpt, all four tonic chords are identical in their construction, further reinforcing the sense of familiarity when E♭ sounds in the bass.

HD4–6.

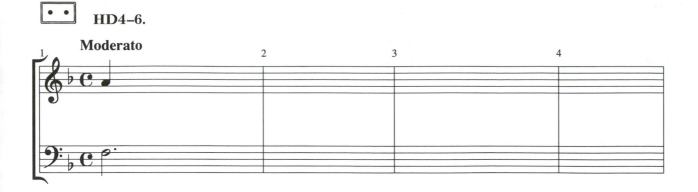

- As in Melodic Dictations, passing notes are employed in Harmonic Dictations to connect chord members.

CASSETTE PROGRAM (TAPE 1, SIDE A)

C4–1.   Six melodies are performed, twice each. During the silence after each playing, respond in one of the following ways: (1) Sing the melody using solmization syllables; (2) Play the melody on the piano or on your primary instrument; (3) Write the melody on staff paper.

C4–2.   Four chord progressions are performed, four times each. During the silence after each playing, respond in one of the following ways: (1) Sing the soprano after the first and second playings and the bass after the third and fourth playings, using solmization syllables; (2) Play the soprano on the piano or your primary instrument after the first and second playings and the bass after the third and fourth playings; (3) Play both the soprano and bass on the piano after each playing; (4) Write the soprano and bass on staff paper and provide an analysis.

Chapter 5

PITCH

The **key of A minor** and the key of C major share the same collection of seven diatonic pitches (A, B, C, D, E, F, and G). In A minor, A serves as tonic; in C major, C serves as tonic. A minor and C major are **relative keys.** A minor is the **relative minor** of C major; C major is the **relative major** of A minor. All of the keys introduced in chapters 1–4 are major keys and thus share many attributes. Your familiarity with these attributes (e.g., the major third between $\hat{1}$ and $\hat{3}$) enables you to classify a melody you may hear as major even if you cannot name the tonic pitch. Minor keys possess different attributes and thus offer possibilities for musical expression not available in major keys.

The **natural minor scale** for A minor, shown in Example 5–1, differs from that of its **parallel key** (A major) at $\hat{3}$, $\hat{6}$, and $\hat{7}$. These pitches serve as the thirds of the tonic ($\hat{1}$-$\underline{\hat{3}}$-$\hat{5}$), subdominant ($\hat{4}$-$\underline{\hat{6}}$-$\hat{8}$), and dominant ($\hat{5}$-$\underline{\hat{7}}$-$\hat{2}$) triads. In A minor, the tonic, subdominant, and dominant chords are minor. In A major, they are major. Any divergence from this norm requires the insertion of accidentals on the staff.

EXAMPLE 5–1

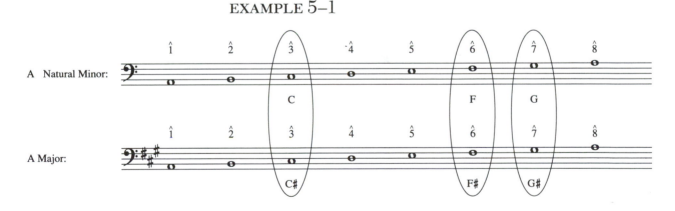

The $\hat{7}$ of major is often borrowed for use in the minor mode, especially when it precedes $\hat{8}$. G♯, when employed in the context of A minor, is labeled "♯$\hat{7}$" ("*sharp* seven" or "*raised* seven") because "$\hat{7}$" refers to the *diatonic* seventh scale degree, G, indicated by the A minor key signature of no sharps or flats. In minor, $\hat{7}$ is called the **subtonic**, while #$\hat{7}$ (like $\hat{7}$ in major) is called the ***leading tone***. Compare the two progressions in Example 5–2. Only the second leads convincingly to tonic.[1]

EXAMPLE 5–2

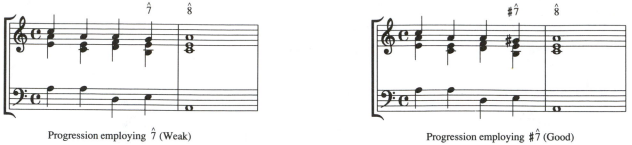

Progression employing $\hat{7}$ (Weak)   Progression employing #$\hat{7}$ (Good)

Two distinct methods of analysis will be presented in this chapter. Method Two analyses will appear in a different typeface and positioned either to the right of or below Method One analyses. Follow the method that coincides more closely with your harmony text.

<u>Method One</u> emphasizes the distinction between what is diatonic and what is not. A capital Roman numeral represents a chord composed entirely of *diatonic* pitches unless that numeral is modified by an accidental. The first progression of Example 5–2 would be analyzed as follows:

A Minor: I — IV   V   I

We know that each of these chords is minor because all *diatonic* I, IV, and V chords in the minor mode are minor. The second progression of Example 5–2 would be analyzed as follows:

A Minor: I — IV   V#   I

Because the V is *followed* by a sharp, we understand that the *third* above the root has been raised, from G to G♯.

<u>Method Two</u> emphasizes the quality of each chord. A major chord is analyzed using a capital Roman numeral. A minor chord is analyzed using a small Roman numeral. The two progressions of Example 5–2 would be analyzed as follows:

A Minor: i — iv   v   i
A Minor: i — iv   V   i

The figured bass for a major dominant chord in the key of A minor requires a sharp to the left or right of the figure "3." In fact, a sharp may appear *instead of* the figure "3." By convention, the absence of a figured-bass symbol under a bass note implies $^5_3$, so if a

---

1. #$\hat{7}$, as well as #$\hat{6}$, will be considered in greater detail in chapter 6.

"♯" appears alone, "$\frac{5}{\sharp}$" is understood. Any of the following symbols may be used for a major dominant chord in the key of A minor:

$$\begin{array}{cccc} 5 & 5 & 5 & \\ \sharp 3 & 3\sharp & \sharp & \sharp \end{array}$$

METER AND RHYTHM

A melody's sense of motion can be enhanced if a "weak" beat precedes the "strong" first beat of the first measure. Whatever precedes the first **downbeat** (beat 1) is called an **upbeat** (also called an **anacrusis** or **pickup**). Usually an equivalent amount of time is missing from the final measure of the composition. Upbeats that fill one beat are explored in this chapter; partial- and multiple-beat upbeats will be introduced in chapter 7.

When counting, begin with the number that would normally precede 1: "2" in $\frac{2}{4}$ meter, "3" in $\frac{3}{4}$ meter, or "4" in $\frac{4}{4}$ meter. Example 5–3 shows appropriate counting syllables for a melody in $\frac{3}{4}$ meter. Observe how the measures are numbered.

EXAMPLE 5–3

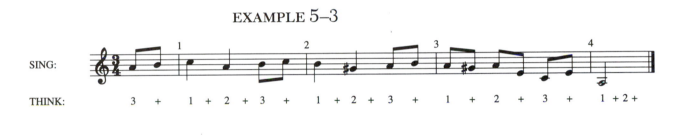

SING:

THINK: 3 + 1 + 2 + 3 + 1 + 2 + 3 + 1 + 2 + 3 + 1 + 2 +

SOLO MELODIES

Note: *The Scale Degrees system is used in the Arpeggiation Workshop, so take note of those instructions if you employ another system for the other activities.*

SCALE DEGREES: *The number $\hat{1}$ represents tonic, whether the key is major or minor. In A minor, both G and G♯ may appear. Use $\hat{7}$ ("sev") for G and "raised" for G♯ in the* **inflected** *Scale Degrees system. (Use "raised" rather than "sharp" because in some keys a natural or a double sharp will occur instead of a sharp. "Raised" applies equally well in all contexts, and it is easier to sing than "natural" or "double sharp.") If your instructor prefers* **uninflected** *syllables, use $\hat{7}$ ("sev") for both G and G♯.*

MOVABLE DO (DO TONIC IN MINOR): *The syllable "do" represents tonic, whether the key is major or minor. The appropriate syllables for the ascending natural minor scale are "do," "re," "me," "fa," "sol," "le," "te," and "do." When ♯$\hat{7}$ substitutes for $\hat{7}$, use "ti."*

MOVABLE DO (LA TONIC IN MINOR): *The syllable "la" represents tonic when the key is minor. Thus the syllables for any minor key correspond exactly to those for its relative major key (a minor third higher). The appropriate syllables for the ascending natural minor scale are "la," "ti," "do," "re," "mi," "fa," "sol," and "la." When #7̂ substitutes for 7̂, use "si."*

FIXED DO: *Because the context of a pitch does not affect its solmization syllable, the key of A minor poses no new difficulties in the Fixed Do system.*

LETTER NAMES: *Because the context of a pitch does not affect its solmization syllable, the key of A minor poses no new difficulties in the Letter Names system.*

SAMPLE SOLMIZATION

SCALE DEGREES:	3̂	1̂	7̂	6̂	5̂	1̂	raised		2̂	5̂	1̂
		(or 8̂				8̂	7̂			8̂)
MOVABLE DO (Do = Tonic):	me	do	te	le	sol	do	ti	re	sol	do
MOVABLE DO (La = Tonic):	do	la	sol	fa	mi	la	si	ti	mi	la
FIXED DO:	do	la	sol	fa	mi	la	si (or sol)	ti	mi	la
LETTER NAMES:	C	A	G	F	E	A	Gis (or G)	B	E	A

MELODIES IN A MINOR

S5–1.

- Before singing, find the C of measure 1 in your internal ear to prevent yourself from ascending to C♯ by mistake.

S5–2.

Andante con moto

S5–3.

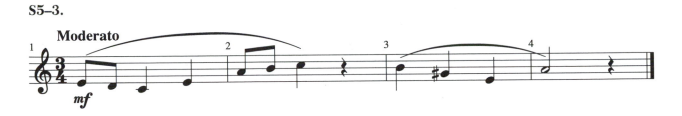

- There is nothing within measure 1 that suggests A minor as tonic, instead of C major. Only in measure 2 are the key and mode confirmed. Think of tonic A before you begin to prevent yourself from singing G instead of A on beat 1 of measure 2. As preparation, sing the following:

S5–4.

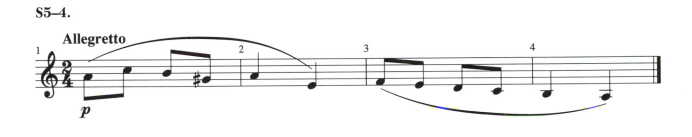

S5–5.

- In this melody, minor tonic and subdominant chords are outlined. (The dominant of measure 3 is major.) The Cs of measures 1 and 4 and the F of measure 2 deserve special attention. It would be easy to sing C♯ instead of C and F♯ instead of F, but the composer (your author) insists on minor!

S5–6.

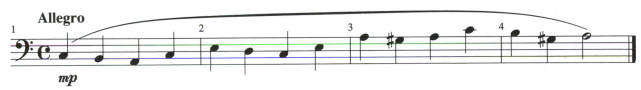

S5–7.

- In measures 5 through 7, each of the three pitches of the major dominant triad is preceded by its upper neighbor. Because the key is minor, each of these neighbors is a half step above the pitch that it embellishes, reinforcing the characteristic "melancholy" mood of the mode. If you understand the underlying structure, you should not find the ascending diminished fourth (G♯ to C) from measure 6 to measure 7 daunting. Practice by singing E, G♯, B, then F E, A G♯, C B.

S5–8.

S5–9.

- Do not sing G♯ at the end of measure 3 by mistake. Though melodies that employ $\hat{7}$ rather than ♯$\hat{7}$ when ascending to $\hat{8}$ are rare, they do occur.

S5–10.

MELODIES THAT FEATURE
ONE-BEAT UPBEATS

S5–11.

· Your performance will be enhanced if you take a breath after the B♭ of measure 4. Why?

MOZART: SYMPHONY NO. 40 IN G MINOR, K. 550, MVMT. 3

S5–12.

BEETHOVEN: SYMPHONY NO. 6 IN F MAJOR ("PASTORALE"), OP. 68, MVMT. 3

S5–13.

· In your performance, convey a distinction between the pitches that are part of the tonic arpeggiation (D, F♯, and A) and the pitches that serve as neighboring notes (C♯ lower neighbor to D, B upper neighbor to A, G upper neighbor to F♯).

BEETHOVEN: SYMPHONY NO. 2 IN D MAJOR, OP. 36, MVMT. 3

S5–14.

DUETS

D5–1.

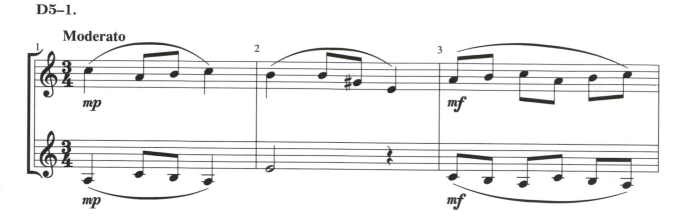

D5–2.

ACCOMPANIED SOLO MELODIES

AS5–1.

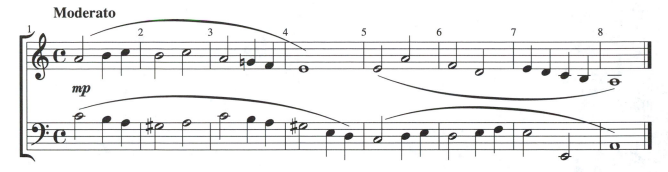

AS5–2.

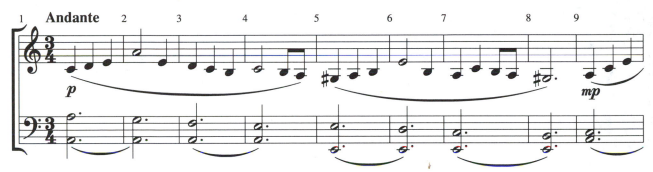

RHYTHMS

R5–1.

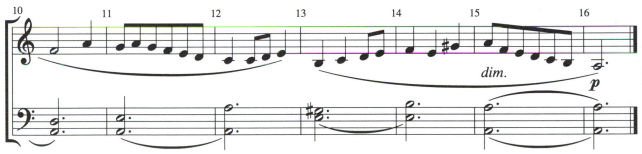

R5–2.

R5–3.

R5–4.

R5–5.

R5–6.

INTERVAL WORKSHOP

I5–1.   Play a pitch that is low in your vocal range at a keyboard. Sing it. Then sing the pitch a minor third higher. Use the keyboard to confirm your performance. Then sing ascending thirds starting on other pitches.

I5–2.   Play a pitch that is high in your vocal range at a keyboard. Sing it. Then sing the pitch a minor third lower. Use the keyboard to confirm your performance. Then sing descending thirds starting on other pitches.

I5–3.   Practice singing the interval of a minor third higher than a sounding pitch. The sounding pitch should be at or beyond the lower limit of your vocal range, and could be sung by a classmate or your instructor or performed on the piano or another instrument such as the cello. Also practice singing compound versions of this interval.

I5–4.   Practice singing the interval of a minor third lower than a sounding pitch. The sounding pitch should be at or beyond the upper limit of your vocal range, and could be sung by a classmate or your instructor or performed on the piano or another instrument such as the flute. Also practice singing compound versions of this interval.

ARPEGGIATION WORKSHOP

A5–1.   Play an A that is low in your vocal range at a keyboard. Let this pitch be 1̂ in a minor key. Sing each of the following arpeggiations, either in the order given or in random order.

> ***Note on Performance:*** *Sing "raised" when you see the symbol "#7̂."*

a.	1̂	3̂	5̂	3̂	❀	4̂	6̂	8̂	6̂	❀	5̂	#7̂	2̂	#7̂	❀	8̂	5̂	3̂	1̂
b.	1̂	3̂	5̂	3̂	❀	4̂	6̂	8̂	6̂	❀	5̂	3̂	1̂	3̂	❀	5̂	7̂	2̂	5̂
c.	1̂	3̂	5̂	3̂	❀	4̂	6̂	8̂	6̂	❀	5̂	3̂	1̂	3̂	❀	5̂	#7̂	2̂	5̂
d.	1̂	3̂	5̂	3̂	❀	5̂	#7̂	2̂	#7̂	❀	8̂	5̂	3̂	1̂	❀	5̂	7̂	2̂	5̂
e.	1̂	3̂	5̂	3̂	❀	5̂	#7̂	2̂	#7̂	❀	8̂	5̂	3̂	1̂	❀	5̂	#7̂	2̂	5̂
f.	3̂	1̂	5̂	3̂	❀	6̂	4̂	8̂	6̂	❀	5̂	#7̂	2̂	#7̂	❀	8̂	5̂	3̂	1̂
g.	3̂	1̂	5̂	3̂	❀	6̂	4̂	8̂	6̂	❀	3̂	5̂	1̂	3̂	❀	5̂	7̂	2̂	5̂
h.	3̂	1̂	5̂	3̂	❀	6̂	4̂	8̂	6̂	❀	3̂	5̂	1̂	3̂	❀	5̂	#7̂	2̂	5̂
i.	3̂	1̂	5̂	3̂	❀	5̂	#7̂	2̂	#7̂	❀	8̂	5̂	1̂	5̂	❀	7̂	5̂	2̂	5̂
j.	3̂	1̂	5̂	3̂	❀	5̂	#7̂	2̂	#7̂	❀	8̂	5̂	1̂	5̂	❀	#7̂	5̂	2̂	5̂

A5–2.   Play an A that is near the middle of your vocal range at a keyboard. Let this pitch be 1̂ in a minor key. Sing each of the following arpeggiations, either in the order given or in the order given or in random order.

a.	1̂	3̂	1̂	❀	4	6	1̂	4	❀	5	#7	2̂	5	❀	1̂	3̂	1̂		
b.	1̂	3̂	1̂	❀	4	6	1̂	4	❀	1̂	3̂	1̂	❀	5	7	2̂	5		
c.	1̂	3̂	1̂	❀	4	6	1̂	4	❀	1̂	3̂	1̂	❀	5	#7	2̂	5		
d.	1̂	3̂	1̂	❀	5	#7	2̂	5	❀	1̂	3̂	1̂	❀	5	7	2̂	5̂		
e.	1̂	3̂	1̂	❀	5	#7	2̂	5	❀	1̂	3̂	1̂	❀	5	#7	2̂	5̂		
f.	1̂	3̂	1̂	❀	6	4	1̂	6	❀	5	#7	2̂	#7	❀	1̂	3̂	1̂		
g.	1̂	3̂	1̂	❀	6	4	1̂	6	❀	1̂	3̂	1̂	❀	7	5	2̂	5̂		
h.	1̂	3̂	1̂	❀	6	4	1̂	6	❀	1̂	3̂	1̂	❀	#7	5	2̂	5̂		
i.	1̂	3̂	1̂	❀	#7	5	2̂	#7	❀	1̂	3̂	1̂	❀	7	5	2̂	5̂		
j.	1̂	3̂	1̂	❀	#7	5	2̂	#7	❀	1̂	3̂	1̂	❀	#7	5	2̂	5̂		

QUICK SWITCH

Q5–1.

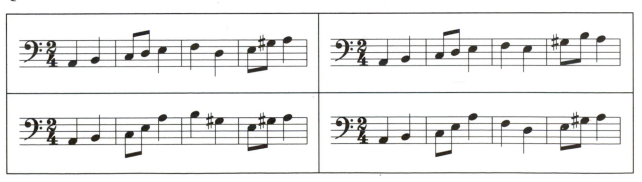

Q5–2.

Q5–3.

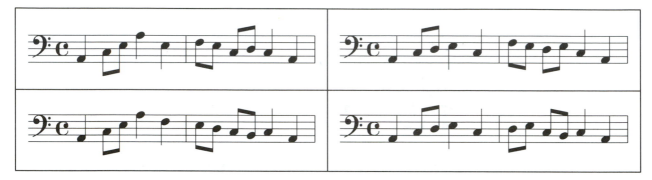

Q5–4.

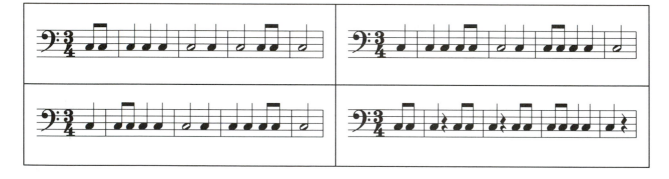

IDENTIFICATIONS

ID5–1.   An interval is performed melodically (ascending or descending) or as a simultaneity. Identify it as a minor third, major third, perfect fourth, perfect fifth, or perfect octave.

ID5–2.   A triad is performed. Identify it as a major triad, a minor triad, or neither.

ID5–3.   A minor triad is performed. Then two of its three pitches are performed melodically: root-third, root-fifth, third-root, third-fifth, fifth-root, or fifth-third. Identify which of these choices is performed.

ID5–4. $\hat{1}, \hat{3}, \hat{5},$ and $\hat{8}$ in A minor are performed simultaneously. Then two of these four scale degrees are performed simultaneously. Identify the scale degrees performed from among the following choices: $\hat{1}$-$\hat{3}$, $\hat{1}$-$\hat{5}$, $\hat{1}$-$\hat{8}$, $\hat{3}$-$\hat{5}$, or $\hat{5}$-$\hat{8}$.

ID5–5. $\hat{1}, \hat{3}, \hat{5},$ and $\hat{8}$ in a major key are performed simultaneously. Then two of these four scale degrees are performed simultaneously. Identify the two scale degrees performed from among the following choices: $\hat{1}$-$\hat{3}$, $\hat{1}$-$\hat{5}$, $\hat{1}$-$\hat{8}$, $\hat{3}$-$\hat{5}$, or $\hat{5}$-$\hat{8}$.

ID5–6.   A minor chord is performed. The root serves as the bass. Does the root, the third, or the fifth serve as the soprano?

ID5–7.   A melody is performed. Identify the correct score notation.

ID5–8.   A chord progression in the minor mode is performed. Identify a suitable
Roman-numeral analysis from among the following choices:

Group 1

a.	I	IV	I	a.	i	iv	i
b.	I	V♯	I	b.	i	V	i
c.	I	IV	V♯	c.	i	iv	V

Group 2

a.	I	IV	I	V♯	a.	i	iv	i	V
b.	I	IV	V♯	I	b.	i	iv	V	i
c.	I	V♯	I	V♯	c.	i	V	i	V

ID5–9.   A chord progression is performed. Identify the correct score notation for
the outer voices. Figured-bass symbols have been placed below the bass where appropriate. If you wish, add Roman numerals.

e.

f.

RHYTHMIC DICTATIONS

RD5–1.

RD5–2.

MELODIC DICTATIONS

MD5–1.

Allegro

- Only five pitches of this melody (1 each in measures 1, 3, and 4; 2 in measure 2) would not occur in A major. Circle those five pitches as you write them down.

HAYDN: SYMPHONY NO. 97 IN C MAJOR, MVMT. 3

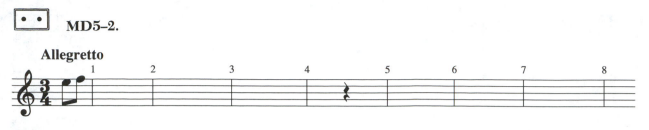

MD5–2.

Allegretto

- The descent to $\hat{1}$ in measure 2 should not prevent you from hearing a linear connection between the downbeats of measures 1 and 3.

J. STRAUSS: *DIE FLEDERMAUS*, ACT 1

MD5–3.

Allegro moderato

- The pitch on beat 3 of measure 2 is *not* G. Is it higher or lower than G? What is its melodic relationship with G?

BEETHOVEN: PIANO SONATA NO. 21 IN C MAJOR ("WALDSTEIN"), OP. 53, MVMT. 3

MD5–4.

Allegro moderato

- Three of the diatonic pitches of A minor differ from those of A major, but only one of them occurs within this melody.

SCHUBERT: PIANO SONATA IN B♭ MAJOR, D. 960, MVMT. 1

MD5–5.

Molto moderato

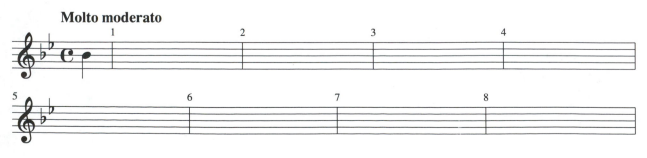

· Listen for a linear connection among the following pitches: measure 2, beat 1; measure 5, beat 1; measure 6, beat 1; and measure 7, beat 3.

R. STRAUSS: *DEATH AND TRANSFIGURATION*, OP. 24

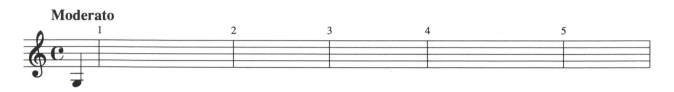

MD5–6.

· Though this melody spans a wide range, none of its intervals is larger than an octave. What scale degree is the third pitch of measure 1? What scale degree is the fourth (last) pitch of measure 1?

HARMONIC DICTATIONS

Instruction: *Write down the outer voices and provide a Roman-numeral analysis, as usual. Construct your Roman numerals following one of the two methods introduced in this chapter.*

HD5–1.

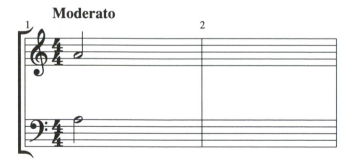

· Three of the four soprano pitches in the progression are the same. Determine whether the pitch that begins measure 2 is a whole step or a half step below the other pitches. Remember that the key signature for A minor indicates G, not G♯. Whenever G♯ is used, a sharp must be inserted beside the notehead.

HD5–2.

Allegro

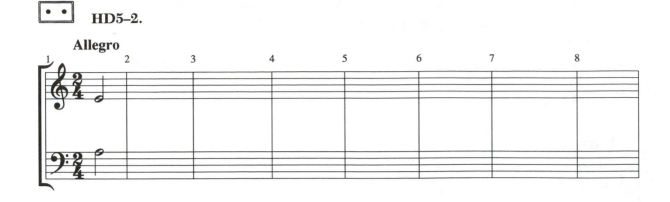

- Measures 3 and 7 are more active than the other measures. Be careful to assess *where* the activity takes place. Is the soprano involved? Is the bass involved?

HD5–3.

Moderato

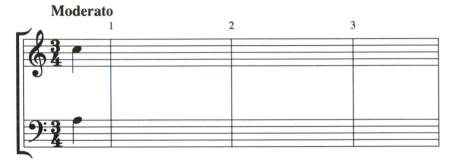

- This progression would be adequate even if the chord on beat 3 of measure 2 were omitted. Its presence intensifies the dominant-to-tonic harmonic progression because both $\hat{2}$ and $\sharp\hat{7}$ appear before $\hat{1}$ in the soprano.

HD5–4.

Andante

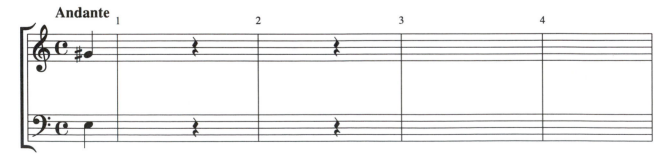

· The soprano pitch on beat 4 of measure 2 creates an uncommon interval with the preceding soprano pitch. No problem! You should not hear beat 4 of measure 2 in relation to beat 1 of measure 2, but instead as a repetition of the upbeat that precedes measure 1. What other chords do the two halves of this harmonic progression have in common?

HD5–5.

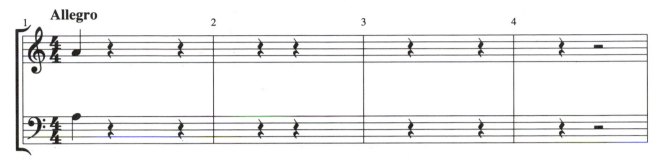

· Though this progression contains seven chords, you should use only four Roman numerals. There is no "progression" from tonic to tonic to tonic in measures 1 and 2. Think instead of a single *harmony* being prolonged through several *chords*. How do the soprano pitches of these three chords contribute to the prolongation of tonic?

 **HD5–6.**

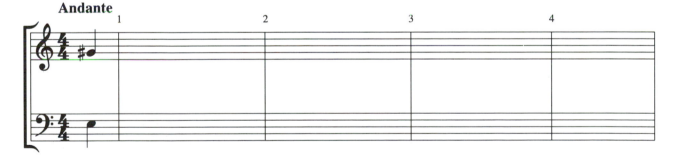

· A passing note appears within the soprano voice of this progression.

⟦··⟧ CASSETTE PROGRAM (TAPE 1, SIDE A)

C5–1.   Six melodies are performed, twice each. During the silence after each playing, respond in one of the following ways: (1) Sing the melody, using solmization syllables; (2) Play the melody on the piano or on your primary instrument; (3) Write the melody on staff paper.

C5–2.   Four chord progressions are performed, four times each. During the silence after each playing, respond in one of the following ways: (1) Sing the soprano after the first and second playings and the bass after the third and fourth playings, using solmization syllables; (2) Play the soprano on the piano or your primary instrument after the first and second playings and the bass after the third and fourth playings; (3) Play both the soprano and bass on the piano after each playing; (4) Write the soprano and bass on staff paper and provide an analysis.

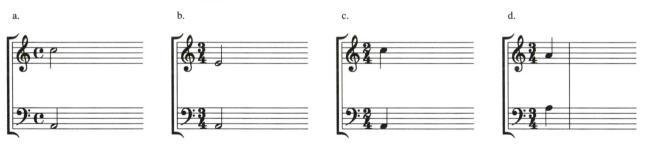

Chapter 6

PITCH

The natural minor scale conforms to the minor key signature. The ***harmonic minor scale*** results when #$\hat{7}$ substitutes for $\hat{7}$. The pitches of the natural minor scale form a succession of major seconds (whole steps) and minor seconds (half steps). In the harmonic minor scale, $\hat{6}$ and #$\hat{7}$ form a rarer, less melodious interval, the ***augmented second.*** Composers seldom juxtapose $\hat{6}$ and #$\hat{7}$ in melodies. When a stepwise ascent to the leading tone is desired, the $\hat{6}$ of major (labeled #$\hat{6}$ in the context of A minor) is generally employed. The ***ascending melodic minor scale*** codifies this practice. These ascending scales are displayed and analyzed in Example 6–1. The standard abbreviations used are "m" (for "minor"), "M" (for "major"), and "A" (for "augmented").

EXAMPLE 6–1

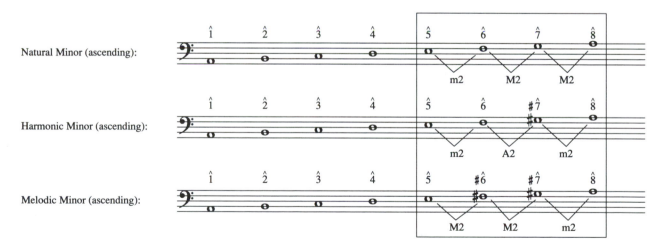

In descending stepwise from $\hat{8}$ to $\hat{5}$, the leading tone (#$\hat{7}$) is often inappropriate. (The leading tone *leads* to $\hat{8}$, not to $\hat{6}$!) The presence of #$\hat{7}$ is sometimes warranted, however, especially when the descending melody connects the third and root of the major dominant chord. Compare the two music excerpts in Example 6–2.

EXAMPLE 6–2

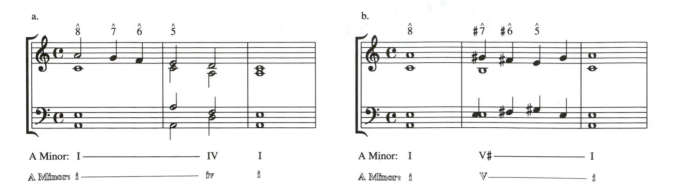

The ***descending melodic minor scale*** is identical to the descending natural minor scale. Be aware, however, that the pitches of the ascending melodic minor scale are sometimes employed during a descending melody as well, as in Example 6–2b. All three descending minor scales are displayed and analyzed in Example 6–3. Melodic minor is the only common scale whose descent varies the path of its ascent.

EXAMPLE 6–3

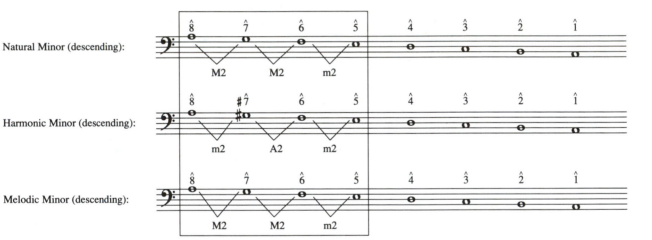

As you sing and listen to melodies in the minor mode, consider how the sixth and seventh scale degrees are treated. A greater upward pull toward $\hat{8}$ results from #$\hat{6}$ and #$\hat{7}$. A greater downward pull toward $\hat{5}$ results from $\hat{7}$ and $\hat{6}$. An unusual interval results when $\hat{6}$ and #$\hat{7}$ are juxtaposed. Though you might initially find this variety disconcerting, go beyond the mere memorization of intervallic successions and explore the underlying forces that make these options necessary.

In Example 6–4, both #$\hat{6}$ and #$\hat{7}$ are employed. In the Method One analysis, sharps appear to the right of the Roman numerals IV and V to indicate that the *third* above each chord's root is raised. The figured bass for these two chords is displayed as

$\frac{5}{\sharp}$, one of the four options given in chapter 5.[1] In the Method Two analysis, the use of capital and small numerals indicates which chords are major and which are minor.

EXAMPLE 6–4

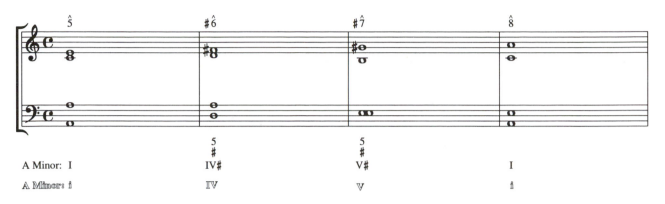

The **key of E minor** and the **key of D minor** are introduced in this chapter. Their key signatures contain one sharp and one flat, respectively. E minor is the relative minor of G major; D minor is the relative minor of F major.

Because $\hat{6}$ in D minor (B♭) is raised by a natural, not a sharp, the appropriate scale degree symbol for B♮ in the context of D minor is "♮$\hat{6}$" ("*natural* $\hat{6}$" or "*raised* $\hat{6}$"), not "♯$\hat{6}$." Use "♯$\hat{6}$" when a sharp is used or when referring to the raised sixth in general, without reference to a specific key. Use "♮$\hat{6}$" only when a natural is used in a specified key. Example 6–5 shows the progression of Example 6–4 transposed to the key of D minor. Observe the correct usage of symbols for scale degrees, figured bass, and Roman numerals.

EXAMPLE 6–5

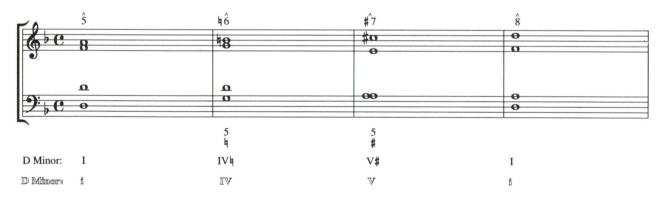

---

1. The use of a sharp both beside the Roman numeral and in the figured bass may seem redundant. This issue will be explored more fully when the inversions of these chords are introduced in chapter 9.

METER AND RHYTHM

Eighth notes need not occur in pairs, as they did in chapters 4 and 5. A single eighth note (♪) may occur if preceded or followed by an **eighth rest** (𝄾) or if preceded by a **dotted quarter note** (♩.). An eighth rest may also be used after a dotted quarter note to fill two beats in $\frac{2}{4}$, $\frac{3}{4}$, or $\frac{4}{4}$ meter. Example 6–6 demonstrates these various possibilities.

EXAMPLE 6–6

SING:																				
THINK:	4	+	1	+	2	+	3	+	4	+	1	+	2	+	3	+	4	+	1	+	2	+	3	+

SOLO MELODIES

MOVABLE DO (DO TONIC IN MINOR): *Sing "le" for* $\hat{6}$ *and "la" for* $\sharp\hat{6}$ *in minor keys.*

MOVABLE DO (LA TONIC IN MINOR): *Sing "fa" for* $\hat{6}$ *and "fi" for* $\sharp\hat{6}$ *in minor keys.*

FIXED DO: *In the key of E minor, sing "ri" for* $\sharp\hat{7}$.

LETTER NAMES: *In the key of E minor, sing "Dis" (= D♯) for* $\sharp\hat{7}$.

SAMPLE SOLMIZATION: *Comments: (1) "Courtesy" accidentals are often employed in minor even when the bar line would adequately cancel the effect of preceding accidentals. The natural and flat in the second measure of this melody, though not required, help prevent errors in performance. They do not deserve special treatment in solmization. C♮ and B♭ are* $\hat{7}$ *and* $\hat{6}$, *not "lowered"* $\hat{7}$ *and "lowered"* $\hat{6}$. *(2) From this point on, only inflected solmization syllables will be demonstrated. The principles described in earlier chapters prevail for uninflected solmization.*

SCALE DEGREES:	$\hat{6}$	$\hat{5}$	raised	raised	$\hat{8}$	$\hat{7}$	$\hat{6}$	$\hat{5}$	$\hat{8}$
MOVABLE DO (Do = Tonic):	le	sol	la	ti	do	te	le	sol	do
MOVABLE DO (La = Tonic):	fa	mi	fi	si	la	sol	fa	mi	la
FIXED DO:	te	la	ti	di	re	do	te	la	re
LETTER NAMES:	Bes	A	B	Cis	D	C	Bes	A	D

MELODIES IN A, D, AND E MINOR, EMPHASIZING $\hat{6}$, #$\hat{6}$, $\hat{7}$, AND #$\hat{7}$

S6-1.

- Observe that the neighboring notes in measures 1 and 2 are not the same. $\hat{1}$ to $\hat{2}$ is a whole step; $\hat{5}$ to $\hat{6}$ is a half step.

S6–2.

S6–3.

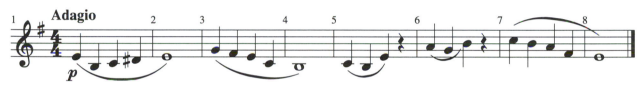

- An augmented second occurs in measure 1. Practice by replacing D# with B (sing E-B-C-B-E). Then sing just E-D#-E. Finally, merge these two ideas.

- The A that begins measure 6 might be difficult to find at first. Practice by replacing the A and G of measure 6 with a G half note. With this alteration, a clear arpeggiation of tonic pitches occurs in measures 5 and 6 (B-E-G-B). When this version is secure, embellish the G of measure 6 with its upper neighbor A, as written.

DVOŘÁK: *RUSALKA*, OP. 114, ACT 2

S6–4.

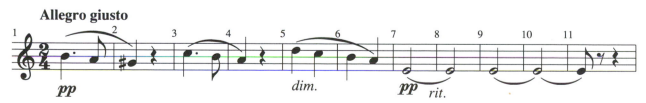

S6–5.

- Aim for the E that begins measure 2 by descending from G (upbeat to measure 1) through F♯ (measure 1) to E (measure 2). The E of measure 1 is a passing note connecting F♯ and D♯, which lead from above and below to E in measure 2.

- The C-B succession of measures 2 and 3 is repeated in measure 5. This neighboring-note motive is repeated in measure 6, with E embellishing D♯. Your performance should project a return to tonic in measure 7, *not* measure 6.

S6–6.

S6–7.

- Measure 3 contains an augmented second. Practice this passage by singing G♯-B-G♯-F♯-E and G♯-B-G♯-F♮-E in alternation.

S6–8.

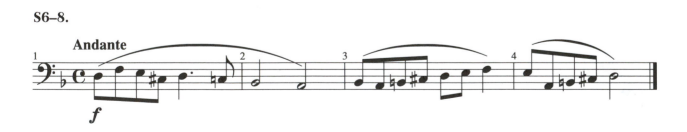

MELODIES THAT EMPLOY DOTTED QUARTER NOTES OR EIGHTH RESTS

GOUNOD: *FAUST*, ACT 3

S6–9.

- Three consecutive descending thirds occur in the opening measures of this melody. The first is unembellished (A-F), the second is embellished by a passing note (Bb-A-G), and the third is embellished by both an upper neighbor and a passing note (D-C-Bb-A).

BEETHOVEN: *FIDELIO*, OP. 72, ACT 1

S6–10.

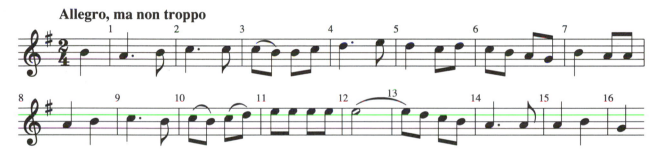

VERDI: *OTELLO*, ACT 2

S6–11.

- Secure tonic carefully in your mind before you begin. The opening two measures expand the 3̂-1̂ of tonic. The next two measures expand the 7̂-5̂ of dominant.

DVOŘÁK: SYMPHONY NO. 9 IN E MINOR ("FROM THE NEW WORLD"), OP. 95, MVMT. 4

S6–12.

LISZT: DANTE SYMPHONY, MVMT. 2 ("PURGATORY")

S6–13.

- The large-scale tonic arpeggiation that spans the entire excerpt incorporates a brief dominant arpeggiation in measures 1 and 2: B♭, D, F. The C that begins measure 2 is a passing note.

TCHAIKOVSKY: SYMPHONY NO. 4 IN F MINOR, OP. 36, MVMT. 4

S6–14.

SCHUBERT: SYMPHONY NO. 9 IN C MAJOR ("THE GREAT"), D. 944, MVMT. 1

S6–15.

· The accented F that begins measure 3 serves as a neighbor to the E that follows on beat 3. Do the Ds in measures 6 and 7 play a similar role?

SCHUBERT: SONATA FOR ARPEGGIONE AND PIANO IN A MINOR, D. 821, MVMT. 3

S6–16.

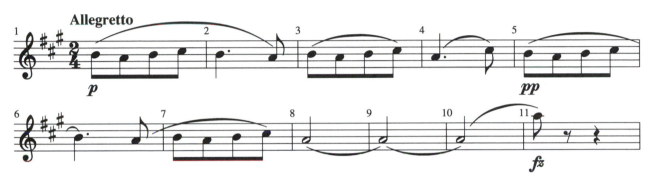

DUETS

D6–1.

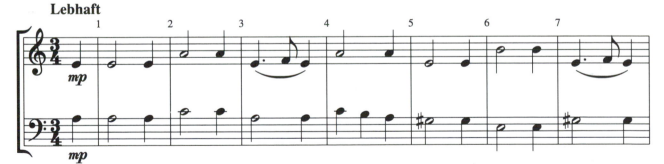

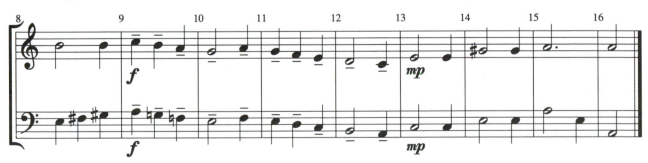

D6–2.

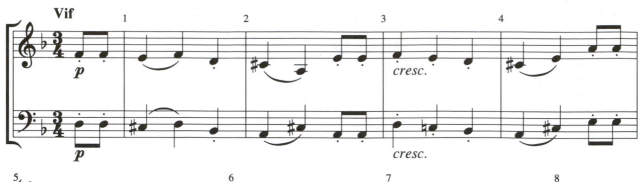

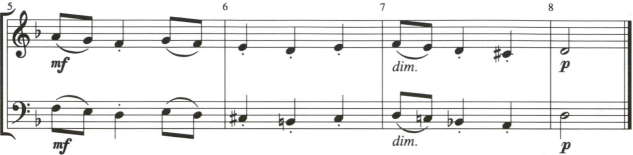

ACCOMPANIED SOLO MELODIES

AS6–1.

AS6–2.

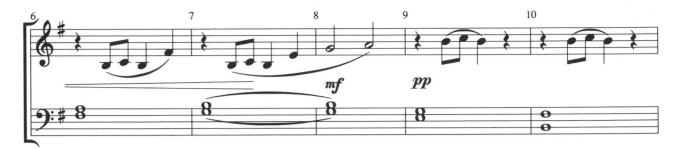

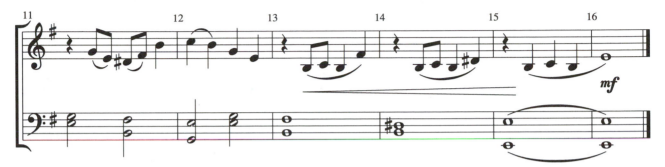

RHYTHMS

R6–1.

R6–2.

R6–3.

R6–4.

R6–5.

R6–6.

INTERVAL WORKSHOP

I6–1.   At the keyboard, play an A, D, or E that is low in your vocal range. Sing it. Then sing each of the following, using solmization syllables:

    a.   An ascending major scale
    b.   An ascending natural minor scale
    c.   An ascending melodic minor scale
    d.   An ascending harmonic minor scale

I6–2.   At the keyboard, play an A, D, or E that is high in your vocal range. Sing it. Then sing each of the following, using solmization syllables:

    a.   A descending major scale
    b.   A descending natural minor or melodic minor scale
    c.   A descending harmonic minor scale

ARPEGGIATION WORKSHOP

A6–1.   Play an A, D, or E that is low in your vocal range at a keyboard. Let this pitch be $\hat{1}$ in a minor key. Sing each of the following arpeggiations, either in the order given or in random order.

Note on Performance: *Sing "raised" when you see the symbol "♯6̂."*

a.	1̂	3̂	5̂	3̂	✿	4̂	6̂	8̂	6̂	✿	5̂	♯7̂	2̂	♯7̂	✿	8̂	5̂	3̂	1̂
b.	1̂	3̂	5̂	3̂	✿	4̂	♯6̂	8̂	♯6̂	✿	5̂	♯7̂	2̂	♯7̂	✿	8̂	5̂	3̂	1̂
c.	1̂	5̂	3̂	1̂	✿	4̂	8̂	6̂	4̂	✿	5̂	2̂	♯7̂	5̂	✿	8̂	5̂	3̂	1̂
d.	1̂	5̂	3̂	1̂	✿	4̂	8̂	♯6̂	4̂	✿	5̂	2̂	♯7̂	5̂	✿	8̂	5̂	3̂	1̂
e.	3̂	1̂	3̂	5̂	✿	6̂	4̂	6̂	8̂	✿	♯7̂	5̂	♯7̂	2̂	✿	8̂	5̂	3̂	1̂
f.	3̂	1̂	3̂	5̂	✿	♯6̂	4̂	♯6̂	8̂	✿	♯7̂	5̂	♯7̂	2̂	✿	8̂	5̂	3̂	1̂
g.	3̂	5̂	1̂	5̂	✿	6̂	8̂	4̂	8̂	✿	♯7̂	2̂	5̂	2̂	✿	8̂	5̂	3̂	1̂
h.	3̂	5̂	1̂	5̂	✿	♯6̂	8̂	4̂	8̂	✿	♯7̂	2̂	5̂	2̂	✿	8̂	5̂	3̂	1̂

A6–2. Play an A, D, or E that is at least a perfect fifth above the lowest note of your vocal range at a keyboard. Let this pitch be 1̂ in a minor key. Sing each of the following arpeggiations, either in the order given or in random order.

a.	1̂	3̂	1̂	✿	4̂	6̂	1̂	4̂	✿	5̂	♯7̂	2̂	5̂	✿	1̂	3̂	1̂		
b.	1̂	3̂	1̂	✿	4̂	♯6̂	1̂	4̂	✿	5̂	♯7̂	2̂	5̂	✿	1̂	3̂	1̂		
c.	1̂	3̂	1̂	✿	4̂	1̂	6̂	4̂	✿	5̂	2̂	♯7̂	5̂	✿	1̂	3̂	1̂		
d.	1̂	3̂	1̂	✿	4̂	1̂	♯6̂	4̂	✿	5̂	2̂	♯7̂	5̂	✿	1̂	3̂	1̂		
e.	1̂	3̂	1̂	✿	6̂	4̂	1̂	6̂	✿	♯7̂	5̂	2̂	♯7̂	✿	1̂	3̂	1̂		
f.	1̂	3̂	1̂	✿	♯6̂	4̂	1̂	♯6̂	✿	♯7̂	5̂	2̂	♯7̂	✿	1̂	3̂	1̂		
g.	1̂	3̂	1̂	✿	6̂	1̂	4̂	6̂	✿	♯7̂	2̂	5̂	♯7̂	✿	1̂	3̂	1̂		
h.	1̂	3̂	1̂	✿	♯6̂	1̂	4̂	♯6̂	✿	♯7̂	2̂	5̂	♯7̂	✿	1̂	3̂	1̂		

QUICK SWITCH

Q6–1.

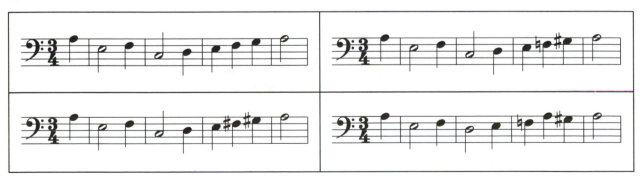

Q6–2.

Q6–3.

Q6–4.

IDENTIFICATIONS

ID6–1.   An interval is performed melodically, either ascending or descending. Identify it as a minor second, major second, or augmented second.

ID6–2.   A scale is performed, ascending and descending. Identify it as a major scale, natural minor scale, harmonic minor scale, or melodic minor scale.

ID6–3. A melody is performed. Identify the correct score notation.

ID6–4. A chord progression in the minor mode is performed. Identify a suitable Roman-numeral analysis from among the following choices:

Group 1

a.	I	IV	I	a.	i	iv	i
b.	I	V♯	I	b.	i	V	i
c.	I	IV	V♯	c.	i	iv	V
d.	I	IV♯	V♯	d.	i	IV	V

<u>Group 2</u>

a.	I	IV	I	V#	a.	i	iv	i	V
b.	I	IV	V#	I	b.	i	iv	V	i
c.	I	IV#	V#	I	c.	i	IV	V	i
d.	I	V#	I	V#	d.	i	V	i	V

ID6–5.   A chord progression is performed. Identify the correct score notation for the outer voices. Figured-bass symbols have been placed below the bass where appropriate. If you wish, add Roman numerals.

a.

b.

c.

d.

e.

f.

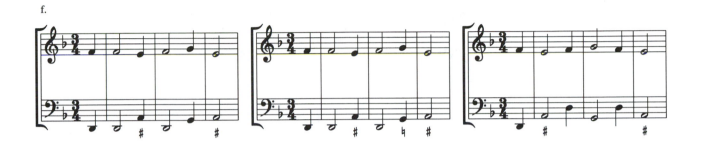

RHYTHMIC DICTATIONS

RD6–1.

RD6–2.

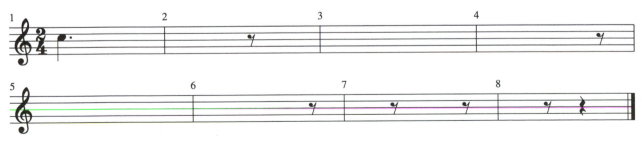

MELODIC DICTATIONS

MENDELSSOHN: SONG WITHOUT WORDS, OP. 30, NO. 5 (BOOK 2)

MD6–1.

Andante grazioso

- After you hear the melody once, "perform" the descending arpeggiation 8̂-5̂-3̂-1̂ in your mind. How does Mendelssohn use this basic structure?

GOUNOD: *FAUST*, ACT 5

MD6–2.

Adagio

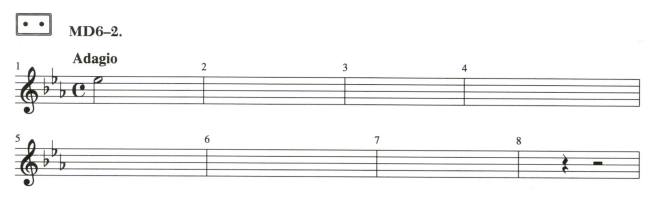

- Composers rarely position a dotted quarter note on beat 2 in ⁴₄ meter. Instead, a quarter note is tied to an eighth note. Use this notation in measures 4 and 6. Similarly, tie a half note to an eighth note in measure 2.

BEETHOVEN: SYMPHONY NO. 9 IN D MINOR ("CHORAL"), OP. 125, MVMT. 3

MD6–3.

Adagio molto e cantabile

- As in Exercise 1, a descending arpeggiation plays a prominent role in this excerpt. This time, the initial pitch is 3̂. "Perform" the descending arpeggiation 3̂-8̂-5̂-3̂ in your mind after you have heard the melody once. Beethoven, unlike Mendelssohn, ascends back to his starting point (at beat 1 of measure 4).

MD6–4.

Moderato

- Compare the first three pitches of this melody (the pickup beat and beat 1 of measure 1) with the three pitches on beat 3 of measure 2 and beat 1 of measure 3.

MD6–5.

- Distinguish carefully between F and F♯ and between G and G♯. All four of these pitches occur during this melody.

FRANCK: SYMPHONY IN D MINOR, MVMT. 1

MD6–6.

- How do beats 1 and 3 of measures 1 and 2 relate?

- How do the first three pitches of measure 3 relate to the preceding measures? How do measures 5 and 6 relate to measures 3 and 4?

HARMONIC DICTATIONS

HD6–1.

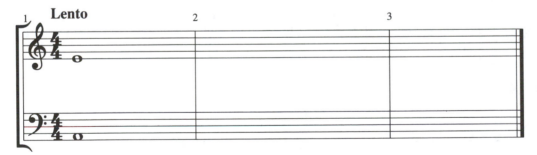

- The melody of this progression ascends from $\hat{5}$ to $\hat{8}$. Are the second and third soprano pitches leaning upward toward $\hat{8}$? Are the chords that support these soprano pitches major or minor?

HD6–2.

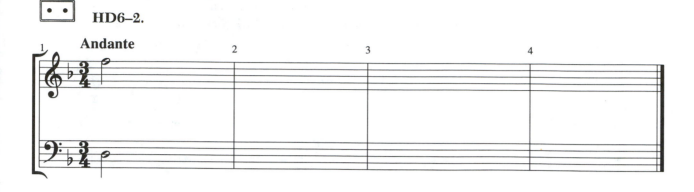

- Is the quality of the first chord in measure 3 major or minor? If major, your Roman numeral will be affected even though an accidental is not required in either the soprano or bass.

HD6–3.

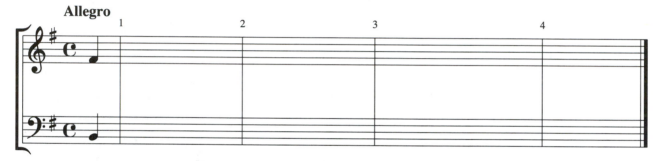

- The fifth through eighth chords are closely related to the first through fourth chords. Listen carefully for any differences, including but not limited to a change in rhythm.

HD6–4.

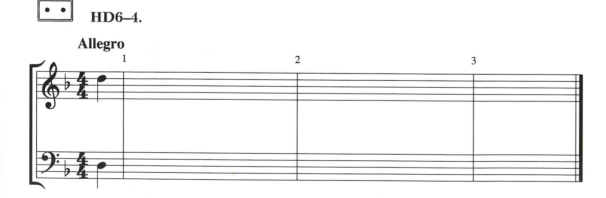

· What interval is formed by the first two soprano pitches in measure 1? To help answer that question, listen to the relationship between the first soprano pitch of measure 1 and the pitch that *precedes* it, and to the relationship between the second soprano pitch of measure 1 and the pitch that *follows* it.

HD6–5.

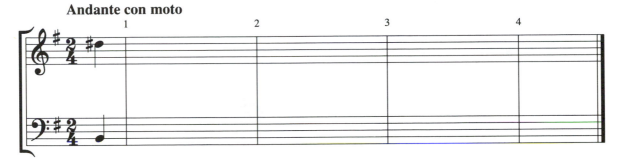

· Which of the two soprano pitches that fill beat 2 of measure 1 belongs to the harmony? Remember that a passing note may appear in either an accented or an unaccented position.

HD6–6.

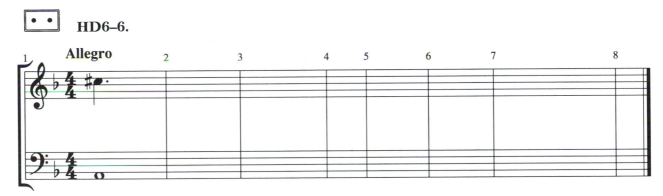

· The second pitch of measure 1 functions as a neighboring note to the leading tone C♯. Is that function better fulfilled using an augmented second (C♯-B♭-C♯) or a major second (C♯-B♮-C♯)? The second pitch of measure 2 serves as a neighboring note to tonic D. Would a major second (D-C-D) or a minor second (D-C♯-D) better fulfill that function?

CASSETTE PROGRAM (TAPE 1, SIDE B)

C6–1.   Six melodies are performed, twice each. During the silence after each playing, respond in one of the following ways: (1) Sing the melody, using solmization syllables; (2) Play the melody on the piano or on your primary instrument; (3) Write the melody on staff paper.

a.   b.   c.   d.   e.   f.

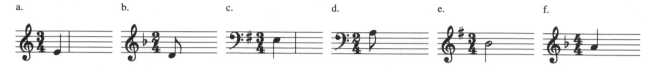

C6–2.   Six chord progressions are performed, four times each. During the silence after each playing, respond in one of the following ways: (1) Sing the soprano after the first and second playings and the bass after the third and fourth playings, using solmization syllables; (2) Play the soprano on the piano or your primary instrument after the first and second playings and the bass after the third and fourth playings; (3) Play both the soprano and bass on the piano after each playing; (4) Write the soprano and bass on staff paper and provide an analysis.

a.   b.   c.   d.   e.   f.

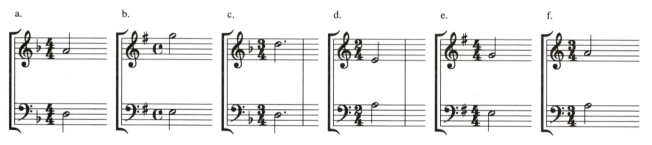

Chapter 7

PITCH

No progression better reinforces the stability of tonic than that from V to I. Example 7–1a shows its characteristic root movement from $\hat{5}$ to $\hat{1}$ (bass), the stepwise ascent from $\hat{7}$ to $\hat{1}$ (tenor), and the stepwise descent from $\hat{2}$ to $\hat{1}$ (soprano). It also shows, in the alto, how a passing note may connect $\hat{5}$ and $\hat{3}$. Like most passing notes, this F is dissonant, forming a ***minor seventh*** (abbreviated m7) against the bass G. Unlike most passing notes, this F may be adopted by V as a chord member (Ex. 7–1b) and may occur even when its context does not imply a passing function (Ex. 7–1c).

EXAMPLE 7–1

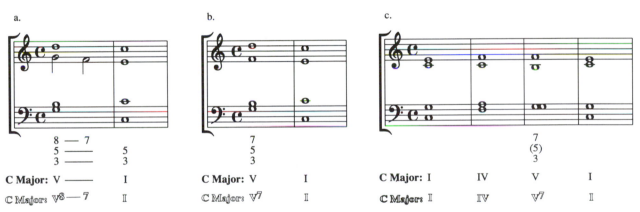

a.

8 — 7
5 ——— 5
3 ——— 3

C Major: V ——— I

C Major: V⁸ — 7   I

b.

7
5
3

C Major: V   I

C Major: V⁷   I

c.

7
(5)
3

C Major: I   IV   V   I

C Major: I   IV   V⁷   I

A chord that contains a major third, perfect fifth (sometimes omitted, as in Ex. 7–1c), and minor seventh above its root is called a ***major-minor seventh chord***. When its root is $\hat{5}$, a major-minor seventh chord is also called a ***dominant seventh chord***. Its figured bass is $\substack{7\\5\\3}$, often abbreviated as 7.

Dissonance is an important attribute of the dominant seventh chord. The minor seventh formed by the root and seventh and the ***diminished fifth*** (or its inversion, the ***augmented fourth***) formed by the third and seventh foster forward momentum. Consonance is more satisfying if the contrasting dissonance of the dominant seventh chord is employed.

You can learn to recognize the characteristic sound of the dominant seventh chord, just as you by now recognize major and minor chords in $\substack{5\\3}$ position. In this and the next two chapters, the dominant seventh will be the only dissonant chord employed in the text's exercises. Though it may contain all the pitches of a major chord, it also contains a minor seventh above the bass.

Observe the following points regarding Example 7–2:

(1) 7 and $\hat{7}$ are not the same. 7 (figured bass indicating a seventh above the bass: G above the dominant's bass A) here refers to $\hat{4}$ (the fourth scale degree: G above tonic D). $\hat{7}$ (the seventh scale degree: C♯ above tonic D in major) and $\sharp\hat{7}$ (the raised seventh scale degree: C♯ above tonic D in minor) here correspond to the figured bass symbols 3 in major and ♯ in minor (figured bass indicating a third or raised third above the bass: C♯ above the dominant's bass A).

(2) Whether a chord contains a diminished fifth (d5) or augmented fourth (A4) depends on whether $\hat{4}$ appears above or below $\hat{7}$ (♯$\hat{7}$ in minor). The augmented fourth is often called a ***tritone***. (Three whole steps, or "tones," come between $\hat{4}$ and $\hat{7}$.) Some musicians also apply this term to the diminished fifth, which differs from an augmented fourth in spelling but not in sound.

(3) In Method One analysis, Roman numerals and figured bass appear in separate rows. In Method Two analysis, Roman numerals and figured bass appear within a single symbol cluster.[1]

EXAMPLE 7–2

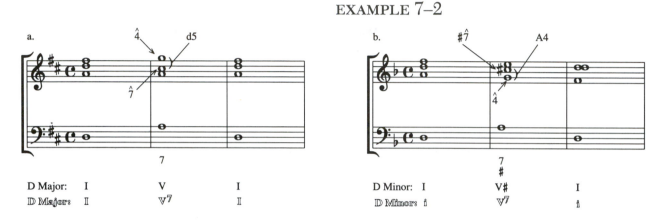

The dominant seventh chord often participates in the drive to a ***cadence***, or resting point, on tonic. Other factors, including the contour of the melody and the segmentation of music into ***phrases*** of typically four, eight, or sixteen measures in length, contribute to this sense of closure as well. When V (in either $\frac{5}{3}$ or $\frac{7}{3}$ position) leads to I at the end of a phrase, the cadence is classified as a ***full cadence*** or ***authentic cadence***. Such a cadence may conclude the composition or one of its sections.

A composer may also cadence on the dominant, in a ***half cadence***. Because a dissonant seventh would be inappropriate at a cadence (which by definition is a point of rest), a dominant chord that serves as the goal of a phrase will generally appear in $\frac{5}{3}$ position, not in $\frac{7}{3}$ position. I and IV are among the most common choices for the chord that precedes this dominant. In the minor mode, the dominant chord at a half cadence may be either minor ($\hat{5}$-$\hat{7}$-$\hat{2}$) or major ($\hat{5}$-♯$\hat{7}$-$\hat{2}$).

The composition must continue after a half cadence. Most often the next phrase begins with tonic and ends in a full cadence. Such a pairing of two phrases, the first ending in a half cadence and the second ending in a full cadence, is one of the most common organizing principles of tonal music. Because the two phrases appear as an ordered pair,

---

1. Baroque figured-bass practice is followed only in Method One analysis. For example, Bach or Handel would have included the sharp below the 7 in Example 7–2b. Roman numerals were first used for analysis in the 1770s by Abbé Georg Joseph Vogler, who placed figured-bass symbols above and capital Roman numerals below the bass. Method Two analysis, in which the size of the numeral conveys some of the information formerly contained in the figured bass, evolved during the nineteenth century.

they are called *antecedent* and *consequent* phrases. Example 7–3 shows the basic elements of this standard binary structure. The entire structure is called a *period*.

EXAMPLE 7–3

I . . . . V,   I V   I
               Half Cadence   Full Cadence
——— Antecedent Phrase ———   ——— Consequent Phrase ———

Many of the melodies and harmonic progressions of this and future chapters will follow the model of Example 7–3. Before analyzing in detail a melody's contour or a progression's succession of chords, determine the goal of the phrase. Does the phrase lead to V, or to I? Does the melody lead to $\hat{2}$, to $\hat{1}$, or to some other scale degree? Assess how a consequent phrase expands upon the musical ideas of its antecedent. For example, a melody will often lead to $\hat{2}$ at the end of an antecedent phrase, and *through* $\hat{2}$ to $\hat{1}$ at the end of a consequent phrase. This strategy works best when the two phrases of the period begin in the same way. When that is the case, the phrases form a *parallel period*.

The *key of B minor* and the *key of G minor* are introduced in this chapter. Their key signatures contain two sharps and two flats, respectively. B minor is the relative minor of D major. G minor is the relative minor of B♭ major.

METER AND RHYTHM

To this point, only *simple meters* have been employed. The word "simple" refers to the fact that the beat divides into two halves. In *compound meters* such as $^6_8$ *meter*, the beat instead divides into three thirds. In $^6_8$ meter, the beat is represented by the dotted quarter note. Three eighth notes fill the same time as a dotted quarter note, and two dotted quarter notes fill a measure. Thus $^6_8$ meter corresponds closely to $^2_4$ meter, where two eighth notes fill the same time as a quarter note, and two quarter notes fill a measure. These relationships are displayed in Example 7–4.

EXAMPLE 7–4

Compound meter ($^6_8$)   Simple meter ($^2_4$)

The syllables "and" and "uh" indicate the second and third thirds of each beat in compound meters, as demonstrated in Example 7–5.

EXAMPLE 7–5

SING:

THINK: 1 + uh 2 + uh   1 + uh 2 + uh   1 + uh 2 + uh   1 + uh 2 + uh

Upbeats need not fill exactly one beat. Other alternatives will be introduced beginning in this chapter. For example, an upbeat might fill one-half beat in simple meters or one-third beat in compound meters, or two beats in simple meters such as $^3_4$ or $^4_4$.

SOLO MELODIES

FIXED DO: *In the key of B minor, sing "li" for #$\hat{7}$.*

LETTER NAMES: *In the key of B minor, sing "Ais" (= A#) for #$\hat{7}$.*

MELODIES THAT EMPLOY ANTECEDENT/CONSEQUENT CONSTRUCTION

BEETHOVEN: SYMPHONY NO. 9 IN D MINOR ("CHORAL"), OP. 125, MVMT. 4

S7–1.

- Although there are no visible signs to indicate it, think of these eight measures as two four-measure phrases. Observe how measures 5 through 7 repeat exactly the contents of measures 1 through 3. The differences in the two halves of the period occur in the cadential measures (measures 4 and 8). Measure 4 ends on $\hat{2}$ in a half cadence. Measure 8 ends on $\hat{1}$ in a full cadence. These phrases form a parallel period.

BRAHMS: SYMPHONY NO. 1 IN C MINOR, OP. 68, MVMT. 4

S7–2.

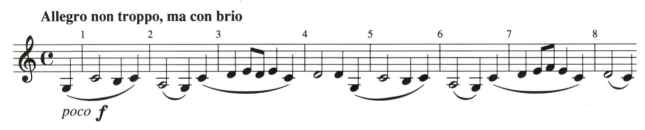

MELODIES THAT EMPLOY A MINOR SEVENTH

BEETHOVEN: *FIDELIO*, OP. 72, ACT 1

S7–3.

- In your mind, develop a harmonic context for the dramatic downward leap of a minor seventh between measures 2 and 3 (and again between measures 6 and 7). As a practice strategy, change the last two pitches of measure 2 to G and E. In this way, C serves as the culmination of a downward arpeggiation of all four pitches of the dominant seventh chord. Eventually learn to sing the score as written.

BEETHOVEN: *FIDELIO*, OP. 72, ACT 1

S7–4.

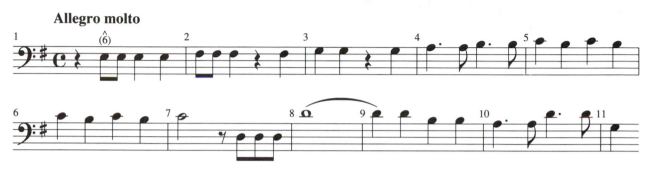

MELODIES IN B MINOR OR G MINOR

TCHAIKOVSKY: SYMPHONY NO. 2 IN C MINOR ("LITTLE RUSSIAN"), OP. 17, MVMT. 1

S7–5.

- Sing the following eight pitches; then sing measures 1 and 2. Think of the C at the end of measure 1 as a note that connects the D at the beginning of measure 1 and the B♭ on beat 3 of measure 2.

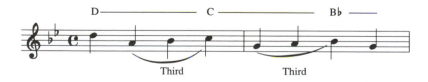

BRAHMS: PIANO TRIO NO. 1 IN B MAJOR, OP. 8, MVMT. 2

S7–6.

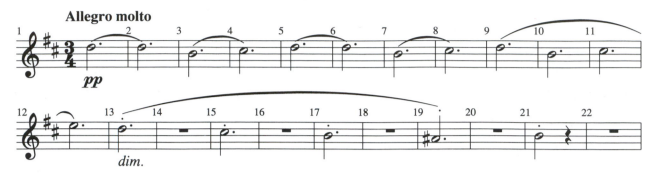

MELODIES THAT EMPLOY PARTIAL- OR MULTIPLE-BEAT UPBEATS

BRAHMS: SONATA FOR VIOLIN AND PIANO NO. 1 IN G MAJOR, OP. 78, MVMT. 3

S7–7.

- Observe how Brahms employed slurs to emphasizes the repetition of the opening rhythmic pattern.

WEBER: CLARINET CONCERTO NO. 1 IN F MINOR, OP. 73, MVMT. 3

S7–8.

MELODIES IN $\frac{6}{8}$ METER

ROSSINI: *WILLIAM TELL*, ACT 1

S7–9.

- Measures 1 and 2 (the first half of the antecedent phrase) are identical to measures 5 and 6 (the first half of the consequent phrase). The antecedent continues by emphasizing $\hat{3}$-$\hat{2}$, while the consequent continues by emphasizing $\hat{2}$-$\hat{1}$.

GOUNOD: *FAUST*, ACT 1

S7–10.

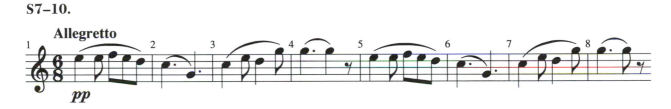

BEETHOVEN: STRING QUARTET NO. 9 IN C MAJOR, OP. 59, NO. 3, MVMT. 2

S7–11.

- In descending (measures 0 through 2), Beethoven follows the model of the harmonic minor scale. In ascending (measures 3 and 4), he follows the model of the melodic minor scale.

BEETHOVEN: VIOLIN CONCERTO IN D MAJOR, OP. 61, MVMT. 3

S7–12.

DUETS

D7–1.

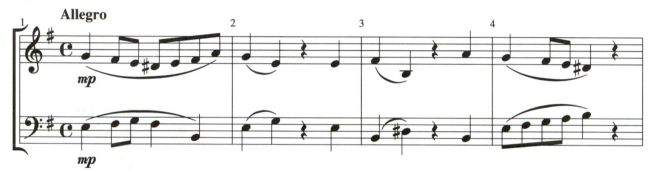

D7–2.

ACCOMPANIED SOLO MELODIES

AS7–1.

AS7–2.

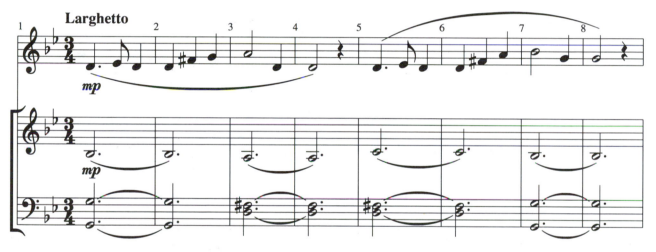

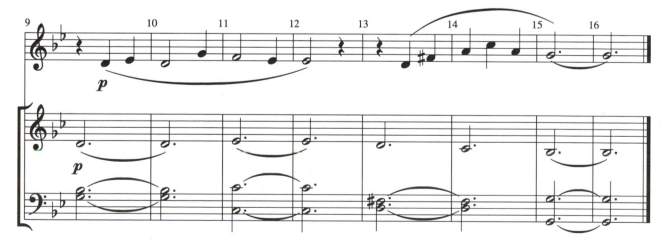

RHYTHMS

INTERVAL WORKSHOP

I7–1.   Play a pitch that is low in your vocal range at a keyboard. Sing it. Then sing the pitch a minor seventh higher. Use the keyboard to confirm your performance. Then sing ascending sevenths starting on other pitches.

I7–2.   Play a pitch that is high in your vocal range at a keyboard. Sing it. Then sing the pitch a minor seventh lower. Use the keyboard to confirm your performance. Then sing descending sevenths starting on other pitches.

I7–3.   Practice singing the interval of a minor seventh higher than a sounding pitch. The sounding pitch should be at or beyond the lower limit of your vocal range, and could be sung by a classmate or your instructor or performed on the piano or another instrument such as the cello. Also practice singing compound versions of this interval.

I7–4.   Practice singing the interval of a minor seventh lower than a sounding pitch. The sounding pitch should be at or beyond the upper limit of your vocal range, and could be sung by a classmate or your instructor or performed on the piano or another instrument such as the flute. Also practice singing compound versions of this interval.

ARPEGGIATION WORKSHOP

A7–1.   Play a C, D, E♭, F, G, A, or B♭ that is at least a perfect fifth above the lowest note of your vocal range at a keyboard. Let this pitch be $\hat{1}$ in a major key. Sing each of the following arpeggiations, either in the order given or in random order.

a. $\hat{1}$ $\hat{3}$ $\hat{5}$ $\hat{1}$ ✲ $\hat{4}$ $\hat{6}$ $\hat{1}$ $\hat{6}$ ✲ $\hat{5}$ $\hat{7}$ $\hat{2}$ $\hat{4}$ ✲ $\hat{3}$ $\hat{5}$ $\hat{3}$ $\hat{1}$

b. $\hat{1}$ $\hat{3}$ $\hat{5}$ $\hat{1}$ ✲ $\hat{4}$ $\hat{6}$ $\hat{1}$ $\hat{6}$ ✲ $\hat{7}$ $\hat{2}$ $\hat{4}$ $\hat{5}$ ✲ $\hat{1}$ $\hat{3}$ $\hat{5}$ $\hat{1}$

c. $\hat{1}$ $\hat{3}$ $\hat{5}$ $\hat{1}$ ✲ $\hat{4}$ $\hat{1}$ $\hat{6}$ $\hat{4}$ ✲ $\hat{5}$ $\hat{7}$ $\hat{2}$ $\hat{4}$ ✲ $\hat{3}$ $\hat{5}$ $\hat{3}$ $\hat{1}$

d. $\hat{1}$ $\hat{3}$ $\hat{5}$ $\hat{1}$ ✲ $\hat{4}$ $\hat{1}$ $\hat{6}$ $\hat{4}$ ✲ $\hat{5}$ $\hat{2}$ $\hat{4}$ $\hat{5}$ ✲ $\hat{1}$ $\hat{3}$ $\hat{5}$ $\hat{1}$

e. $\hat{1}$ $\hat{3}$ $\hat{5}$ $\hat{1}$ ✲ $\hat{4}$ $\hat{6}$ $\hat{1}$ $\hat{4}$ ✲ $\hat{5}$ $\hat{7}$ $\hat{2}$ $\hat{4}$ ✲ $\hat{3}$ $\hat{5}$ $\hat{3}$ $\hat{1}$

f. $\hat{1}$ $\hat{3}$ $\hat{5}$ $\hat{1}$ ✲ $\hat{4}$ $\hat{6}$ $\hat{1}$ $\hat{4}$ ✲ $\hat{2}$ $\hat{4}$ $\hat{5}$ $\hat{7}$ ✲ $\hat{1}$ $\hat{3}$ $\hat{5}$ $\hat{1}$

A7–2.   Play a D, E, G, A, or B that is at least a perfect fifth above the lowest note of your vocal range at a keyboard. Let this pitch be $\hat{1}$ in a minor key. Sing each of the following arpeggiations, either in the order given or in random order.

a. $\hat{1}$ $\hat{3}$ $\hat{5}$ $\hat{1}$ ✲ $\hat{4}$ $\hat{6}$ $\hat{1}$ $\hat{6}$ ✲ $\hat{5}$ $\hat{\sharp 7}$ $\hat{2}$ $\hat{4}$ ✲ $\hat{3}$ $\hat{5}$ $\hat{3}$ $\hat{1}$

b. $\hat{1}$ $\hat{3}$ $\hat{5}$ $\hat{1}$ ✲ $\hat{4}$ $\hat{6}$ $\hat{1}$ $\hat{6}$ ✲ $\hat{\sharp 7}$ $\hat{2}$ $\hat{4}$ $\hat{5}$ ✲ $\hat{1}$ $\hat{3}$ $\hat{5}$ $\hat{1}$

c. $\hat{1}$ $\hat{3}$ $\hat{5}$ $\hat{1}$ ✲ $\hat{4}$ $\hat{\sharp 6}$ $\hat{1}$ $\hat{\sharp 6}$ ✲ $\hat{\sharp 7}$ $\hat{2}$ $\hat{4}$ $\hat{5}$ ✲ $\hat{1}$ $\hat{3}$ $\hat{5}$ $\hat{1}$

d. $\hat{1}$ $\hat{3}$ $\hat{5}$ $\hat{1}$ ✲ $\hat{4}$ $\hat{1}$ $\hat{6}$ $\hat{4}$ ✲ $\hat{5}$ $\hat{\sharp 7}$ $\hat{2}$ $\hat{4}$ ✲ $\hat{3}$ $\hat{5}$ $\hat{3}$ $\hat{1}$

e. $\hat{1}$ $\hat{3}$ $\hat{5}$ $\hat{1}$ ✲ $\hat{4}$ $\hat{1}$ $\hat{6}$ $\hat{4}$ ✲ $\hat{5}$ $\hat{2}$ $\hat{4}$ $\hat{5}$ ✲ $\hat{1}$ $\hat{3}$ $\hat{5}$ $\hat{1}$

f. $\hat{1}$ $\hat{3}$ $\hat{5}$ $\hat{1}$ ✲ $\hat{4}$ $\hat{6}$ $\hat{1}$ $\hat{4}$ ✲ $\hat{5}$ $\hat{\sharp 7}$ $\hat{2}$ $\hat{4}$ ✲ $\hat{3}$ $\hat{5}$ $\hat{3}$ $\hat{1}$

g. $\hat{1}$ $\hat{3}$ $\hat{5}$ $\hat{1}$ ✲ $\hat{4}$ $\hat{6}$ $\hat{1}$ $\hat{4}$ ✲ $\hat{2}$ $\hat{4}$ $\hat{5}$ $\hat{\sharp 7}$ ✲ $\hat{1}$ $\hat{3}$ $\hat{5}$ $\hat{1}$

QUICK SWITCH

Q7–1.

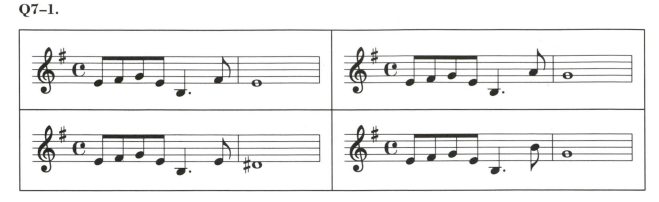

Q7–2.

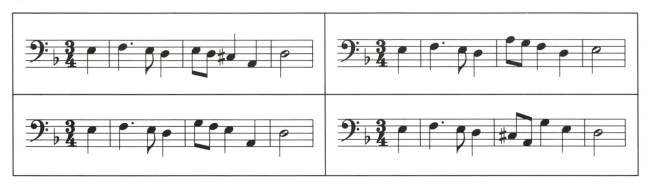

Q7–3.

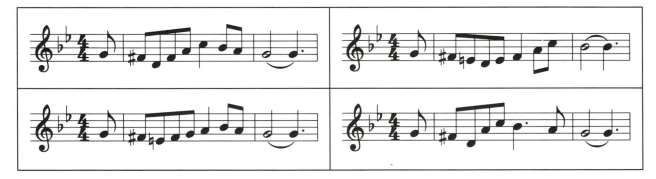

Q7–4.

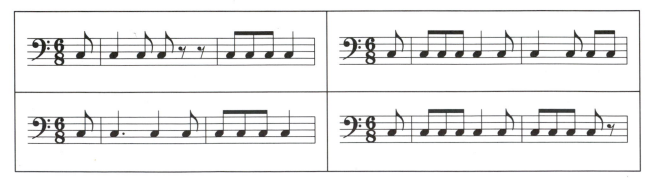

IDENTIFICATIONS

ID7–1.　　An interval is performed melodically, either ascending or descending. Identify it as a minor second, major second, minor third, major third, perfect fourth, perfect fifth, minor seventh, or perfect octave.

ID7–2.　　An interval is performed as a simultaneity. Identify it as a minor third, major third, perfect fourth, perfect fifth, minor seventh, or perfect octave.

ID7–3.　　A four-note chord is performed. Identify it as a major chord, a minor chord, or a major-minor (dominant) seventh chord.

ID7–4.　　$\hat{5}$, $\hat{7}$, $\hat{2}$, and $\hat{4}$ in a major key are performed simultaneously. Then two of these four scale degrees are performed simultaneously. Identify the two scale degrees performed, from among the following choices: $\hat{5}$-$\hat{7}$, $\hat{5}$-$\hat{2}$, $\hat{5}$-$\hat{4}$, $\hat{7}$-$\hat{2}$, $\hat{2}$-$\hat{4}$.

ID7–5.　　A major-minor (dominant) seventh chord is performed. The root serves as the bass. Does the root, the third, the fifth, or the seventh serve as the soprano?

ID7–6.　　A melody is performed. Identify the correct score notation.

e.   f.

ID7–7.   A chord progression in the major mode is performed. Identify a suitable Roman-numeral/figured-bass analysis from among the following choices.

Group 1

a.	I	IV	I
b.	I	IV	V
c.	I	V	I
d.	I	$\overset{7}{V}$	I

a.	I	IV	I
b.	I	IV	V
c.	I	V	I
d.	I	V^7	I

Group 2

a.	I	IV	V	I
b.	I	IV	$\overset{7}{V}$	I
c.	I	V	I	V
d.	I	$\overset{7}{V}$	I	V

a.	I	IV	V	I
b.	I	IV	V^7	I
c.	I	V	I	V
d.	I	V^7	I	V

ID7–8.   A chord progression in the minor mode is performed. Identify a suitable Roman-numeral/figured-bass analysis from among the following choices:

Group 1

a.	I	IV	I
b.	I	IV	$\overset{\#}{V\sharp}$
c.	I	$\overset{\#}{V\sharp}$	I
d.	I	$\overset{7}{\underset{}{\overset{\#}{V\sharp}}}$	I

a.	i	iv	i
b.	i	iv	V
c.	i	V	i
d.	i	V^7	i

Group 2

a.	I	IV	$\overset{\#}{V\sharp}$	I
b.	I	IV	$\overset{7}{\overset{\#}{V\sharp}}$	I
c.	I	$\overset{\#}{V\sharp}$	I	$\overset{\#}{V\sharp}$
d.	I	$\overset{7}{\overset{\#}{V\sharp}}$	I	$\overset{\#}{V\sharp}$

a.	i	iv	V	i
b.	i	iv	V^7	i
c.	i	V	i	V
d.	i	V^7	i	V

ID7–9. A chord progression is performed. Identify the correct score notation for the outer voices. Figured-bass symbols have been placed below the bass where appropriate. If you wish, add Roman numerals.

a.

b.

c.

d.

e.

f.

RHYTHMIC DICTATIONS

RD7–1.

RD7–2.

MELODIC DICTATIONS

SCHUBERT: SYMPHONY NO. 8 IN B MINOR ("UNFINISHED"), D. 759, MVMT. 1

MD7–1.

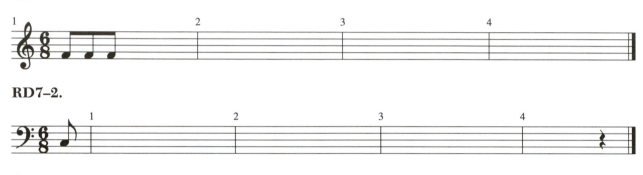

- After the excerpt is performed, recall its first and last pitches in your internal ear. What interval do they form? Among the various pitches in between are some that traverse a segment of the descending melodic minor scale, connecting $\hat{8}$ and the goal pitch.

MENDELSSOHN: SYMPHONY NO. 3 IN A MINOR ("SCOTTISH"), OP. 56, MVMT. 1

 **MD7–2.**

Allegro un poco agitato

- Use the first pitch ($\hat{5}$) to gauge how high or low various other pitches are. Where within measure 2 does $\hat{5}$ recur? Is the last pitch higher than $\hat{5}$, lower than $\hat{5}$, or $\hat{5}$ itself?

PUCCINI: *LA BOHÈME*, ACT 1

MD7–3.

- What role does the descent $\hat{8}$-$\hat{7}$-$\hat{6}$-$\hat{5}$ play in the structure of this melody?

HAYDN: SYMPHONY NO. 99 IN E♭ MAJOR, MVMT. 3

MD7–4.

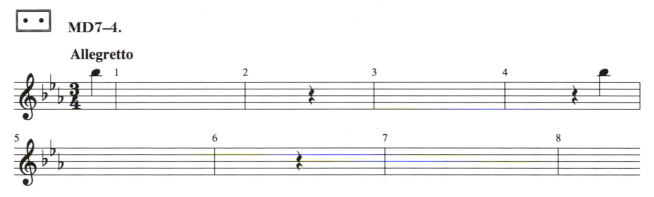

- How does the consequent phrase differ from the antecedent? Which of the two covers the larger total span? What pitch ends each phrase?

MENDELSSOHN: SONG WITHOUT WORDS, OP. 19, NO. 6 (BOOK 1)

MD7–5.

- The first, third, and fourth pitches of measure 1 form a neighboring-note figure. Likewise the first, third, and fourth pitches of measure 4 form a passing-note figure.

- Is this excerpt in the key of B♭ major or the key of G minor?

TCHAIKOVSKY: SYMPHONY NO. 3 IN D MAJOR ("POLISH"), OP. 29, MVMT. 1

MD7–6.

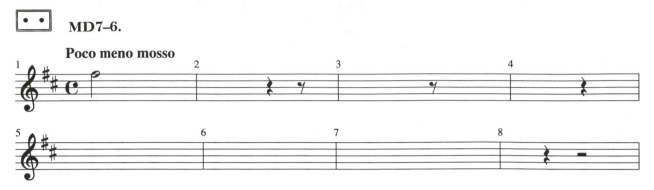

· Three descending lines (four pitches each) occur within the first four measures. How do they differ? What do they have in common?

HARMONIC DICTATIONS

Instruction: *From this chapter onward, include figured bass as well as Roman numerals in your analyses.*

HD7–1.

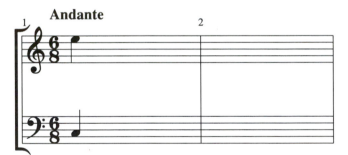

· As in earlier chapters, the choice of bass pitches is limited to three scale degrees ($\hat{1}$, $\hat{4}$, and $\hat{5}$). Unlike earlier chapters, $\hat{5}$ may serve as the root of either a dominant $^5_3$ or a dominant seventh chord.

HD7–2.

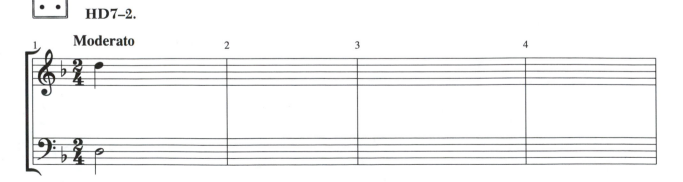

- In this excerpt the dominant harmony is introduced in $^5_3$ position, with the seventh added nearer to the cadence point. In a Method One analysis, the figured bass should be written $^{8-7}_{}$. In a Method Two analysis, the analysis symbol should be written V^{8-7}.

HD7–3.

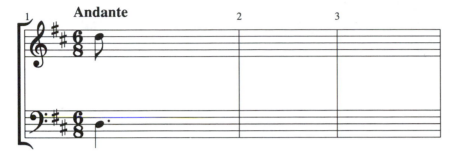

- The second pitch of this progression's soprano forms the interval of a seventh against the bass. The figured bass for the first half of measure 1 remains $^5_3$, however, because the seventh is a nonharmonic passing note. In contrast, the seventh that appears in the second half of measure 2 is a chord member and should appear in the figured bass.

HD7–4.

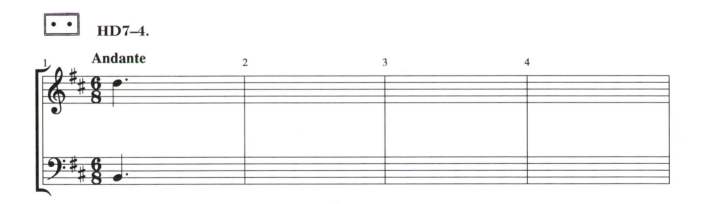

- What do the two phrases of the progression have in common? Do they form a parallel period? Place a comma after the Roman numeral V♯ or V in measure 2 to indicate that this chord *ends* the antecedent phrase. It does not *resolve* to the tonic chord of measure 3. That chord is, instead, a new beginning.

HD7–5.

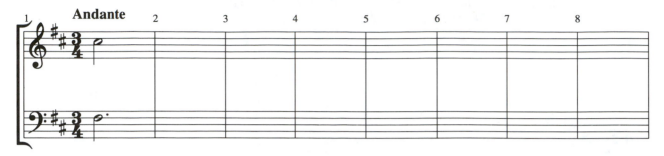

- The dominant seventh chord is prolonged in measures 1 and 2. Tonic does not appear until measure 3.

- The soprano pitch that begins measure 6 is not a member of the dominant harmony. How does it relate to the pitch that begins measure 5?

HD7–6.

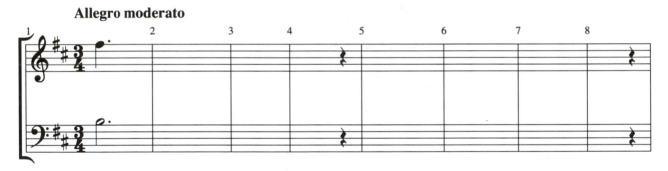

- Observe what your *eyes* do as you write down the outer voices of measures 5 and 6. They look left to measures 1 and 2! Your *ears* should also make this sort of comparison whenever a parallel period is performed.

⊡ CASSETTE PROGRAM
(TAPE 1, SIDE B)

C7–1.   Six melodies are performed, twice each. During the silence after each playing, respond in one of the following ways: (1) Sing the melody, using solmization syllables; (2) Play the melody on the piano or on your primary instrument; (3) Write the melody on staff paper.

C7–2.   Six chord progressions are performed, four times each. During the silence after each playing, respond in one of the following ways: (1) Sing the soprano after the first and second playings and the bass after the third and fourth playings, using solmization syllables; (2) Play the soprano on the piano or your primary instrument after the first and second playings and the bass after the third and fourth playings; (3) Play both the soprano and bass on the piano after each playing; (4) Write the soprano and bass on staff paper and provide an analysis.

Chapter 8

PITCH

When a chord is in *first inversion*, its third—not its root—serves as the bass. Example 8–1 displays three related chords. Example 8–1a is a C-major triad. The terms "root" and "third" refer to the placement of pitches within this triad. The chord in Example 8–1b is in root position (or $_3^5$ position). The root serves as the bass. Example 8–1c shows a chord in first inversion (or $_3^6$ *position*). Here the third serves as the bass.[1]

EXAMPLE 8–1

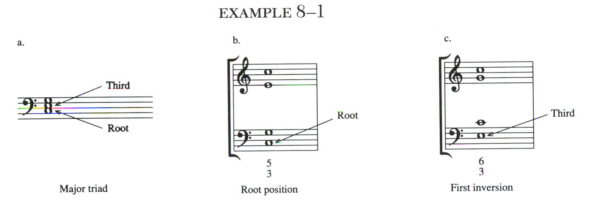

a.   b.   c.

Major triad   Root position   First inversion

Play the three chords of Example 8–1 at a keyboard. Their sounds are very similar. In comparing Examples 8–1b and 8–1c, observe that root position is more stable than first inversion, and thus more appropriate for contexts that require maximum stability, such as the cadence at the end of a period. As you develop the ability to distinguish between these two similar sounds, listen particularly for whether a perfect fifth or a *minor sixth* (the inversion of the triad's major third) is formed with the bass. To do this, first isolate the bass among the sounding pitches and sing it internally. (Avoid the mistake of singing the root even when the third is in the bass.) Then sing a third above the bass internally. Finally sing the next pitch in an ascending arpeggiation of the chord. Is that pitch a fifth or a sixth above the bass? (Or, is it a third or a fourth above the pitch you just sang?) This process is outlined in Example 8–2.

---

1. Caution: The term "third" has two different meanings. When one says that the third serves as the bass, "third" means the third of the triad from which the first-inversion chord is derived (i.e., E in Ex. 8–1c). When discussing the construction of a $_3^6$-position chord, however, one often refers to the sixth and "third" above the bass (i.e., G in Ex. 8–1c).

EXAMPLE 8–2

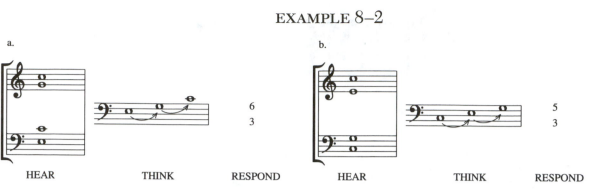

HEAR   THINK   RESPOND   HEAR   THINK   RESPOND

$^6_3$-position I, IV, and V chords in major keys are introduced in this chapter. With these additions, six of the seven diatonic pitches may occur in the bass. (Only $\hat{2}$ is not used at this point.) Inversion allows for a more melodious bass, with fewer leaps of fourths and fifths and more stepwise motions and leaps of thirds. Example 8–3 demonstrates some of the new possibilities.

EXAMPLE 8–3

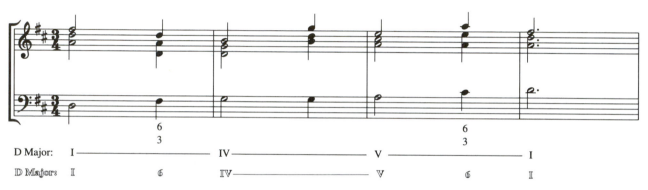

When a major third is inverted, a minor sixth results (as noted above). Example 8–4a displays this relationship. Minor sixths occur in both major and minor keys. Example 8–4b shows a melody in C major. C and E correspond to $\hat{8}$ and $\hat{3}$. In A minor (Ex. 8–4c), E and C correspond to $\hat{\underset{5}{}}$ and $\hat{3}$. Example 8–4d shows a context in which $\hat{6}$ serves as a neighbor to $\hat{5}$. In this instance, the principle of inversion is not a factor.

EXAMPLE 8–4

a.

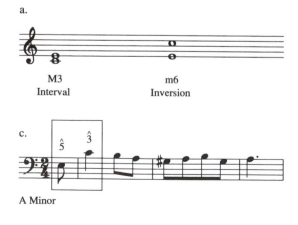

M3   m6
Interval   Inversion

c.

A Minor

b.

C Major

d.

E Minor

The **key of F♯ minor** and the **key of C minor** are introduced in this chapter. Their key signatures contain three sharps and three flats, respectively. F♯ minor is the relative minor of A major; C minor is the relative minor of E♭ major.

METER AND RHYTHM

Two **sixteenth notes** (♬) fill the same musical time as an eighth note. Four sixteenth notes fill a full beat in simple meters such as $\frac{2}{4}$, $\frac{3}{4}$, and $\frac{4}{4}$. Six sixteenth notes fill a full beat in compound meters such as $\frac{6}{8}$. Example 8–5 shows two melodies that contain sixteenth notes, along with appropriate counting syllables. Although you might choose to omit the "ee" syllables (in consultation with your instructor), they may prove useful in future chapters, especially as an aid in performing syncopation (chapter 11).

EXAMPLE 8–5

a.

SING:

THINK: 1 ee + ee   2 ee + ee   3 ee + ee   1 ee + ee   2 ee + ee   3 ee + ee

b.

SING:

THINK: 1 ee + ee uh ee   2 ee + ee uh ee   1 ee + ee uh ee   2 ee + ee uh ee

SOLO MELODIES

FIXED DO: *In the key of F♯ minor, sing "mis" for ♯$\hat{7}$. As a general rule, add "s" (the first letter of the word "sharp") to a syllable ending in "i" to indicate the pitch a half step higher. For example, because "mi" is used for E, the syllable for E♯ is "mis."*

LETTER NAMES: *In the key of F♯ minor, sing "Eis" (= E♯) for ♯$\hat{7}$.*

MAJOR-MODE MELODIES THAT EMPLOY A MINOR SIXTH

TCHAIKOVSKY: 1812 OVERTURE, OP. 49

S8–1.

Allegro giusto

f marc.

- The ascending minor sixth A-F in measure 3 will be easier to sing if you think of F as a descending whole step from the G in measure 2.

MOZART: *DIE ENTFÜHRUNG AUS DEM SERAIL*, K. 384, ACT 3

S8–2.

MOZART: *COSÌ FAN TUTTE*, K. 588, ACT 2

S8–3.

- At first sing only the pitches that occur on beats 1 and 2 of each measure. Then add the remaining pitches. By following this strategy, you can avoid thinking of the Es in measures 2 and 3 as descending sevenths from D. They are instead descending seconds from F♯.

MAHLER: SYMPHONY NO. 9 IN D MAJOR, MVMT. 2

S8–4.

MINOR-MODE MELODIES THAT EMPLOY A MINOR SIXTH

BEETHOVEN: SYMPHONY NO. 9 IN D MINOR ("CHORAL"), OP. 125, MVMT. 2

S8–5.

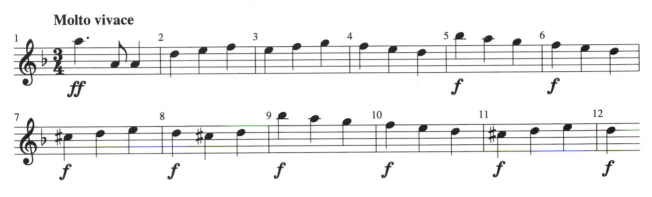

- Find the B♭ of measure 5 by remembering the A that you sang on beat 1 of measure 1.

MENDELSSOHN: ORGAN SONATA NO. 5 IN D MAJOR

S8–6.

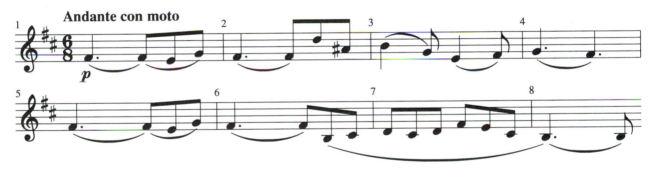

MELODIES IN F♯ MINOR OR C MINOR

GLUCK: *IPHIGÉNIE EN TAURIDE*, ACT 3

S8–7.

- Gluck has employed an augmented second in the ascent from $\hat{5}$ to $\hat{8}$ in measures 4 through 7. As a practice strategy, sing G-A♮-B♮-C. Then sing G-A♭-B♮-C. Then sing measures 4 through 7.

TCHAIKOVSKY: INCIDENTAL MUSIC TO *HAMLET*, OP. 67 BIS, ACT 4

S8–8.

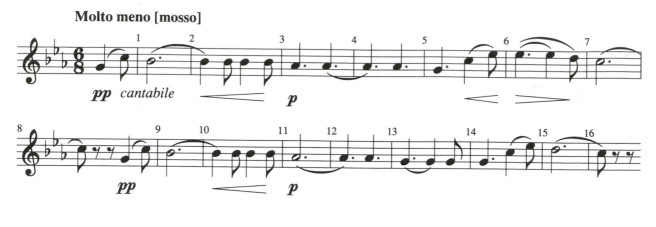

S8–9.

- The mode of this melody will not be apparent to your listeners until the D of measure 3. Remind yourself that the melody is in F♯ minor to prevent yourself from singing D♯ in measure 3 by mistake.

SCHUBERT: LÄNDLER, D. 355, NO. 6

S8–10.

MELODIES THAT EMPLOY SIXTEENTH NOTES

BRAHMS: INTERMEZZO, OP. 117, NO. 1

S8–11.

- Observe that measures 1 and 3 are identical. How does measure 2 promote the melody's continuation? How does measure 4 bring it to a close?

VERDI: *FALSTAFF*, ACT 1

S8–12.

DVOŘÁK: SYMPHONY NO. 7 IN D MINOR, OP. 70, MVMT. 1

S8–13.

- This melody employs pitches of the natural minor scale. Make sure that you approach the Ds of measures 3 and 4 by whole step (from C) rather than by half step (from C♯).

MOZART: *IDOMENEO, RE DI CRETA*, K. 366, ACT 3

S8–14.

DVOŘÁK: SYMPHONY NO. 9 IN E MINOR ("FROM THE NEW WORLD"), OP. 95, MVMT. 1

S8–15.

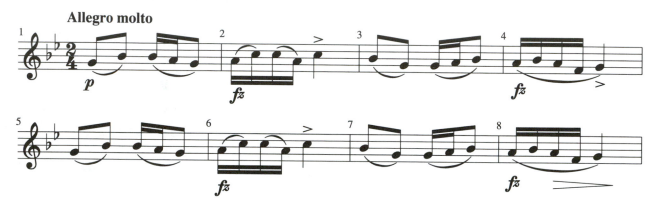

- This melody is similar in structure to Solo Melody #13, though somewhat more complex. The diagram below shows that it contains two melodic strands that run in parallel thirds until the cadence on G.

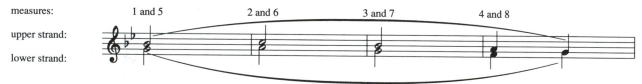

MOZART: *DIE ENTFÜHRUNG AUS DEM SERAIL*, K. 384, ACT 2

S8–16.

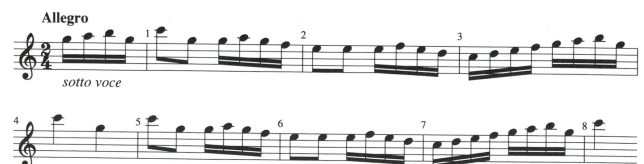

DUETS

D8–1.

D8–2.

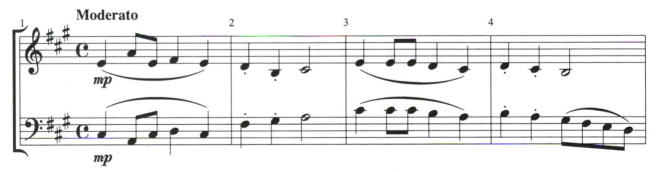

ACCOMPANIED SOLO MELODIES

AS8–1.

AS8–2.

RHYTHMS

R8–1.

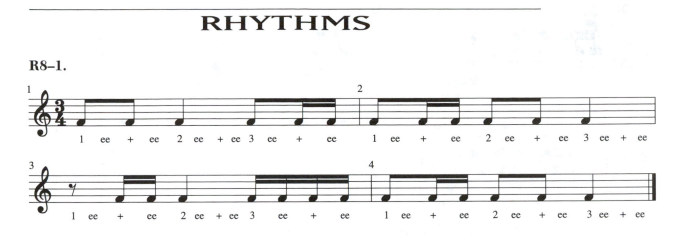

R8–2.

R8–3.

R8–4.

R8–5.

R8–6.

INTERVAL WORKSHOP

I8–1.   Play a pitch that is low in your vocal range at a keyboard. Sing it. Then sing the pitch a minor sixth higher. Use the keyboard to confirm your performance. Then sing ascending sixths starting on other pitches.

I8–2.   Play a pitch that is high in your vocal range at a keyboard. Sing it. Then sing the pitch a minor sixth lower. Use the keyboard to confirm your performance. Then sing descending sixths starting on other pitches.

I8–3.   Practice singing the interval of a minor sixth higher than a sounding pitch. The sounding pitch should be at or beyond the lower limit of your vocal range, and could be sung by a classmate or your instructor or performed on the piano or another instrument such as the cello. Also practice singing compound versions of this interval.

I8–4.   Practice singing the interval of a minor sixth lower than a sounding pitch. The sounding pitch should be at or beyond the upper limit of your vocal range, and could be sung by a classmate or your instructor or performed on the piano or another instrument such as the flute. Also practice singing compound versions of this interval.

I8–5.   At the keyboard, select a pitch in the middle of your vocal range as the "starting pitch." Then sing the following groups of four pitches on "la," forming inversionally related intervals. Practice a. through h. from first to last, from last to first, and in random order.

a.	Starting pitch	Major third higher	Starting pitch	Minor sixth lower
b.	Starting pitch	Perfect fourth higher	Starting pitch	Perfect fifth lower
c.	Starting pitch	Perfect fifth higher	Starting pitch	Perfect fourth lower
d.	Starting pitch	Minor sixth higher	Starting pitch	Major third lower
e.	Starting pitch	Minor sixth lower	Starting pitch	Major third higher
f.	Starting pitch	Perfect fifth lower	Starting pitch	Perfect fourth higher
g.	Starting pitch	Perfect fourth lower	Starting pitch	Perfect fifth higher
h.	Starting pitch	Major third lower	Starting pitch	Minor sixth higher

I8–6.   Choose a classmate with a similar vocal range as a partner. Then perform the following exercises, using each of the following four pairs of intervals.

X	**Inv(X)**
Major third	Minor sixth
Perfect fourth	Perfect fifth
Perfect fifth	Perfect fourth
Minor sixth	Major third

   a. Your partner sings a pitch that is low in your vocal range. Then your partner sings the pitch a second time, while you sing the pitch that is **X** higher than your partner's. Then you sing the pitch you just sang a second time, while your partner sings the pitch that is **Inv(X)** higher than yours.

   b. Your partner sings a pitch that is high in your vocal range. Then your partner sings the pitch a second time, while you sing the pitch that is **X** lower than your partner's. Then you sing the pitch you just sang a second time, while your partner sings the pitch that is **Inv(X)** lower than yours.

ARPEGGIATION WORKSHOP

A8–1.   Play a C, D, E♭, F, G, A, or B♭ that is low in your vocal range at a keyboard. Let this pitch be $\hat{1}$ in a major key. Sing each of the following arpeggiations, either in the order given or in random order.

a.	$\hat{1}$	$\hat{3}$	$\hat{5}$	∘	$\hat{3}$	$\hat{5}$	$\hat{8}$	∘	$\hat{4}$	$\hat{6}$	$\hat{8}$	∘	$\hat{5}$	$\hat{7}$	$\hat{2}$	∘	$\hat{8}$	$\hat{5}$	$\hat{3}$ $\hat{1}$
b.	$\hat{1}$	$\hat{3}$	$\hat{5}$	∘	$\hat{3}$	$\hat{5}$	$\hat{8}$	∘	$\hat{4}$	$\hat{6}$	$\hat{8}$	∘	$\hat{7}$	$\hat{2}$	$\hat{5}$	∘	$\hat{8}$	$\hat{5}$	$\hat{3}$ $\hat{1}$
c.	$\hat{1}$	$\hat{3}$	$\hat{5}$	∘	$\hat{3}$	$\hat{5}$	$\hat{8}$	∘	$\hat{6}$	$\hat{8}$	$\hat{4}$	∘	$\hat{5}$	$\hat{7}$	$\hat{2}$	∘	$\hat{8}$	$\hat{5}$	$\hat{3}$ $\hat{1}$
d.	$\hat{1}$	$\hat{3}$	$\hat{5}$	∘	$\hat{4}$	$\hat{6}$	$\hat{8}$	∘	$\hat{6}$	$\hat{8}$	$\hat{4}$	∘	$\hat{5}$	$\hat{7}$	$\hat{2}$	∘	$\hat{8}$	$\hat{5}$	$\hat{3}$ $\hat{1}$
e.	$\hat{1}$	$\hat{3}$	$\hat{5}$	∘	$\hat{4}$	$\hat{6}$	$\hat{8}$	∘	$\hat{5}$	$\hat{7}$	$\hat{2}$	∘	$\hat{7}$	$\hat{2}$	$\hat{5}$	∘	$\hat{8}$	$\hat{5}$	$\hat{3}$ $\hat{1}$
f.	$\hat{3}$	$\hat{5}$	$\hat{8}$	∘	$\hat{4}$	$\hat{6}$	$\hat{8}$	∘	$\hat{6}$	$\hat{8}$	$\hat{4}$	∘	$\hat{5}$	$\hat{7}$	$\hat{2}$	∘	$\hat{8}$	$\hat{5}$	$\hat{3}$ $\hat{1}$
g.	$\hat{3}$	$\hat{5}$	$\hat{8}$	∘	$\hat{6}$	$\hat{8}$	$\hat{4}$	∘	$\hat{5}$	$\hat{7}$	$\hat{2}$	∘	$\hat{7}$	$\hat{2}$	$\hat{5}$	∘	$\hat{8}$	$\hat{5}$	$\hat{3}$ $\hat{1}$

A8–2.   Play a C, D, E♭, F, G, A, or B♭ that is at least a minor sixth above the lowest note of your vocal range at a keyboard. Let this pitch be $\hat{1}$ in a major key. Sing each of the following arpeggiations, either in the order given or in random order.

a.	$\hat{1}$	$\hat{3}$	$\hat{1}$	∘	$\hat{6}$	$\hat{1}$	$\hat{4}$	∘	$\hat{5}$	$\hat{7}$	$\hat{2}$	∘	$\hat{7}$	$\hat{2}$	$\hat{5}$	∘	$\hat{1}$	$\hat{3}$	$\hat{5}$	$\hat{1}$
b.	$\hat{1}$	$\hat{3}$	$\hat{1}$	∘	$\hat{6}$	$\hat{1}$	$\hat{4}$	∘	$\hat{4}$	$\hat{6}$	$\hat{1}$	∘	$\hat{5}$	$\hat{7}$	$\hat{2}$	∘	$\hat{1}$	$\hat{3}$	$\hat{5}$	$\hat{1}$
c.	$\hat{1}$	$\hat{3}$	$\hat{1}$	∘	$\hat{6}$	$\hat{1}$	$\hat{4}$	∘	$\hat{7}$	$\hat{2}$	$\hat{5}$	∘	$\hat{5}$	$\hat{7}$	$\hat{2}$	∘	$\hat{1}$	$\hat{3}$	$\hat{5}$	$\hat{1}$
d.	$\hat{1}$	$\hat{3}$	$\hat{1}$	∘	$\hat{3}$	$\hat{5}$	$\hat{1}$	∘	$\hat{5}$	$\hat{7}$	$\hat{2}$	∘	$\hat{7}$	$\hat{2}$	$\hat{5}$	∘	$\hat{1}$	$\hat{3}$	$\hat{5}$	$\hat{1}$
e.	$\hat{1}$	$\hat{3}$	$\hat{1}$	∘	$\hat{3}$	$\hat{5}$	$\hat{1}$	∘	$\hat{4}$	$\hat{6}$	$\hat{1}$	∘	$\hat{5}$	$\hat{7}$	$\hat{2}$	∘	$\hat{1}$	$\hat{3}$	$\hat{5}$	$\hat{1}$
f.	$\hat{1}$	$\hat{3}$	$\hat{1}$	∘	$\hat{3}$	$\hat{5}$	$\hat{1}$	∘	$\hat{4}$	$\hat{6}$	$\hat{1}$	∘	$\hat{6}$	$\hat{1}$	$\hat{4}$	∘	$\hat{1}$	$\hat{3}$	$\hat{5}$	$\hat{1}$

QUICK SWITCH

Q8–1.

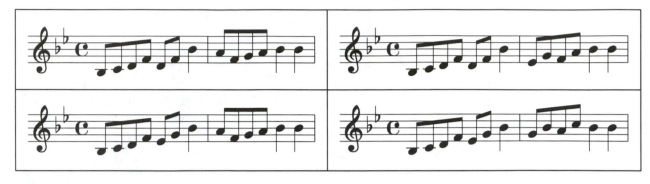

Q8–2.

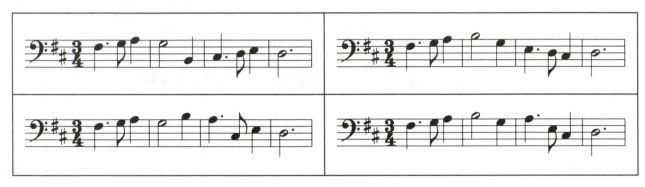

Q8–3.

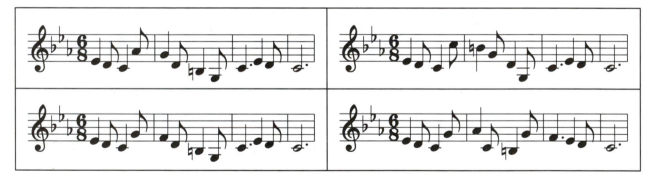

Q8–4.

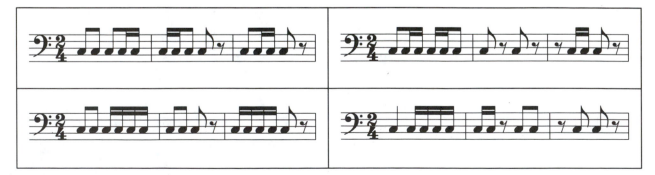

IDENTIFICATIONS

ID8–1. An interval is performed melodically, either ascending or descending. Identify it as a minor second, major second, minor third, major third, perfect fourth, perfect fifth, minor sixth, minor seventh, or perfect octave.

ID8–2. An interval is performed as a simultaneity. Identify it as a minor third, major third, perfect fourth, perfect fifth, minor sixth, minor seventh, or perfect octave.

ID8–3. $\hat{1}$, $\hat{3}$, $\hat{5}$, and $\hat{8}$ in a major key are performed simultaneously. Then two of these four scale degrees are performed simultaneously. Identify the two scale degrees performed, from among the following choices: $\hat{1}$-$\hat{3}$, $\hat{1}$-$\hat{5}$, $\hat{1}$-$\hat{8}$, $\hat{3}$-$\hat{5}$, $\hat{3}$-$\hat{8}$, $\hat{5}$-$\hat{8}$.

ID8–4. $\hat{1}$, $\hat{3}$, $\hat{5}$, and $\hat{8}$ in a major key are performed simultaneously. Then either $\hat{1}$, $\hat{3}$, and $\hat{5}$ or $\hat{3}$, $\hat{5}$, and $\hat{8}$ are performed simultaneously. Is the resulting chord in $\frac{5}{3}$ or $\frac{6}{3}$ position?

ID8–5. Two chords are performed. Interpret the first chord as I in $\frac{5}{3}$ position in a major key. What is the appropriate Roman numeral and figured bass for the second chord? Suitable choices are listed below.

$$\begin{array}{cccccc} & & & & & 7 \\ 6 & & 6 & & 6 & 5 \\ 3 & & 3 & & 3 & 3 \\ \text{I} & \text{IV} & \text{IV} & \text{V} & \text{V} & \text{V} \\ \text{I}^6 & \text{IV} & \text{IV}^6 & \text{V} & \text{V}^6 & \text{V}^7 \end{array}$$

ID8–6. A melody is performed. Identify the correct score notation.

e.

f.

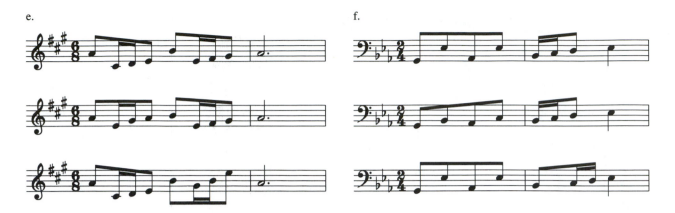

ID8–7.   A chord progression in the major mode is performed. Identify a suitable Roman-numeral/figured-bass analysis from among the following choices:

Group 1

a.   I———————IV   I
b.   I———————V   I
c.   I   IV   V   I
d.   I   V———————I

a.   I ^{6} IV   I
b.   I ^{6} V^7 I
c.   I   IV   V^7 I
d.   I   V ^{6} I

Group 2

a.   I———————IV———————I
b.   I———————IV———————I
c.   I———————V———————I
d.   I———————V   I   V

a.   I ^{6} IV ^{6} I
b.   I ^{6} IV ^{6} I^6
c.   I ^{6} V ^{6} I
d.   I ^{6} V   I   V^6

Group 3

a.   I   IV   V^7 I   V^6
b.   I   IV   V^6 I^6 V^6
c.   I^6 IV^6 V^7 I   V^6
d.   I^6 IV^6 V^6 I   V

a.   I   IV   V^7 I   V^6
b.   I   IV^6 V^6 I   V
c.   I^6 IV   V^7 I   V^6
d.   I^6 IV^6 V^6 I   V

Group 4

a.   I   V   I———————V
b.   I   V   I———————V
c.   I   V   I———————V
d.   I   V   I———————V

a.   I   V   I ^{6} V
b.   I   V^6 I ^{6} V
c.   I   V   I^6 $^5_3$ V
d.   I   V   I^6 $^5_3$ V^6

ID8–8.   A chord progression is performed. Identify the correct score notation for the outer voices. Figured-bass symbols have been placed below the bass where appropriate. If you wish, add Roman numerals.

a.

b.

c.

d.

e.

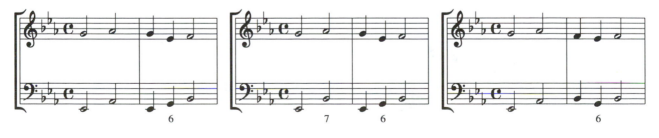

f.

RHYTHMIC DICTATIONS

RD8–1.

RD8–2.

MELODIC DICTATIONS

J.S. BACH: WELL-TEMPERED CLAVIER, VOL. 1, FUGUE 16, BWV 861

MD8–1.

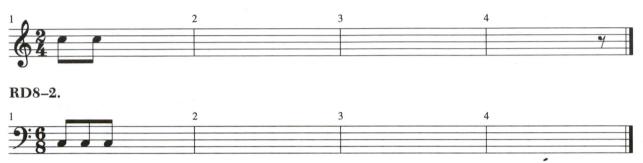

- Measure 1 juxtaposes D and the G below it. Because D is embellished by an incomplete upper neighbor, the descending interval is a minor sixth, rather than a perfect fifth.

GOUNOD: *FAUST*, ACT 3

MD8–2.

Moderato quasi andante

- What is the last pitch of measure 1? Why does Gounod employ it as the seventh scale degree in this context? What is the fourth pitch of measure 3? Why does Gounod employ it as the seventh scale degree in this context?

TCHAIKOVSKY: FESTIVAL OVERTURE ON THE DANISH NATIONAL ANTHEM, OP. 15

MD8–3.

Andante non troppo

- The fourth pitch of measure 1 is the leading tone, B♮. When and to what pitch does it resolve?

SCHUBERT: PIANO SONATA IN B MAJOR, D. 575, OP. POST. 147, MVMT. 3

MD8–4.

Allegretto

- At first, concentrate on the pitches that appear on beat 1 of each measure. The remaining pitches will fit very nicely into the framework they form.

MENDELSSOHN: SYMPHONY NO. 4 IN A MAJOR ("ITALIAN"), OP. 90, MVMT. 1

MD8–5.

Allegro vivace

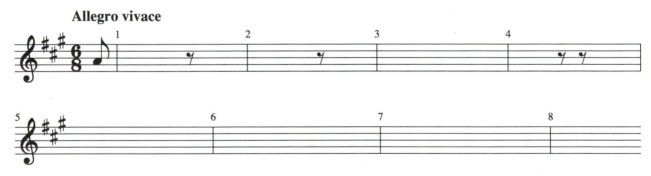

- Observe that the dominant seventh chord's seventh, D, appears in two different registers during measures 3 and 4. Thus it is no coincidence that C♯ appears in both of those registers during measure 5.

MAHLER: SYMPHONY NO. 4 IN G MAJOR, MVMT. 1

MD8–6.

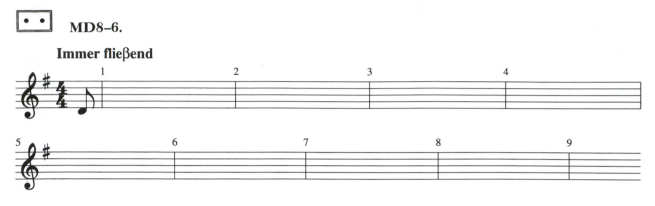

- The melody ascends gradually, like a balloon, higher and higher above the earth (tonic). In the opening measures, the tonic triad (G, B, D) is weighted down. In measures 3 and 4, D's upper neighbor E launches the initial surge of ascent, while the root G is left behind. In measures 5 and 6, the height of G above the triad's D is attained. Beginning in measure 7, the high G is supreme, with only brief reminders of the world below.

HARMONIC DICTATIONS

HD8–1.

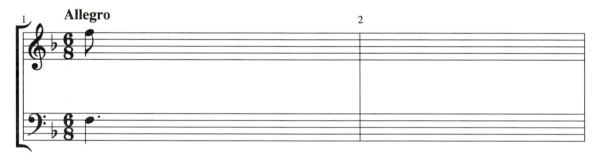

- Compare the chords that appear on beats 1 and 2 of measure 1. Do they represent the same harmony or different harmonies? If they are the same harmony, do they appear in the same inversion or in different inversions?

HD8–2.

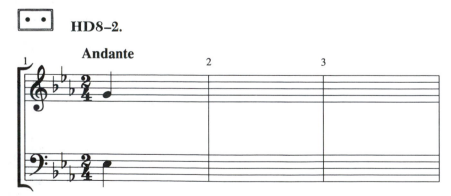

- Do not assume that an abundance of notes must coordinate with an abundance of different harmonies. Sometimes many notes prolong a single harmony, such as tonic in measure 1.

HD8–3.

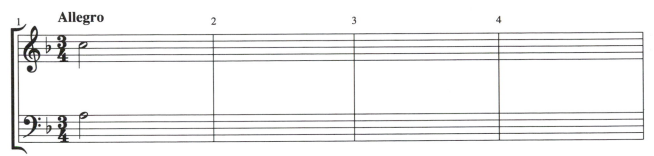

- Where does the first F appear in the bass? What pitch immediately precedes it? Where does the second F appear in the bass? What pitch immediately precedes it? In one case, tonic is preceded by the subdominant in first inversion. In the other, tonic is preceded by the dominant in first inversion.

BEETHOVEN: PIANO SONATA NO. 3 IN C MAJOR, OP. 2, NO. 3, MVMT. 1

 HD8–4.

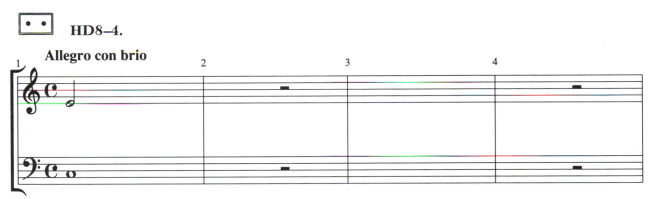

- Do not allow the neighboring notes in measures 1 and 3 to obscure the basic shape of the melody. Write down the first soprano pitch of each measure before dealing with the figuration.

- The first soprano pitch of measure 3 forms a dissonance against the bass. To what pitch should it resolve? Where does the resolution occur?

HD8–5.

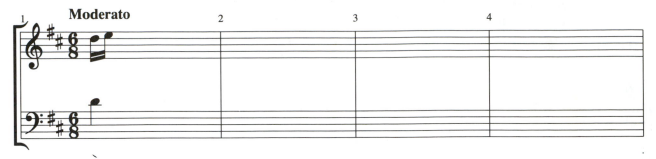

· Measures 2 and 4 are similar but not identical. Contrast the treatment of the dominant's seventh in these two measures.

HD8–6.

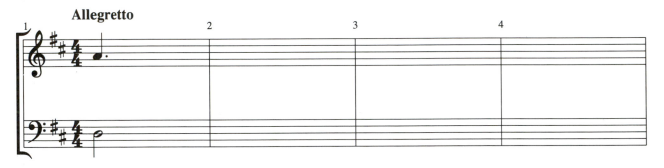

· Measure 2 contains passing notes in the bass. They connect notes that serve as chord members. The chord on the first beat of measure 2 is in $\frac{5}{3}$ position; that on the second beat is in $\frac{6}{3}$ position.

⊡ CASSETTE PROGRAM
(TAPE 1, SIDE B)

C8–1.   Six melodies are performed, twice each. During the silence after each playing, respond in one of the following ways: (1) Sing the melody, using solmization syllables; (2) Play the melody on the piano or on your primary instrument; (3) Write the melody on staff paper.

a.   b.   c.   d.   e.   f.

C8–2.   Six chord progressions are performed, four times each. During the silence after each playing, respond in one of the following ways: (1) Sing the soprano after the first and second playings and the bass after the third and fourth playings, using solmization syllables; (2) Play the soprano on the piano or your primary instrument after the first and second playings and the bass after the third and fourth playings; (3) Play both the soprano and bass on the piano after each playing; (4) Write the soprano and bass on staff paper and provide an analysis.

a.   b.   c.   d.   e.   f.

Chapter 9

PITCH

The principles of inversion introduced in chapter 8 apply in minor keys as well. In Method One analysis, give special attention to altered pitches. Example 9–1 shows that *when a raised scale degree appears in the bass, the figured bass does not show an accidental*. That is because the bass itself, rather than one of the pitches above the bass (which is what the figures account for), contains the altered pitch. An accidental to the right of a Roman numeral (a practice introduced in chapters 5 and 6) indicates that a chord's quality is major. In Method Two analysis, also shown in Example 9–1, the altered subdominant and dominant chords are analyzed exactly as they would be in the parallel major key (from which they are borrowed). Major quality is indicated, as always, by a capital Roman numeral.

EXAMPLE 9–1

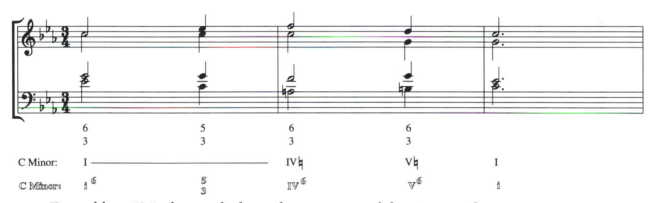

Figured-bass "6," when applied to a *diatonic* tonic, subdominant, or dominant chord in minor keys, indicates a ***major sixth***, the inversion of the minor third formed by the root and third of a minor triad (see Ex. 9–2a). The interval formed by E♭ and C in the first chord in Example 9–1 is a major sixth.[1] Examples 9–2b, 9–2c, and 9–2d show samples of the major sixth in the context of both minor and major keys.

---

1. When "6" is applied to an *altered* subdominant or dominant chord containing #$\hat{6}$ or #$\hat{7}$, as in measure 2 of Example 1, it indicates a minor sixth, just as it does in major keys.

EXAMPLE 9–2

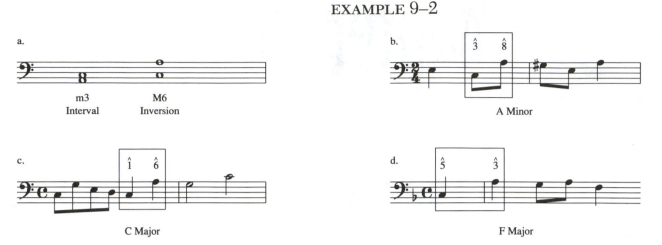

Four new keys are introduced in this chapter. Both the **key of E major** and its relative minor, the **key of C♯ minor**, employ a key signature of four sharps. Both the **key of A♭ major** and its relative minor, the **key of F minor**, employ a key signature of four flats.

METER AND RHYTHM

Sixteenth notes do not always occur in pairs. In simple meters such as $\frac{2}{4}$, $\frac{3}{4}$, or $\frac{4}{4}$ a single sixteenth note (♪) may occur if preceded or followed by a **sixteenth rest** (𝄿) or if preceded by a **dotted eighth note** (♪.). A sixteenth rest may also occur after a dotted eighth note to fill a beat. A **dotted eighth rest** (𝄾·) may occur *before* a sixteenth note to fill a beat. If a sixteenth note is *followed* by silence for the remainder of a beat, the combination of a sixteenth rest and an eighth rest would generally be used. Similar conventions prevail in compound meters such as $\frac{6}{8}$, where six sixteenth notes or their equivalent fill a beat. Example 9–3 demonstrates most of these possibilities. Beams may be employed (instead of flags) to indicate eighth, dotted eighth, and sixteenth notes.

EXAMPLE 9–3

SOLO MELODIES

FIXED DO: *Sing "tis" for B♯. Sing "ra" for D♭.*

LETTER NAMES: *Sing "Bis" for B♯. Sing "Des" for D♭.*

MAJOR-MODE MELODIES THAT EMPLOY A MAJOR SIXTH

DVOŘÁK: *RUSALKA*, OP. 114, ACT 2

S9–1.

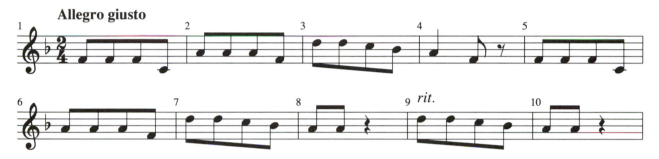

- The D of measure 3 comes as a surprise. The basic shape $\hat{1}$-$\hat{5}$-$\hat{3}$-$\hat{1}$ in measures 1 and 2 would logically continue with $\hat{5}$. As a practice strategy, sing $\hat{1}$-$\hat{5}$-$\hat{3}$-$\hat{1}$-$\hat{5}$, then sing $\hat{1}$-$\hat{5}$-$\hat{3}$-$\hat{1}$-$\hat{6}$.

WEBER: *DER FREISCHÜTZ*, ACT 2

S9–2.

HANDEL: *SUSANNA*, ACT 1

S9–3.

- Arpeggiate D♯-F♯-B in your internal ear during measure 4 (while singing D♯) to find the B of measure 5.

MOZART: PIANO CONCERTO NO. 22 IN E♭ MAJOR, K. 482, MVMT. 3

S9–4.

MINOR-MODE MELODIES THAT EMPLOY A MAJOR SIXTH

HANDEL: *SUSANNA*, ACT 2

S9–5.

· Think of the E♭ in measure 2 as a neighbor to the following D. As a practice strategy, sing D (upbeat to measure 1) and then the E♭ and D of measure 2.

S9–6.

MELODIES IN E MAJOR OR C♯ MINOR

HANDEL: *SUSANNA*, ACT 1

S9–7.

- Though it looks like this melody is in C♯ minor, the E of measure 2 sounds like tonic.

VIVALDI: CONCERTO IN E MAJOR ("THE FOUR SEASONS: SPRING"), RV 269, OP. 8, NO. 1, MVMT. 1

S9–8.

BRAHMS: SYMPHONY NO. 1 IN C MINOR, OP. 68, MVMT. 2

S9–9.

- Sing 5̂-3̂-1̂-3̂-5̂-8̂ as preparation for this melody. Locate where each of these scale degrees occurs within the melody.

BRAHMS: INTERMEZZO, OP. 117, NO. 3

S9–10.

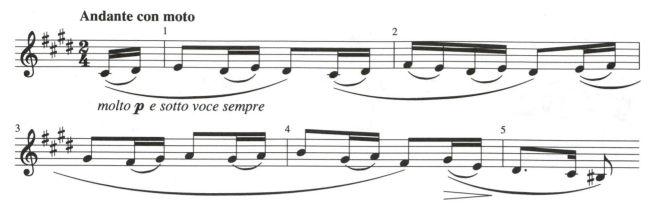

MELODIES IN A♭ MAJOR OR F MINOR

MOZART: STRING QUARTET NO. 15 IN D MINOR, K. 421, MVMT. 2

S9–11.

- Observe the symmetrical construction of this phrase. Where does each pitch of the following diagram occur within the melody?

FIELD: PIANO CONCERTO NO. 2 IN A♭ MAJOR, MVMT. 3

S9–12.

MELODIES THAT EMPLOY DOTTED EIGHTH OR INDIVIDUAL SIXTEENTH NOTES

MOZART: PIANO SONATA NO. 11 IN A MAJOR, K. 331, MVMT. 1

S9–13.

- Leaps connect notes that form two concurrent stepwise descending lines. In the antecedent phrase, follow the lines C#-B-A (on beat 1 of measures 1 through 3) and, a third higher, E-D-C#. The structure of the consequent phrase is similar.

TCHAIKOVSKY: *CAPRICCIO ITALIEN*, OP. 45

S9–14.

MOZART: *THE MAGIC FLUTE*, K. 620, ACT 1

S9–15.

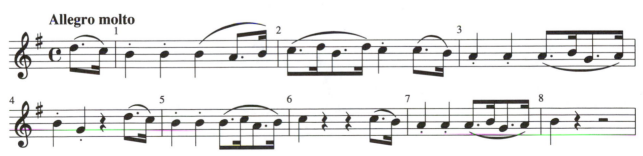

- Circle the two Ds of measure 2, the B of measures 3 and 7, and the C of measure 5. At first, practice the melody without these notes (converting the dotted eighth notes preceding circled notes into quarter notes). When you feel confident, add the circled notes.

GOUNOD: *FAUST*, ACT 2

S9–16.

DUETS

D9–1.

AFTER DVOŘÁK: *RUSALKA*, OP. 114, ACT 2

D9–2.

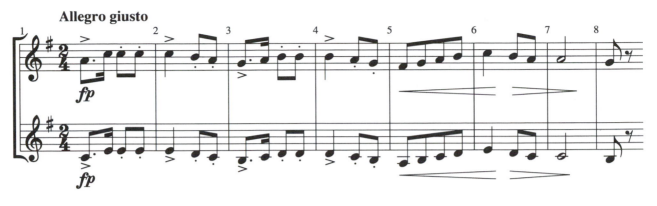

ACCOMPANIED SOLO MELODIES

AFTER BEETHOVEN: SYMPHONY NO. 3 IN E♭ MAJOR ("EROICA"), OP. 55, MVMT. 4

AS9–1.

AS9–2.

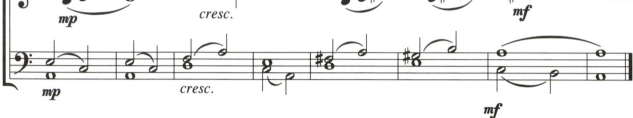

RHYTHMS

R9–1.

R9–2.

R9–3.

R9–4.

R9–5.

R9–6.

INTERVAL WORKSHOP

I9–1.   Play a pitch that is low in your vocal range at a keyboard. Sing it. Then sing the pitch a major sixth higher. Use the keyboard to confirm your performance. Then sing ascending sixths starting on other pitches.

I9–2.   Play a pitch that is high in your vocal range at a keyboard. Sing it. Then sing the pitch a major sixth lower. Use the keyboard to confirm your performance. Then sing descending sixths starting on other pitches.

I9–3.   Practice singing the interval of a major sixth higher than a sounding pitch. The sounding pitch should be at or beyond the lower limit of your vocal range, and could be sung by a classmate or your instructor or performed on the piano or another instrument such as the cello. Also practice singing compound versions of this interval.

I9–4.   Practice singing the interval of a major sixth lower than a sounding pitch. The sounding pitch should be at or beyond the upper limit of your vocal range, and could be sung by a classmate or your instructor or performed on the piano or another instrument such as the flute. Also practice singing compound versions of this interval.

I9–5.   At the keyboard, select a pitch in the middle of your vocal range as the "starting pitch." Then sing the following groups of four pitches on "la," forming inversionally related intervals. Practice a. through l. from first to last, from last to first, and in random order.

a.	Starting pitch	Minor third higher	Starting pitch	Major sixth lower
b.	Starting pitch	Major third higher	Starting pitch	Minor sixth lower
c.	Starting pitch	Perfect fourth higher	Starting pitch	Perfect fifth lower
d.	Starting pitch	Perfect fifth higher	Starting pitch	Perfect fourth lower
e.	Starting pitch	Minor sixth higher	Starting pitch	Major third lower
f.	Starting pitch	Major sixth higher	Starting pitch	Minor third lower
g.	Starting pitch	Major sixth lower	Starting pitch	Minor third higher
h.	Starting pitch	Minor sixth lower	Starting pitch	Major third higher
i.	Starting pitch	Perfect fifth lower	Starting pitch	Perfect fourth higher
j.	Starting pitch	Perfect fourth lower	Starting pitch	Perfect fifth higher
k.	Starting pitch	Major third lower	Starting pitch	Minor sixth higher
l.	Starting pitch	Minor third lower	Starting pitch	Major sixth higher

I9–6.   Choose a classmate with a similar vocal range as a partner. Then perform the following exercises, using each of the following six pairs of intervals.

X	Inv(X)
Minor third	Major sixth
Major third	Minor sixth
Perfect fourth	Perfect fifth
Perfect fifth	Perfect fourth
Minor sixth	Major third
Major sixth	Minor third

a.   Your partner sings a pitch that is low in your vocal range. Then your partner sings the pitch a second time, while you sing the pitch that is **X** higher than your partner's. Then you sing the pitch you just sang a second time, while your partner sings the pitch that is **Inv(X)** higher than yours.

b.   Your partner sings a pitch that is high in your vocal range. Then your partner sings the pitch a second time, while you sing the pitch that is **X** lower than your partner's. Then you sing the pitch you just sang a second time, while your partner sings the pitch that is **Inv(X)** lower than yours.

ARPEGGIATION WORKSHOP

A9–1.   Play a C, C♯, D, E, F, F♯, G, A, or B that is low in your vocal range at a keyboard. Let this pitch be $\hat{1}$ in a minor key. Sing each of the following arpeggiations, either in the order given or in random order.

a. 1̂ 3̂ 5̂ ⬦ 3̂ 5̂ 8̂ ⬦ 4̂ 6̂ 8̂ ⬦ 5̂ #7̂ 2̂ ⬦ 8̂ 5̂ 3̂ 1̂

b. 1̂ 3̂ 5̂ ⬦ 3̂ 5̂ 8̂ ⬦ 4̂ 6̂ 8̂ ⬦ #7̂ 2̂ 5̂ ⬦ 8̂ 5̂ 3̂ 1̂

c. 1̂ 3̂ 5̂ ⬦ 3̂ 5̂ 8̂ ⬦ 6̂ 8̂ 4̂ ⬦ 5̂ #7̂ 2̂ ⬦ 8̂ 5̂ 3̂ 1̂

d. 1̂ 3̂ 5̂ ⬦ 4̂ 6̂ 8̂ ⬦ 6̂ 8̂ 4̂ ⬦ 5̂ #7̂ 2̂ ⬦ 8̂ 5̂ 3̂ 1̂

e. 1̂ 3̂ 5̂ ⬦ 4̂ #6̂ 8̂ ⬦ #6̂ 8̂ 4̂ ⬦ 5̂ #7̂ 2̂ ⬦ 8̂ 5̂ 3̂ 1̂

f. 1̂ 3̂ 5̂ ⬦ 4̂ 6̂ 8̂ ⬦ 5̂ #7̂ 2̂ ⬦ #7̂ 2̂ 5̂ ⬦ 8̂ 5̂ 3̂ 1̂

g. 3̂ 5̂ 8̂ ⬦ 4̂ 6̂ 8̂ ⬦ 6̂ 8̂ 4̂ ⬦ 5̂ #7̂ 2̂ ⬦ 8̂ 5̂ 3̂ 1̂

h. 3̂ 5̂ 8̂ ⬦ 6̂ 8̂ 4̂ ⬦ 5̂ #7̂ 2̂ ⬦ #7̂ 2̂ 5̂ ⬦ 8̂ 5̂ 3̂ 1̂

i. 3̂ 5̂ 8̂ ⬦ #6̂ 8̂ 4̂ ⬦ 5̂ #7̂ 2̂ ⬦ #7̂ 2̂ 5̂ ⬦ 8̂ 5̂ 3̂ 1̂

A9–2. Play a C, C♯, D, E, F, F♯, G, A, or B that is at least a major sixth above the lowest note of your vocal range at a keyboard. Let this pitch be 1̂ in a minor key. Sing each of the following arpeggiations, either in the order given or in random order.

a. 1̂ 3̂ 1̂ ⬦ 6̂ 1̂ 4̂ ⬦ 5̂ #7̂ 2̂ ⬦ #7̂ 2̂ 5̂ ⬦ 1̂ 3̂ 5̂ 1̂

b. 1̂ 3̂ 1̂ ⬦ 6̂ 1̂ 4̂ ⬦ 4̂ 6̂ 1̂ ⬦ 5̂ #7̂ 2̂ ⬦ 1̂ 3̂ 5̂ 1̂

c. 1̂ 3̂ 1̂ ⬦ #6̂ 1̂ 4̂ ⬦ #7̂ 2̂ 5̂ ⬦ 5̂ #7̂ 2̂ ⬦ 1̂ 3̂ 5̂ 1̂

d. 1̂ 3̂ 1̂ ⬦ 3̂ 5̂ 1̂ ⬦ 5̂ #7̂ 2̂ ⬦ #7̂ 2̂ 5̂ ⬦ 1̂ 3̂ 5̂ 1̂

e. 1̂ 3̂ 1̂ ⬦ 3̂ 5̂ 1̂ ⬦ 4̂ 6̂ 1̂ ⬦ 5̂ #7̂ 2̂ ⬦ 1̂ 3̂ 5̂ 1̂

f. 1̂ 3̂ 1̂ ⬦ 3̂ 5̂ 1̂ ⬦ 4̂ #6̂ 1̂ ⬦ 5̂ #7̂ 2̂ ⬦ 1̂ 3̂ 5̂ 1̂

g. 1̂ 3̂ 1̂ ⬦ 3̂ 5̂ 1̂ ⬦ 4̂ 6̂ 1̂ ⬦ 6̂ 1̂ 4̂ ⬦ 5̂ #7̂ 2̂ 5̂

QUICK SWITCH

Q9–1.

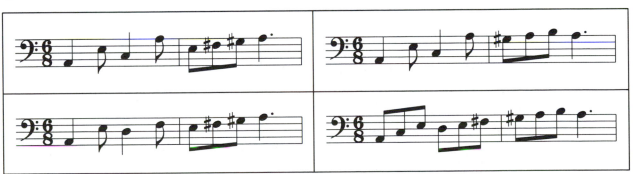

Q9–2.

Q9–3.

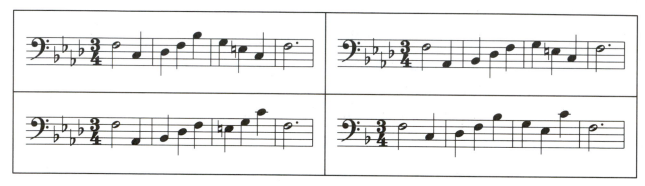

Q9–4.

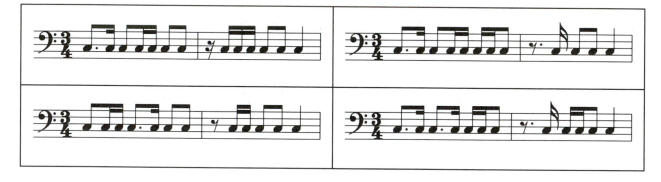

IDENTIFICATIONS

ID9–1.   An interval is performed melodically, either ascending or descending. Identify it as a minor second, major second, minor third, major third, perfect fourth, perfect fifth, minor sixth, major sixth, minor seventh, or perfect octave.

ID9–2.   An interval is performed as a simultaneity. Identify it as a minor third, major third, perfect fourth, perfect fifth, minor sixth, major sixth, minor seventh, or perfect octave.

ID9–3. $\hat{1}$, $\hat{3}$, $\hat{5}$, and $\hat{8}$ in a minor key are performed simultaneously. Then two of these four scale degrees are performed simultaneously. Identify the two scale degrees performed, from among the following choices: $\hat{1}$-$\hat{3}$, $\hat{1}$-$\hat{5}$, $\hat{1}$-$\hat{8}$, $\hat{3}$-$\hat{5}$, $\hat{3}$-$\hat{8}$, $\hat{5}$-$\hat{8}$.

ID9–4. $\hat{1}$, $\hat{3}$, $\hat{5}$, and $\hat{8}$ in a minor key are performed simultaneously. Then either $\hat{1}$, $\hat{3}$, and $\hat{5}$ or $\hat{3}$, $\hat{5}$, and $\hat{8}$ are performed simultaneously. Is the resulting chord in $\frac{5}{3}$ or $\frac{6}{3}$ position?

ID9–5. A chord in $\frac{6}{3}$ position is performed. Is its quality major or minor?

ID9–6. Two chords are performed. Interpret the first chord as I in $\frac{5}{3}$ position or i in a minor key. What is the appropriate Roman numeral and figured bass for the second chord? Suitable choices are listed below.

| $\begin{smallmatrix}6\\3\end{smallmatrix}$ | | $\begin{smallmatrix}5\\\sharp\end{smallmatrix}$ | $\begin{smallmatrix}6\\3\end{smallmatrix}$ | $\begin{smallmatrix}6\\3\end{smallmatrix}$ | | $\begin{smallmatrix}5\\\sharp\end{smallmatrix}$ | $\begin{smallmatrix}6\\3\end{smallmatrix}$ | $\begin{smallmatrix}6\\3\end{smallmatrix}$ | $\begin{smallmatrix}7\\5\\\sharp\end{smallmatrix}$ |
| I | IV | IV♯ | IV | IV♯ | V | V♯ | V | V♯ | V♯ |

i^6 iv   IV   iv^6 IV^6 v   V   v^6 V^6 V^7

ID9–7. A melody is performed. Identify the correct score notation.

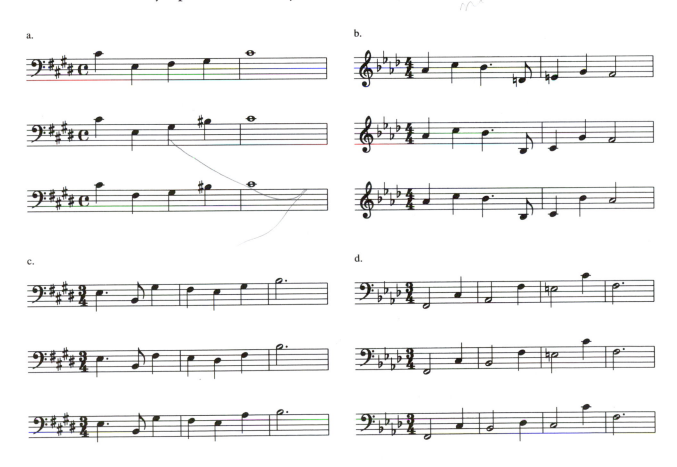

ID9–8.   A chord progression in the minor mode is performed. Identify a suitable Roman-numeral/figured-bass analysis from among the following choices:

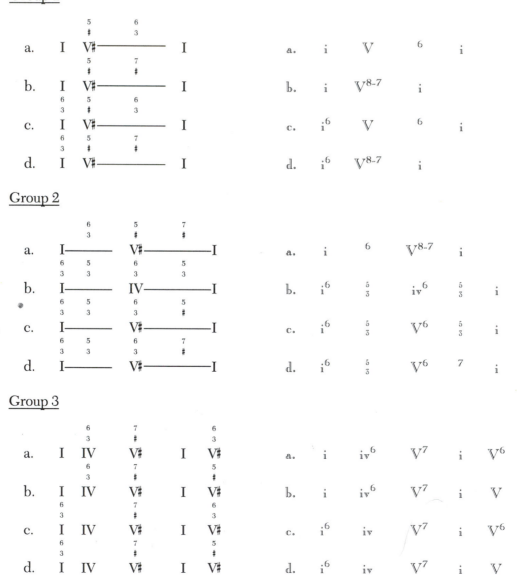

Group 4

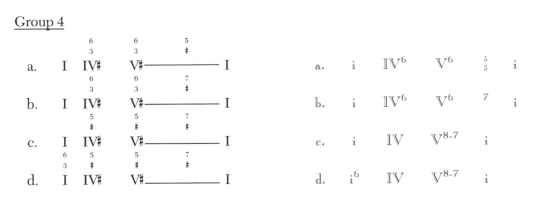

a.	I	IV♯ (6 3)	V♯ (5)———	I		a.	i	IV⁶	V⁶ (5 3)		i
b.	I	IV♯ (6 3)	V♯ (6 3)———7	I		b.	i	IV⁶	V⁶ 7		i
c.	I	IV♯ (5 ♯)	V♯ (5 ♯)———7	I		c.	i	IV	V⁸⁻⁷		i
d.	I	IV♯ (6 3)	V♯ (5 ♯)———7	I		d.	i⁶	IV	V⁸⁻⁷		i

ID9–9.   A chord progression is performed. Identify the correct score notation for the outer voices. Figured-bass symbols have been placed below the bass where appropriate. If you wish, add Roman numerals.

d.

e.

f.

RHYTHMIC DICTATIONS

RD9–1.

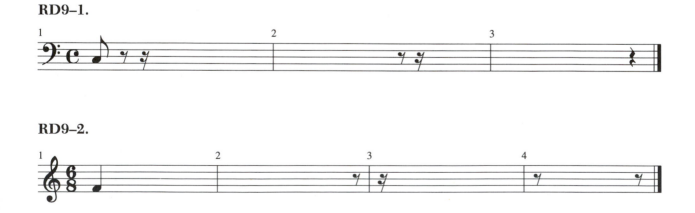

RD9–2.

MELODIC DICTATIONS

J. STRAUSS: *DIE FLEDERMAUS*, ACT 1

MD9–1.

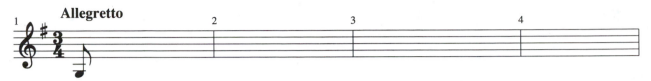

- The second pitch in each of the first three measures is an upper neighboring note. Listen at first for the pitches that occur *on* the beats. Once that basic structure is established, add the embellishing pitches.

HANDEL: *RODELINDA*, ACT 3

MD9–2.

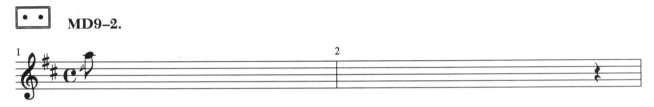

- Melodic forces, as well as harmonic forces, can generate a sixth. B (which occurs twice in measure 1) is a neighbor to A, as the following diagram shows.

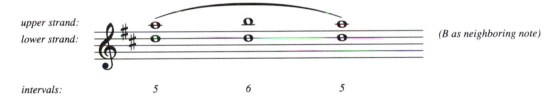

BEETHOVEN: PIANO SONATA NO. 31 IN A♭ MAJOR, OP. 110, MVMT. 2

MD9–3.

- Before writing down any other pitches, write down the first pitch of measures 3 and 5.

CHOPIN: NOCTURNE, OP. 48, NO. 1

MD9–4.

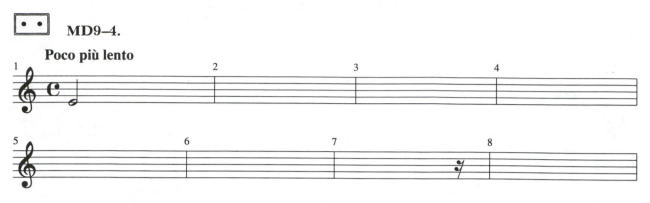

- What harmony do the pitches of measures 2 and 3 arpeggiate?
- What is the relationship between measures 1 and 5?

MOZART: *COSÌ FAN TUTTE*, K. 588, ACT 2

MD9–5.

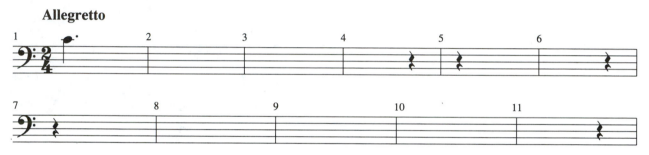

- Write down the first pitch of measures 4, 5, 6, 7, and 8 before writing down any other pitches of those measures.

WEBER: *DER FREISCHÜTZ*, ACT 2

MD9–6.

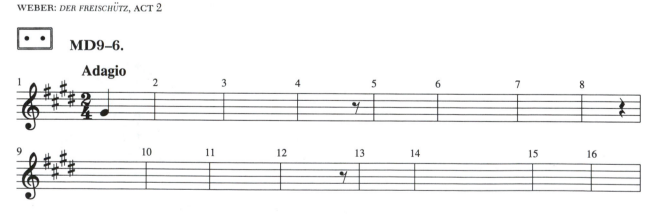

- Some of what occurs in the second half of this excerpt is derived from materials of the first half. For example, the three pitches of measure 9 are closely related to the four pitches of measures 1 and 2.
- What harmony do the first pitches of measures 9 through 13 arpeggiate?

HARMONIC DICTATIONS

HD9–1.

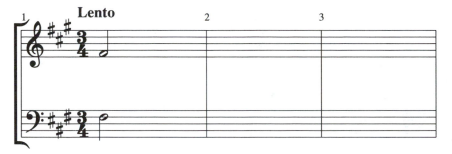

- The two chords in measure 1 are linked by leaps in both outer voices. Do not allow this disjunct motion to camouflage what these chords have in common.

 HD9–2.

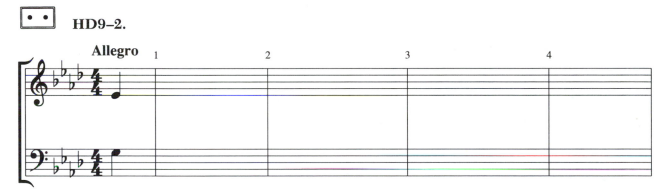

- What characteristics of the two chords that precede measure 1 prevent you from interpreting them as tonic?

HD9–3.

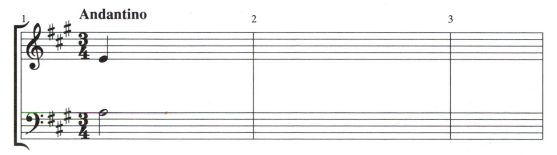

- How do the four soprano pitches of measure 2 relate to the four soprano pitches of measure 1?

BEETHOVEN: SYMPHONY NO. 5 IN C MINOR, OP. 67, MVMT. 4

HD9–4.

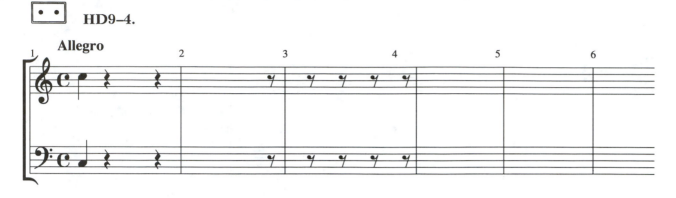

· The number of different harmonies used in this excerpt is surprisingly small.

HD9–5.

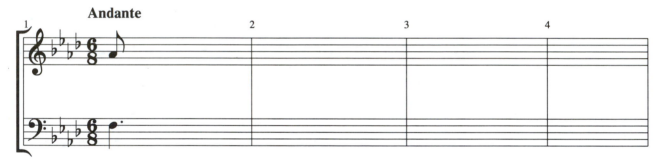

· The second chord of measure 1 often leads to the dominant. Here, tonic returns instead in measure 2. An identical pre–dominant chord occurs in the middle of measure 3. How does the progression differ in this measure?

HD9–6.

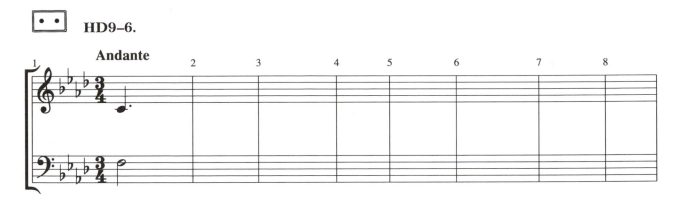

· The neighboring-note motive of measures 1 and 3 recurs with varied rhythm in measure 6.

CASSETTE PROGRAM (TAPE 2, SIDE A)

C9–1.   Six melodies are performed, twice each. During the silence after each playing, respond in one of the following ways: (1) Sing the melody, using solmization syllables; (2) Play the melody on the piano or on your primary instrument; (3) Write the melody on staff paper.

C9–2.   Six chord progressions are performed, four times each. During the silence after each playing, respond in one of the following ways: (1) Sing the soprano after the first and second playings and the bass after the third and fourth playings, using solmization syllables; (2) Play the soprano on the piano or your primary instrument after the first and second playings and the bass after the third and fourth playings; (3) Play both the soprano and bass on the piano after each playing; (4) Write the soprano and bass on staff paper and provide an analysis.

Chapter 10

PITCH

The dominant seventh chord contains the pitches of two of the major mode's seven diatonic triads: the dominant triad (V) and the **leading-tone** triad (VII or vii°). These chords are displayed in the context of C major in Example 10–1. Each employs the leading tone ($\hat{7}$). Each typically precedes tonic. Both the dominant seventh chord and the leading-tone chord contain the dissonant interval of a diminished fifth (or its inversion, an augmented fourth). When you hear a chord that you think belongs to this group, ask yourself the following questions: (1) Is the chord consonant or dissonant? (2) What scale degree occurs in the bass? (3) Is there a seventh above the bass? If not, is there a fifth or a sixth? With practice, you can learn to distinguish among these similar sounds.

EXAMPLE 10–1

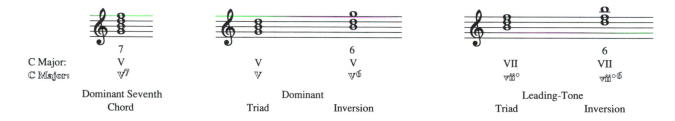

C Major:					
	V	V	V	VII	VII
C Majors	V⁷	V	V⁶	vii°	vii°⁶
	Dominant Seventh Chord	Dominant Triad	Inversion	Leading-Tone Triad	Inversion

Just as the leading tone is borrowed from major to form major dominant chords in minor keys, it is borrowed for the leading-tone chord as well. In Method One analysis, the alteration of a chord's *root* is indicated by placing the appropriate accidental to the *left* of the Roman numeral. When the leading-tone chord appears in first inversion, that accidental will also appear in the figured bass. A circle [°] to the right of a small Roman numeral indicates diminished quality in Method Two analysis. Example 10–2 demonstrates these notational conventions in both major and minor keys.

Four new keys are introduced in this chapter. Both the **key of B major** and its relative minor, the **key of G♯ minor**, employ a key signature of five sharps. Both the **key of D♭ major** and its relative minor, the **key of B♭ minor**, employ a key signature of five flats.

EXAMPLE 10–2

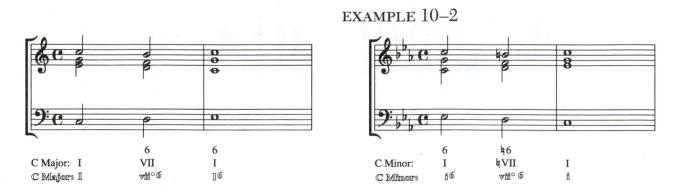

		6		6			
C Major: I		VII		I			
C Major: I		vii° 6		I 6			

6	4 6		
C Minor: I	♮VII	I	
C Minor: i 6	vii° 6	i	

METER AND RHYTHM

In $\frac{2}{2}$ *meter*, also known as ***alla breve*** or ***cut time*** and often indicated by the symbol ₵, the beat is represented by a half note. Two half notes fill a measure in $\frac{2}{2}$ meter, just as two quarter notes fill a measure in $\frac{2}{4}$ meter. Example 10–3 shows two melodies in alla breve, along with appropriate counting syllables.

EXAMPLE 10–3

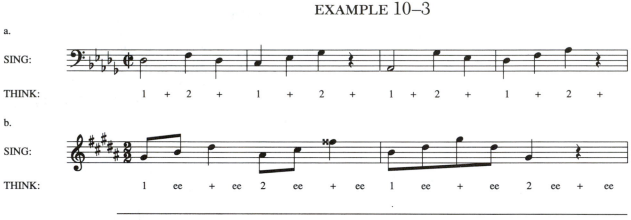

a.

SING:

THINK: 1   +   2   +   1   +   2   +   1   +   2   +   1   +   2   +

b.

SING:

THINK: 1   ee   +   ee   2   ee   +   ee   1   ee   +   ee   2   ee   +   ee

SOLO MELODIES

FIXED DO: *Sing "fis" for F✗. Sing "se" for G♭.*

LETTER NAMES: *Sing "Fisis" for F✗. Sing "Ges" for G♭.*

MELODIES THAT OUTLINE A DIMINISHED FIFTH OR AUGMENTED FOURTH

MOZART: *THE MAGIC FLUTE,* K. 620, ACT 2

S10–1.

- Despite the numerous changes of direction, the overall trajectory of this melody is downward. Your performance should be guided by the stepwise descent from G (measure 1) through F (measure 2), E (measure 3), and D (measure 4) to C (measure 5).

MOZART: *COSÌ FAN TUTTE*, K. 588, ACT 2

S10–2.

TCHAIKOVSKY: SYMPHONY NO. 5 IN E MINOR, OP. 64, MVMT. 3

S10–3.

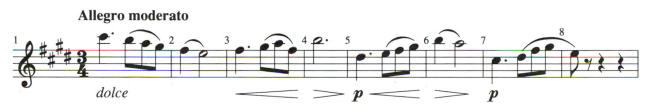

- Observe that measures 5 and 6 outline a diminished fifth (D♯ to A). The B on beat 1 of measure 6 is an upper neighbor to the A. How do the last two pitches of the excerpt (G♯ and E) relate to this diminished fifth?

GOUNOD: *FAUST*, ACT 3

S10–4.

MENDELSSOHN: INCIDENTAL MUSIC TO *A MIDSUMMER NIGHT'S DREAM*, OP. 61

S10–5.

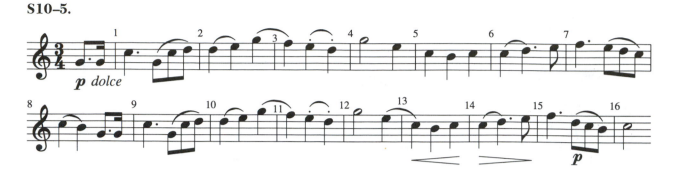

- Isolate the two phrase endings in your practice. In alternation, sing F-E-D-C-B (measures 7 and 8) and F-D-C-B-C (measures 15 and 16). Both emphasize the F-B diminished fifth, but only in the second case does the leading tone B resolve to tonic C.

MOZART: STRING QUARTET NO. 17 IN B♭ MAJOR ("HUNTING"), K. 458, MVMT. 1

S10–6.

SCHUBERT: STRING QUINTET IN C MAJOR, D. 956, OP. 163, MVMT. 4

S10–7.

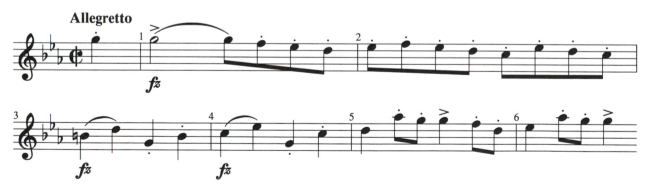

- Your performance should project the ascending line B♮-C-D-E♭ (beat 1 of measures 4 through 7). G occurs on beat 3 of each of these measures, either below or above the other pitches. In measures 5 and 6, G is embellished by a neighboring note, A♭.

BEETHOVEN: PIANO SONATA NO. 18 IN E♭ MAJOR, OP. 31, NO. 3, MVMT. 2

S10–8.

MELODIES IN B MAJOR OR G♯ MINOR

BRAHMS: PIANO TRIO NO. 1 IN B MAJOR, OP. 8, MVMT. 2

S10–9.

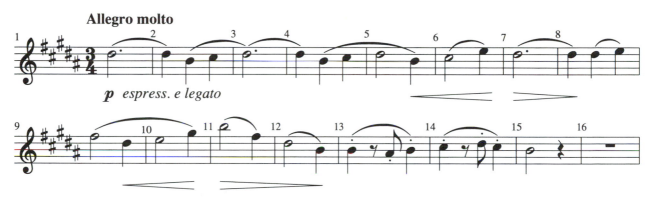

- D♯ (measures 1 through 5) is embellished by neighboring note E in measure 6. F♯ (measure 9) is embellished by neighboring note G♯ in measure 10. B (measures 11 through 13) is embellished by neighboring note C♯ in measure 14.

S10–10.

MELODIES IN Dь MAJOR OR Bь MINOR

DVOŘÁK: SYMPHONY NO. 9 IN E MINOR ("FROM THE NEW WORLD"), OP. 95, MVMT. 2

S10–11.

- This melody is constructed after the model of an antecedent/consequent phrase pair. Measures 1 and 2 lead from $\hat{3}$ to $\hat{2}$; measures 3 and 4 lead from $\hat{3}$ through $\hat{2}$ to $\hat{1}$.

CHOPIN: SONATA NO. 2 IN Bь MINOR, MVMT. 3 ("MARCHE FUNÈBRE")

S10–12.

MELODIES IN $\frac{2}{2}$ METER

MOZART: *DON GIOVANNI*, K. 527, ACT 1

S10–13.

- From measure 1 into measure 2 Mozart establishes a descending motion, from C to F (via A). In measures 3 and 4 he extends this descending motion, reaching D, a seventh below C. Practice this leap by at first singing a succession of descending thirds, based on the model of measures 1 and 2: C-A-F-D. Eventually learn to sing C-D without the intervening A and F.

HAYDN: SYMPHONY NO. 104 IN D MAJOR ("LONDON"), MVMT. 4

S10–14.

HAYDN: PIANO SONATA IN C MAJOR, HOB. XVI/35, MVMT. 1

S10–15.

· Haydn has juxtaposed seemingly unmatched motives: C-E-G (the opening three pitches) and B-C-D (measures 3 and 4). C leads to B; E leads to D. But what about the G of the earlier motive? That question should be on every listener's (and the performer's!) mind during the two rests of measure 4. Fortunately F arrives in measure 5. The line continues with E in measure 5, D in measure 7, and C in measure 8.

MOZART: *COSÌ FAN TUTTE*, K. 588, ACT 2

S10–16.

DUETS

D10–1.

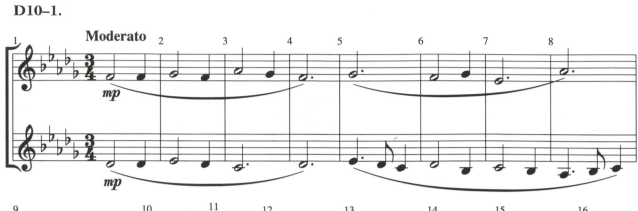

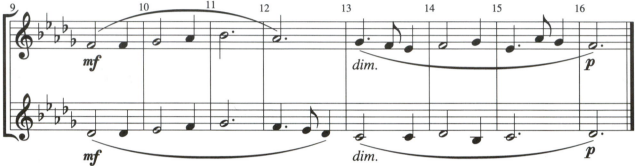

D10–2.

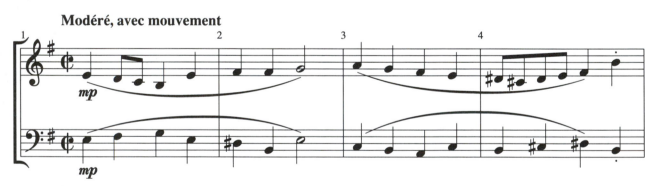

ACCOMPANIED SOLO MELODIES

AS10–1.

AS10–2.

RHYTHMS

R10–1.

R10–2.

R10–3.

R10–4.

R10–5.

R10–6.

INTERVAL WORKSHOP

I10–1.   Play a pitch that is low in your vocal range at a keyboard. Sing it. Then sing the pitch an augmented fourth or diminished fifth higher. Use the keyboard to confirm your performance. Then sing ascending fourths or fifths starting on other pitches.

I10–2.   Play a pitch that is high in your vocal range at a keyboard. Sing it. Then sing the pitch an augmented fourth or diminished fifth lower. Use the keyboard to confirm your performance. Then sing descending fourths or fifths starting on other pitches.

I10–3.   Practice singing the interval of an augmented fourth or diminished fifth higher than a sounding pitch. The sounding pitch should be at or beyond the lower limit of your vocal range, and could be sung by a classmate or your instructor or performed on the piano or another instrument such as the cello. Also practice singing compound versions of this interval.

I10–4.   Practice singing the interval of an augmented fourth or diminished fifth lower than a sounding pitch. The sounding pitch should be at or beyond the upper limit of your vocal range, and could be sung by a classmate or your instructor or performed on the piano or another instrument such as the flute. Also practice singing compound versions of this interval.

I10–5.   At the keyboard, select a pitch in the middle of your vocal range as the "starting pitch." Then sing the following groups of four pitches on "la," forming inversionally related intervals. Practice a. through n. from first to last, from last to first, and in random order.

a.	Starting pitch	Minor third higher	Starting pitch	Major sixth lower
b.	Starting pitch	Major third higher	Starting pitch	Minor sixth lower
c.	Starting pitch	Perfect fourth higher	Starting pitch	Perfect fifth lower
d.	Starting pitch	Augmented fourth higher	Starting pitch	Diminished fifth lower
e.	Starting pitch	Perfect fifth higher	Starting pitch	Perfect fourth lower
f.	Starting pitch	Minor sixth higher	Starting pitch	Major third lower
g.	Starting pitch	Major sixth higher	Starting pitch	Minor third lower
h.	Starting pitch	Major sixth lower	Starting pitch	Minor third higher
i.	Starting pitch	Minor sixth lower	Starting pitch	Major third higher
j.	Starting pitch	Perfect fifth lower	Starting pitch	Perfect fourth higher
k.	Starting pitch	Augmented fourth lower	Starting pitch	Diminished fifth higher
l.	Starting pitch	Perfect fourth lower	Starting pitch	Perfect fifth higher
m.	Starting pitch	Major third lower	Starting pitch	Minor sixth higher
n.	Starting pitch	Minor third lower	Starting pitch	Major sixth higher

I10–6.   Choose a classmate with a similar vocal range as a partner. Then perform the following exercises, using each of the following seven pairs of intervals.

X	**Inv(X)**
Minor third	Major sixth
Major third	Minor sixth
Perfect fourth	Perfect fifth
Augmented fourth	Diminished fifth
Perfect fifth	Perfect fourth
Minor sixth	Major third
Major sixth	Minor third

a.   Your partner sings a pitch that is low in your vocal range. Then your partner sings the pitch a second time, while you sing the pitch that is **X** higher than your partner's. Then you sing the pitch you just sang a second time, while your partner sings the pitch that is **Inv(X)** higher than yours.

b.   Your partner sings a pitch that is high in your vocal range. Then your partner sings the pitch a second time, while you sing the pitch that is **X** lower than your partner's. Then you sing the pitch you just sang a second time, while your partner sings the pitch that is **Inv(X)** lower than yours.

ARPEGGIATION WORKSHOP

A10–1.   Play a C, D♭, D, E♭, E, F, G, A♭, A, B♭, or B that is low in your vocal range at a keyboard. Let this pitch be $\hat{1}$ in a major key. Sing each of the following arpeggiations, either in the order given or in random order.

a. $\hat{1}$ $\hat{3}$ $\hat{5}$ ° $\hat{2}$ $\hat{4}$ $\hat{7}$ ° $\hat{3}$ $\hat{5}$ $\hat{8}$ ° $\hat{5}$ $\hat{7}$ $\hat{2}$ ° $\hat{8}$ $\hat{5}$ $\hat{3}$ $\hat{1}$

b. $\hat{1}$ $\hat{3}$ $\hat{5}$ ° $\hat{2}$ $\hat{4}$ $\hat{7}$ ° $\hat{3}$ $\hat{5}$ $\hat{8}$ ° $\hat{4}$ $\hat{6}$ $\hat{8}$ ° $\hat{5}$ $\hat{7}$ $\hat{2}$ $\hat{5}$

c. $\hat{3}$ $\hat{5}$ $\hat{8}$ ° $\hat{2}$ $\hat{4}$ $\hat{7}$ ° $\hat{1}$ $\hat{3}$ $\hat{8}$ ° $\hat{5}$ $\hat{7}$ $\hat{2}$ ° $\hat{8}$ $\hat{5}$ $\hat{3}$ $\hat{1}$

d. $\hat{3}$ $\hat{5}$ $\hat{8}$ ° $\hat{2}$ $\hat{4}$ $\hat{7}$ ° $\hat{1}$ $\hat{3}$ $\hat{8}$ ° $\hat{4}$ $\hat{6}$ $\hat{8}$ ° $\hat{5}$ $\hat{7}$ $\hat{2}$ $\hat{5}$

e. $\hat{1}$ $\hat{5}$ $\hat{3}$ ° $\hat{2}$ $\hat{7}$ $\hat{4}$ ° $\hat{3}$ $\hat{8}$ $\hat{5}$ ° $\hat{5}$ $\hat{2}$ $\hat{7}$ ° $\hat{8}$ $\hat{3}$ $\hat{5}$ $\hat{1}$

f. $\hat{1}$ $\hat{5}$ $\hat{3}$ ° $\hat{2}$ $\hat{7}$ $\hat{4}$ ° $\hat{3}$ $\hat{8}$ $\hat{5}$ ° $\hat{4}$ $\hat{8}$ $\hat{6}$ ° $\hat{5}$ $\hat{2}$ $\hat{7}$ $\hat{5}$

g. $\hat{3}$ $\hat{8}$ $\hat{5}$ ° $\hat{2}$ $\hat{7}$ $\hat{4}$ ° $\hat{1}$ $\hat{8}$ $\hat{3}$ ° $\hat{5}$ $\hat{2}$ $\hat{7}$ ° $\hat{8}$ $\hat{3}$ $\hat{5}$ $\hat{1}$

h. $\hat{3}$ $\hat{8}$ $\hat{5}$ ° $\hat{2}$ $\hat{7}$ $\hat{4}$ ° $\hat{1}$ $\hat{8}$ $\hat{3}$ ° $\hat{4}$ $\hat{8}$ $\hat{6}$ ° $\hat{5}$ $\hat{2}$ $\hat{7}$ $\hat{5}$

A10–2.   Play a C, C♯, D, E, F, F♯, G, G♯, A, B♭, or B that is low in your vocal range at a keyboard. Let this pitch be $\hat{1}$ in a minor key. Sing each of the following arpeggiations, either in the order given or in random order.

a. $\hat{1}$ $\hat{3}$ $\hat{5}$ ° $\hat{2}$ $\hat{4}$ $\sharp\hat{7}$ ° $\hat{3}$ $\hat{5}$ $\hat{8}$ ° $\hat{5}$ $\sharp\hat{7}$ $\hat{2}$ ° $\hat{8}$ $\hat{5}$ $\hat{3}$ $\hat{1}$

b. $\hat{1}$ $\hat{3}$ $\hat{5}$ ° $\hat{2}$ $\hat{4}$ $\sharp\hat{7}$ ° $\hat{3}$ $\hat{5}$ $\hat{8}$ ° $\hat{4}$ $\hat{6}$ $\hat{8}$ ° $\hat{5}$ $\sharp\hat{7}$ $\hat{2}$ $\hat{5}$

c. $\hat{3}$ $\hat{5}$ $\hat{8}$ ° $\hat{2}$ $\hat{4}$ $\sharp\hat{7}$ ° $\hat{1}$ $\hat{3}$ $\hat{8}$ ° $\hat{5}$ $\sharp\hat{7}$ $\hat{2}$ ° $\hat{8}$ $\hat{5}$ $\hat{3}$ $\hat{1}$

d. $\hat{3}$ $\hat{5}$ $\hat{8}$ ° $\hat{2}$ $\hat{4}$ $\sharp\hat{7}$ ° $\hat{1}$ $\hat{3}$ $\hat{8}$ ° $\hat{4}$ $\hat{6}$ $\hat{8}$ ° $\hat{5}$ $\sharp\hat{7}$ $\hat{2}$ $\hat{5}$

e. $\hat{1}$ $\hat{5}$ $\hat{3}$ ° $\hat{2}$ $\sharp\hat{7}$ $\hat{4}$ ° $\hat{3}$ $\hat{8}$ $\hat{5}$ ° $\hat{5}$ $\hat{2}$ $\sharp\hat{7}$ ° $\hat{8}$ $\hat{3}$ $\hat{5}$ $\hat{1}$

f. $\hat{1}$ $\hat{5}$ $\hat{3}$ ° $\hat{2}$ $\sharp\hat{7}$ $\hat{4}$ ° $\hat{3}$ $\hat{8}$ $\hat{5}$ ° $\hat{4}$ $\hat{8}$ $\hat{6}$ ° $\hat{5}$ $\hat{2}$ $\sharp\hat{7}$ $\hat{5}$

g. $\hat{3}$ $\hat{8}$ $\hat{5}$ ° $\hat{2}$ $\sharp\hat{7}$ $\hat{4}$ ° $\hat{1}$ $\hat{8}$ $\hat{3}$ ° $\hat{5}$ $\hat{2}$ $\sharp\hat{7}$ ° $\hat{8}$ $\hat{3}$ $\hat{5}$ $\hat{1}$

h. $\hat{3}$ $\hat{8}$ $\hat{5}$ ° $\hat{2}$ $\sharp\hat{7}$ $\hat{4}$ ° $\hat{1}$ $\hat{8}$ $\hat{3}$ ° $\hat{4}$ $\hat{8}$ $\hat{6}$ ° $\hat{5}$ $\hat{2}$ $\sharp\hat{7}$ $\hat{5}$

QUICK SWITCH

Q10–1.

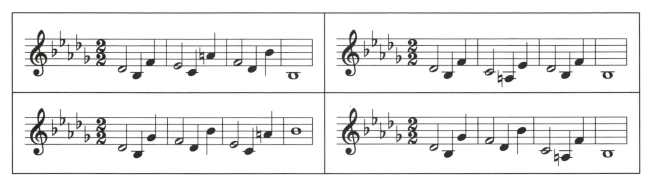

Q10–2.

Q10–3.

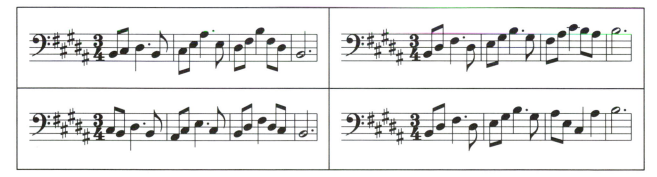

Q10–4.

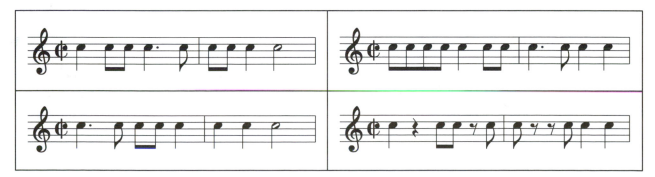

IDENTIFICATIONS

ID10–1.   An interval is performed melodically, either ascending or descending. Identify it as a minor second, major second, minor third, major third, perfect fourth, augmented fourth (or diminished fifth), perfect fifth, minor sixth, major sixth, minor seventh, or perfect octave.

ID10–2.   An interval is performed as a simultaneity. Identify it as a minor third, major third, perfect fourth, augmented fourth (or diminished fifth), perfect fifth, minor sixth, major sixth, minor seventh, or perfect octave.

ID10–3.   A triad is performed. Identify it as a major triad, a minor triad, or a diminished triad.

ID10–4.   A diminished triad is performed. Then two of its three pitches are performed melodically: root-third, root-fifth, third-root, third-fifth, fifth-root, or fifth-third. Identify which of these choices is performed.

ID10–5. $\hat{2}$, $\hat{4}$, $\hat{7}$, and $\hat{\dot{2}}$ in a major key are performed simultaneously. Then two of these four scale degrees are performed simultaneously. Identify the two scale degrees performed, from among the following choices: $\hat{2}$-$\hat{4}$, $\hat{2}$-$\hat{7}$, $\hat{2}$-$\hat{\dot{2}}$, $\hat{4}$-$\hat{7}$, $\hat{4}$-$\hat{\dot{2}}$, $\hat{7}$-$\hat{\dot{2}}$.

ID10–6. $\hat{5}$, $\hat{7}$, $\hat{\dot{2}}$, and $\hat{\dot{4}}$ in a major key are performed simultaneously. Then two of these four scale degrees are performed simultaneously. Identify the two scale degrees performed, from among the following choices: $\hat{5}$-$\hat{7}$, $\hat{5}$-$\hat{\dot{2}}$, $\hat{5}$-$\hat{\dot{4}}$, $\hat{7}$-$\hat{\dot{2}}$, $\hat{7}$-$\hat{\dot{4}}$, $\hat{\dot{2}}$-$\hat{\dot{4}}$.

ID10–7. $\hat{\dot{7}}$, $\hat{2}$, $\hat{4}$, and $\hat{7}$ in a major key are performed simultaneously. Then either $\hat{\dot{7}}$, $\hat{2}$, and $\hat{4}$ or $\hat{2}$, $\hat{4}$, and $\hat{7}$ are performed simultaneously. Is the resulting chord in $\frac{5}{3}$ or $\frac{6}{3}$ position?

ID10–8.   A chord in $\frac{6}{3}$ position is performed. Is its quality major, minor, or diminished?

ID10–9.   Two chords are performed. Interpret the first chord as I in $\frac{5}{3}$ position in a major key. What is the appropriate Roman numeral and figured bass for the second chord? Suitable choices are listed below.

I	IV	$\overset{6}{IV}$	V	$\overset{6}{V}$	$\overset{7}{V}$	VII	$\overset{6}{VII}$
I^6	IV	IV^6	V	V^6	V^7	vii^o	vii^{o6}

ID10–10.   Two chords are performed. Interpret the first chord as I in $\frac{5}{3}$ position or i in a minor key. What is the appropriate Roman numeral and figured bass for the second chord? Suitable choices are listed below.

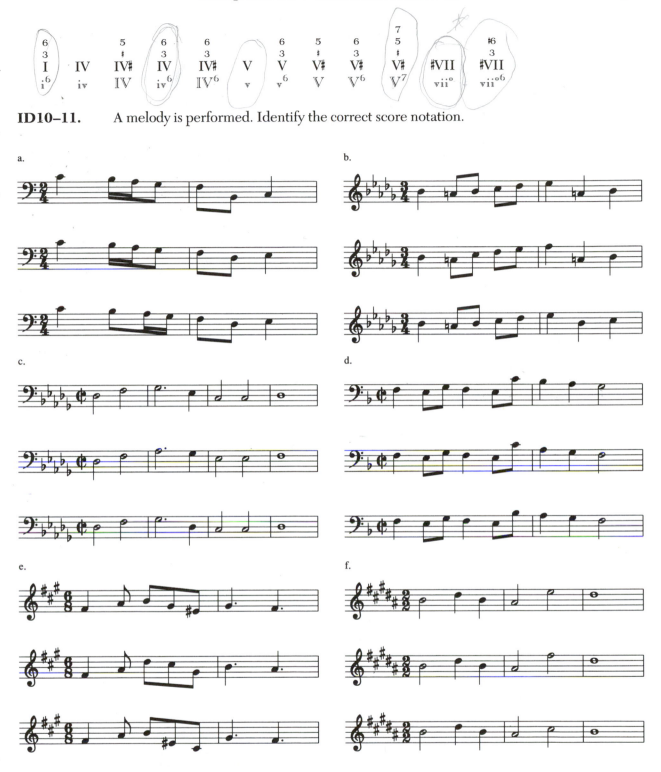

6 3		5 #	6 3	6 3		6 3	5 #	6 3	7 5 #		#6 3
I	IV	IV#	IV	IV#	V	V	V#	V#	V#	#VII	#VII
.6 1	iv	IV	iv 6	IV 6	v	v 6	V	V 6	V 7	vii o	vii o6

ID10–11. A melody is performed. Identify the correct score notation.

a.

b.

c.

d.

e.

f.

ID10–12. A chord progression in the major mode is performed. Identify a suitable Roman-numeral/figured-bass analysis from among the following choices:

Group 1

Left:

a. I VII^{6} I^{6} V I
b. I^{6} VII^{6} I V I
c. I^{6} VII^{6} I^{6} V I
d. I VII I V I

Right:

a. I $vii^{\circ 6}$ I^{6} V I
b. I^{6} $vii^{\circ 6}$ I V I
c. I^{6} $vii^{\circ 6}$ I^{6} V I
d. I vii° I V I

Group 2

Left:

a. V^{6}_{3} I VII^{6}_{3} I^{6}_{3} ——— $^{5}_{3}$ V
b. V^{6}_{3} I VII^{6}_{3} I^{6}_{3} ——— $^{5}_{3}$ V^{6}
c. V I^{6} VII^{6} I ——— ^{6} V
d. V I^{6} VII^{6} I ——— ^{6} V^{6}

Right:

a. V^{6} I $vii^{\circ 6}$ I^{6} $^{5}_{3}$ V
b. V^{6} I $vii^{\circ 6}$ I^{6} $^{5}_{3}$ V^{6}
c. V I^{6} $vii^{\circ 6}$ I ^{6} V
d. V I^{6} $vii^{\circ 6}$ I ^{6} V^{6}

ID10–13. A chord progression in the minor mode is performed. Identify a suitable Roman-numeral/figured bass analysis from among the following choices:

Group 1

Left:

a. $V\sharp^{6}$ I $\sharp VII^{6\sharp}$ I^{6} $V\sharp^{\sharp}$
b. $V\sharp^{\sharp}$ I $\sharp VII^{6\sharp}$ I^{6} $V\sharp^{\sharp}$
c. $V\sharp^{\sharp}$ I^{6} $\sharp VII^{6\sharp}$ I $V\sharp^{\sharp}$
d. $V\sharp^{\sharp}$ I^{6} $\sharp VII^{6\sharp}$ I^{6} $V\sharp^{\sharp}$

Right:

a. V^{6} i $vii^{\circ 6}$ i^{6} V
b. V i $vii^{\circ 6}$ i^{6} V
c. V i^{6} $vii^{\circ 6}$ i V
d. V i^{6} $vii^{\circ 6}$ i^{6} V

Group 2

Left:

a. I $\sharp VII^{6\sharp}$ I^{6} IV $V\sharp^{\sharp}$
b. I^{6} $\sharp VII^{6\sharp}$ I IV $V\sharp^{\sharp}$
c. I^{6} $\sharp VII^{6\sharp}$ I IV^{6} $V\sharp^{\sharp}$
d. I^{6} $\sharp VII^{6\sharp}$ I^{6} IV $V\sharp^{\sharp}$

Right:

a. i $vii^{\circ 6}$ i^{6} iv V
b. i^{6} $vii^{\circ 6}$ i iv V
c. i^{6} $vii^{\circ 6}$ i iv^{6} V
d. i^{6} $vii^{\circ 6}$ i^{6} iv V

ID10–14. A chord progression is performed. Identify the correct score notation for the outer voices. Figured-bass symbols have been placed below the bass where appropriate. If you wish, add Roman numerals.

a.

b.

c.

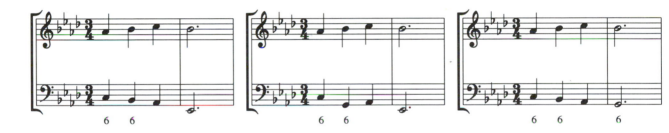

d.

e.

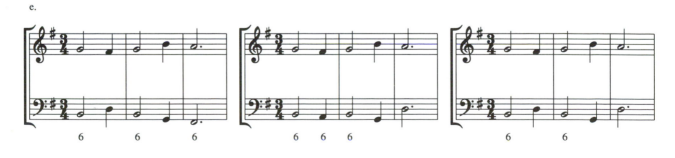

f.

RHYTHMIC DICTATIONS

RD10–1.

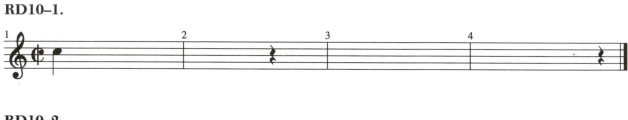

RD10–2.

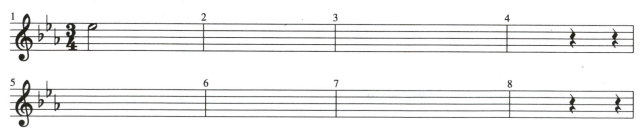

MELODIC DICTATIONS

MOZART: SYMPHONY NO. 39 IN E♭ MAJOR, K. 543, MVMT. 3

MD10–1.

- The shape of measures 5 and 6 is similar to that of measures 1 and 2, but not identical.

BEETHOVEN: SYMPHONY NO. 3 IN E♭ MAJOR ("EROICA"), OP. 55, MVMT. 4

MD10–2.

Allegro molto

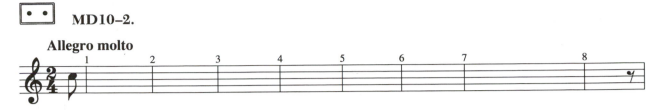

- Beethoven employs many thirds in this melody. Measure 7 is no exception. The notes that occur on the beats in measure 7 are embellishments of the notes that immediately follow them. Though each half of the measure may appear visually to span the interval of a fourth, the *structural* interval is a third.

- How does the descending melodic second in measure 8 relate to the motivic ideas of measure 7?

J. S. BACH: SUITE FOR UNACCOMPANIED CELLO NO. 3 IN C MAJOR, BWV 1009, BOURRÉE II

MD10–3.

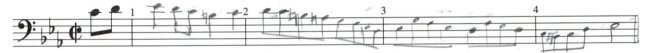

- Be particularly careful with accidentals in measure 2. Why did Bach choose to descend as he did?

MAHLER: SYMPHONY NO. 5 IN C♯ MINOR, MVMT. 1

MD10–4.

Trauermarsch

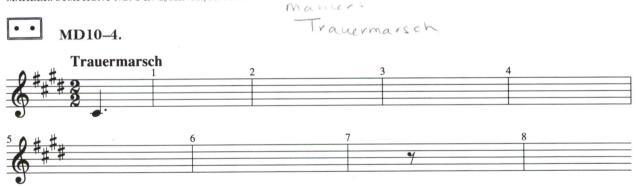

- As you write down the pitches of this melody, consider the following performance question: Both F♯ and E appear in measure 2. Should F♯ be performed as a passing note connecting G♯ and E (thus prolonging tonic), or should E be performed as a passing note connecting F♯ and the D♯ that begins measure 3 (thus initiating the dominant seventh or leading-tone chord)? What factors influence your decision? What means are at a performer's disposal to differentiate between these two conflicting interpretations?

HAYDN: SYMPHONY NO. 101 IN D MAJOR ("THE CLOCK"), MVMT. 4

MD10–5.

- The diminished fifth C#–G is outlined in measures 4 through 7. How and where does this dissonant interval resolve?

DVOŘÁK: *RUSALKA*, OP. 114, ACT 2

MD10–6.

- Listen for the descent 5̂-4̂-3̂-2̂ in measures 5 through 8. The 5̂'s upper neighbor, 6̂, occurs in measures 1, 3, and 5. The 4̂'s upper neighbor, 5̂, occurs in measure 6.

HARMONIC DICTATIONS

HD10–1.

- Do not confuse the passing notes in measure 2 with a change of harmony. The entire measure is tonic harmony.

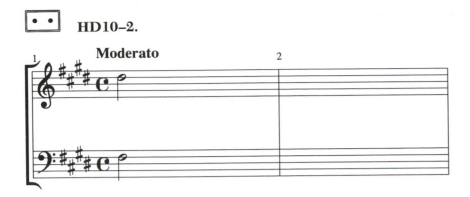

HD10–2.

- In this progression, the first chord is dissonant and thus not a candidate for tonic. What is its harmonic function?

HD10–3.

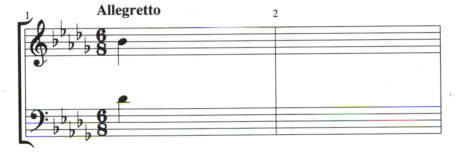

- The leading-tone chord in measure 1 is part of a progression that, while connecting the $^6_3$ and $^5_3$ positions of tonic, makes use of contrary motion in the outer voices. The contrary motion continues beyond tonic to the dominant in measure 2.

HD10–4.

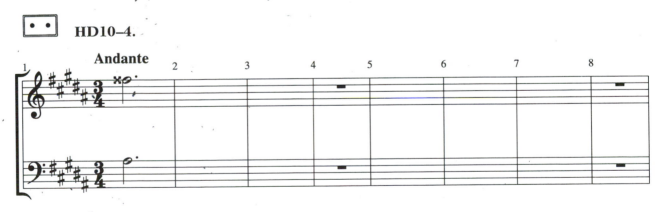

- This progression provides opportunities to compare the dominant and the leading-tone harmonies. F𝄪, the raised seventh scale degree in G♯ minor ($\mathrm{x}\hat{7}$ = F𝄪), appears in both outer voices. Remember to add accidentals on the system (and beside the Roman numeral and/or figured bass if you are completing a Method One analysis).

HD10–5.

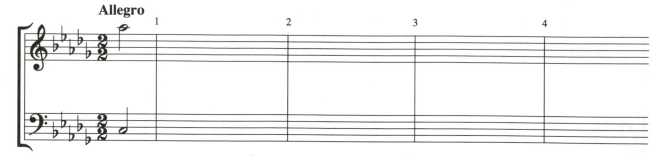

· What is the relationship between the first chord of measure 1 and the first chord of measure 2? What chord is employed to connect these two chords?

HD10–6.

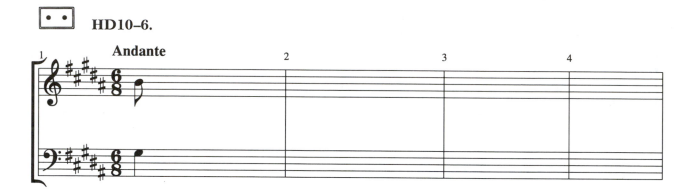

· Listen beyond the passing notes to the parallel tenths in the outer voices during the first measure and a half. The following diagram shows the underlying structure:

m.	1		2	
	B	C#	D#	B
	G#	A#	B	G#
	10 -	- 10 -	- 10 -	- 10

⟦··⟧ CASSETTE PROGRAM (TAPE 2, SIDE A)

C10–1.   Six melodies are performed, twice each. During the silence after each playing, respond in one of the following ways: (1) Sing the melody, using solmization syllables; (2) Play the melody on the piano or on your primary instrument; (3) Write the melody on staff paper.

C10–2.   Six chord progressions are performed, four times each. During the silence after each playing, respond in one of the following ways: (1) Sing the soprano after the first and second playings and the bass after the third and fourth playings, using solmization syllables; (2) Play the soprano on the piano or your primary instrument after the first and second playings and the bass after the third and fourth playings; (3) Play both the soprano and bass on the piano after each playing; (4) Write the soprano and bass on staff paper and provide an analysis.

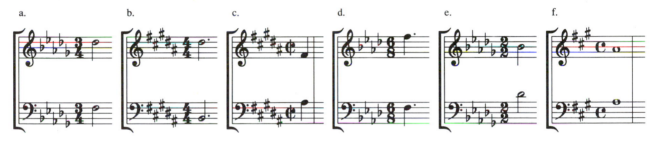

Chapter 11

PITCH

The **supertonic** chord offers a new alternative when $\hat{2}$ or $\hat{4}$ serves as the bass. The **submediant** chord offers a new alternative when $\hat{6}$ or $\hat{1}$ serves as the bass. Example 11–1 displays $^5_3$ and $^6_3$ positions of these chords in major and minor keys, as well as similar chords that share the same bass. Distinguishing between such alternatives will be one of your main preoccupations during this and future chapters.

EXAMPLE 11–1

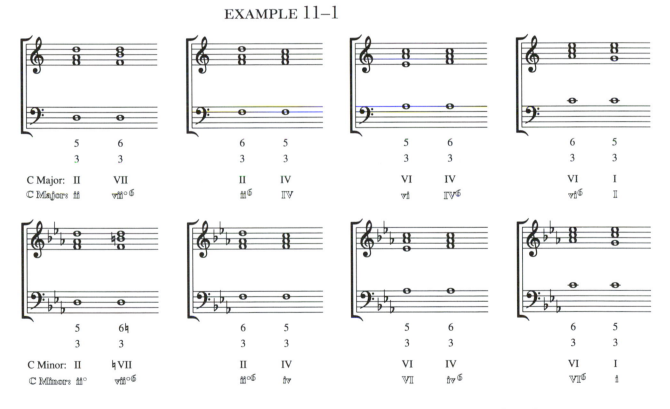

Use the following three listening strategies to determine Roman numerals and figured bass for a harmonic progression's chords.

   (1) *Determine the contexts in which each chord's outer voices might occur.* For example, in C major the bass pitch F and the soprano pitch D are sufficient to identify

the chord as supertonic in $^6_3$ position, given the chords and positions introduced to this point. If the outer voices do not uniquely distinguish the chord, make a list—either mentally or in writing—of potential chords. Then continue with the steps listed below.

(2) *Determine each chord's figured bass.* Locate the bass among a chord's sounding pitches, and "sing" it internally. Quickly arpeggiate the chord internally, just as you do in Arpeggiation Workshop exercises. Write down the figured bass and then the Roman numeral. (A third step, explained below, may be required before you select the Roman numeral.) This procedure is outlined in Example 11–2.

EXAMPLE 11–2

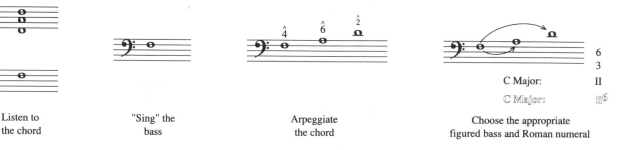

<table>
<tr><td>Listen to
the chord</td><td>"Sing" the
bass</td><td>Arpeggiate
the chord</td><td>Choose the appropriate
figured bass and Roman numeral</td></tr>
</table>

(3) *Determine each chord's quality.*[1] The information of Example 11–3 will help narrow your choices to a single Roman numeral and will remind you of any accidentals that should be added to Method One figured bass.

EXAMPLE 11–3

	Major Chords	Minor Chords	Diminished Chords
MAJOR KEYS	I, IV, V	II, VI	VII
	I, IV, V	ii, vi	vii°
MINOR KEYS	IV♯, V♯, VI	I, IV, V	II, ♯VII
	IV, V, VI	i, iv, v	ii°, vii°

Also consider how each chord functions in its musical context. By applying the label II or ii to a chord, for example, you tap a store of knowledge regarding how the supertonic typically behaves. Use this information! Does the supertonic lead to the dominant, confirming its most prominent role as a dominant preparation? Or does the subdominant follow? Such analyses can be made with confidence, because they coincide with your understanding of music theory. If, however, you analyze a progression as

C Major: I   II   I   V

C Major: I   ii   I⁶   V

---

1. At present this step is required only for subdominant and dominant chords in the minor mode. Its usefulness will increase as more chords are introduced.

you should suspect an error. The leading-tone chord, *not* supertonic, connects the $\frac{5}{3}$ and $\frac{6}{3}$ positions of tonic. Or perhaps the third chord is instead the supertonic $\frac{6}{3}$, prolonging the dominant preparation.

Knowledge of the submediant's typical behavior will also prove useful. The submediant chord is often used when the bass descends from $\hat{8}$ to $\hat{4}$. $\hat{8}$ generally supports tonic, while $\hat{4}$ may support subdominant or supertonic $\frac{6}{3}$ (as in Ex. 11–4). $\hat{6}$ may support submediant (Ex. 11–4) or subdominant $\frac{6}{3}$.

EXAMPLE 11–4

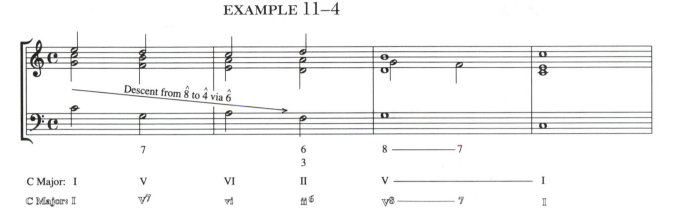

Four new keys are introduced in this chapter. Both the **key of F♯ major** and its relative minor, the **key of D♯ minor**, employ a key signature of six sharps. Both the **key of G♭ major** and its relative minor, the **key of E♭ minor**, employ a key signature of six flats.

METER AND RHYTHM

Meters are distinguished by the number of beats per measure and the note that represents the beat. By convention, some beats are emphasized or accented. The first beat of a measure is accented in all meters. In $\frac{4}{4}$ meter, the third beat is also somewhat accented. The subdivisions of the beat are weighted as well. In simple meters, the first and third fourths of a beat are stronger than the second and fourth fourths (e.g., $\frac{4}{4}$♪♪♪♪ or $\frac{3}{8}$♪♪♪). Likewise, the first, third, and fifth sixths of a beat are the strongest in compound meters (e.g., $\frac{3}{8}$♪♪♪♪♪♪).

Composers sometimes arrange notes in such a way that the meter's characteristic accents are negated. This procedure, called **syncopation**, may be applied both at the level of the beat (e.g., offsetting the accent of the third beat in $\frac{4}{4}$ meter, as in $\frac{4}{4}$ ♩♩ ♩ |) or at the submetrical level (e.g., making the second of the four sixteenths of the beat stronger than the third, as in $\frac{4}{4}$ ♫♫ ♩♩|).

Syncopation requires no special notation, though conventional symbols will be arranged in new ways. Example 11–5 shows examples of syncopation in both simple and compound meters.

EXAMPLE 11–5

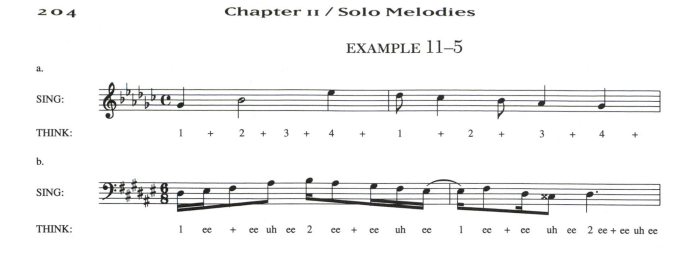

SOLO MELODIES

FIXED DO: *Sing "de" for C♭. Sing "dis" for C✕.*

LETTER NAMES: *Sing "Ces" for C♭. Sing "Cisis" for C✕.*

MELODIES THAT OUTLINE THE SUPERTONIC OR SUBMEDIANT CHORD

MOZART: *THE MAGIC FLUTE*, K. 620, ACT 1

S11–1.

- This melody takes advantage of the fact that the tonic and submediant share two pitches, and that the submediant and subdominant share two pitches.

FANNY MENDELSSOHN: NOTTURNO

S11–2.

SCHUBERT: PIANO SONATA IN A MINOR, D. 845, OP. 42, MVMT. 3

S11–3.

- This melody challenges your ability to maintain several layers of pitches at the same time. Keep the following relationships in mind: The A of measure 2 reinstates the A of measure 1; the D-C of measures 3 and 4 reverses the C-D of measure 1; the G and A of measures 4 and 5 ascend from the F of measure 2; and the C of measure 5 reinstates the C of measure 4.

MOZART: STRING QUARTET NO. 22 IN B♭ MAJOR, K. 589, MVMT. 4

S11–4.

SCHUBERT: *FIERRABRAS*, D. 796, ACT 1

S11–5.

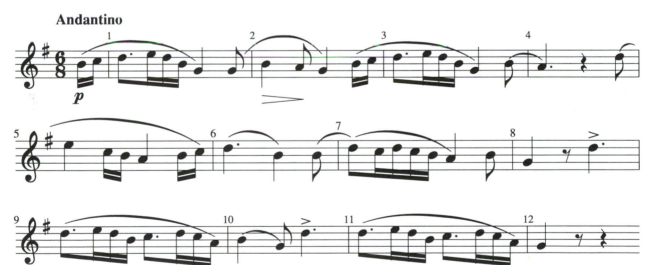

- Your performance will be enhanced if you take a breath at the following points: after the third note of measure 2; during the rest in measure 4; after the second note in measure 6; during the rest in measure 8; and after the second note in measure 10.

BEETHOVEN: VIOLIN CONCERTO IN D MAJOR, OP. 61, MVMT. 1

S11–6.

MELODIES IN F♯ MAJOR OR D♯ MINOR

S11–7.

- The descending minor third F♯-D♯ in measure 1 is followed by other descending thirds in an ascending trajectory: G♯-E♯ in measures 3 and 4; A♯-F♯ in measure 5; and B-G♯ in measure 6.

S11–8.

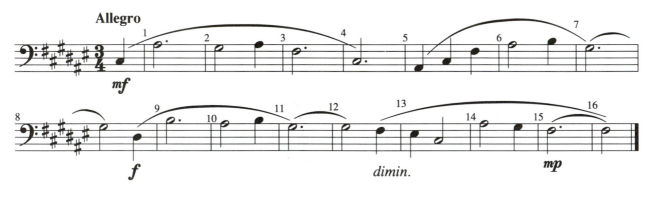

MELODIES IN G♭ MAJOR OR E♭ MINOR

SCHUBERT: PIANO SONATA IN B♭ MAJOR, D. 960, MVMT. 1

S11–9.

- In what key is the melody written?

TCHAIKOVSKY: 1812 OVERTURE, OP. 49

S11–10.

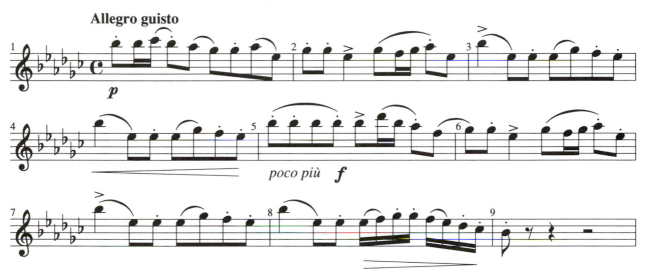

MELODIES THAT EMPLOY SYNCOPATION

R. STRAUSS: *AUS ITALIEN*

S11–11.

- Observe that the basic shape of this melody is a downward arpeggiation of a tonic chord (G-D-B-G).

BEETHOVEN: SYMPHONY NO. 6 IN F MAJOR ("PASTORALE"), OP. 68, MVMT. 5

S11–12.

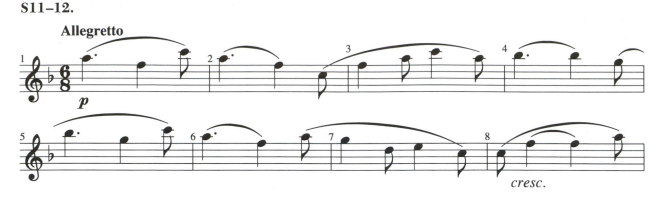

SCHUBERT: PIANO SONATA IN D MAJOR, D. 850, OP. 53, MVMT. 2

S11–13.

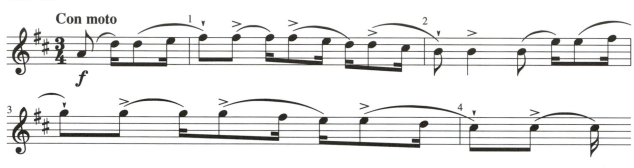

· Schubert's accent marks emphasize the syncopated character of this melody. Observe these marks carefully, as well as the slurs that span the interval of a third.

PUCCINI: *LA BOHÈME*, ACT 2

S11–14.

SCHUBERT: PIANO SONATA IN A MAJOR, D. 959, MVMT. 4

S11–15.

- Schubert's slur in measure 4 indicates only that the pitches are to be performed legato. He did not intend that you emphasize a subdominant triad, as the end points of the slur might seem to imply. Instead, measure 4 concludes the antecedent phrase, where the dominant harmony prevails. G♯ (the second pitch of measure 4) is the dominant's third (the leading tone). The motion from A to G♯ parallels that from B to A in measure 8, the end of the consequent phrase. The F♯ of measure 4 serves as a passing note to E, the dominant's root.

R. STRAUSS: *DEATH AND TRANSFIGURATION*, OP. 24

S11–16.

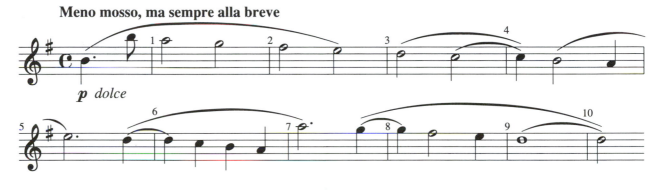

DUETS

D11–1.

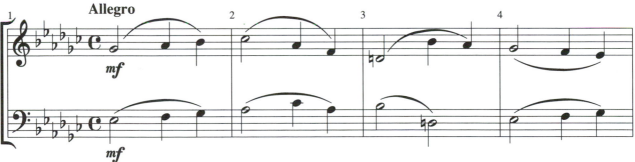

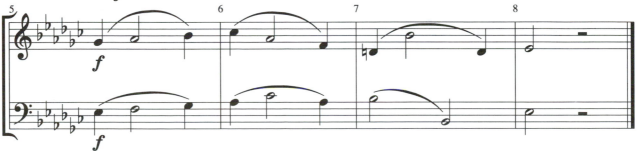

D11–2.

ACCOMPANIED SOLO MELODIES

AS11–1.

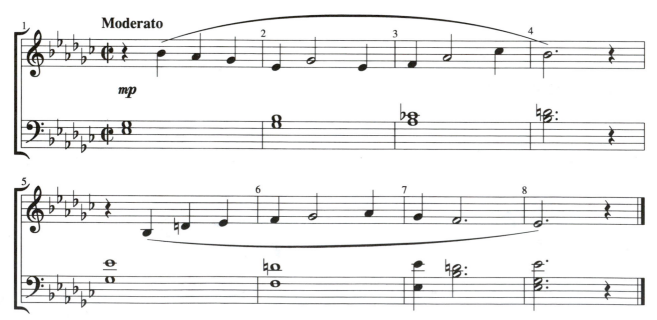

AS11–2.

RHYTHMS

R11–1.

R11–2.

R11–3.

R11–4.

R11–5.

R11–6.

ARPEGGIATION WORKSHOP

A11–1.   Play a pitch that is low in your vocal range at a keyboard. Let this pitch be $\hat{1}$ in a major key. Sing each of the following arpeggiations, either in the order given or in random order.

A11–2. Play a pitch that is at least a major sixth above the lowest note of your vocal range at a keyboard. Let this pitch be $\hat{1}$ in a minor key. Sing each of the following arpeggiations, either in the order given or in random order.

a. $\hat{1}$ $\hat{3}$ $\hat{1}$ ✿ $\hat{3}$ $\hat{5}$ $\hat{1}$ ✿ $\hat{4}$ $\hat{6}$ $\hat{1}$ ✿ $\hat{5}$ $\sharp\hat{7}$ $\hat{2}$ ✿ $\hat{1}$ $\hat{3}$ $\hat{5}$ $\hat{1}$

b. $\hat{1}$ $\hat{3}$ $\hat{1}$ ✿ $\hat{3}$ $\hat{5}$ $\hat{1}$ ✿ $\hat{4}$ $\hat{6}$ $\hat{2}$ ✿ $\hat{5}$ $\sharp\hat{7}$ $\hat{2}$ ✿ $\hat{1}$ $\hat{3}$ $\hat{5}$ $\hat{1}$

c. $\hat{1}$ $\hat{3}$ $\hat{1}$ ✿ $\hat{6}$ $\hat{1}$ $\hat{3}$ ✿ $\hat{4}$ $\hat{6}$ $\hat{1}$ ✿ $\hat{5}$ $\sharp\hat{7}$ $\hat{2}$ ✿ $\hat{1}$ $\hat{3}$ $\hat{5}$ $\hat{1}$

d. $\hat{1}$ $\hat{3}$ $\hat{1}$ ✿ $\hat{6}$ $\hat{1}$ $\hat{3}$ ✿ $\hat{4}$ $\hat{6}$ $\hat{2}$ ✿ $\hat{5}$ $\sharp\hat{7}$ $\hat{2}$ ✿ $\hat{1}$ $\hat{3}$ $\hat{5}$ $\hat{1}$

e. $\hat{1}$ $\hat{3}$ $\hat{1}$ ✿ $\hat{6}$ $\hat{1}$ $\hat{4}$ ✿ $\hat{4}$ $\hat{6}$ $\hat{1}$ ✿ $\hat{5}$ $\sharp\hat{7}$ $\hat{2}$ ✿ $\hat{1}$ $\hat{3}$ $\hat{5}$ $\hat{1}$

f. $\hat{1}$ $\hat{3}$ $\hat{1}$ ✿ $\hat{6}$ $\hat{1}$ $\hat{4}$ ✿ $\hat{4}$ $\hat{6}$ $\hat{2}$ ✿ $\hat{5}$ $\sharp\hat{7}$ $\hat{2}$ ✿ $\hat{1}$ $\hat{3}$ $\hat{5}$ $\hat{1}$

g. $\hat{1}$ $\hat{3}$ $\hat{1}$ ✿ $\hat{6}$ $\hat{1}$ $\hat{3}$ ✿ $\hat{4}$ $\hat{6}$ $\hat{1}$ ✿ $\hat{4}$ $\hat{6}$ $\hat{2}$ ✿ $\hat{5}$ $\sharp\hat{7}$ $\hat{2}$ $\hat{5}$

QUICK SWITCH

Q11–1.

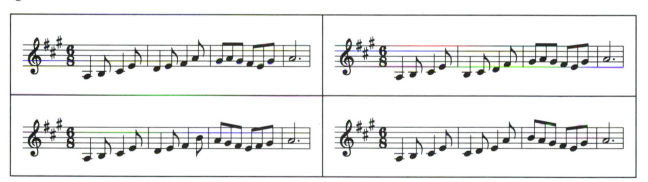

Q11–2.

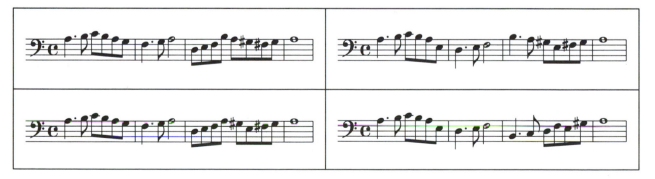

Q11–3.

Q11–4.

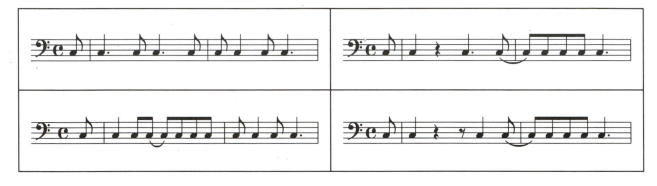

IDENTIFICATIONS

ID11–1.   Two chords are performed. Interpret the first chord as I in $\frac{5}{3}$ position in a major key. What is the appropriate Roman numeral and figured bass for the second chord? Suitable choices are listed below.

I	II	II	IV	IV	V	V	V	VI	VI	VII	VII
I^6	ii	ii^6	IV	IV^6	V	V^6	V^7	vi	vi^6	vii^o	vii^{o6}

(with superscript 6 above I, II, IV, V, VI, VII respectively)

ID11–2.   Two chords are performed. Interpret the first chord as I in $\frac{5}{3}$ position or i in a minor key. What is the appropriate Roman numeral and figured bass for the second chord? Suitable choices are listed below.

I	II	II	IV	IV	V	V	V♯	V♯	V♯	VI	VI	♯VII	♯VII
i^6	ii^o	ii^{o6}	iv	iv^6	v	v^6	V	V^6	V^7	VI	VI^6	vii^o	vii^{o6}

ID11–3.   What chord occurs at **X**? Suitable choices are listed below.

C Major: I   **X**   V

Choices:

I	II	II	IV	IV	VI
I^6	ii	ii^6	IV	IV^6	vi

ID11–4. What chord occurs at **Y**? Suitable choices are listed below.

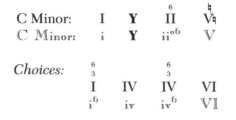

Choices:

ID11–5. A melody is performed. Identify the correct score notation.

ID11–6.   A chord progression in the major mode is performed. Identify a suitable Roman-numeral/figured-bass analysis from among the following choices:

<u>Group 1</u>

a.   I   VII⁶   I⁶₃ ————⁵₃ V   a.   I   vii°⁶   I⁶   ⁵₃   V

b.   I   VII⁶   I⁶   II   V   b.   I   vii°⁶   I⁶   ii   V

c.   I   VII⁶   I⁶   II⁶   V   c.   I   vii°⁶   I⁶   ii⁶   V

d.   I   VII⁶   I⁶   IV   V   d.   I   vii°⁶   I⁶   IV   V

<u>Group 2</u>

a.   I   VI   IV   V⁷   I   a.   I   vi   IV   V⁷   I

b.   I   VI   II⁶   V⁷   I   b.   I   vi   ii⁶   V⁷   I

c.   I   VI   II   V⁷   I   c.   I   vi   ii   V⁷   I

d.   I   IV⁶   II⁶   V⁷   I   d.   I   IV⁶   ii⁶   V⁷   I

ID11–7.   A chord progression in the minor mode is performed. Identify a suitable Roman-numeral/figured-bass analysis from among the following choices:

<u>Group 1</u>

a.   I   IV   V♯⁶   I   V♯   a.   i   iv⁶   V⁷   i   V

b.   I   VI   V♯⁷   I   V♯   b.   i   VI   V⁷   i   V

c.   I   IV♯⁶   V♯⁶   I   V♯   c.   i   IV⁶   V⁶   i   V

d.   I   VI⁶   V♯⁶   I   V♯   d.   i   VI⁶   V⁶   i   V

<u>Group 2</u>

a.   I   V♯⁷   VI   II⁶   V♯   a.   i   V⁷   VI   ii°⁶   V

b.   I   V♯⁷   IV⁶   II⁶   V♯   b.   i   V⁷   iv⁶   ii°⁶   V

c.   I   V♯⁷   VI   IV   V♯   c.   i   V⁷   VI   iv   V

d.   I   V♯⁷   IV⁶₃ ————⁵₃ V♯   d.   i   V⁷   iv⁶   ⁵₃   V

ID11–8. A chord progression is performed. Identify the correct score notation for the outer voices. Figured-bass symbols have been placed below the bass where appropriate. If you wish, add Roman numerals.

a.

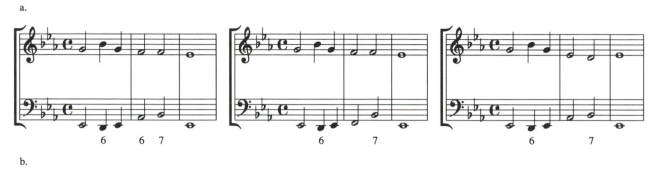

b.

c.

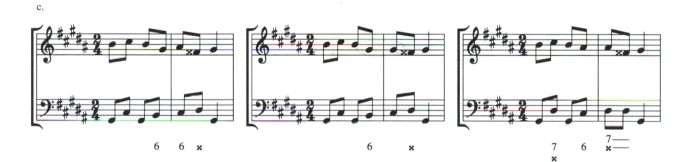

d.

e.

f.

RHYTHMIC DICTATIONS

RD11–1.

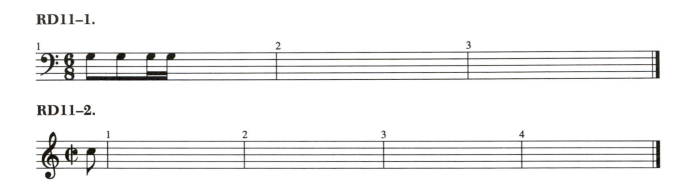

RD11–2.

MELODIC DICTATIONS

J. S. BACH: SUITE FOR ORCHESTRA NO. 2 IN B MINOR, BWV 1067, OUVERTURE

MD11–1.

- At first you might wonder whether the initial F♯ represents $\hat{3}$ in D major or $\hat{5}$ in B minor. By the end of measure 2, its function should be clear.

MOZART: SYMPHONY NO. 36 IN C MAJOR ("LINZ"), K. 425, MVMT. 1

MD11–2.

- As an aid to understanding how Mozart creates such a beautiful cadence, work on the second half of the excerpt in the following order:

    First, write down the pitches on beat 3 of measure 3, beat 1 of measure 4, and beat 1 of measure 5.

    Second, write down the pitches on beats 3 and 4 of measure 4.

    Third, write down the remaining pitches of measure 4.

MOZART: *COSÌ FAN TUTTE*, K. 588, ACT 2

MD11–3.

- Several different pitches seem to be vying for the role of tonic during the opening measures. The cadence distinguishes the true tonic from the impostors.

SCHUBERT: PIANO SONATA IN B MAJOR, D. 575, OP. POST. 147, MVMT. 1

MD11–4.

- Do not allow the leaps to distract you from hearing the melody's linear path. Before considering the details, establish a firm foundation by writing down the pitches on beats 1 and 3 of both measures.

BRAHMS: PIANO TRIO NO. 1 IN B MAJOR, OP. 8, MVMT. 1

MD11–5.

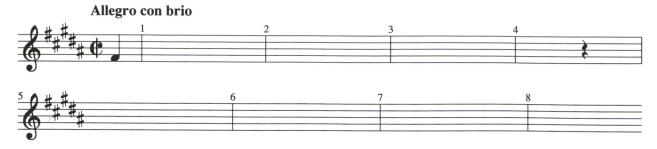

- Supertonic, as its name suggests, is a step higher than tonic. In this melody, Brahms arpeggiates tonic in measures 1 and 2 and supertonic in measures 5 and 6. The transposition is not exact. Obeying the B major key signature, the pitches of tonic form a major chord, while those of supertonic form a minor chord.

MOZART: PIANO SONATA IN F MAJOR, K. 332, MVMT. 1

MD11–6.

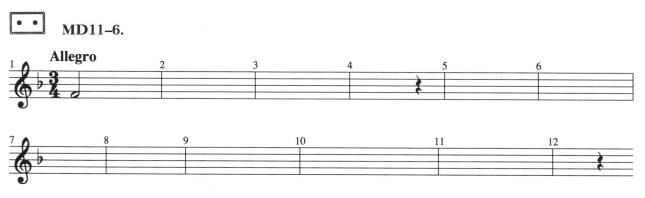

- B♭ and E form an augmented fourth. Listen both for an outline of this interval by nonadjacent pitches in measures 3 and 4 and for Mozart's response to this dissonance in measure 5.

HARMONIC DICTATIONS

HD11–1.

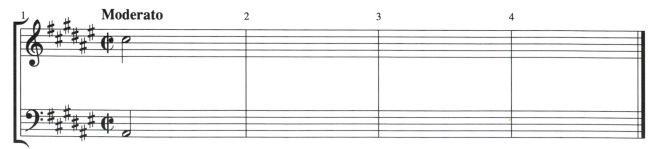

- Only two $^5_3$-position chords occur in this excerpt: D♯ minor on beat 1 of measure 2 and F♯ major on beat 1 of measure 4. The key signature could support either as tonic. Which of these chords *sounds* like tonic when you hear it?

BEETHOVEN: PIANO SONATA NO. 15 IN D MAJOR, OP. 28, MVMT. 3

 **HD11–2.**

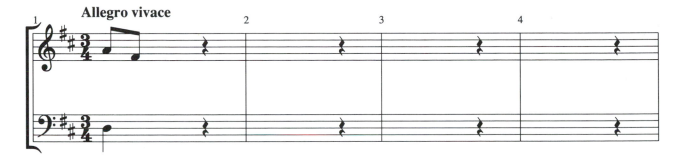

- Beethoven's soprano demonstrates that chords are built of "stacked thirds." Do not assume, however, that in each case he arpeggiates fifth-third-root. (In measure 3 he does not.) The chord of measure 2 is *not* in $^5_3$ position, even though the soprano of that measure resembles that of measure 1, whose chord *is* in $^5_3$ position.

J. S. BACH: SUITE FOR UNACCOMPANIED CELLO NO. 4 IN E♭ MAJOR, BWV 1010, BOURRÉE II

HD11–3.

- Bach could do more with fewer pitches than almost any other composer. The cello sometimes sounds two pitches, but more often sounds only one pitch at a time in this excerpt. The twenty pitches that you hear result in a sophisticated chord progression. Do not worry about adding rests when only one pitch is sounding.

MOZART: PIANO SONATA NO. 13 IN Bb MAJOR, K. 333, MVMT. 3

HD11–4.

- Give special attention to the two chords in the second half of measure 3. Which of their outer-voice pitches are dissonant? How does Mozart respond to their tendencies for resolution?

BEETHOVEN: BAGATELLE IN A MAJOR, OP. 33, NO. 4

HD11–5.

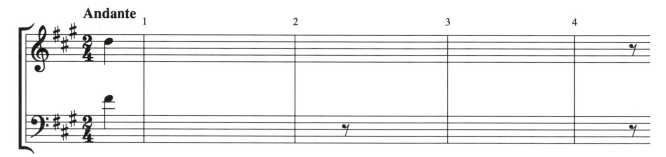

- You may want to refer to the first half of this excerpt when completing the second half. Why?

MOZART: PIANO SONATA NO. 8 IN A MINOR, K. 310, MVMT. 1

HD11–6.

Allegro maestoso

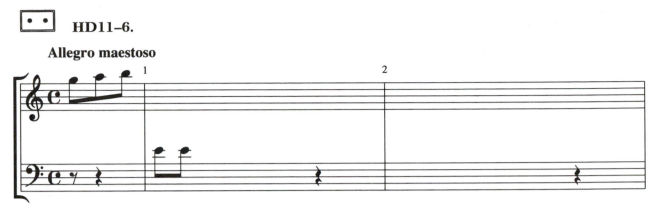

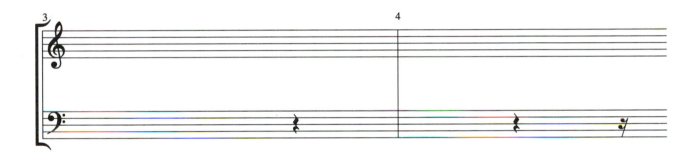

- Write down the first soprano pitch of each measure before dealing with the notes that follow them. How do these four soprano pitches relate? The figuration of measure 1 serves as a model for that in measures 2 and 3.

⊡ CASSETTE PROGRAM
(TAPE 2, SIDE A)

C11–1.   Six melodies are performed, twice each. During the silence after each playing, respond in one of the following ways: (1) Sing the melody, using solmization syllables; (2) Play the melody on the piano or on your primary instrument; (3) Write the melody on staff paper.

C11–2.   Six chord progressions are performed, four times each. During the silence after each playing, respond in one of the following ways: (1) Sing the soprano after the first and second playings and the bass after the third and fourth playings, using solmization syllables; (2) Play the soprano on the piano or your primary instrument after the first and second playings and the bass after the third and fourth playings; (3) Play both the soprano and bass on the piano after each playing; (4) Write the soprano and bass on staff paper and provide an analysis.

Chapter 12

PITCH

E and C in Example 12–1 embellish two of the three members of a G major triad. The $^6_4$ chord has no independent *harmonic* role. It is instead a *melodic* and *rhythmic* embellishment of G major. Using the numbers $^6_4$ as the chord's figured bass is appropriate, because a sixth and a fourth appear above the bass. The label "second inversion" should not be employed in this context, however, because C is not the chord's root.[1]

EXAMPLE 12–1

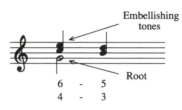

A $^6_4$ chord that embellishes a cadential dominant is called a ***cadential*** $^6_4$ ***chord***. The delay of the dominant's fifth and third intensifies the cadential effect. In Example 12–2, a cadential $^6_4$ chord enhances an authentic cadence. The sixth and fourth occur in a strong metrical position, resolving to the fifth and third on the comparatively weak third beat. In this case the dominant's seventh accompanies the fifth and third.

EXAMPLE 12–2

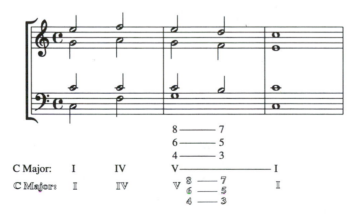

---

1. Second-inversion chords, to which the figured bass $^6_4$ is also applied, will be explored beginning in chapter 16.

The cadential $^6_4$ chord may embellish an authentic cadence, a half cadence, or a **deceptive cadence**, in which the tonic chord that would resolve the dominant's tendencies is replaced by a substitute, such as the submediant in Example 12–3.

EXAMPLE 12–3

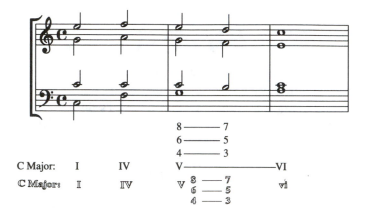

In contrast to the other cadences, the **plagal cadence** does not employ the dominant harmony. Instead, the subdominant precedes tonic. A plagal cadence generally appears just after an authentic cadence, as in Example 12–4.

EXAMPLE 12–4

A cadential $^6_4$ *delays* the arrival of harmony pitches. An **anticipation**, in contrast, introduces a member of a new harmony *before* it is expected. An anticipation occurs most often just before a bar line, after which the remainder of the new harmony arrives. For a moment components of two harmonies are juxtaposed. Example 12–5 demonstrates its use in an authentic cadence. An anticipation is rarely acknowledged by figured bass.

EXAMPLE 12–5

Four new keys are introduced in this chapter. Both the **key of C♯ major** and its relative minor, the **key of A♯ minor**, employ a key signature of seven sharps. Both the **key of C♭ major** and its relative minor, the **key of A♭ minor**, employ a key signature of seven flats.

Beginning in this chapter some melodies, such as that in Example 12–6, will be written in **alto clef**. Its symbol (𝄡) is centered on the middle line of the staff to indicate the location of middle C. Alto clef was once commonly used in the notation of vocal music. It remains the standard clef for the viola.

EXAMPLE 12–6

TCHAIKOVSKY: SYMPHONY NO. 6 IN B MINOR ("PATHÉTIQUE"), OP. 74, MVMT. 4

METER AND RHYTHM

In $\frac{9}{8}$ and $\frac{12}{8}$ **meters**, as in $\frac{6}{8}$ meter, a dotted quarter note or three eighth notes fill a beat. Three beats occur within each measure of $\frac{9}{8}$ meter, while four beats occur within each measure of $\frac{12}{8}$ meter. Example 12–7 demonstrates both meters and their counting syllables.[2]

---

2. The syllable "ee" should be used only when the rhythm contains some sixteenth notes.

EXAMPLE 12–7

a.

SING:

THINK: 1 + uh 2 + uh 3 + uh 4 + uh   1 + uh 2   +   uh 3 + uh 4 + uh

b.

SING:

THINK: 1 ee + ee uh ee 2 ee + ee uh ee 3 ee + ee uh ee

SING:

THINK: 1   ee + ee uh   ee   2 ee + ee   uh ee   3 ee + ee uh ee

Though one beat of silence in $^6_8$, $^9_8$, and $^{12}_8$ meters is usually written as a quarter rest followed by an eighth rest (≹ 7), a **dotted quarter rest** (≹·) may be used instead. In $^{12}_8$ meter, a **dotted half rest** (—·) may be used when either the first half or the second half of a measure is silent. Example 12–8 demonstrates these possibilities.

EXAMPLE 12–8

Repeat signs will be employed beginning in this chapter. These common symbols (‖: before material to be repeated; :‖ after material to be repeated) reduce the chore of writing or typesetting music notation.

SOLO MELODIES

FIXED DO: *Sing "fe" for F♭. Sing "sis" for G𝄪.*

LETTER NAMES: *Sing "Fes" for F♭. Sing "Gisis" for G𝄪.*

MELODIES WRITTEN IN ALTO CLEF

TCHAIKOVSKY: SYMPHONY NO. 6 IN B MINOR ("PATHÉTIQUE"), OP. 74, MVMT. 4

S12–1.

- Breathe at the following spots: After beat 2 of measure 2 (deep breath); after beat 2 of measure 4 (deep breath); after beat 2 of measure 5 (short breath); after beat 2 of measure 6 (short breath).

BEETHOVEN: STRING QUARTET NO. 8 IN E MINOR, OP. 59, NO. 2, MVMT. 3

S12–2.

J. S. BACH: BRANDENBURG CONCERTO NO. 6 IN B♭ MAJOR, BWV 1051, MVMT. 3

S12–3.

- Label the arpeggiations of the following chords in the score: tonic in $^6_3$ position; dominant in $^5_3$ position; tonic in $^5_3$ position.

HANDEL: *GIULIO CESARE*, ACT 1

S12–4.

MELODIES IN C♯ MAJOR OR A♯ MINOR

S12–5.

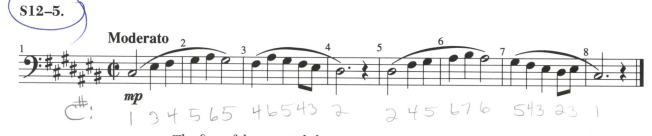

- The first of the two eighth notes in measure 3 is a passing note. The second of the two eighth notes in measure 7 is a neighboring note.

S12–6.

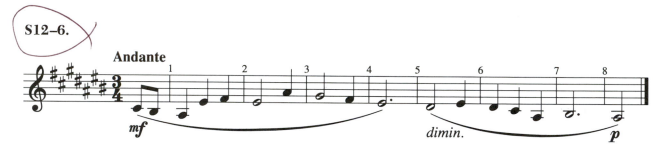

MELODIES IN C♭ MAJOR OR A♭ MINOR

S12–7.

- Sing this melody both in the key of C♭ major and in the key of C major (by paying no attention to the key signature). In some solmization systems (Scale Degrees; Movable Do), the syllables are exactly the same in both keys. In others (Fixed Do; Letter Names), they are all different!

BRAHMS: SYMPHONY NO. 1 IN C MINOR, OP. 68, MVMT. 3

S12–8.

Un poco Allegretto e grazioso

MELODIES THAT EMPLOY AN ANTICIPATION

HANDEL: *WATER MUSIC*

S12–9.

F:

- How does measure 4 fulfill the melodic tendencies left unresolved in measures 1 and 2?

HANDEL: *ROYAL FIREWORKS MUSIC*

S12–10.

MOZART: *IDOMENEO, RE DI CRETA*, K. 366, ACT 2

S12–11.

- If you find the B♭ of measure 4 difficult to sing accurately, practice the first four measures with measure 4 transposed up an octave. Once you are comfortable with the ascending third G-B♭ you should have less difficulty with the descending sixth G-B♭.

HANDEL: *SUSANNA*, ACT 2

S12–12.

Non troppo presto

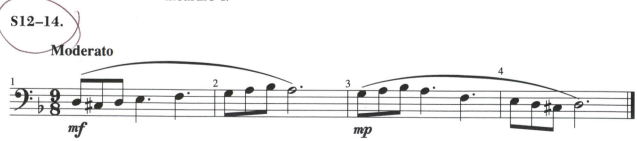

MELODIES IN $\frac{9}{8}$ OR $\frac{12}{8}$ METER

HANDEL: *ROYAL FIREWORKS MUSIC*

S12–13.

Largo alla Siciliana

- *Complete* neighboring notes occur during beat 1 of measures 1 through 3 and beat 3 of measure 3. *Incomplete* neighboring notes occur during beats 2 and 3 of measure 4.

S12–14.

Moderato

MELODIES THAT EMPLOY A REPEAT SIGN

WEBER: *DER FREISCHÜTZ*, ACT 1

S12–15.

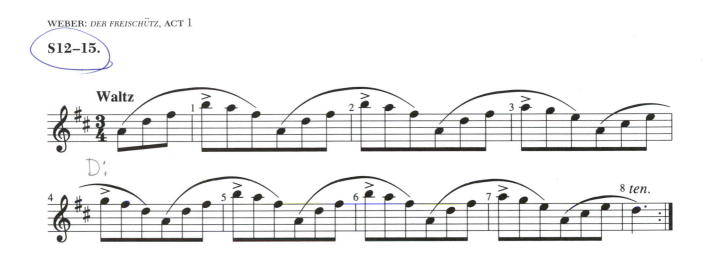

- The first pitch of each measure except the last functions as an accented upper neighbor to the following pitch. As a practice strategy, omit the first pitch of each measure and sing the second pitch as a quarter note. Once this is secure, reinstate the neighbors.

SCHUBERT: LÄNDLER, D. 370, NO. 6

S12–16.

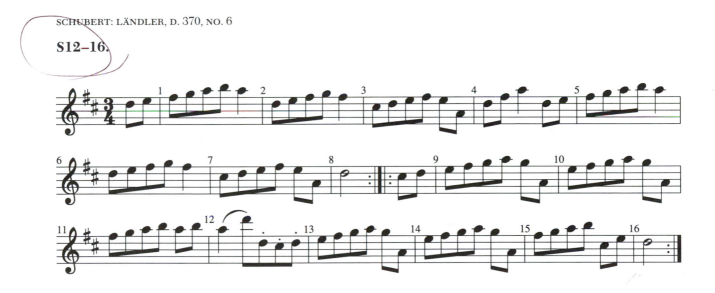

DUETS

D12–1.

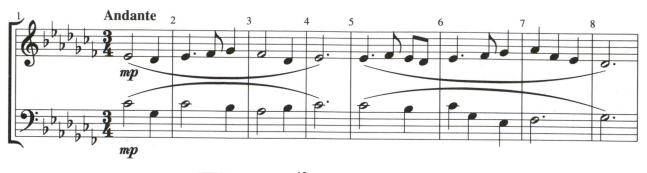

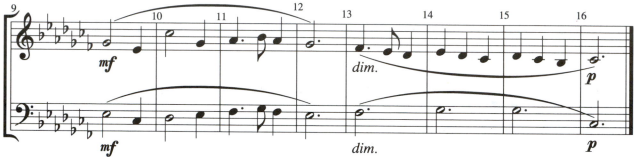

D12–2.

ACCOMPANIED SOLO MELODIES

AS12–1.

AS12–2.

RHYTHMS

R12–1.

uh   1 + uh 2 + uh 3 + uh 4 + uh   1 + uh 2 + uh 3 + uh 4 + uh   1 + uh 2 + uh 3 + uh 4 +

R12–2.

R12–3.

R12–4.

R12–5.

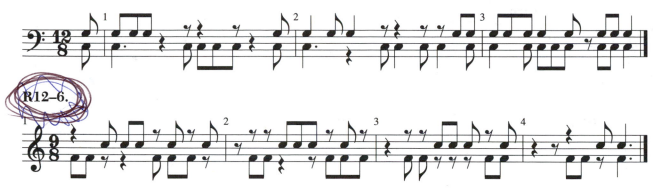

R12–6.

ARPEGGIATION WORKSHOP

A12–1.   Play a pitch that is low in your vocal range at a keyboard. Let this pitch be $\hat{1}$ in a major key. Sing each of the following arpeggiations, either in the order given or in random order.

a.	$\hat{1}$	$\hat{3}$	$\hat{5}$	✿	$\hat{3}$	$\hat{5}$	$\hat{8}$	✿	$\hat{4}$	$\hat{6}$	$\hat{8}$	✿	$\hat{5}$	$\hat{7}$	$\hat{2}$	✿	$\hat{6}$	$\hat{8}$	$\hat{3}$
b.	$\hat{1}$	$\hat{3}$	$\hat{5}$	✿	$\hat{3}$	$\hat{5}$	$\hat{8}$	✿	$\hat{4}$	$\hat{6}$	$\hat{2}$	✿	$\hat{5}$	$\hat{7}$	$\hat{2}$	✿	$\hat{6}$	$\hat{8}$	$\hat{4}$
c.	$\hat{1}$	$\hat{3}$	$\hat{5}$	✿	$\hat{5}$	$\hat{7}$	$\hat{2}$	✿	$\hat{8}$	$\hat{5}$	$\hat{3}$	✿	$\hat{4}$	$\hat{6}$	$\hat{8}$	✿	$\hat{8}$	$\hat{5}$	$\hat{1}$
d.	$\hat{1}$	$\hat{3}$	$\hat{5}$	✿	$\hat{2}$	$\hat{4}$	$\hat{6}$	✿	$\hat{5}$	$\hat{8}$	$\hat{3}$	✿	$\hat{5}$	$\hat{7}$	$\hat{2}$	✿	$\hat{8}$	$\hat{5}$	$\hat{1}$
e.	$\hat{1}$	$\hat{3}$	$\hat{5}$	✿	$\hat{4}$	$\hat{6}$	$\hat{8}$	✿	$\hat{5}$	$\hat{8}$	$\hat{3}$	✿	$\hat{5}$	$\hat{7}$	$\hat{2}$	✿	$\hat{6}$	$\hat{8}$	$\hat{3}$
f.	$\hat{1}$	$\hat{3}$	$\hat{5}$	✿	$\hat{4}$	$\hat{6}$	$\hat{2}$	✿	$\hat{5}$	$\hat{8}$	$\hat{3}$	✿	$\hat{5}$	$\hat{7}$	$\hat{2}$	✿	$\hat{6}$	$\hat{8}$	$\hat{4}$
g.	$\hat{1}$	$\hat{3}$	$\hat{5}$	✿	$\hat{3}$	$\hat{5}$	$\hat{8}$	✿	$\hat{5}$	$\hat{8}$	$\hat{3}$	✿	$\hat{5}$	$\hat{7}$	$\hat{2}$	✿	$\hat{8}$	$\hat{5}$	$\hat{1}$

A12–2.   Play a pitch that is at least a perfect fifth above the lowest note of your vocal range at a keyboard. Let this pitch be $\hat{1}$ in a minor key. Sing each of the following arpeggiations, either in the order given or in random order.

a.	$\hat{1}$	$\hat{3}$	$\hat{1}$	✿	$\hat{6}$	$\hat{1}$	$\hat{3}$	✿	$\hat{4}$	$\hat{6}$	$\hat{1}$	✿	$\hat{5}$	$\sharp\hat{7}$	$\hat{2}$	✿	$\hat{6}$	$\hat{1}$	$\hat{3}$	$\hat{6}$
b.	$\hat{1}$	$\hat{3}$	$\hat{1}$	✿	$\hat{6}$	$\hat{1}$	$\hat{3}$	✿	$\hat{4}$	$\hat{6}$	$\hat{2}$	✿	$\hat{5}$	$\sharp\hat{7}$	$\hat{2}$	✿	$\hat{6}$	$\hat{1}$	$\hat{4}$	$\hat{6}$
c.	$\hat{1}$	$\hat{3}$	$\hat{1}$	✿	$\hat{6}$	$\hat{1}$	$\hat{3}$	✿	$\hat{5}$	$\hat{1}$	$\hat{3}$	✿	$\hat{5}$	$\sharp\hat{7}$	$\hat{2}$	✿	$\hat{1}$	$\hat{3}$	$\hat{1}$	
d.	$\hat{1}$	$\hat{3}$	$\hat{1}$	✿	$\hat{6}$	$\hat{1}$	$\hat{4}$	✿	$\hat{5}$	$\hat{1}$	$\hat{3}$	✿	$\hat{5}$	$\sharp\hat{7}$	$\hat{2}$	✿	$\hat{1}$	$\hat{3}$	$\hat{1}$	
e.	$\hat{1}$	$\hat{3}$	$\hat{1}$	✿	$\hat{6}$	$\hat{1}$	$\hat{3}$	✿	$\hat{5}$	$\hat{1}$	$\hat{3}$	$\hat{5}$	✿	$\hat{5}$	$\sharp\hat{7}$	$\hat{2}$	$\hat{4}$	✿	$\hat{3}$	$\hat{5}$	$\hat{1}$
f.	$\hat{1}$	$\hat{3}$	$\hat{1}$	✿	$\hat{6}$	$\hat{1}$	$\hat{3}$	✿	$\hat{5}$	$\hat{1}$	$\hat{3}$	$\hat{5}$	✿	$\hat{5}$	$\sharp\hat{7}$	$\hat{2}$	$\hat{4}$	✿	$\hat{6}$	$\hat{1}$	$\hat{3}$
g.	$\hat{1}$	$\hat{3}$	$\hat{1}$	✿	$\hat{4}$	$\hat{6}$	$\hat{1}$	✿	$\hat{5}$	$\hat{1}$	$\hat{3}$	✿	$\hat{5}$	$\sharp\hat{7}$	$\hat{2}$	✿	$\hat{1}$	$\hat{3}$	$\hat{1}$	
h.	$\hat{1}$	$\hat{3}$	$\hat{1}$	✿	$\hat{4}$	$\hat{6}$	$\hat{2}$	✿	$\hat{5}$	$\hat{1}$	$\hat{3}$	✿	$\hat{5}$	$\sharp\hat{7}$	$\hat{2}$	✿	$\hat{1}$	$\hat{3}$	$\hat{1}$	
i.	$\hat{1}$	$\hat{3}$	$\hat{1}$	✿	$\hat{4}$	$\hat{6}$	$\hat{1}$	✿	$\hat{5}$	$\hat{1}$	$\hat{3}$	$\hat{5}$	✿	$\hat{5}$	$\sharp\hat{7}$	$\hat{2}$	$\hat{4}$	✿	$\hat{3}$	$\hat{5}$	$\hat{1}$
j.	$\hat{1}$	$\hat{3}$	$\hat{1}$	✿	$\hat{4}$	$\hat{6}$	$\hat{1}$	✿	$\hat{5}$	$\hat{1}$	$\hat{3}$	$\hat{5}$	✿	$\hat{5}$	$\sharp\hat{7}$	$\hat{2}$	$\hat{4}$	✿	$\hat{6}$	$\hat{1}$	$\hat{3}$

QUICK SWITCH

IDENTIFICATIONS

ID12–1. A chord progression is performed. Indicate the type of cadence that ends the progression, from among the following choices:

> Deceptive cadence
> Full cadence
> Half cadence
> Plagal cadence

ID12–2. $\hat{5}, \hat{8}, \hat{3}$, and $\hat{5}$ in a major or minor key are performed simultaneously. Then two of these four scale degrees are performed simultaneously. Identify the two scale degrees performed, from among the following choices: $\hat{5}\text{-}\hat{8}, \hat{5}\text{-}\hat{3}, \hat{5}\text{-}\hat{5}, \hat{8}\text{-}\hat{3}, \hat{8}\text{-}\hat{5}, \hat{3}\text{-}\hat{5}$.

ID12–3. $\hat{1}, \hat{3}, \hat{5}, \hat{8}$, and $\hat{3}$ in a major or minor key are performed simultaneously. Then either $\hat{1}, \hat{3}$, and $\hat{5}$; $\hat{3}, \hat{5}$, and $\hat{8}$; or $\hat{5}, \hat{8}$, and $\hat{3}$ are performed simultaneously. Is the resulting chord in $^5_3$, $^6_3$, or $^6_4$ position?

ID12–4. A chord is performed. Identify its position from among the following choices: $^5_3$, $^6_3$, $^6_4$, or ^{7}.

ID12–5. What chord occurs at **X**? Suitable choices are listed below.

C Major: I   II   V   **X**
C Major: I   ii   V   **X**

Choices:

I   I^6 IV^6 V^6 VI
I   I^6 IV^6 V^6 vi

ID12–6. What chord occurs at **Y**? Suitable choices are listed below.

C Minor: I——**Y**   I   (with $^5_3$ $^6_3$)
C Minor: i ^{6} **Y**   i

Choices:

IV   V   V♮   V♮   ♮VII
iv   v   V   V^7 vii^{o6}

ID12–7.   A melody is performed. Identify the correct score notation.

ID12–8. A chord progression in the major mode is performed. Identify a suitable Roman-numeral/figured-bass analysis from among the following choices:

Group 1

a. I VII$^6_3$ I IV V–$^{6-5}_{4-3}$ I   a. I vii^{o6} I^6 IV V$^{6-5}_{4-3}$ I

b. I VII$^6_3$ I II$^6_3$ V–$^{6-5}_{4-3}$ I   b. I vii^{o6} I^6 ii^6 V$^{6-5}_{4-3}$ I

c. I VII$^6_3$ I IV V–$^{8-7}_{6-5\ 4-3}$ I   c. I vii^{o6} I^6 IV V$^{8-7}_{6-5\ 4-3}$ I

d. I VII$^6_3$ I II$^6_3$ V-$^{8-7}_{6-5\ 4-3}$ I   d. I vii^{o6} I^6 ii^6 V$^{8-7}_{6-5\ 4-3}$ I

Group 2

a. I IV V–$^{6-5}_{4-3}$ I IV I   a. I IV V$^{6-5}_{4-3}$ I IV I

b. I IV V–$^{6-5}_{4-3}$ VI IV I   b. I IV V$^{6-5}_{4-3}$ vi IV I

c. I IV V–$^{6-5}_{4-3}$ VI IV V   c. I IV V$^{6-5}_{4-3}$ vi IV V

d. I IV I$^6_3$ V I IV I   d. I IV I^6 V I IV I

ID12–9. A chord progression in the minor mode is performed. Identify a suitable Roman-numeral/figured-bass analysis from among the following choices:

Group 1

a. I VI II$^6_3$ V♯–$^{6-5}_{4-♯}$ I   a. i VI ii^{o6} V$^{6-5}_{4-3}$ i

b. I VI II$^6_3$ V♯–$^{8-7}_{6-5\ 4-♯}$ I   b. i VI ii^{o6} V$^{8-7}_{6-5\ 4-3}$ i

c. I VI II$^6_3$ V♯–$^{6-5}_{4-♯}$ VI   c. i VI ii^{o6} V$^{6-5}_{4-3}$ VI

d. I VI II$^6_3$ V♯–$^{8-7}_{6-5\ 4-♯}$ VI   d. i VI ii^{o6} V$^{8-7}_{6-5\ 4-3}$ VI

Group 2

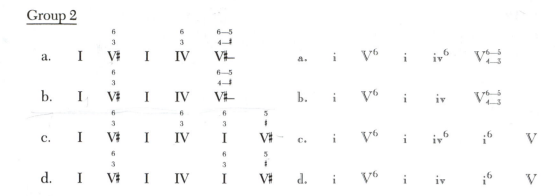

ID12–10.   A chord progression is performed. Identify the correct score notation for the outer voices. Figured-bass symbols have been placed below the bass where appropriate. If you wish, add Roman numerals.

a.

b.

c.

d.

e.

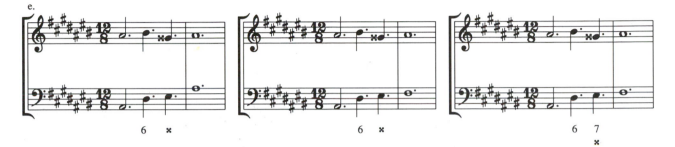

f.

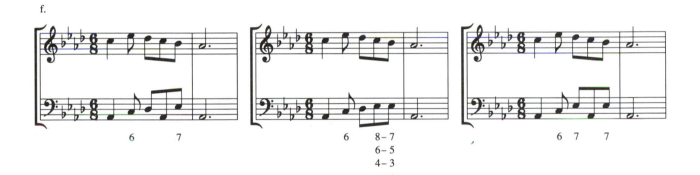

RHYTHMIC DICTATIONS

RD12–1.

RD12–2.

MELODIC DICTATIONS

SCHUBERT: PIANO QUINTET IN A MAJOR ("TROUT"), D. 667, OP. 114, MVMT. 3

MD12–1.

- The first pitches of measures 1, 2, and 4 descend by step from $\hat{5}$ to $\hat{3}$.

J. S. BACH: WELL-TEMPERED CLAVIER, VOL. 1, FUGUE 3, BWV 848

MD12–2.

- Though sixths and sevenths abound in this melody, focus instead on stepwise lines formed by nonadjacent pitches. You should hear two distinct strands, one a sixth above the other.

HANDEL: *SUSANNA*, ACT 2

MD12–3.

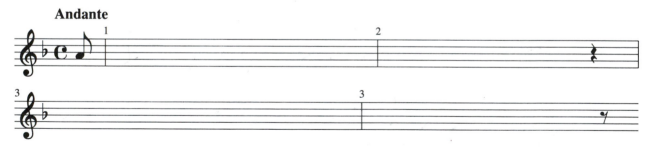

- The rhythm of a dotted eighth note followed by a sixteenth note is employed three times during this melody. In two of those cases, the sixteenth note functions as an anticipation.

HANDEL: *GIULIO CESARE*, ACT 2

MD12–4.

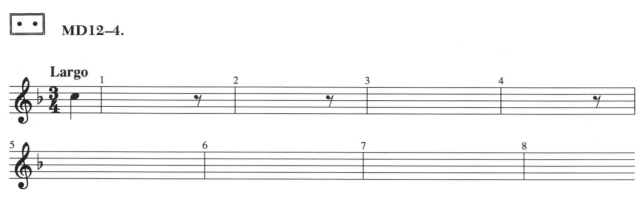

· Compare the melodic and rhythmic content of measure 7, beat 1, with that of measure 7, beats 2 and 3.

J. S. BACH: SUITE FOR ORCHESTRA NO. 2 IN B MINOR, BWV 1067, RONDEAU

MD12–5.

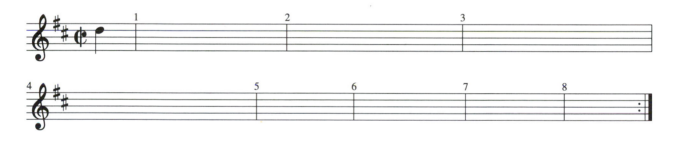

· What two pitches would best continue the pattern established by the following four pitches:

| D-C♯ | E–D | ?–? |

How are these six pitches employed in Bach's melody?

MENDELSSOHN: SYMPHONY NO. 3 IN A MINOR ("SCOTTISH"), OP. 56, MVMT. 1

MD12–6.

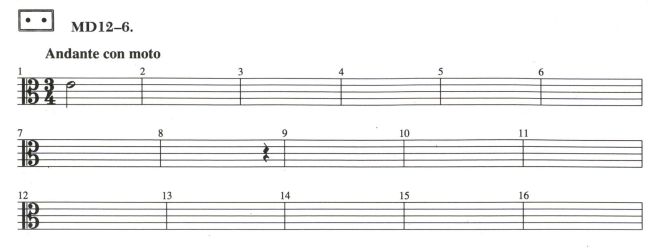

Andante con moto

- These sixteen measures form a parallel period. First write down the pitches of measure 1 through 4 and 9 through 12, focusing on what the two phrases have in common. Next write down the two cadential measures (measures 8 and 16). Finally write down how Mendelssohn leads to each cadence (measures 5 through 7 and 13 through 15).

HARMONIC DICTATIONS

SCHUBERT: *FIERRABRAS*, D. 796, OVERTURE

HD12–1.

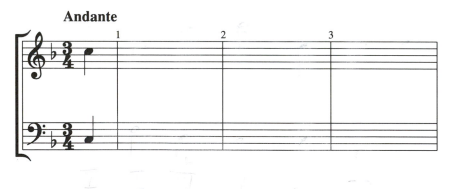

Andante

- The opening Cs in the outer voices are preparation for the root-position tonic chord that occurs after the bar line.

MASSENET: *MANON*, ACT 1

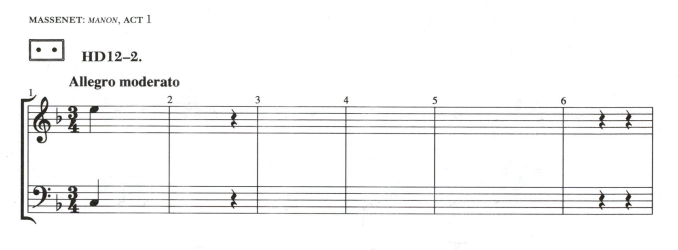

HD12–2.

· The leading note E is present in both measures 1 and 5. How does E resolve in each case? What harmony follows the harmony to which E belongs in each case?

ROSSINI: *THE BARBER OF SEVILLE*, ACT 1

HD12–3.

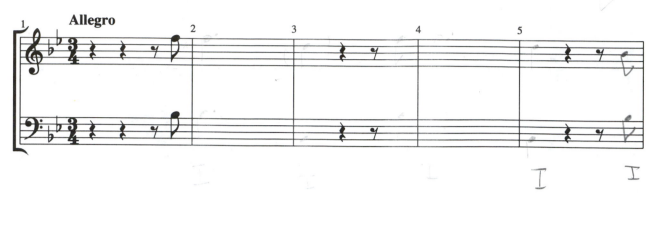

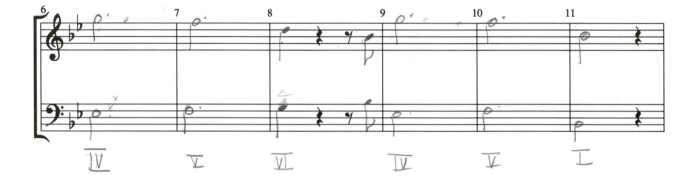

- Four segments of music are separated by rests. The first two segments are identical. The fourth differs from the third in important ways, though they remain very similar.

MOZART: *THE MAGIC FLUTE*, K. 620, ACT 1

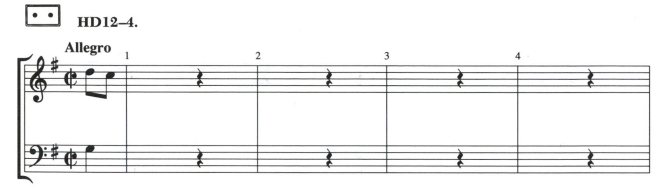

HD12–4.

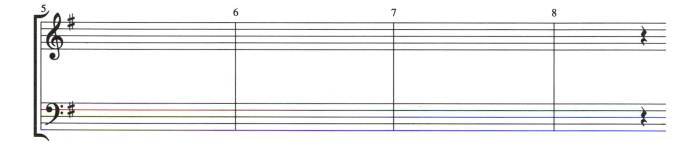

· Although the pitch C does not occur in measure 3, its sound lingers in your mind from measure 2. (It is a dissonance that requires resolution.) Use the figured-bass symbol "7" for both measures 2 and 3. Does measure 4 contain the expected resolution?

J. S. BACH: SUITE FOR UNACCOMPANIED CELLO NO. 6 IN D MAJOR, BWV 1012, GIGUE

HD12–5.

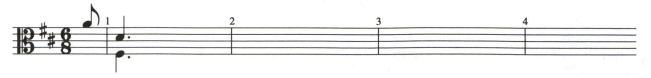

· The first bass pitch (given) is a dotted quarter note. Bach used eighth notes for the remaining bass pitches. Don't worry about adding rests when this lower voice is not sounding.

SCHUMANN: *DICHTERLIEBE*, OP. 48, NO. 10

 HD12–6.

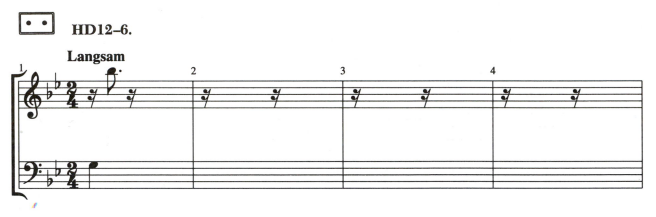

· The first half of measure 3 should be interpreted contextually, not literally. Only D and B♭ sound during this beat. This chord does *not* function as a first inversion of the mediant (the chord whose root is B♭, not yet introduced in this text). Instead, our internal ear supplies the missing G, with which we can succeed in making sense of this measure's structure.

⊡ CASSETTE PROGRAM
(TAPE 2, SIDE B)

C12–1.   Six melodies are performed, twice each. During the silence after each playing, respond in one of the following ways: (1) Sing the melody, using solmization syllables; (2) Play the melody on the piano or on your primary instrument; (3) Write the melody on staff paper.

C12–2.   Six chord progressions are performed, four times each. During the silence after each playing, respond in one of the following ways: (1) Sing the soprano after the first and second playings and the bass after the third and fourth playings, using solmization syllables; (2) Play the soprano on the piano or your primary instrument after the first and second playings and the bass after the third and fourth playings; (3) Play both the soprano and bass on the piano after each playing; (4) Write the soprano and bass on staff paper and provide an analysis.

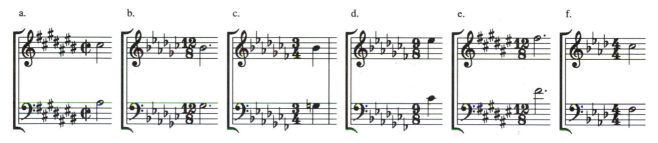

Chapter 13

PITCH

$^6_3$ position is the first inversion of $^5_3$ position; $^6_5$ ***position***[1] is the first inversion of $^7_5$ position. In Example 13–1, the dominant $^6_5$'s bass forms a dissonant diminished fifth against the soprano and ascends by half step (#$\hat{7}$ to $\hat{8}$) as the dominant resolves to tonic. To distinguish among the various forms of dominant ($^5_3$, $^6_3$, ^{7}, and $^6_5$), focus your listening on the bass and on whether the chord is consonant or dissonant.

EXAMPLE 13–1

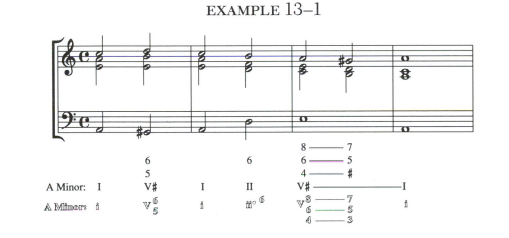

The fifteen major and fifteen minor keys employ an abundance of notes, but in fact there are even more.[2] With the exception of #$\hat{6}$ and #$\hat{7}$ in minor, the pitches employed to this point are those indicated by a key signature. F♯ is a *diatonic* pitch in D major, E minor, and A major, because F♯ is indicated by their key signatures. In C major, how-ever, F♯ is a ***chromatic*** pitch, because it counters the F natural indicated by the key signature for C major. An accidental must appear beside its notehead on the staff.

The ***chromatic passing note*** that connects $\hat{4}$ and $\hat{5}$ is usually spelled #$\hat{4}$. In C major, that pitch is F♯. The melody in Example 13–2a arpeggiates the three pitches of the tonic chord in C major: E (measure 1), G (measure 3), and C (measure 4). F (mea-

---

1. $^6_3$ is usually abbreviated to $^6_5$.

2. No more new *sounds* will be introduced, just more ways of naming and employing the twelve sounds per octave that have been used all along.

sure 2) connects E and G. In Example 13–2b, the leap from F to A (a detour on the ascending path E-F-G) is replaced by F♯. The line ascends from F *through* F♯ to G. When you sing two consecutive half steps, keep the whole step that they form in mind. Do not think F to F♯, and then F♯ to G. Think F to G, via F♯.

EXAMPLE 13–2

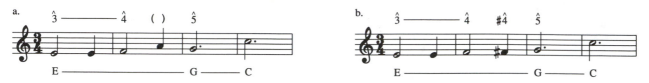

A chromatic passing note (also usually spelled ♯4̂) may be employed in descending from 5̂ to 4̂ as well. Example 13–3a shows the basic shape of a melody by Mozart. In Example 13–3b, diatonic passing notes connect the pitches that outline the tonic triad. Example 13–3c, Mozart's melody, includes a chromatic passing note, F♯.

EXAMPLE 13–3

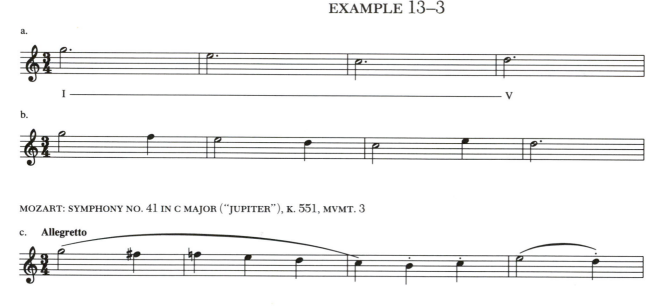

The connection between 4̂ and 5̂ will be explored in this chapter. Other contexts for chromaticism will be introduced in future chapters.

METER AND RHYTHM

$\frac{2}{2}$ meter is similar to $\frac{2}{4}$ meter. Both are simple meters of two beats per measure. They differ in that the beat is represented by the half note in $\frac{2}{2}$ meter and by the quarter note in $\frac{2}{4}$ meter. An equivalent relationship exists between $\frac{6}{4}$ ***meter*** and $\frac{6}{8}$ meter. Both are compound meters of two beats per measure. They differ in that the beat is represented by the dotted half note in $^6_4$ meter and by the dotted quarter note in $^6_8$ meter. As Example 13–4 shows, the counting syllables for $^6_4$ meter are identical to those of $^6_8$ meter.

EXAMPLE 13–4

SING:

THINK: 1 ee + ee uh ee 2 ee + ee uh ee 1 ee + ee uh ee 2 ee + ee uh ee

In $^6_8$ meter, a dotted half note fills an entire measure. In $^6_4$ meter, a **_dotted whole note_** (o.) fills an entire measure. In both $^6_8$ and $^6_4$ meters, a whole rest is employed to indicate that no sound occurs for an entire measure. When either the first or the second half of a measure in $^6_4$ meter contains no pitches, a dotted half rest (▬·) is employed.

SOLO MELODIES

SCALE DEGREES: *As with ♯$\hat{6}$ and ♯$\hat{7}$ in the ascending melodic minor scale, sing "raised" whenever you encounter ♯$\hat{4}$.*

MOVABLE DO (DO TONIC IN MINOR): *Sing "fi" for ♯$\hat{4}$ in any major or minor key.*

MOVABLE DO (LA TONIC IN MINOR): *In any major key, sing "fi" for ♯$\hat{4}$. In any minor key, sing "ri" for ♯$\hat{4}$.*

FIXED DO: *The pitches that function as ♯$\hat{4}$ in twenty-nine of the thirty keys have already been introduced in a diatonic context. Use the same syllable in both diatonic and chromatic contexts. If you encounter D✗ in the key of A♯ minor, sing "ris."*

LETTER NAMES: *The pitches that function as ♯$\hat{4}$ in twenty-nine of the thirty keys have already been introduced in a diatonic context. Use the same syllable in both diatonic and chromatic contexts. If you encounter D✗ in the key of A♯ minor, sing "Disis."*

SAMPLE SOLMIZATION

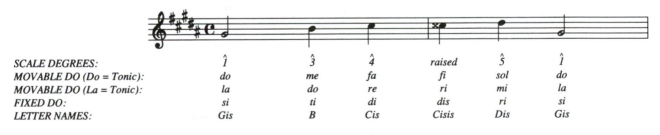

SCALE DEGREES:	$\hat{1}$	$\hat{3}$	$\hat{4}$	raised	$\hat{5}$	$\hat{1}$
MOVABLE DO (Do = Tonic):	do	me	fa	fi	sol	do
MOVABLE DO (La = Tonic):	la	do	re	ri	mi	la
FIXED DO:	si	ti	di	dis	ri	si
LETTER NAMES:	Gis	B	Cis	Cisis	Dis	Gis

MELODIES THAT OUTLINE A DOMINANT $^6_5$ CHORD

BEETHOVEN: PIANO SONATA NO. 28 IN A MAJOR, OP. 101, MVMT. 1

S13–1.

- Before singing the melody, arpeggiate the diminished triad G#-B-D.

S13–2.

MELODIES THAT CONTAIN $\hat{4}$-#$\hat{4}$-$\hat{5}$

SCHUBERT: QUARTET NO. 13 IN A MINOR, D. 804, OP. 29, MVMT. 1

S13–3.

- Sing E-C-A (from measures 1 and 2). Then sing B-C-D-E (the first pitches of measures 5 through 8). Then sing the entire melody as written.

WAGNER: *LOHENGRIN*, ACT 2

S13–4.

WAGNER: *TANNHÄUSER*, ACT 2

S13–5.

· Sometimes an intervening pitch will occur between a chromatic passing note
and its continuation. The linear motion of measures 3 and 4 (B ascending to D)
is temporarily diverted by the E that comes between C♯ and D.

TCHAIKOVSKY: *CAPRICCIO ITALIEN*, OP. 45

S13–6.

BEETHOVEN: SYMPHONY NO. 8 IN F MAJOR, OP. 93, MVMT. 1

S13–7.

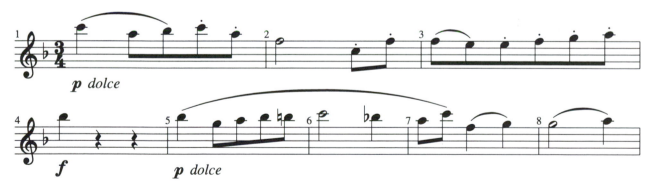

· Composers are often especially careful with their notation in a chromatic context. Though the flat beside the B notehead in measure 6 is not required,
Beethoven wrote it to prevent confusion. Of course, such a "courtesy" accidental does not imply a further lowering of an already flat pitch. Sing B♭ in measure
6, *not* B♭♭.

MOZART: PIANO SONATA NO. 13 IN B♭ MAJOR, K. 333, MVMT. 1

S13–8.

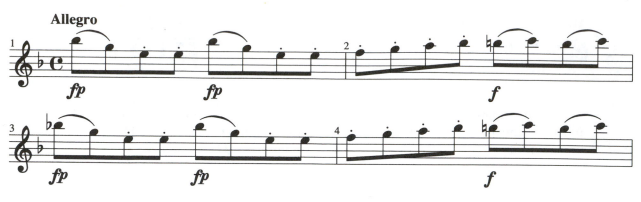

MELODIES THAT CONTAIN $\hat{5}$-#$\hat{4}$-$\hat{4}$

MOZART: SYMPHONY NO. 41 IN C MAJOR ("JUPITER"), K. 551, MVMT. 3

S13–9.

- The first phrase of this excerpt was discussed in the chapter introduction. The second phrase contains chromaticism as well. In the first phrase, the chromatic pitch (F#) occurs on a weak beat; in the second phrase, it occurs on a downbeat.

S13–10.

CHOPIN: MAZURKA, OP. 56, NO. 2

S13–11.

· To explore the function of F♯, sing each of the following descending lines.

measure	1		2				
	G					E	(tonic fifth and third)
	G				F	E	(with diatonic passing note)
	G		F♯		F	E	(with chromatic passing note)
	G	A	F♯	D	F	E	(with further embellishment)

BEETHOVEN: PIANO SONATA NO. 20 IN G MAJOR, OP. 49, NO. 2, MVMT. 2

S13–12.

MELODIES IN ⁶₄ METER

S13–13.

· The leading tone occurs in two different registers in measure 3. So does the tonic pitch (its resolution) in measure 4.

S13–14.

DUETS

D13–1.

D13–2.

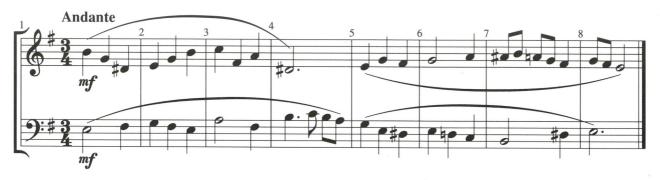

ACCOMPANIED SOLO
MELODIES

AS13–1.

AS13–2.

RHYTHMS

R13–1.

1 + uh 2 + uh   1 + uh 2 + uh   1 + uh 2 + uh   1 + uh 2 + uh

R13–2.

R13–3.

R13–4.

R13–5.

R13–6.

INTERVAL WORKSHOP

I13–1.   Practice singing the interval of a major second higher than a sounding pitch. The sounding pitch should be near the low end of your vocal range, and could be sung by a classmate or your instructor or performed on the piano or another instrument such as the cello. Also practice singing compound versions of this interval.

I13–2.   Practice singing the interval of a major second lower than a sounding pitch. The sounding pitch should be near the high end of your vocal range, and could be sung by a classmate or your instructor or performed on the piano or another instrument such as the flute. Also practice singing compound versions of this interval.

I13–3.   Choose a classmate with a similar vocal range as a partner. Then perform the following exercise. When no partner is available, perform the major seconds at a keyboard.
   a.   Your partner sings two pitches that form an ascending major second (e.g., F-G). Then you sing three pitches: the two that your partner sang plus a chromatic passing note connecting them (e.g., F-F♯-G).
   b.   Your partner sings two pitches that form a descending major second (e.g., C-B♭). Then you sing three pitches: the two that your partner sang plus a chromatic passing note connecting them (e.g., C–B–B♭).

I13–4.   At the keyboard, select a pitch in the middle of your vocal range as the "Starting pitch." Then sing the following groups of four pitches on "la," forming inversionally related intervals. Practice a. through r. from first to last, from last to first, and in random order.

a.	Starting pitch	Major second higher	Starting pitch	Minor seventh lower
b.	Starting pitch	Minor third higher	Starting pitch	Major sixth lower
c.	Starting pitch	Major third higher	Starting pitch	Minor sixth lower
d.	Starting pitch	Perfect fourth higher	Starting pitch	Perfect fifth lower
e.	Starting pitch	Augmented fourth higher	Starting pitch	Diminished fifth lower
f.	Starting pitch	Perfect fifth higher	Starting pitch	Perfect fourth lower
g.	Starting pitch	Minor sixth higher	Starting pitch	Major third lower
h.	Starting pitch	Major sixth higher	Starting pitch	Minor third lower
i.	Starting pitch	Minor seventh higher	Starting pitch	Major second lower
j.	Starting pitch	Minor seventh lower	Starting pitch	Major second higher
k.	Starting pitch	Major sixth lower	Starting pitch	Minor third higher
l.	Starting pitch	Minor sixth lower	Starting pitch	Major third higher
m.	Starting pitch	Perfect fifth lower	Starting pitch	Perfect fourth higher
n.	Starting pitch	Augmented fourth lower	Starting pitch	Diminished fifth higher

o.	Starting pitch	Perfect fourth lower	Starting pitch	Perfect fifth higher
p.	Starting pitch	Major third lower	Starting pitch	Minor sixth higher
q.	Starting pitch	Minor third lower	Starting pitch	Major sixth higher
r.	Starting pitch	Major second lower	Starting pitch	Minor seventh higher

I13–5. Choose a classmate with a similar vocal range as a partner. Then perform the following exercises, using each of the following nine pairs of intervals.

X	**Inv(X)**
Major second	Minor seventh
Minor third	Major sixth
Major third	Minor sixth
Perfect fourth	Perfect fifth
Augmented fourth	Diminished fifth
Perfect fifth	Perfect fourth
Minor sixth	Major third
Major sixth	Minor third
Minor seventh	Major second

a. Your partner sings a pitch that is low in your vocal range. Then your partner sings the pitch a second time, while you sing the pitch that is **X** higher than your partner's. Then you sing the pitch you just sang a second time, while your partner sings the pitch that is **Inv(X)** higher than yours.

b. Your partner sings a pitch that is high in your vocal range. Then your partner sings the pitch a second time, while you sing the pitch that is **X** lower than your partner's. Then you sing the pitch you just sang a second time, while your partner sings the pitch that is **Inv(X)** lower than yours.

ARPEGGIATION WORKSHOP

A13–1. Play a pitch that is at least a perfect fourth above the lowest note of your vocal range at a keyboard. Let this pitch be $\hat{1}$ in a major key. Sing each of the following arpeggiations, either in the order given or in random order.

a. $\hat{1}$ $\hat{3}$ $\hat{5}$ $\hat{1}$ ❋ $\hat{7}$ $\hat{2}$ $\hat{4}$ $\hat{5}$ ❋ $\hat{1}$ $\hat{3}$ $\hat{5}$ $\hat{1}$ ❋ $\hat{5}$ $\hat{7}$ $\hat{2}$ $\hat{5}$

b. $\hat{1}$ $\hat{3}$ $\hat{5}$ $\hat{1}$ ❋ $\hat{7}$ $\hat{2}$ $\hat{4}$ $\hat{5}$ ❋ $\hat{5}$ $\hat{7}$ $\hat{2}$ $\hat{4}$ ❋ $\hat{3}$ $\hat{5}$ $\hat{3}$ $\hat{1}$

c. $\hat{1}$ $\hat{3}$ $\hat{5}$ $\hat{1}$ ❋ $\hat{5}$ $\hat{7}$ $\hat{2}$ $\hat{4}$ ❋ $\hat{7}$ $\hat{2}$ $\hat{4}$ $\hat{5}$ ❋ $\hat{1}$ $\hat{3}$ $\hat{5}$ $\hat{1}$

d. $\hat{1}$ $\hat{3}$ $\hat{5}$ $\hat{1}$ ❋ $\hat{6}$ $\hat{1}$ $\hat{4}$ $\hat{6}$ ❋ $\hat{7}$ $\hat{2}$ $\hat{4}$ $\hat{5}$ ❋ $\hat{1}$ $\hat{3}$ $\hat{5}$ $\hat{1}$

e. $\hat{3}$ $\hat{5}$ $\hat{8}$ $\hat{3}$ ❋ $\hat{7}$ $\hat{2}$ $\hat{4}$ $\hat{5}$ ❋ $\hat{1}$ $\hat{3}$ $\hat{5}$ $\hat{1}$ ❋ $\hat{5}$ $\hat{7}$ $\hat{2}$ $\hat{5}$

f. $\hat{3}$ $\hat{5}$ $\hat{8}$ $\hat{3}$ ❋ $\hat{7}$ $\hat{2}$ $\hat{4}$ $\hat{5}$ ❋ $\hat{5}$ $\hat{7}$ $\hat{2}$ $\hat{4}$ ❋ $\hat{3}$ $\hat{5}$ $\hat{3}$ $\hat{1}$

g. $\hat{3}$ $\hat{5}$ $\hat{8}$ $\hat{3}$ ❋ $\hat{5}$ $\hat{7}$ $\hat{2}$ $\hat{5}$ ❋ $\hat{7}$ $\hat{2}$ $\hat{4}$ $\hat{5}$ ❋ $\hat{1}$ $\hat{3}$ $\hat{5}$ $\hat{1}$

A13–2.   Play a pitch that is at least a perfect fourth above the lowest note of your vocal range at a keyboard. Let this pitch be $\hat{1}$ in a minor key. Sing each of the following arpeggiations, either in the order given or in random order.

a. $\hat{1}$ $\hat{3}$ $\hat{5}$ $\hat{1}$ ❋ $\sharp\hat{7}$ $\hat{2}$ $\hat{4}$ $\hat{5}$ ❋ $\hat{1}$ $\hat{3}$ $\hat{5}$ $\hat{1}$ ❋ $\hat{5}$ $\sharp\hat{7}$ $\hat{2}$ $\hat{5}$

b. $\hat{1}$ $\hat{3}$ $\hat{5}$ $\hat{1}$ ❋ $\sharp\hat{7}$ $\hat{2}$ $\hat{4}$ $\hat{5}$ ❋ $\hat{5}$ $\sharp\hat{7}$ $\hat{2}$ $\hat{4}$ ❋ $\hat{3}$ $\hat{5}$ $\hat{3}$ $\hat{1}$

c. $\hat{1}$ $\hat{3}$ $\hat{5}$ $\hat{1}$ ❋ $\hat{5}$ $\sharp\hat{7}$ $\hat{2}$ $\hat{4}$ ❋ $\sharp\hat{7}$ $\hat{2}$ $\hat{4}$ $\hat{5}$ ❋ $\hat{1}$ $\hat{3}$ $\hat{5}$ $\hat{1}$

d. $\hat{1}$ $\hat{3}$ $\hat{5}$ $\hat{1}$ ❋ $\sharp\hat{6}$ $\hat{1}$ $\hat{4}$ $\sharp\hat{6}$ ❋ $\sharp\hat{7}$ $\hat{2}$ $\hat{4}$ $\hat{5}$ ❋ $\hat{1}$ $\hat{3}$ $\hat{5}$ $\hat{1}$

e. $\hat{3}$ $\hat{5}$ $\hat{8}$ $\hat{3}$ ❋ $\sharp\hat{7}$ $\hat{2}$ $\hat{4}$ $\hat{5}$ ❋ $\hat{1}$ $\hat{3}$ $\hat{5}$ $\hat{1}$ ❋ $\hat{5}$ $\sharp\hat{7}$ $\hat{2}$ $\hat{5}$

f. $\hat{3}$ $\hat{5}$ $\hat{8}$ $\hat{3}$ ❋ $\sharp\hat{7}$ $\hat{2}$ $\hat{4}$ $\hat{5}$ ❋ $\hat{5}$ $\sharp\hat{7}$ $\hat{2}$ $\hat{4}$ ❋ $\hat{3}$ $\hat{5}$ $\hat{3}$ $\hat{1}$

g. $\hat{3}$ $\hat{5}$ $\hat{8}$ $\hat{3}$ ❋ $\hat{5}$ $\sharp\hat{7}$ $\hat{2}$ $\hat{5}$ ❋ $\sharp\hat{7}$ $\hat{2}$ $\hat{4}$ $\hat{5}$ ❋ $\hat{1}$ $\hat{3}$ $\hat{5}$ $\hat{1}$

QUICK SWITCH

Q13–1.

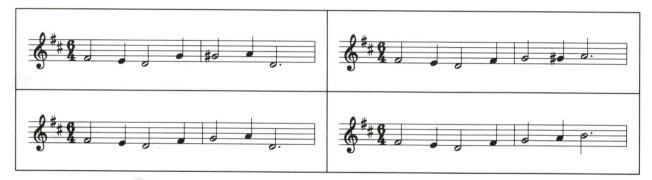

Q13–2.

Q13–3.

Q13–4.

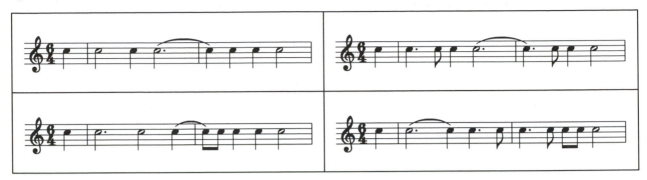

IDENTIFICATIONS

ID13–1. An interval is performed as a simultaneity. Identify it as a major second, minor third, major third, perfect fourth, augmented fourth (or diminished fifth), perfect fifth, minor sixth, major sixth, minor seventh, or perfect octave.

ID13–2. A brief melody of three ascending or three descending pitches is performed. Which of the following combinations of half and whole steps corresponds to the melody?

    a.   Half-Half (for example, F-F♯-G or G-F♯-F)
    b.   Half-Whole (for example, E-F-G or F-E-D)
    c.   Whole-Half (for example, D-E-F or G-F-E)
    d.   Whole-Whole (for example, F-G-A or A-G-F)

ID13–3. $\hat{7}$, $\hat{2}$, $\hat{4}$, and $\hat{5}$ in a major key are performed simultaneously. Then two of these four scale degrees are performed simultaneously. Identify the two scale degrees performed, from among the following choices: $\hat{7}$-$\hat{2}$, $\hat{7}$-$\hat{4}$, $\hat{7}$-$\hat{5}$, $\hat{2}$-$\hat{4}$, $\hat{2}$-$\hat{5}$, $\hat{4}$-$\hat{5}$.

ID13–4. $\hat{5}$, $\hat{7}$, $\hat{2}$, $\hat{4}$, and $\hat{5}$ in a major key are performed simultaneously. Then either $\hat{5}$, $\hat{7}$, $\hat{2}$, and $\hat{4}$ or $\hat{7}$, $\hat{2}$, $\hat{4}$, and $\hat{5}$ are performed simultaneously. Is the resulting chord in ^{7} or $^6_5$ position?

ID13–5. A chord is performed. Identify its position from among the following choices: $^5_3$, $^6_3$, $^6_4$, $^6_5$, or ^{7}.

ID13–6.   What chord occurs at **X**? Suitable choices are listed below.

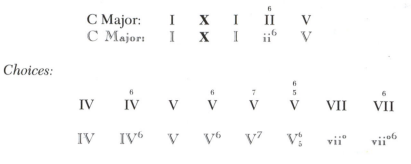

C Major: I   **X**   I   II^6 V

C Major: I   **X**   I   ii^6 V

Choices:

IV   IV^6 V   V^6 V^7 V$^6_5$ VII   VII^6

IV   IV^6 V   V^6 V^7 V$^6_5$ vii$^\circ$ vii$^{\circ 6}$

ID13–7.   What chord occurs at **Y**? Suitable choices are listed below.

A Minor: I   IV♯^{6} **Y**   I   V♯

A Minor: i   IV^6 **Y**   i   V

Choices:

IV♯   V♯   V♯^{6} V♯^{7} V♯$^6_5$ ♯VII

IV   V   V^6 V^7 V$^6_5$ vii$^\circ$

ID13–8.   A melody is performed. Identify the correct score notation.

a.

b.

c.

d.

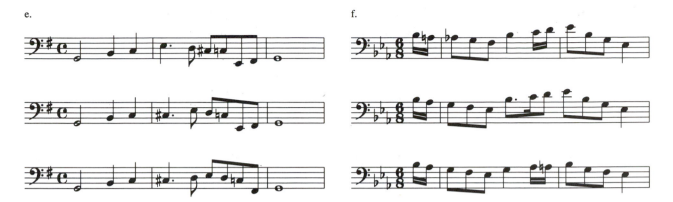

e.

f.

ID13–9.   A chord progression in the major mode is performed. Identify a suitable Roman-numeral/figured-bass analysis from among the following choices:

Group 1

a.	I	V	I———V			a.	I	V	I ^{6}	V	
b.	I	V^7	I^6———V			b.	I	V^7	I ^{6}	V	
c.	I	V^6	I^6———V			c.	I	V^6	I ^{6}	V	
d.	I	V$^6_5$	I$^6_3$———V			d.	I	V$^6_5$	I ^{6}	V	

Group 2

a.	I	IV$^6_3$	V$^6_5$	I	V		a.	I	IV^6	V$^6_5$	I	V
b.	I	VI	V$^6_5$	I	V		b.	I	vi	V$^6_5$	I	V
c.	I	IV^6	V^7	I	V		c.	I	IV^6	V^7	I	V
d.	I	V^7——$^6_5$	I	V			d.	I	V^7	$^6_5$	I	V

$y = x, \quad y = x^2 \quad$ about x axis

$$\pi \int_0^1 \left[x - x^2 \right] dx$$

$$= \pi \left(\tfrac{1}{2} x^2 - \tfrac{1}{3} x^3 \right) \Big|_0^1$$

$$\pi \left(\tfrac{1}{2} - \tfrac{1}{3} \right) \quad \tfrac{3}{6} - \tfrac{2}{6}$$

$y = \sqrt{x} \qquad y = x^2 \qquad$ about

$$\pi \int_0^1 \left[(\sqrt{x} + 7) - (x^2 \right.$$

$$\pi \left(\tfrac{2}{3} x^{\frac{3}{2}} + 7 \right.$$

$$\tfrac{2}{3} x^{\frac{3}{2}} - 3 x$$

ID13–10.   A chord progression in the minor mode is performed. Identify a suitable Roman-numeral/figured-bass analysis from among the following choices:

Group 1

a.   I   IV#$^6_3$ V#$^6_5$ I   V#$^\sharp$ a.   i   IV^6 V$^6_5$ i   V

b.   I   IV#^{6} V#$^{7}_{\sharp}$ I   V#$^\sharp$ b.   i   IV^6 V^7 i   V

c.   I   VI   V#$^{7}_{\sharp}$ I   V#$^\sharp$ c.   i   VI   V^7 i   V

d.   I   V#$^{7}_{\sharp}$——— $^6_5$ I   V#$^\sharp$ d.   i   V^7 $^6_5$ i   V

Group 2

a.   I^6 IV   V#$^{\sharp}$——— $^6_5$ I   a.   i^6 iv   V $^6_5$ i

b.   I^6 IV   V#$^{7}_{\sharp}$——— $^6_5$ I   b.   i^6 iv   V^7 $^6_5$ i

c.   I^6 IV   V#$^{\sharp}$——— ^{6} I   c.   i^6 iv   V ^{6} i

d.   I^6 IV   V#$^{8-7}_{\sharp}$—   I   d.   i^6 iv   V ^{7} i

ID13–11.   A chord progression is performed. Identify the correct score notation for the outer voices. Figured-bass symbols have been placed below the bass where appropriate. If you wish, add Roman numerals.

a.

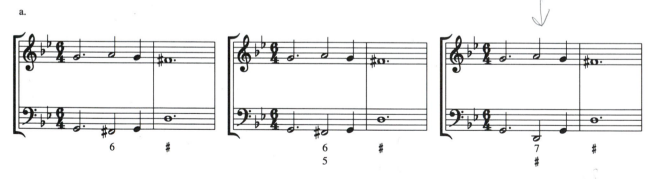

b.

c.

d.

e.

f.

RHYTHMIC DICTATIONS

RD13–1.

RD13–2.

MELODIC DICTATIONS

MENDELSSOHN: SONG WITHOUT WORDS, OP. 19, NO. 5 (BOOK 1)

MD13–1.

Poco agitato

· The rhythm of measure 1 requires the use of a tie.

FIELD: PIANO CONCERTO NO. 1 IN E♭ MAJOR, MVMT. 2 ("AIR ECOSSAIS: WITHIN A MILE OF EDINBURGH TOWN")

MD13–2.

Adagio non troppo

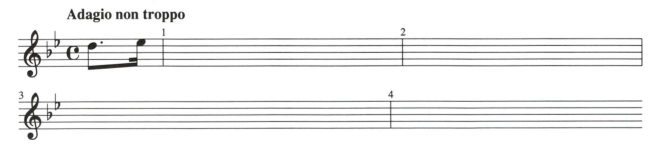

· The rhythmic notation confirms the following arithmetic:
$$1 = \tfrac{1}{2} + \tfrac{1}{2} = \tfrac{3}{4} + \tfrac{1}{4} = \tfrac{1}{4} + \tfrac{3}{4} = \tfrac{1}{4} + \tfrac{1}{4} + \tfrac{1}{4} + \tfrac{1}{4}$$

WAGNER: *LOHENGRIN*, ACT 3

MD13–3.

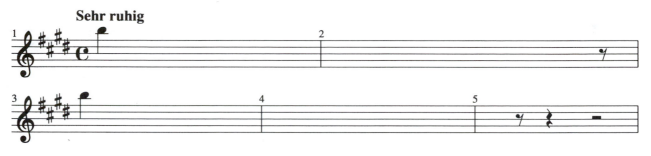

- Find the next-to-last pitch of measure 4 through reference to the first pitch of that measure.

MOZART: *COSÌ FAN TUTTE*, K. 588, ACT 1

MD13–4.

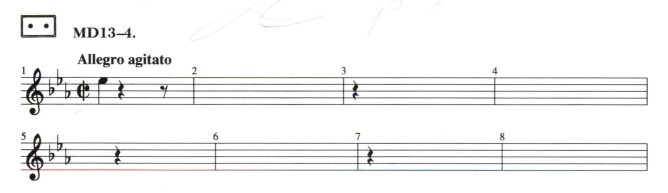

- Where and how does the diminished fifth of measure 4 resolve?

J. S. BACH: VIOLIN PARTITA NO. 2 IN D MINOR, BWV 1004, GIGUE

MD13–5.

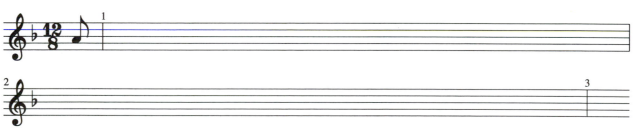

- The dominant $^6_5$'s diminished fifth is outlined in the first half of measure 2. Where and how does this dissonant interval resolve?

MOZART: PIANO CONCERTO NO. 23 IN A MAJOR, K. 488, MVMT. 1

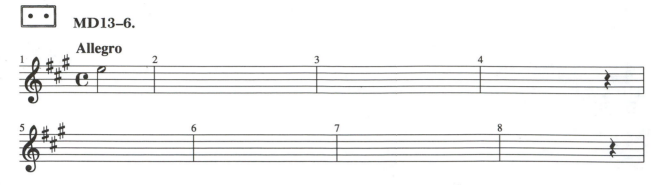

MD13–6.

- Write down the first, third, and fifth pitches of measure 2 before the second, fourth, and sixth pitches.

HARMONIC DICTATIONS

BRAHMS: SYMPHONY NO. 1 IN C MINOR, OP. 68, MVMT. 2

HD13–1.

- Brahms's bass includes a melodic interval that seldom occurs in such an exposed context.

J. S. BACH: SUITE FOR UNACCOMPANIED CELLO NO. 3 IN C MAJOR, BWV 1009, BOURRÉE I

HD13–2.

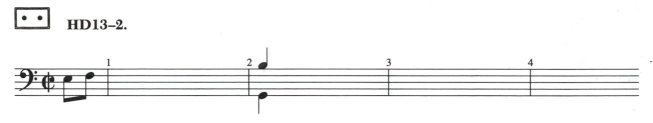

· The leading tone that occurs on beat 1 of measure 2 is transferred to a lower register in measure 3 and resolves in that register during measure 4.

BEETHOVEN: PIANO SONATA NO. 24 IN F♯ MAJOR, OP. 78, MVMT. 1

HD13–3.

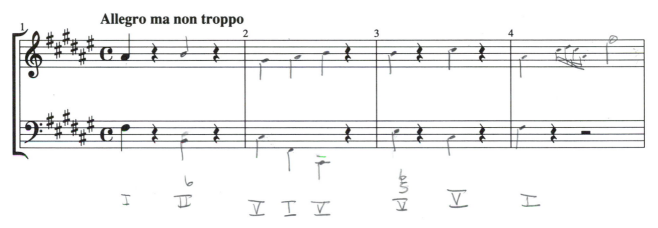

· Both $\hat{7}$ and $\hat{4}$, which form a diminished fifth, occur on beat 1 of measure 3. How and when does this dissonant interval resolve?

BEETHOVEN: PIANO SONATA NO. 13 IN E♭ MAJOR, OP. 27, NO. 1, MVMT. 4

HD13–4.

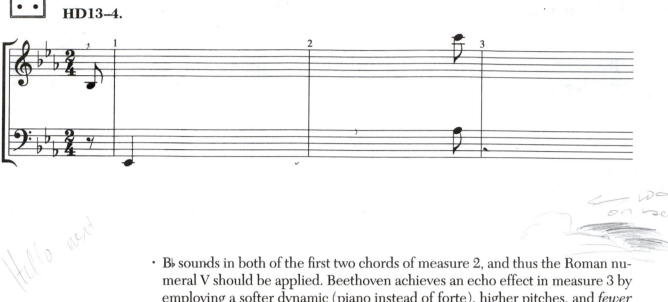

- B♭ sounds in both of the first two chords of measure 2, and thus the Roman numeral V should be applied. Beethoven achieves an echo effect in measure 3 by employing a softer dynamic (piano instead of forte), higher pitches, and *fewer* pitches. B♭ is omitted from the second chord of measure 3. Because measure 3 is an echo of measure 2 and because the root B♭ sounds in the first chord of measure 3, the Roman numeral V is appropriate for the second chord nevertheless. In short, the chord is a dominant $^6_5$ with omitted root.

MOZART: PIANO CONCERTO NO. 18 IN B♭ MAJOR, K. 456, MVMT. 3

HD13–5.

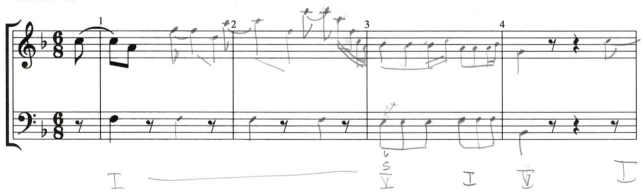

- Compare the two halves of this parallel period. Is the soprano pitch B♭ in measure 3 consonant or dissonant? How is it harmonized? Is the soprano pitch B♭ in measure 7 consonant or dissonant? How is it harmonized?

MOZART: *DIE ENTFÜHRUNG AUS DEM SERAIL*, K. 384, ACT 2

HD13–6.

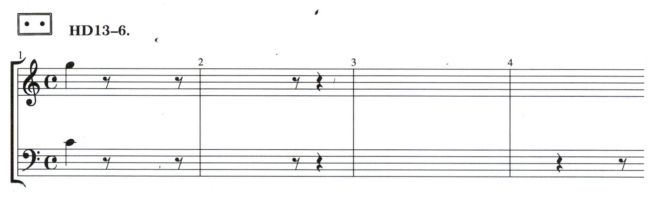

- Compare the first halves of measures 3 and 4. In both measures, the melody spans an ascending minor third, complementing the descending minor thirds of measure 1.

CASSETTE PROGRAM (TAPE 2, SIDE B)

C13–1.   Six melodies are performed, twice each. During the silence after each playing, respond in one of the following ways: (1) Sing the melody, using solmization syllables; (2) Play the melody on the piano or on your primary instrument; (3) Write the melody on staff paper.

C13–2.   Six chord progressions are performed, four times each. During the silence after each playing, respond in one of the following ways: (1) Sing the soprano after the first and second playings and the bass after the third and fourth playings, using solmization syllables; (2) Play the soprano on the piano or your primary instrument after the first and second playings and the bass after the third and fourth playings; (3) Play both the soprano and bass on the piano after each playing; (4) Write the soprano and bass on staff paper and provide an analysis.

Chapter 14

PITCH

A dissonant pitch increases a chord's instability and therefore its forward momentum. Carefully applied, dissonance is a crucial ingredient of tonal music. A seventh may be added to any $\frac{5}{3}$ chord, resulting in a $\frac{7}{3}$ chord. Likewise a fifth may be added to any $\frac{6}{3}$ chord, resulting in a $\frac{6}{5}$ chord. $\frac{7}{5}$ and $\frac{6}{3}$ dominant chords have appeared in previous chapters. In this chapter these configurations are applied to tonic, supertonic, subdominant, and submediant chords as well.

Just as $\frac{5}{3}$ chords and their $\frac{6}{3}$ inversions may be major, minor, or diminished, a seventh chord and its $\frac{6}{5}$ inversion belong to one of several classifications. Example 14–1 displays the characteristics of the ***major seventh chord***, the major-minor seventh chord, the ***minor seventh chord***, and the ***half-diminished seventh chord***. Sample chords are displayed with analysis in Example 14–2.

EXAMPLE 14–1

Seventh chord quality	Triad quality	Seventh quality
Major	Major	Major
Major-minor	Major	Minor
Minor	Minor	Minor
Half-diminished	Diminished	Minor

EXAMPLE 14–2

MAJOR KEYS

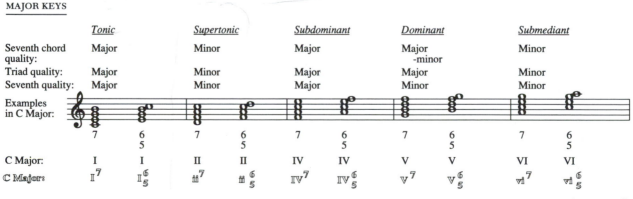

	Tonic	Supertonic	Subdominant	Dominant	Submediant
Seventh chord quality:	Major	Minor	Major	Major-minor	Minor
Triad quality:	Major	Minor	Major	Major	Minor
Seventh quality:	Major	Minor	Major	Minor	Minor

(continued)

EXAMPLE 14–2 (*continued*)

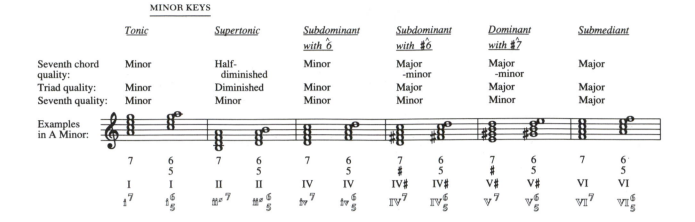

	Tonic	Supertonic	Subdominant with $\hat{6}$	Subdominant with #$\hat{6}$	Dominant with #$\hat{7}$	Submediant
Seventh chord quality:	Minor	Half-diminished	Minor	Major-minor	Major-minor	Major
Triad quality:	Minor	Diminished	Minor	Major	Major	Major
Seventh quality:	Minor	Minor	Minor	Minor	Minor	Major

The symbol for the half-diminished seventh chord in Method Two harmonic analysis is a small Roman numeral followed by a slashed degree circle ($^{\varnothing}$). The capital Roman numeral is used for both major-minor and major seventh chords, while the small Roman numeral is used for minor seventh chords.

Apply the listening strategies you have developed for the dominant harmony with these new choices. First isolate the bass in your internal ear and bring to mind the choices that are available for that scale degree. (For example, bass $\hat{4}$ could support the supertonic $^6_3$ or $^6_5$ or the subdominant $^5_3$ or $^7_3$.) Then arpeggiate upward from the bass in your mind to determine the figured bass for the chord. In minor keys, consider whether #$\hat{6}$ substitutes for $\hat{6}$ in the subdominant or subdominant seventh chord or whether #$\hat{7}$ substitutes for $\hat{7}$ in the dominant chord.[1]

#$\hat{4}$ may serve not only as a chromatic passing note (introduced in chapter 13), but also as a **chromatic neighboring note**. Example 14–3 demonstrates both of these roles.

EXAMPLE 14–3

BERLIOZ: *LA DAMNATION DE FAUST*, OP. 24, PART 1

---

1. For the time being, $\hat{6}$ will always be used in the supertonic and supertonic seventh chords and #$\hat{7}$ will always be used in the dominant seventh chord in minor keys.

METER AND RHYTHM

In simple meters such as $\frac{2}{4}$, $\frac{3}{4}$, $\frac{4}{4}$, and $\frac{2}{2}$, the beat divides into two halves, as shown in Example 14–4a. To divide the beat into three thirds (as would occur without special notation in compound meters), three notes are positioned within the space that would normally be occupied by two and the number 3, indicating a *triplet*, appears either adjacent to the beam when three eighth notes are employed or adjacent to a *bracket* inserted in the score to bind notes (or rests) that are not connected by a beam. These possibilities are displayed in Example 14–4b.

EXAMPLE 14–4

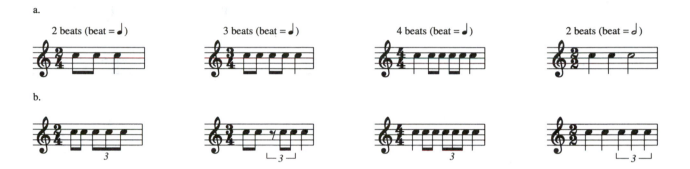

Whenever triplets are juxtaposed with duple or quadruple subdivisions of the beat, be especially careful to keep the beats evenly spaced in time. Do not allow a beat that contains triplets to take up more time than the other beats. To promote the even spacing of beats, count only the beat numbers, as demonstrated in Example 14–5. If necessary, use a metronome to keep these beats uniform. What fills the beat (two eighth notes, four sixteenth notes, triplets, etc.) will correspond to subdivisions encountered in the simple and (for the triplets) compound meters introduced in earlier chapters.

EXAMPLE 14–5

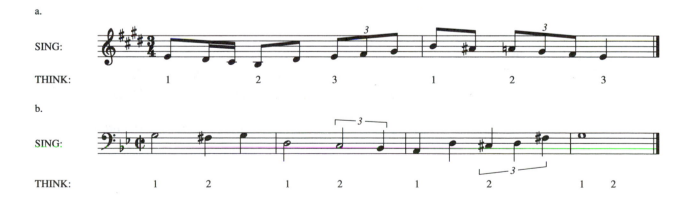

SOLO MELODIES

MELODIES THAT EMPLOY A MAJOR SEVENTH

MOZART: *DON GIOVANNI*, K. 527, ACT 1

S14–1.

- In measure 16, F ascends to A. In measure 20, F descends (via C) to A. In both cases, B♭ occurs on the following downbeat. In alternation, sing measures 20 and 21 (where A and B♭ form a minor second) and measure 16 and 17 (where A and B♭ form a major seventh).

BEETHOVEN: PIANO SONATA NO. 32 IN C MINOR, OP. 111, MVMT. 1

S14–2.

MELODIES THAT EMPLOY ♯4̂ AS LOWER NEIGHBOR TO 5̂

HAYDN: SYMPHONY NO. 104 IN D MAJOR ("LONDON"), MVMT. 3

S14–3.

- Though neighboring notes that occur on third beats of $\frac{3}{4}$ measures would generally attract little attention, Haydn instructs you to give them forzando accentuation.

MOZART: PIANO CONCERTO NO. 20 IN D MINOR, K. 466, MVMT. 3

S14–4.

MENDELSSOHN: SYMPHONY NO. 4 IN A MAJOR ("ITALIAN"), OP. 90, MVMT. 3

S14–5.

- D in measure 1 forms a diminished fifth with G♯ in measure 2. This interval is resolved by the major third C♯-A in measures 4 and 5. The A in measure 2 is a passing note that connects G♯ and B, *not* the resolution of the leading tone.

DVOŘÁK: *RUSALKA*, OP. 114, ACT 1

S14–6.

BERLIOZ: *LA DAMNATION DE FAUST*, OP. 24, PART 1

S14–7.

- If you think only in terms of adjacent pitches, you have some difficult melodic leaps to traverse in this melody: an ascending major seventh (measure 4) and two ascending augmented fourths (measures 5 and 6). If you think instead in terms of longer-range connections, the C♯s are merely minor seconds below Ds that were recently sounded. You decide which way to think about the C♯s!

MENDELSSOHN: FANTASY IN F♯ MINOR, OP. 28

S14–8.

MELODIES THAT EMPLOY ONE-BEAT
TRIPLETS

DVOŘÁK: SYMPHONY NO. 9 IN E MINOR ("FROM THE NEW WORLD"), OP. 95, MVMT. 4

S14–9.

- In measures 1 and 2, the melody ascends from E to G and then returns to E. The F♯ passing notes that enliven this basic structure occur on strong beats, thereby creating a tension between harmonic and metric forces. The harmonically "strong" G in measure 1 occurs in a metrically "weak" position. Your performance must come to terms with these conflicting forces. G should not come across as a neighbor between the two F♯s, as its rhythmic placement would suggest.

ROSSINI: *WILLIAM TELL*, ACT 3

S14–10.

PUCCINI: *LA BOHÈME*, ACT 4

S14–11.

- This melody follows the contour of the descending melodic minor scale, one scale degree per measure. By conforming to the scale with absolute rigidity, Puccini creates an impression of inevitability. The contour of the melody reflects the unhappy fate of the operatic character who sings it.

WEBER: *DER FREISCHÜTZ*, ACT 1

S14–12.

BRAHMS: VIOLONCELLO SONATA NO. 2 IN F MAJOR, OP. 99, MVMT. 1

S14–13.

· How do measures 3 and 4 relate?

J. S. BACH: BRANDENBURG CONCERTO NO. 5 IN D MAJOR, BWV 1050, MVMT. 3

S14–14.

DUETS

D14–1.

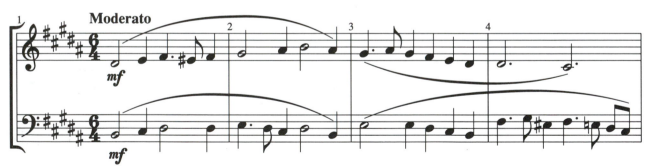

D14–2.

ACCOMPANIED SOLO MELODIES

AFTER CHOPIN: MAZURKA, OP. 33, NO. 2

AS14–1.

AS14–2.

RHYTHMS

R14–1.

R14–2.

R14–3.

R14–4.

R14–5.

R14–6.

INTERVAL WORKSHOP

I14–1.   Practice singing the interval of a minor second higher than a sounding pitch. The sounding pitch should be near the low end of your vocal range, and could be sung by a classmate or your instructor or performed on the piano or another instrument such as the cello. Also practice singing compound versions of this interval.

I14–2.   Practice singing the interval of a minor second lower than a sounding pitch. The sounding pitch should be near the high end of your vocal range, and could be sung by a classmate or your instructor or performed on the piano or another instrument such as the flute. Also practice singing compound versions of this interval.

I14–3.   Play a pitch that is low in your vocal range at a keyboard. Sing it. Then sing the pitch a major seventh higher. Use the keyboard to confirm your performance. Then sing ascending sevenths starting on other pitches.

I14–4.   Play a pitch that is high in your vocal range at a keyboard. Sing it. Then sing the pitch a major seventh lower. Use the keyboard to confirm your performance. Then sing descending sevenths starting on other pitches.

I14–5.   Practice singing the interval of a major seventh higher than a sounding pitch. The sounding pitch should be at or beyond the lower limit of your vocal range, and could be sung by a classmate or your instructor or performed on the piano or another instrument such as the cello. Also practice singing compound versions of this interval.

I14–6.   Practice singing the interval of a major seventh lower than a sounding pitch. The sounding pitch should be at or beyond the upper limit of your vocal range, and could be sung by a classmate or your instructor or performed on the piano or another instrument such as the flute. Also practice singing compound versions of this interval.

I14–7.   At the keyboard, select a pitch in the middle of your vocal range as the "starting pitch." Then sing the following groups of four pitches on "la," forming inversionally related intervals. Practice a. through v. from first to last, from last to first, and in random order.

a.	Starting pitch	Minor second higher	Starting pitch	Major seventh lower
b.	Starting pitch	Major second higher	Starting pitch	Minor seventh lower
c.	Starting pitch	Minor third higher	Starting pitch	Major sixth lower
d.	Starting pitch	Major third higher	Starting pitch	Minor sixth lower
e.	Starting pitch	Perfect fourth higher	Starting pitch	Perfect fifth lower
f.	Starting pitch	Augmented fourth higher	Starting pitch	Diminished fifth lower
g.	Starting pitch	Perfect fifth higher	Starting pitch	Perfect fourth lower
h.	Starting pitch	Minor sixth higher	Starting pitch	Major third lower
i.	Starting pitch	Major sixth higher	Starting pitch	Minor third lower
j.	Starting pitch	Minor seventh higher	Starting pitch	Major second lower
k.	Starting pitch	Major seventh higher	Starting pitch	Minor second lower
l.	Starting pitch	Major seventh lower	Starting pitch	Minor second higher
m.	Starting pitch	Minor seventh lower	Starting pitch	Major second higher
n.	Starting pitch	Major sixth lower	Starting pitch	Minor third higher
o.	Starting pitch	Minor sixth lower	Starting pitch	Major third higher
p.	Starting pitch	Perfect fifth lower	Starting pitch	Perfect fourth higher
q.	Starting pitch	Augmented fourth lower	Starting pitch	Diminished fifth higher
r.	Starting pitch	Perfect fourth lower	Starting pitch	Perfect fifth higher
s.	Starting pitch	Major third lower	Starting pitch	Minor sixth higher
t.	Starting pitch	Minor third lower	Starting pitch	Major sixth higher
u.	Starting pitch	Major second lower	Starting pitch	Minor seventh higher
v.	Starting pitch	Minor second lower	Starting pitch	Major seventh higher

I14–8.   Choose a classmate with a similar vocal range as a partner. Then perform the following exercises, using each of the following eleven pairs of intervals.

X	**Inv(X)**
Minor second	Major seventh
Major second	Minor seventh
Minor third	Major sixth
Major third	Minor sixth
Perfect fourth	Perfect fifth
Augmented fourth	Diminished fifth
Perfect fifth	Perfect fourth
Minor sixth	Major third
Major sixth	Minor third
Minor seventh	Major second
Major seventh	Minor second

a. Your partner sings a pitch that is low in your vocal range. Then your partner sings the pitch a second time, while you sing the pitch that is **X** higher than your partner's. Then you sing the pitch you just sang a second time, while your partner sings the pitch that is **Inv(X)** higher than yours.

b. Your partner sings a pitch that is high in your vocal range. Then your partner sings the pitch a second time, while you sing the pitch that is **X** lower than your partner's. Then you sing the pitch you just sang a second time, while your partner sings the pitch that is **Inv(X)** lower than yours.

ARPEGGIATION WORKSHOP

A14–1.　Play a pitch that is low in your vocal range at a keyboard. Let this pitch be $\hat{1}$ in a major key. Sing each of the following arpeggiations, either in the order given or in random order.

a. $\hat{1}$ $\hat{3}$ $\hat{5}$ $\hat{1}$ ✿ $\hat{2}$ $\hat{4}$ $\hat{6}$ $\hat{8}$ ✿ $\hat{5}$ $\hat{7}$ $\hat{2}$ $\hat{7}$ ✿ $\hat{8}$ $\hat{5}$ $\hat{3}$ $\hat{1}$

b. $\hat{1}$ $\hat{3}$ $\hat{5}$ $\hat{1}$ ✿ $\hat{4}$ $\hat{6}$ $\hat{8}$ $\hat{2}$ ✿ $\hat{5}$ $\hat{7}$ $\hat{2}$ $\hat{4}$ ✿ $\hat{3}$ $\hat{8}$ $\hat{5}$ $\hat{1}$

c. $\hat{3}$ $\hat{5}$ $\hat{8}$ $\hat{3}$ ✿ $\hat{2}$ $\hat{4}$ $\hat{6}$ $\hat{8}$ ✿ $\hat{5}$ $\hat{7}$ $\hat{2}$ $\hat{7}$ ✿ $\hat{8}$ $\hat{5}$ $\hat{3}$ $\hat{1}$

d. $\hat{3}$ $\hat{5}$ $\hat{8}$ $\hat{3}$ ✿ $\hat{4}$ $\hat{6}$ $\hat{8}$ $\hat{2}$ ✿ $\hat{5}$ $\hat{7}$ $\hat{2}$ $\hat{4}$ ✿ $\hat{3}$ $\hat{8}$ $\hat{5}$ $\hat{1}$

e. $\hat{1}$ $\hat{3}$ $\hat{5}$ $\hat{1}$ ✿ $\hat{4}$ $\hat{6}$ $\hat{8}$ $\hat{3}$ ✿ $\hat{5}$ $\hat{7}$ $\hat{2}$ $\hat{7}$ ✿ $\hat{8}$ $\hat{5}$ $\hat{3}$ $\hat{1}$

f. $\hat{1}$ $\hat{3}$ $\hat{5}$ $\hat{8}$ ✿ $\hat{6}$ $\hat{8}$ $\hat{3}$ $\hat{4}$ ✿ $\hat{5}$ $\hat{7}$ $\hat{2}$ $\hat{4}$ ✿ $\hat{3}$ $\hat{8}$ $\hat{5}$ $\hat{1}$

g. $\hat{3}$ $\hat{5}$ $\hat{8}$ $\hat{3}$ ✿ $\hat{4}$ $\hat{6}$ $\hat{8}$ $\hat{3}$ ✿ $\hat{5}$ $\hat{7}$ $\hat{2}$ $\hat{7}$ ✿ $\hat{8}$ $\hat{5}$ $\hat{3}$ $\hat{1}$

h. $\hat{1}$ $\hat{3}$ $\hat{5}$ $\hat{8}$ ✿ $\hat{1}$ $\hat{3}$ $\hat{5}$ $\hat{7}$ ✿ $\hat{6}$ $\hat{4}$ $\hat{6}$ $\hat{8}$ ✿ $\hat{7}$ $\hat{2}$ $\hat{7}$ $\hat{5}$

i. $\hat{1}$ $\hat{3}$ $\hat{5}$ $\hat{8}$ ✿ $\hat{3}$ $\hat{5}$ $\hat{7}$ $\hat{8}$ ✿ $\hat{4}$ $\hat{6}$ $\hat{8}$ $\hat{2}$ ✿ $\hat{5}$ $\hat{7}$ $\hat{2}$ $\hat{5}$

j. $\hat{1}$ $\hat{3}$ $\hat{5}$ $\hat{3}$ ✿ $\hat{1}$ $\hat{3}$ $\hat{5}$ $\hat{6}$ ✿ $\hat{7}$ $\hat{2}$ $\hat{4}$ $\hat{5}$ ✿ $\hat{1}$ $\hat{3}$ $\hat{5}$ $\hat{1}$

A14–2.　Play a pitch that is at least a perfect fifth above the lowest note of your vocal range at a keyboard. Let this pitch be $\hat{1}$ in a minor key. Sing each of the following arpeggiations, either in the order given or in random order.

a. $\hat{1}$ $\hat{3}$ $\hat{1}$ ✿ $\hat{6}$ $\hat{1}$ $\hat{3}$ ✿ $\hat{4}$ $\hat{6}$ $\hat{1}$ $\hat{2}$ ✿ $\hat{5}$ $\hat{\sharp7}$ $\hat{2}$ ✿ $\hat{1}$ $\hat{5}$ $\hat{3}$ $\hat{1}$

b. $\hat{1}$ $\hat{3}$ $\hat{1}$ ✿ $\hat{6}$ $\hat{1}$ $\hat{4}$ ✿ $\hat{4}$ $\hat{6}$ $\hat{1}$ $\hat{2}$ ✿ $\hat{5}$ $\hat{\sharp7}$ $\hat{2}$ ✿ $\hat{1}$ $\hat{5}$ $\hat{3}$ $\hat{1}$

c. $\hat{1}$ $\hat{3}$ $\hat{1}$ ✿ $\hat{4}$ $\hat{6}$ $\hat{1}$ $\hat{2}$ ✿ $\hat{5}$ $\hat{1}$ $\hat{3}$ ✿ $\hat{5}$ $\hat{\sharp7}$ $\hat{2}$ ✿ $\hat{1}$ $\hat{5}$ $\hat{3}$ $\hat{1}$

d. $\hat{1}$ $\hat{3}$ $\hat{1}$ ✿ $\hat{\sharp7}$ $\hat{2}$ $\hat{4}$ $\hat{5}$ ✿ $\hat{1}$ $\hat{3}$ $\hat{1}$ ✿ $\hat{4}$ $\hat{6}$ $\hat{1}$ $\hat{2}$ ✿ $\hat{5}$ $\hat{\sharp7}$ $\hat{2}$ $\hat{5}$

e. $\hat{1}$ $\hat{3}$ $\hat{1}$ ✿ $\hat{6}$ $\hat{1}$ $\hat{3}$ $\hat{4}$ ✿ $\hat{4}$ $\hat{6}$ $\hat{1}$ $\hat{3}$ ✿ $\hat{5}$ $\hat{\sharp7}$ $\hat{2}$ ✿ $\hat{1}$ $\hat{5}$ $\hat{3}$ $\hat{1}$

f. $\hat{1}$ $\hat{3}$ $\hat{1}$ ✿ $\hat{6}$ $\hat{1}$ $\hat{3}$ $\hat{4}$ ✿ $\hat{4}$ $\hat{6}$ $\hat{1}$ $\hat{2}$ ✿ $\hat{5}$ $\hat{\sharp7}$ $\hat{2}$ ✿ $\hat{1}$ $\hat{5}$ $\hat{3}$ $\hat{1}$

g. $\hat{1}$ $\hat{3}$ $\hat{1}$ ✿ $\hat{\sharp6}$ $\hat{1}$ $\hat{3}$ $\hat{4}$ ✿ $\hat{\sharp7}$ $\hat{2}$ $\hat{4}$ $\hat{5}$ ✿ $\hat{1}$ $\hat{3}$ $\hat{5}$ $\hat{1}$ ✿ $\hat{5}$ $\hat{\sharp7}$ $\hat{2}$ $\hat{5}$

h. $\hat{1}$ $\hat{3}$ $\hat{1}$ ✿ $\hat{6}$ $\hat{1}$ $\hat{3}$ $\hat{5}$ ✿ $\hat{5}$ $\hat{1}$ $\hat{3}$ $\hat{5}$ ✿ $\hat{5}$ $\hat{\sharp7}$ $\hat{2}$ $\hat{5}$ ✿ $\hat{1}$ $\hat{5}$ $\hat{3}$ $\hat{1}$

QUICK SWITCH

Q14–1.

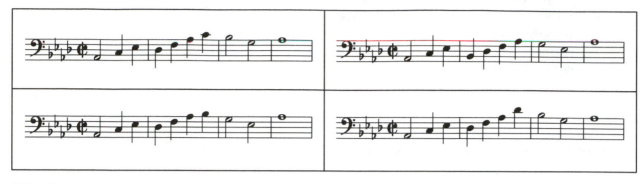

Q14–2.

Q14–3.

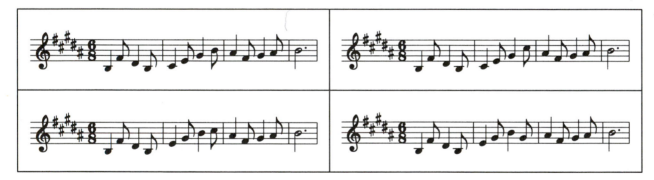

Q14–4.

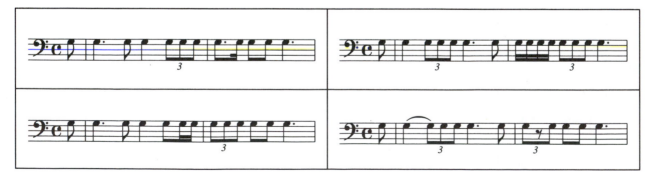

IDENTIFICATIONS

ID14–1. An interval not larger than an octave is performed melodically or as a simultaneity. Identify it.

ID14–2. A seventh chord in ^{7} or $^6_5$ position is performed. Identify it as a major seventh chord, a major-minor seventh chord, a minor seventh chord, or a half-diminished seventh chord.

ID14–3. A major, minor, or half-diminished seventh chord is performed. Then two of its four pitches are performed melodically: root-third, root-fifth, root-seventh, third-root, third-fifth, third-seventh, fifth-root, fifth-third, fifth-seventh, seventh-root, seventh-third, or seventh-fifth. Identify which of these choices is performed.

ID14–4. $\hat{4}, \hat{6}, \hat{8}$, and $\hat{2}$ in a major or minor key are performed simultaneously. Then two of these four scale degrees are performed simultaneously. Identify the two scale degrees performed, from among the following choices: $\hat{4}$-$\hat{6}$, $\hat{4}$-$\hat{8}$, $\hat{4}$-$\hat{2}$, $\hat{6}$-$\hat{8}$, $\hat{6}$-$\hat{2}$, $\hat{8}$-$\hat{2}$.

ID14–5. $\hat{1}, \hat{3}, \hat{5}$, and $\hat{7}$ in a major key are performed simultaneously. Then two of these four scale degrees are performed simultaneously. Identify the two scale degrees performed, from among the following choices: $\hat{1}$-$\hat{3}$, $\hat{1}$-$\hat{5}$, $\hat{1}$-$\hat{7}$, $\hat{3}$-$\hat{5}$, $\hat{3}$-$\hat{7}$, $\hat{5}$-$\hat{7}$.

ID14–6. $\hat{2}, \hat{4}, \hat{6}, \hat{8}$, and $\hat{2}$ in a major or minor key are performed simultaneously. Then either $\hat{2}, \hat{4}, \hat{6}$, and $\hat{8}$ or $\hat{4}, \hat{6}, \hat{8}$, and $\hat{2}$ are performed simultaneously. Is the resulting chord in ^{7} or $^6_5$ position?

ID14–7. $\hat{1}, \hat{3}, \hat{5}, \hat{7}$, and $\hat{8}$ in a major key are performed simultaneously. Then either $\hat{1}, \hat{3}, \hat{5}$, and $\hat{7}$ or $\hat{3}, \hat{5}, \hat{7}$, and $\hat{8}$ are performed simultaneously. Is the resulting chord in ^{7} or $^6_5$ position?

ID14–8. A chord is performed. Identify its position from among the following choices: $^6_3, ^6_3, ^6_4, ^6_5,$ or ^{7}.

ID14–9. What chord occurs at **X**? Suitable choices are listed below.

C Major:	I^6	**X**	V	I	V
C Major:	I^6	**X**	V	I	V

Choices:

II	II^6	II^7	II$^6_5$	IV	IV^6	IV^7
ii	ii^6	ii^7	ii$^6_5$	IV	IV^6	IV^7

ID14–10. What chord occurs at **Y**? Suitable choices are listed below.

A Minor:	I	VI	**Y**	V$\sharp$	I
A Minor:	i	VI	**Y**	V	i

Choices:

I^6	II°	II^{o6}	II^{ø7}	II$^{ø6}_5$	IV	IV^6	IV^7
i^6	ii^o	ii^{o6}	ii^{ø7}	ii$^{ø6}_5$	iv	iv^6	iv^7

ID14–11.   A melody is performed. Identify the correct score notation.

ID14–12. A chord progression in the major mode is performed. Identify a suitable Roman-numeral/figured-bass analysis from among the following choices:

Group 1

a.   I   II$^{6}_{5}$———V^{7} I^{7} *Seventh, minor*
b.   I   II^{6}———V^{7} I^{7} *minor*
c.   I   IV   II^{7} V^{7} I   *major* IV
d.   I   VI^{7} II^{7} V^{7} I   *Bass line Distng.*

a.   I   ii°$^{6}_{5}$ ^{7} V^{7} I
b.   I   ii°^{6} ^{7} V^{7} I
c.   I   IV   ii^{7} V^{7} I
d.   I   vi^{7} ii^{7} V^{7} I

Group 2

a.   I   ♭VI   V^{7} I   V$^{6}_{5}$ *right hand does not change. V minor 7-6*
b.   I   ♭VI$^{6}_{5}$ V   I   V$^{6}_{5}$ *thumb goes stepwise. V minor*
c.   I   ♯IV^{6} V   I   V$^{6}_{5}$ *top changes V major*
d.   I   ♯IV$^{6}_{5}$ V   I   V$^{6}_{5}$ *top doesn't change V major 7th*

a.   I   vi^{7} V$^{6}_{5}$ I   V
b.   I   vi   V$^{6}_{5}$ I   V
c.   I   IV^{6} V$^{6}_{5}$ I   V
d.   I   IV$^{6}_{5}$ V$^{6}_{5}$ I   V

ID14–13. A chord progression in the <u>minor mode</u> is performed. Identify a suitable Roman-numeral/figured-bass analysis from among the following choices:

Group 1

listen for 2nd scale degree

a.   I   II^{6}———V♯^{7} I   (6 5)
b.   I   II^{6}———V♯^{7} I   *3 bassline*
c.   I   IV   II$^{6}_{5}$ V♯^{7} I
d.   I   IV   II^{7} V♯^{7} I

a.   i   ii°^{6} ø$^{6}_{5}$ V^{7} i
b.   i   ii°^{6} ø^{7} V^{7} i
c.   i   iv   ii°ø$^{6}_{5}$ V^{7} i
d.   i   iv   ii°ø^{7} V^{7} i

Group 2

a.   I   VI   II$^{6}_{5}$♯   V♯   I
b.   I   VI   II^{6}♯   V♯   I
c.   I   VI   IV$^{♯}$ V♯   I   *minor*
d.   I   IV$^{6}_{3}$ II$^{6}_{5}$♯   V♯   I

a.   i   VI   ii°ø$^{6}_{5}$ V   i
b.   i   VI   ii°^{6} V   i
c.   i   VI   iv   V   i
d.   i   iv^{6} ii°ø$^{6}_{5}$ V   i

ID14–14.   A chord progression is performed. Identify the correct score notation for the outer voices. Figured-bass symbols have been placed below the bass where appropriate. If you wish, add Roman numerals.

e. minor or major? 7th?
3rd chord.

IV⁷= rich, rich
sound, jazzy

e.

minor

7 7 7   major   6 7 7   6 7 7

IV   5

IV

f.

minor   minor,   diminished
   no

6   x   x   6   x
5

RHYTHMIC DICTATIONS

RD14–1.

RD14–2.

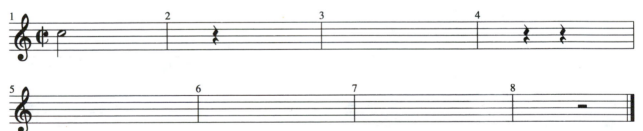

MELODIC DICTATIONS

DVOŘÁK: SYMPHONY NO. 8 IN G MAJOR, OP. 88, MVMT. 1

MD14–1.

- Though measure 3 may sound like a faster version of measures 1 and 2 transposed a minor third higher, the positioning of whole and half steps is revised. The differences are due in part to the fact that 3̂-4̂ and 5̂-6̂ are not the same in the major mode, but also in part to the fact that Dvořák employs an accidental.

J. STRAUSS: *DIE FLEDERMAUS*, ACT 2

MD14–2.

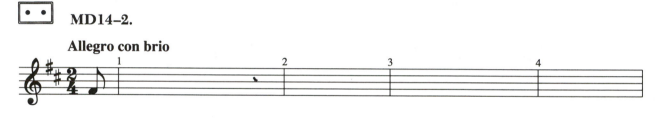

- D major (measure 1) and B minor (measure 2) are juxtaposed. Which is tonic?

PUCCINI: *LA BOHÈME*, ACT 1

MD14–3.

- In this excerpt triplets are used so extensively that for several measures you might think that the meter is $\frac{12}{8}$. Do not write dotted quarter notes for the two pitches of measure 4 by mistake!

(3:20 Review pg. 149)

MENDELSSOHN: VIOLIN CONCERTO IN E MINOR, OP. 64, MVMT. 1

MD14–4.

Allegro molto appassionato

- Focus your attention on the second, fourth, sixth, and eighth pitches of the melody (counting the starting pitch as the first pitch). They form a straightforward arpeggiation. Then focus your attention on the third, fifth, and seventh pitches, all of which have the same function.

R. STRAUSS: *DON JUAN*, OP. 20

MD14–5.

Allegro molto con brio

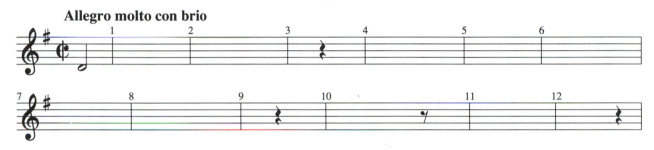

- During most of this melody, a descending contour is emphasized. The rhythm is characterized by quarter, dotted quarter, and eighth notes. Starting in measure 10 an ascending contour prevails. The rhythm is characterized by triplets.

SCHUBERT: PIANO SONATA IN A MINOR, D. 784, OP. POST. 143, MVMT. 1

MD14–6.

Allegro giusto

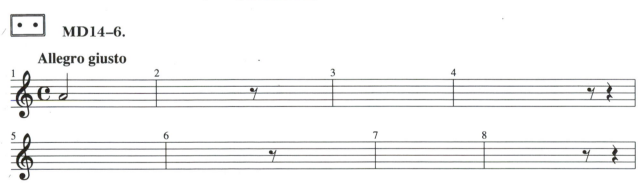

- This melody emphasizes neighbors to $\hat{5}$. The first pitch of measure 2 is an obvious example. Not so obvious is the relationship between $\hat{5}$ (in measures 3 and 7) and the second pitch of measure 5.

HARMONIC DICTATIONS

MOZART: *DIE ENTFÜHRUNG AUS DEM SERAIL,* K. 384, ACT 2

HD14–1.

- As you focus on the first chord of measure 3, first write down the outer voices and create a list of the chords that could be formed with them. Then decide whether the chord is consonant or dissonant and cross out any chords on your list that do not conform. Finally determine the chord's figured bass (by arpeggiating upward from the bass in your imagination) and select the matching chord from your list.

I D F♯ A
II E G B
IV G B D
V A C♯ E
VI B D F♯

HAYDN: *THE CREATION*, PART 1

HD14-2.

Allegro moderato

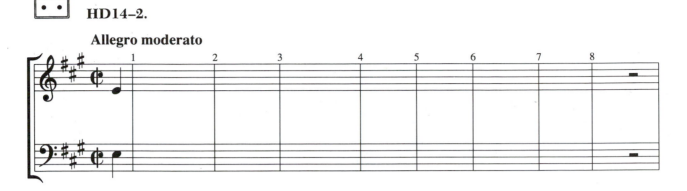

- In Haydn's time, some music theorists allowed only root progressions by fifth or by third (or their inversions). They explained the progression I-IV-V-I as

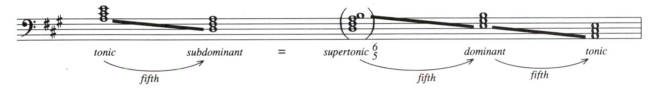

This analysis was advocated even if the "added sixth" did not appear above bass 4̂. Perhaps Haydn was thinking of this prescription when, near the end of measure 6, he added a B to the subdominant chord.

SCHUMANN: *LIEDERKREIS*, OP. 39, NO. 7

HD14–3.

- In measure 1, the alto descends a perfect fifth from B to E (shown). In measure 2, the tenor descends a perfect fifth from B to E (shown). How does the bass respond to these precedents in measures 3 and 4?

BRAHMS: VIOLIN SONATA NO. 1 IN G MAJOR, OP. 78, MVMT. 2

HD14–4.

- The descending fifth $\hat{5}$-$\hat{1}$ that characterizes the bass of an authentic cadence is rarely embellished in any way. This excerpt is an exception. Its distinctive and persistent rhythm is continued even between the $\hat{5}$ and $\hat{1}$ of the cadence. Which scale degree did Brahms select to subdivide the descending fifth? Does that pitch belong to the dominant or to the tonic chord? How does the bass of measure 2 relate to the bass of measure 1?

MOZART: *THE MAGIC FLUTE*, K. 620, ACT 1

HD14–5.

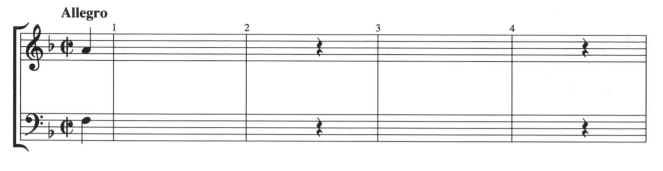

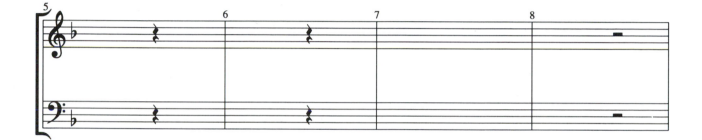

· The outer voices in measure 2 form a dissonant interval. Both pitches have tendencies for resolution, but the resolution pitches are *not* found in measure 3. Instead, the dominant harmony is prolonged from the beginning of measure 2 through the end of measure 3. The dissonant pitches of measure 2 are *repositioned* in measure 3: the bass E is transferred to the soprano, while the soprano B♭ is transferred to the tenor.

MOZART: *THE MAGIC FLUTE*, K. 620, ACT 1

HD14–6.

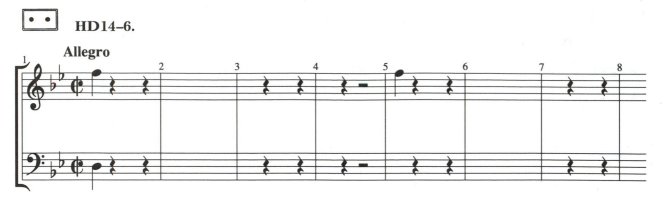

· Mozart employs a deceptive cadence in the antecedent phrase of this parallel period.

CASSETTE PROGRAM (TAPE 2, SIDE B)

C14–1.   Six melodies are performed, twice each. During the silence after each playing, respond in one of the following ways: (1) Sing the melody, using solmization syllables; (2) Play the melody on the piano or on your primary instrument; (3) Write the melody on staff paper.

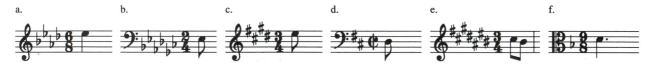

C14–2.   Six chord progressions are performed, four times each. During the silence after each playing, respond in one of the following ways: (1) Sing the soprano after the first and second playings and the bass after the third and fourth playings, using solmization syllables; (2) Play the soprano on the piano or your primary instrument after the first and second playings and the bass after the third and fourth playings; (3) Play both the soprano and bass on the piano after each playing; (4) Write the soprano and bass on staff paper and provide an analysis.

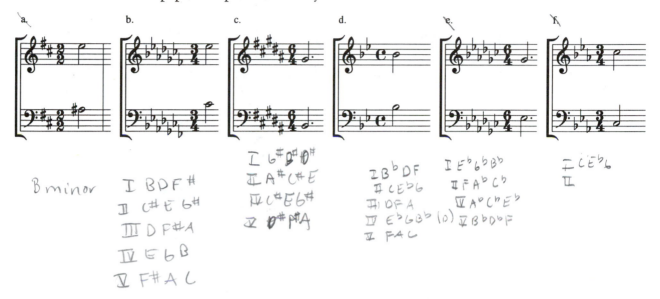

B minor

I B D F#
II C# E G#
III D F# A
IV E G B
V F# A C

I G# B# D#
II A# C# E
III C# E G#
V D# F# A

I Bb D F
II C Eb G
III D F A
IV Eb Gb Bb
V F A C

I Eb Gb Bb
II F Ab Cb
VI Ab Cb Eb
(6) V Bb Db F

I C Eb G
II

Chapter 15

PITCH

If #4̂ *connects* 4̂ and 5̂ or *embellishes* 5̂, the harmonic content of a chord progression is unaffected. The analysis of Example 15–1a would be the same whether or not the pitches shown in parentheses are employed. If on the other hand #4̂ *substitutes for* 4̂, a new harmony is created. In Example 15–1b the supertonic is replaced by ***V of V***, the chord that would function as V in the dominant key. Any chord made to sound like the dominant of the following chord is called an ***applied dominant*** or ***secondary dominant***. In Method One analysis V of V is indicated by the symbol V⌣ pointing toward V, while in Method Two analysis the symbol V/V is used.

EXAMPLE 15–1

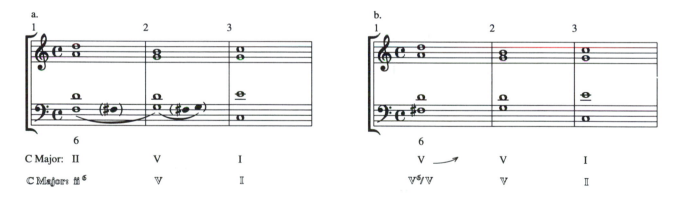

V of V occurs in $^5_3$, $^7_5$, $^6_3$, and $^6_5$ positions and may be applied to a dominant in any of those positions. (In Example 15–2, an applied dominant in $^6_5$ position leads to a dominant in $^7_5$ position.) In minor keys, *two* accidentals are required to transform a supertonic chord into an applied dominant (for example, F♯ and A♮ in Example 15–2). <u>Note</u>: In Method One analysis, figured-bass symbols conform to the prevailing *key signature*, while Roman numerals conform to the immediate and sometimes temporary *key of the*

harmonic analysis. The figured bass $^6_5$ is used for the applied dominant in Example 15–2, while its Roman numeral is simply V⌣ (that is, the *diatonic* V of the key of G major), not V♯⌣. The analysis

C Minor: V⌣   V♮   I

is an abbreviation of

G Major: V   I

C Minor: V♮   I.

EXAMPLE 15–2

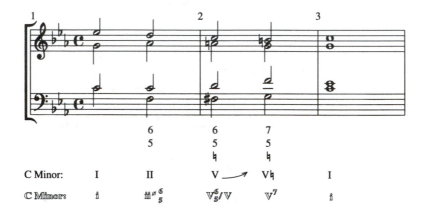

An *applied leading-tone* or *secondary leading-tone* chord functions much like an applied dominant. **VII of V**, or vii° of V, occurs in both $^5_3$ and $^6_3$ positions. Example 15–3 demonstrates its use and indicates appropriate analysis. Example 15–3 also demonstrates that an applied chord may precede a cadential $^6_4$. The applied dominant in measure 3 resolves to the dominant on beat 3 of measure 4.

EXAMPLE 15–3

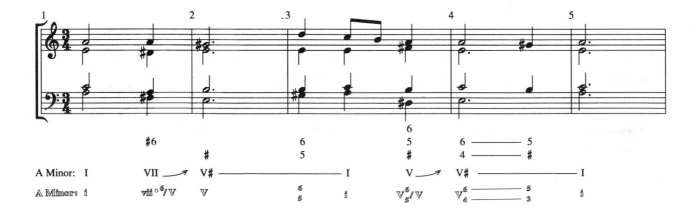

The applied chords introduced in this chapter employ combinations of pitches that are already familiar to you. Only their placement within a key is new. For example, you have had much practice listening to and discriminating among major chords and major-minor seventh chords whose root is $\hat{5}$. Beginning in this chapter these possibilities will occur with root $\hat{2}$ as well, and must be distinguished from minor, diminished, and half-diminished chords that share $\hat{2}$ as root. Likewise, chords with root $\hat{7}$ (or $\sharp\hat{7}$ in minor) will now occur with root $\sharp\hat{4}$ as well.

In the examples containing applied chords, the key of the composition was never severely challenged. Once the applied chord resolved to the dominant, the dominant led immediately to tonic. It is also possible to prolong the dominant for a longer period of time, using a procedure called ***tonicization*** (for prolongations of short duration) or ***modulation*** (for larger-scale prolongations or permanent changes of key). During a tonicization or modulation, a succession of several chords will be analyzed in the dominant key. Often a ***pivot chord*** (or occasionally chords), which is analyzed in both keys, helps in the transition between keys. The pivot chord often precedes the chord that functions as dominant in the dominant key. Example 15–4 shows a modulation from E major to B major.

EXAMPLE 15–4

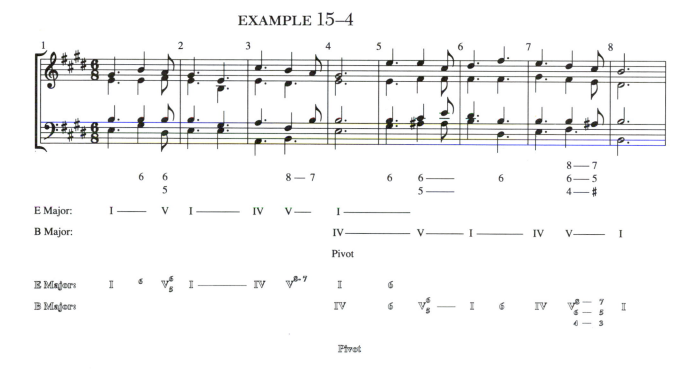

METER AND RHYTHM

In $\frac{3}{8}$ ***meter*** an eighth note fills one beat. Three eighth notes fill a measure in $\frac{3}{8}$ meter, just as three quarter notes fill a measure in $\frac{3}{4}$ meter. $\frac{3}{8}$ is a simple meter because its beats tend to divide into halves (two sixteenth notes). Example 15–5 shows a melody in $\frac{3}{8}$ meter, along with appropriate counting syllables.

EXAMPLE 15–5

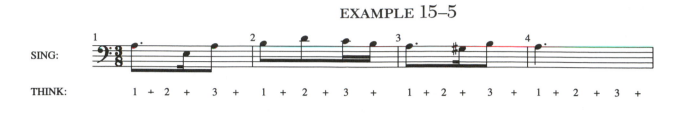

SOLO MELODIES

Note on Performance: *Because the Scale Degrees and Movable Do solmization systems employ tonic as their point of reference, they must reflect the change of tonic that results from tonicization or modulation. Inspect each melody before performing it. If the dominant key is tonicized, choose an appropriate spot to shift reference points. (Solo Melodies #5 and #7 are accompanied by demonstrations of this procedure.) If the melody contains only an occasional applied chord, retain the solmization syllables of the original key, singing "raised" or "fi" for ♯4̂. The Fixed Do and Letter Names solmization systems are unaffected by tonicizations.*

MELODIES THAT OUTLINE AN APPLIED DOMINANT OR APPLIED LEADING-TONE CHORD

HAYDN: SYMPHONY NO. 100 IN G MAJOR ("MILITARY"), MVMT. 1

S15–1.

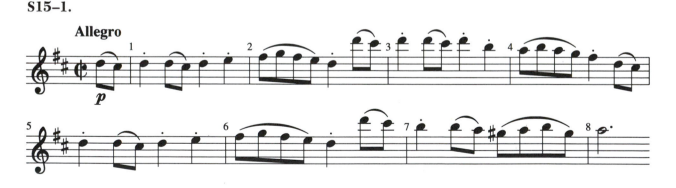

- If the pitches at the end of measure 6 followed the precedent of measures 0-1, 2-3, and 4-5, D would occur on the downbeat of measure 7. The B is a surprise. Like all surprises, it should be kept a secret for as long as possible. Perform the last two pitches of measure 6 exactly as you did those at the end of measure 2, so that the B will have a more powerful impact.

MENDELSSOHN: PIANO SONATA IN E MAJOR, OP. 6, MVMT. 2

S15–2.

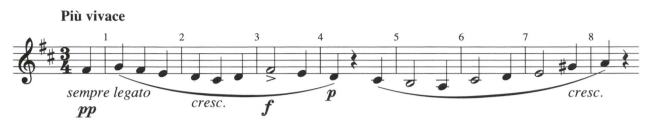

BEETHOVEN: STRING QUARTET NO. 14 IN C♯ MINOR, OP. 131, MVMT. 7

S15–3.

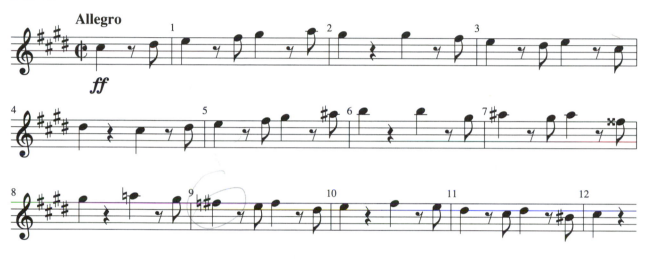

- When performing measures 6 and 7, think of a D♯ sounding below the melodic pitches. The applied dominant (D♯)-F𝄪-A♯ in measure 7 is preceded by a cadential $^6_4$.

BEETHOVEN: PIANO SONATA NO. 20 IN G MAJOR, OP. 49, NO. 2, MVMT. 2

S15–4.

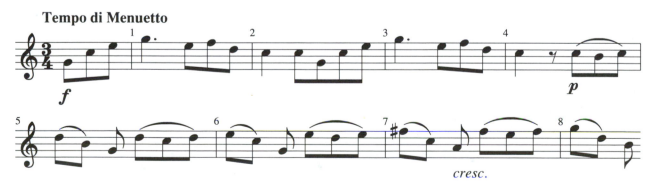

MELODIES THAT TONICIZE THE DOMINANT

BEETHOVEN: SYMPHONY NO. 2 IN D MAJOR, OP. 36, MVMT. 4

S15–5.

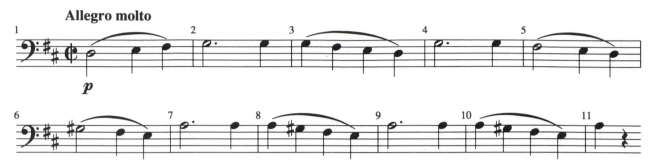

- For students who employ the Scale Degrees or Movable Do solmization system: When the melody begins, D functions as tonic. When it ends, A functions as tonic. At some point, you must shift from one tonal center to the other. Beat 1 of measure 5 is perhaps the best place to make this switch. F♯ (which would be sung as $\hat{3}$ or "mi" in D major) should be sung as $\hat{6}$ or "la" in A major. By converting to A major at this early point, you establish a good foundation for the following measures. For example, the downbeats of measures 5 through 7 are sung as "$\hat{6}$-$\hat{7}$-$\hat{8}$" or as "la-ti-do." The solmization for measures 1 through 7 is as follows:

Scale Degrees: $\hat{1}\ \hat{2}\ \hat{3}\ \hat{4}\ \hat{4}\ \hat{4}\ \hat{3}\ \hat{2}\ \hat{1}\ \hat{4}\ \hat{4}\ /\ \hat{6}\ \hat{5}\ \hat{4}\ \hat{7}\ \hat{6}\ \hat{5}\ \hat{8}\ \ldots$
Movable Do: do re mi fa fa fa mi re do fa fa / la sol fa ti la sol do . . .

SCHUBERT: OCTET IN F MAJOR FOR STRINGS AND WINDS, D. 803, OP. 166, MVMT. 6

S15–6.

BIZET: *CARMEN*, ACT 2

S15–7.

- This melody contains three segments of eight measures each (a ternary form: A-B-A). The outer segments are in the key of B♭ major. The middle segment is in the key of F major. Instead of gradual transitions with pivot chords, the keys are boldly juxtaposed.

- For students who employ the Scale Degrees or Movable Do solmization system: Sing measures 1 through 8 and 17 through 24 with reference to B♭ as tonic, and measures 9 through 16 with reference to F as tonic. The solmization for measures 7 through 9 is as follows:

Scale degrees:	$\hat{5}\ \hat{6}\ \hat{5}\ \hat{3}\ \hat{4}\ \hat{5}\ \hat{8}\ \hat{5}\ ^{\hat{3}\,\hat{3}\,\hat{2}}\hat{5}\ ^{\hat{2}\,\hat{1}} /\ \hat{5}\ \hat{6}\ \hat{5}\ \hat{4}\ \hat{3}\ \hat{2}\ \hat{1}\ \hat{2}\ ...$
Movable Do:	sol la sol mi fa sol do sol mi mi re sol re do / sol la sol fa mi re do re . . .

CHOPIN: MAZURKA, OP. 50, NO. 3

S15–8.

MELODIES IN $\frac{3}{8}$ METER

FIELD: NOCTURNE NO. 2

S15–9.

- Emphasize the second pitch in measures 3, 6, and 7 (A♭, D, and B♮). The C in measure 7 does not represent tonic, but instead connects D in measure 6 and B♮ in measure 7.

DVOŘÁK: SYMPHONY NO. 8 IN G MAJOR, OP. 88, MVMT. 3

S15–10.

SCHUBERT: SYMPHONY NO. 8 IN B MINOR ("UNFINISHED"), D. 759, MVMT. 2

S15–11.

- Measures 5 through 8 do in the context of B major exactly what measures 1 through 4 do in the context of E major. How does measure 7 relate to measure 3?

J. S. BACH: MASS IN B MINOR, BWV 232, GLORIA

S15–12.

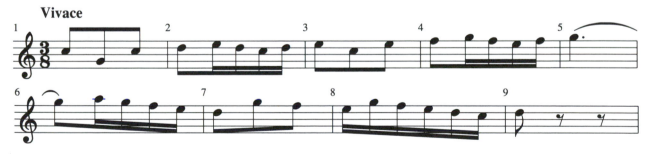

DUETS

AFTER HAYDN: SYMPHONY NO. 94 IN G MAJOR ("SURPRISE"), MVMT. 2

D15–1.

D15–2.

ACCOMPANIED SOLO MELODIES

AFTER MENDELSSOHN: SONG WITHOUT WORDS, OP. 85, NO. 2 (BOOK 7)

AS15–1.

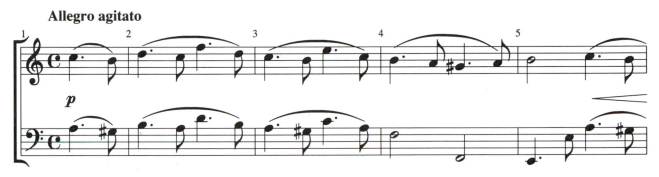

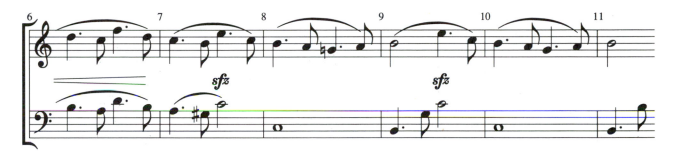

AFTER BRAHMS: SYMPHONY NO. 1 IN C MINOR, OP. 68, MVMT. 3

AS15–2.

Un poco Allegretto e grazioso

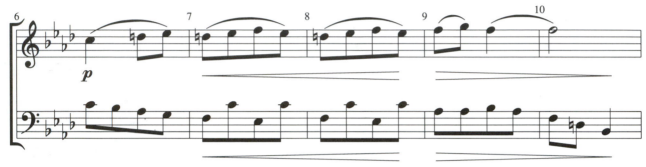

RHYTHMS

R15–1.

R15–2.

R15–3.

R15–4.

R15–5.

R15–6.

ARPEGGIATION WORKSHOP

A15–1.   Play a pitch that is low in your vocal range at a keyboard. Let this pitch be $\hat{1}$ in a major key. Sing each of the following arpeggiations, either in the order given or in random order.

a.	$\hat{1}$	$\hat{3}$	$\hat{5}$	$\hat{1}$	❊	$\hat{2}$	$\hat{\sharp4}$	$\hat{6}$	$\hat{\sharp4}$	❊	$\hat{5}$	$\hat{7}$	$^{\hat{2}}$	$\hat{7}$	❊	$\hat{8}$	$\hat{5}$	$\hat{3}$	$\hat{1}$
b.	$\hat{1}$	$\hat{3}$	$\hat{5}$	$\hat{1}$	❊	$\hat{2}$	$\hat{\sharp4}$	$\hat{6}$	$\hat{8}$	❊	$\hat{7}$	$^{\hat{2}}$	$\hat{7}$	$\hat{5}$	❊	$\hat{8}$	$\hat{5}$	$\hat{3}$	$\hat{1}$
c.	$\hat{1}$	$\hat{3}$	$\hat{5}$	$\hat{3}$	❊	$\hat{\sharp4}$	$\hat{6}$	$^{\hat{2}}$	$\hat{\sharp4}$	❊	$\hat{5}$	$\hat{7}$	$^{\hat{2}}$	$\hat{7}$	❊	$\hat{8}$	$\hat{5}$	$\hat{3}$	$\hat{1}$
d.	$\hat{1}$	$\hat{3}$	$\hat{5}$	$\hat{3}$	❊	$\hat{\sharp4}$	$\hat{6}$	$\hat{8}$	$^{\hat{2}}$	❊	$\hat{5}$	$\hat{7}$	$^{\hat{2}}$	$\hat{7}$	❊	$\hat{8}$	$\hat{5}$	$\hat{3}$	$\hat{1}$
e.	$\hat{1}$	$\hat{3}$	$\hat{5}$	$\hat{3}$	❊	$\hat{\sharp4}$	$\hat{6}$	$\hat{8}$	$^{\hat{2}}$	❊	$\hat{5}$	$\hat{8}$	$^{\hat{3}}$	$\hat{8}$	❊	$\hat{5}$	$\hat{7}$	$^{\hat{2}}$	$\hat{5}$
f.	$\hat{1}$	$\hat{3}$	$\hat{5}$	$\hat{3}$	❊	$\hat{4}$	$\hat{6}$	$\hat{8}$	$^{\hat{2}}$	❊	$\hat{\sharp4}$	$\hat{6}$	$\hat{8}$	$^{\hat{2}}$	❊	$\hat{5}$	$\hat{7}$	$^{\hat{2}}$	$\hat{5}$
g.	$\hat{1}$	$\hat{3}$	$\hat{5}$	$\hat{1}$	❊	$\hat{2}$	$\hat{\sharp4}$	$\hat{6}$	$^{\hat{2}}$	❊	$\hat{5}$	$\hat{7}$	$^{\hat{2}}$	$^{\hat{4}}$	❊	$^{\hat{3}}$	$\hat{8}$	$\hat{5}$	$\hat{1}$
h.	$\hat{1}$	$\hat{3}$	$\hat{5}$	$\hat{1}$	❊	$\hat{2}$	$\hat{\sharp4}$	$\hat{6}$	$\hat{8}$	❊	$\hat{7}$	$\hat{5}$	$^{\hat{2}}$	$^{\hat{4}}$	❊	$^{\hat{3}}$	$\hat{8}$	$\hat{5}$	$\hat{1}$
i.	$\hat{3}$	$\hat{5}$	$\hat{8}$	$\hat{3}$	❊	$\hat{4}$	$\hat{6}$	$\hat{8}$	$\hat{6}$	❊	$\hat{\sharp4}$	$\hat{6}$	$\hat{8}$	$^{\hat{2}}$	❊	$\hat{5}$	$\hat{7}$	$^{\hat{2}}$	$\hat{5}$
j.	$\hat{3}$	$\hat{5}$	$\hat{8}$	$\hat{5}$	❊	$\hat{6}$	$\hat{8}$	$^{\hat{\sharp4}}$	$\hat{6}$	❊	$\hat{5}$	$\hat{8}$	$^{\hat{3}}$	$^{\hat{5}}$	❊	$\hat{5}$	$\hat{7}$	$^{\hat{2}}$	$\hat{5}$

A15–2.   Play a pitch that is at least a diminished fifth above the lowest note of your vocal range at a keyboard. Let this pitch be $\hat{1}$ in a minor key. Sing each of the following arpeggiations, either in the order given or in random order.

a. $\hat{1}$ $\hat{3}$ $\hat{5}$ $\hat{1}$ ❀ $\hat{2}$ $\sharp\hat{4}$ $\sharp\hat{6}$ $\sharp\hat{4}$ ❀ $\hat{5}$ $\hat{2}$ $\flat\hat{7}$ $\hat{5}$ ❀ $\hat{1}$ $\hat{5}$ $\hat{3}$ $\hat{1}$

b. $\hat{1}$ $\hat{3}$ $\hat{5}$ $\hat{1}$ ❀ $\sharp\hat{4}$ $\sharp\hat{6}$ $\hat{2}$ $\sharp\hat{4}$ ❀ $\hat{5}$ $\flat\hat{7}$ $\hat{2}$ $\flat\hat{7}$ ❀ $\hat{1}$ $\hat{5}$ $\hat{3}$ $\hat{1}$

c. $\hat{1}$ $\hat{3}$ $\hat{5}$ $\hat{1}$ ❀ $\sharp\hat{4}$ $\sharp\hat{6}$ $\hat{1}$ $\hat{2}$ ❀ $\hat{5}$ $\hat{1}$ $\hat{3}$ $\hat{5}$ ❀ $\hat{5}$ $\flat\hat{7}$ $\hat{2}$ $\hat{5}$

d. $\hat{1}$ $\hat{3}$ $\hat{5}$ $\hat{1}$ ❀ $\sharp\hat{4}$ $\sharp\hat{6}$ $\hat{2}$ $\sharp\hat{4}$ ❀ $\hat{5}$ $\hat{4}$ $\hat{2}$ $\flat\hat{7}$ ❀ $\hat{1}$ $\hat{5}$ $\hat{3}$ $\hat{1}$

e. $\hat{1}$ $\hat{3}$ $\hat{5}$ $\hat{1}$ ❀ $\sharp\hat{4}$ $\sharp\hat{6}$ $\hat{1}$ $\hat{2}$ ❀ $\hat{5}$ $\flat\hat{7}$ $\hat{2}$ $\hat{4}$ ❀ $\hat{3}$ $\hat{1}$ $\hat{5}$ $\hat{1}$

f. $\hat{1}$ $\hat{3}$ $\hat{5}$ $\hat{1}$ ❀ $\sharp\hat{6}$ $\hat{1}$ $\sharp\hat{4}$ $\sharp\hat{6}$ ❀ $\hat{5}$ $\hat{1}$ $\hat{3}$ $\hat{5}$ ❀ $\hat{5}$ $\flat\hat{7}$ $\hat{2}$ $\hat{5}$

g. $\hat{1}$ $\hat{3}$ $\hat{5}$ $\hat{1}$ ❀ $\sharp\hat{4}$ $\sharp\hat{6}$ $\hat{1}$ $\sharp\hat{6}$ ❀ $\hat{5}$ $\flat\hat{7}$ $\hat{2}$ $\hat{4}$ ❀ $\hat{3}$ $\hat{1}$ $\hat{5}$ $\hat{1}$

h. $\hat{1}$ $\hat{3}$ $\hat{5}$ $\hat{1}$ ❀ $\hat{6}$ $\hat{1}$ $\hat{3}$ $\hat{6}$ ❀ $\sharp\hat{4}$ $\sharp\hat{6}$ $\hat{1}$ $\hat{2}$ ❀ $\hat{5}$ $\flat\hat{7}$ $\hat{2}$ $\hat{5}$

QUICK SWITCH

Q15–1.

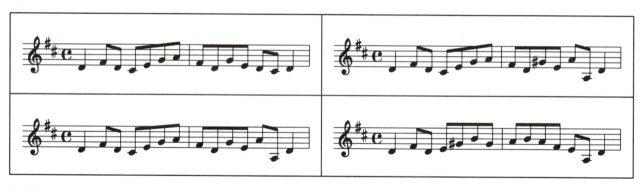

Q15–2.

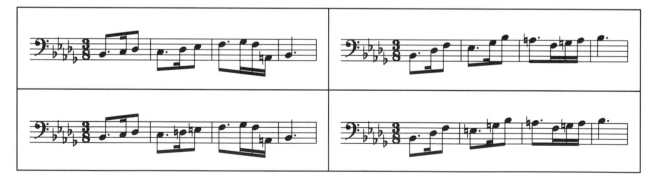

Q15–3.

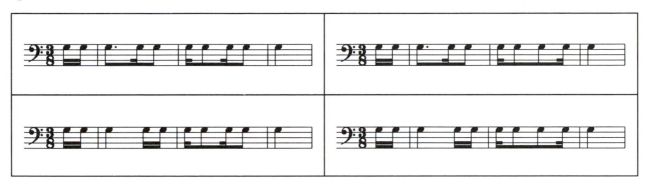

Q15–4.

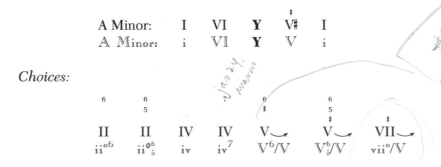

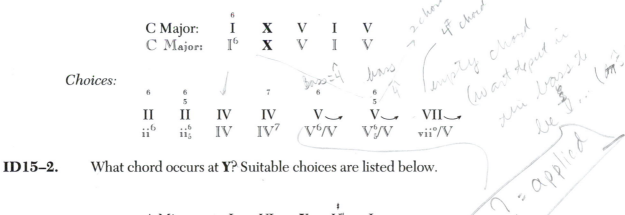

IDENTIFICATIONS

ID15–1.   What chord occurs at **X**? Suitable choices are listed below.

C Major:	I	**X**	V	I	V
C Major:	I⁶	**X**	V	I	V

Choices:

II	II	IV	IV	V	V	VII
ii⁶	ii₅⁶	IV	IV⁷	V⁶/V	V₅⁶/V	vii°/V

ID15–2.   What chord occurs at **Y**? Suitable choices are listed below.

A Minor:	I	VI	**Y**	V♯	I
A Minor:	i	VI	**Y**	V	i

Choices:

II	II	IV	IV	V	V	VII
ii°⁶	iiø₅⁶	iv	iv⁷	V⁶/V	V₅⁶/V	vii°/V

ID15–3.   A melody is performed. Identify the correct score notation.

ID15–4.   A chord progression in the major mode is performed. Identify a suitable Roman-numeral/figured-bass analysis from among the following choices:

Group 1

a.   I   II$^{6}_{5}$ V$^{8-7}$ I   V^{6} I   a.   I   ii$^{6}_{5}$ V$^{8-7}$ I   V$^{6}_{5}$ I

b.   I   V$^{6}_{5}$ V   I   V$^{6}_{5}$ I   b.   I   V$^{6}_{5}$/V   V$^{8-7}$ I   V$^{6}_{5}$ I

c.   I   II^{6} V$^{8-7}$ I   V$^{6}_{5}$ I   c.   I   ii^{6} V$^{8-7}$ I   V$^{6}_{5}$ I

d.   I   V^{6} V   I   V$^{6}_{5}$ I   d.   I   V^{6}/V   V$^{8-7}$ I   V$^{6}_{5}$ I

Group 2

a.   I   V$^{6}_{\sharp 5}$ V   I   V^{6} I   a.   I^{6} V^{7}/V   V$^{6}_{5}$ I   V$^{8-7}$ I

b.   I   II^{6} V$^{7}_{5}$ I   V$^{8-7}$ I   b.   I^{6} ii^{7} V$^{6}_{5}$ I   V$^{8-7}$ I

c.   I   V$^{6}_{\sharp}$ V   I   V$^{6}_{5}$ I   c.   I^{6} V/V   V$^{6}_{5}$ I   V$^{8-7}$ I

d.   I   II^{6} V$^{6}_{5}$ I   V$^{8-7}$ I   d.   I^{6} ii   V$^{6}_{5}$ I   V$^{8-7}$ I

ID15–5.   A chord progression in the minor mode is performed. Identify a suitable Roman-numeral/figured-bass analysis from among the following choices:

Group 1

a.   V$^{6}_{\sharp}$ I   IV$^{6}_{\sharp}$ V$^{6}_{5}$ I   V$^{7}_{\sharp}$ I   a.   V^{6} i   IV^{6} V$^{6}_{5}$ i   V^{7} i

b.   V$^{6}_{\sharp}$ I   VII$^{6\sharp}$ V$^{6}_{5\sharp}$ I   V$^{7}_{\sharp}$ I   b.   V^{6} i   vii$^{\circ 6}$/V   V$^{6}_{5}$ i   V^{7} i

c.   V$^{6}_{\sharp}$ I   IV$^{6\sharp}$ V$^{6}_{\sharp}$ I   V$^{7}_{\sharp}$ I   c.   V^{6} i   IV^{6} V^{6} i   V^{7} i

d.   V$^{6}_{\sharp}$ I   VII^{6} V$^{6}_{\sharp}$ I   V$^{7}_{\sharp}$ I   d.   V^{6} i   vii$^{\circ 6}$/V   V^{6} i   V^{7} i

<u>Group 2</u>

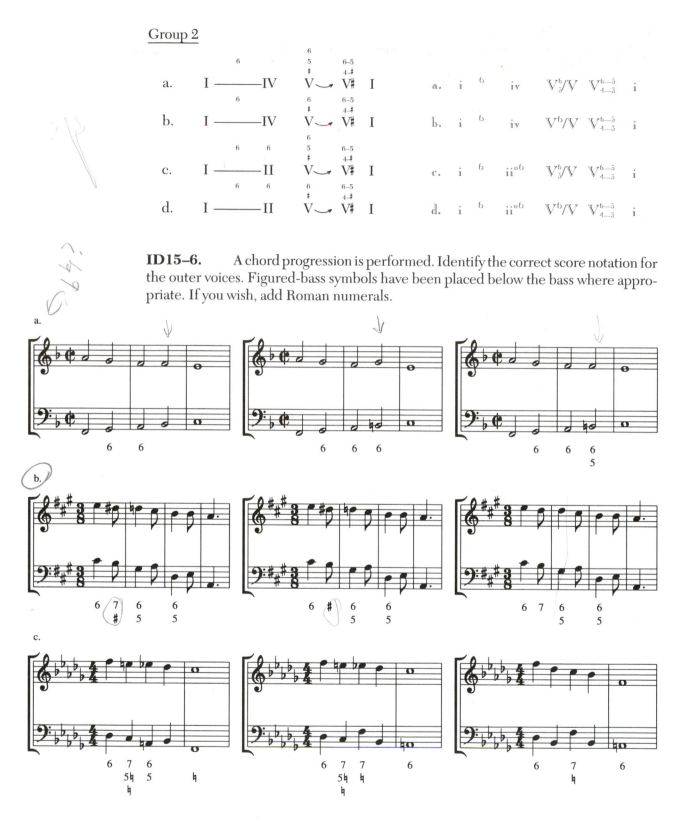

ID15–6.   A chord progression is performed. Identify the correct score notation for the outer voices. Figured-bass symbols have been placed below the bass where appropriate. If you wish, add Roman numerals.

d.

e.

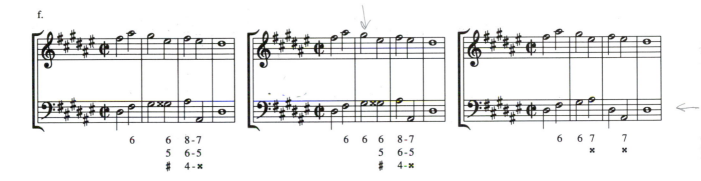

f.

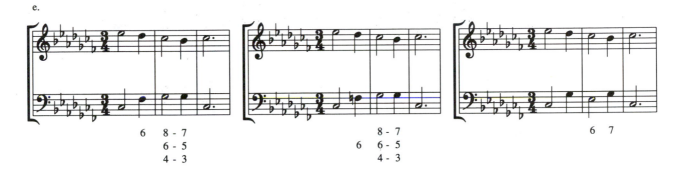

RHYTHMIC DICTATIONS

RD15–1.

RD15–2.

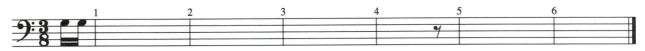

MELODIC DICTATIONS

J. S. BACH: WELL-TEMPERED CLAVIER, VOL. 1, FUGUE 11, BWV 856

MD15–1.

- The diminished fifth E–B♭ is outlined from beat 2 of measure 2 through beat 1 of measure 3. Listen for its resolution in measure 4.

TCHAIKOVSKY: SYMPHONY NO. 2 IN C MINOR ("LITTLE RUSSIAN"), OP. 17, MVMT. 3

 **MD15–2.**

Allegro molto vivace

- An ascending minor second occurs at the beginning of each measure from measure 2 through measure 6. Which are diatonic and which are chromatic? Two sharps are required.

TCHAIKOVSKY: SYMPHONY NO. 3 IN D MAJOR ("POLISH"), OP. 29, MVMT. 4

MD15–3.

Allegro vivo

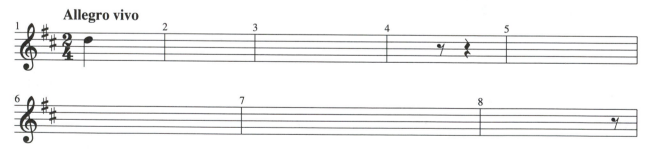

- Which sharp is in the key signature of F♯ minor (the dominant key) but not in that of B minor? Which sharps are used for ♯$\hat{6}$ and ♯$\hat{7}$ in F♯ minor? All three sharps are required for this excerpt.

J. S. BACH: SUITE FOR UNACCOMPANIED CELLO NO. 4 IN E♭ MAJOR, BWV 1010, COURANTE

MD15–4.

- Measures 3 and 4 should be much easier to write down than measures 1 and 2. Why?

J. S. BACH: BRANDENBURG CONCERTO NO. 3 IN G MAJOR, BWV 1048, MVMT. 1

MD15–5.

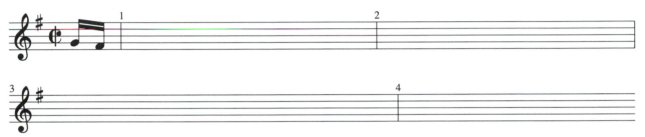

- In what context does Bach employ C as lower neighbor to D? In what context does he instead employ C♯?

BEETHOVEN: PIANO SONATA NO. 18 IN E♭ MAJOR, OP. 31, NO. 3, MVMT. 1

MD15–6.

- What chord is arpeggiated by the four pitches on the beats from beat 1 of measure 5 through beat 1 of measure 6?

- What is the function of the fourth pitch in measure 6 and the fourth pitch in measure 7?

HARMONIC DICTATIONS

MOZART: PIANO SONATA NO. 11 IN A MAJOR, K. 331, MVMT. 2

HD15–1.

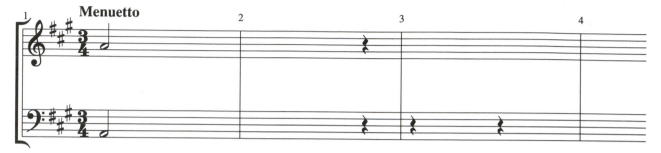

- Interpret all of measure 1 and 2 as tonic in $\frac{5}{3}$ position.

BEETHOVEN: PIANO SONATA NO. 23 IN F MINOR ("APPASSIONATA"), OP. 57, MVMT. 3

HD15–2.

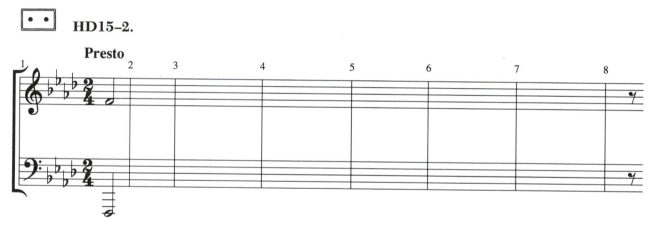

- The applied dominant in measure 7 is preceded by a cadential $\frac{6}{4}$.

- Given what you hear in measure 7, do you interpret the chord of measure 8 as major or minor? The "chord" consists of only the root, doubled at the octave.

SCHUBERT: MENUET, D. 995, NO. 2

HD15–3.

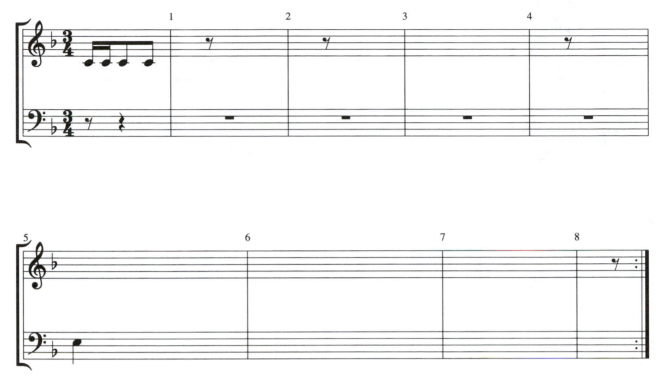

- You might interpret the first bass pitch of measure 5 as the structural bass for the entire measure. Or you could use the figured bass $^4_3$ (to be introduced in chapter 18) for beat 2 of that measure. Whichever method you choose, make sure that your analysis of measure 6 is consistent with that of measure 5.

MOZART: *THE MAGIC FLUTE*, K. 620, ACT 2

HD15–4.

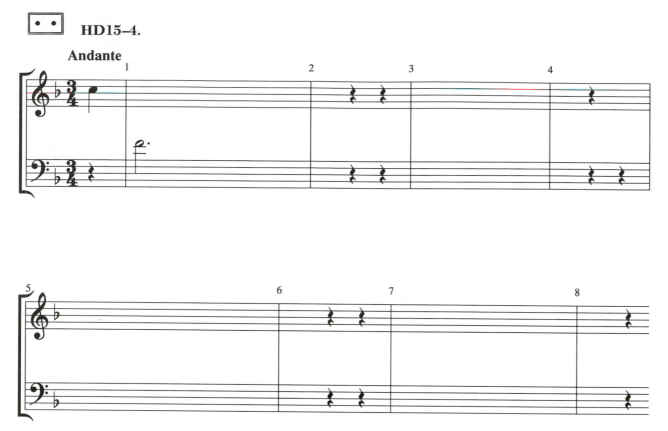

- The harmonic progression is shaped by a descending bass line. To better understand that shape, observe how the following bass pitches relate: measure 1, beat 1; measure 4, beat 1; measure 6, beat 1; measure 7, beat 2; and measure 8, beat 1.

HD15–5.

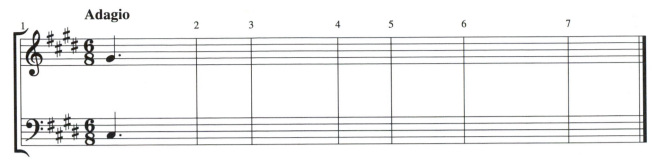

· The major dominant in the key of C♯ minor is G♯ major. There is no key signature for G♯ major, because its scale (G♯ A♯ B♯ C♯ D♯ E♯ F✗ G♯) requires a double sharp. V of V in C♯ minor is V in the key of G♯ major and thus is made from pitches of that scale.

MOZART: PIANO CONCERTO NO. 19 IN F MAJOR, K. 459, MVMT. 3

HD15–6.

Allegro assai

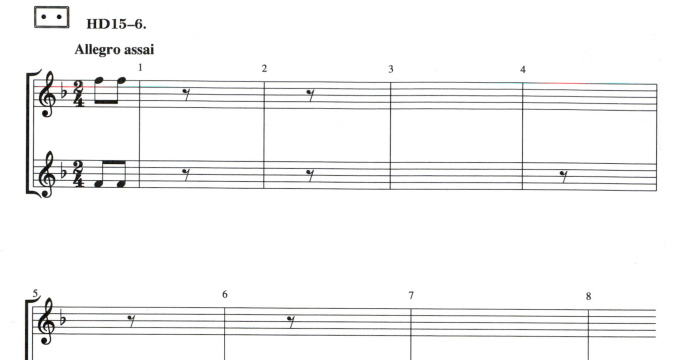

· Both phrases of this excerpt end with a C major chord. C's leading tone, B, precedes both of these chords. Which of the two cadences sounds like a half cadence in the key of F major? Which sounds like an authentic cadence in the key of C major?

⊡ CASSETTE PROGRAM
(TAPE 3, SIDE A)

C15–1.   Six melodies are performed, twice each. During the silence after each playing, respond in one of the following ways: (1) Sing the melody, using solmization syllables; (2) Play the melody on the piano or on your primary instrument; (3) Write the melody on staff paper.

C15–2.   Six chord progressions are performed, four times each. During the silence after each playing, respond in one of the following ways: (1) Sing the soprano after the first and second playings and the bass after the third and fourth playings, using solmization syllables; (2) Play the soprano on the piano or your primary instrument after the first and second playings and the bass after the third and fourth playings; (3) Play both the soprano and bass on the piano after each playing; (4) Write the soprano and bass on staff paper and provide an analysis.

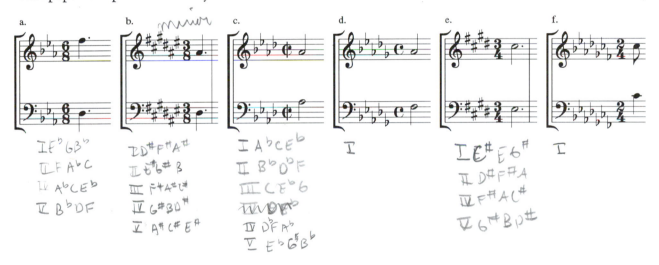

Chapter 16

PITCH

$^6_4$ *position* (usually abbreviated to $^4_2$) is the third inversion of $^7_5$ position. Its bass, the "seventh" of the $^7_5$ position, usually resolves downward by step, as in Example 16–1. Focus your listening especially on the bass, which behaves differently in the progression from each of the three positions of the seventh chord introduced thus far: from $^7_5$ position, the bass generally leaps an ascending fourth or descending fifth; from $^6_5$ position, it generally ascends by step; from $^6_4$ position, it generally descends by step.

EXAMPLE 16–1

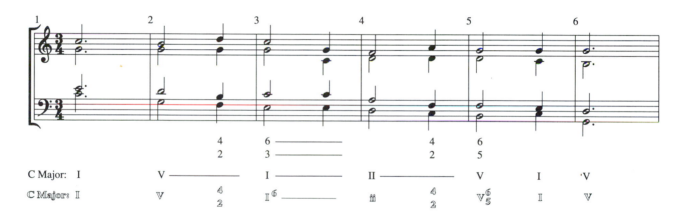

When a cadential $^6_4$ is followed by a dominant $^4_2$, as shown in Example 16–2, its cadential effect is weakened. Tonic $^6_3$—not $^5_3$—generally follows dominant $^4_2$ because the dissonant bass $\hat{4}$ resolves downward *by step* to $\hat{3}$. Occasionally the root of the dominant $^4_2$ (G in Ex. 16–2) is omitted when a $^4_2$ follows the cadential $^6_4$.

The sixth and fourth in a cadential $^6_4$ chord *displace* members of the harmony. Even when the $^6_4$ resolves to the dominant $^4_2$, the sixth and fourth give way to pitches of the dominant harmony (E♭ to D and C to B♮ in Example 16–2). In a ***consonant*** $^6_4$ ***chord***, in contrast, the sixth and fourth *belong to* the harmony. The consonant $^6_4$ is a genuine second inversion. The fourth above the bass is the chord's root. The consonant $^6_4$ often occurs in close proximity to $^5_3$ and $^6_3$ chords with the same root, as in Example 16–3.

EXAMPLE 16–2

EXAMPLE 16–3

In both major and minor keys, $\hat{1}$ and $\hat{2}$ are separated by a whole step. Chromatic passing and neighboring notes often fill that space, as they do the space between $\hat{4}$ and $\hat{5}$. Although the spelling $\sharp\hat{1}$ is more common than $\flat\hat{2}$, both are employed. Example 16–4 demonstrates the use of $\sharp\hat{1}$.[1]

---

1. The use of chromatic pitches such as $\sharp\hat{1}$ to form applied chords will be introduced beginning in chapter 21.

EXAMPLE 16–4

MOZART: *THE MAGIC FLUTE*, K. 620, ACT 2

METER AND RHYTHM

$\frac{2}{2}$ and $\frac{2}{4}$ meters differ only in the note value that represents the beat. In $\frac{2}{2}$ meter, the half note represents the beat; in $\frac{2}{4}$ meter, the quarter note represents the beat. Likewise, $\frac{3}{2}$ ***and*** $\frac{4}{2}$ ***meters*** differ from $\frac{3}{4}$ and $\frac{4}{4}$ meters, respectively, only in that the half note, rather than the quarter note, represents the beat. Two new symbols of notation are employed in Example 16–5: the ***double whole note*** (𝅜), which fills four beats in $\frac{4}{2}$ meter, and the ***double whole rest*** (▬), which fills a full measure in $\frac{4}{2}$ meter. (An entire measure of rest in $\frac{3}{2}$ meter is written using a conventional whole rest.) The dotted whole note, also employed in $\frac{6}{4}$ meter, fills three beats in $\frac{3}{2}$ or $\frac{4}{2}$ meter.

EXAMPLE 16–5

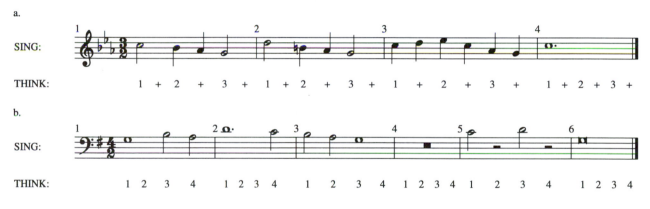

SOLO MELODIES

SCALE DEGREES: *Sing "raised" for* #$\hat{1}$ *and "low" (a single-syllable abbreviation for "lowered") for* ♭$\hat{2}$.

MOVABLE DO (DO TONIC IN MINOR): *Sing "di" for* #$\hat{1}$ *and "ra" for* ♭$\hat{2}$.

MOVABLE DO (LA TONIC IN MINOR): *In any major key, sing "di" for* #$\hat{1}$ *and "ra" for* ♭$\hat{2}$. *In any minor key, sing "li" for* #$\hat{1}$ *and "te" for* ♭$\hat{2}$.

FIXED DO: *Sing "raf" for D♭♭, "mef" for E♭♭, "lef" for A♭♭, "lis" for A𝄪, and "tef" for B♭♭.*

LETTER NAMES: *Sing "Deses" for D♭♭, "Eses" for E♭♭, "Ases" for A♭♭, "Aisis" for A𝄪, and "Beses" for B♭♭.*

MELODIES THAT OUTLINE A CHORD IN $\frac{4}{2}$ POSITION

WEBER: CLARINET CONCERTO NO. 1 IN F MINOR, OP. 73, MVMT. 1

S16–1.

- All the pitches of the dominant seventh chord occur within measures 4 through 6. At the end of measure 6 the dominant's seventh, C, is transferred an octave lower ($\frac{4}{2}$ position) and resolves downward by step to B♭ in measure 7.

MOZART: SYMPHONY NO. 40 IN G MINOR, K. 550, MVMT. 1

S16–2.

MELODIES THAT EMPLOY ♯î OR ♭2̂

SCHUBERT: STRING QUARTET NO. 15 IN G MAJOR, D. 887, OP. 161, MVMT. 4

S16–3.

- The D♮s in measures 13 and 14 are especially potent because of D♯'s prominence earlier in the excerpt.

MOZART: *THE MAGIC FLUTE*, K. 620, ACT 2

S16–4.

BEETHOVEN: SYMPHONY NO. 3 IN E♭ MAJOR ("EROICA"), OP. 55, MVMT. 4

S16–5.

- The last eight pitches pair up to form four ascending half steps. D-E♭, which occurs twice, is diatonic; E♮-F and A♮-B♭ are chromatic. In each case, the second pitch of the pair plays the more fundamental structural role, while the first pitch is the more flamboyant, more interesting one.

SCHUBERT: STRING QUARTET NO. 13 IN A MINOR, D. 804, OP. 29, MVMT. 2

S16–6.

MOZART: *DON GIOVANNI*, K. 527, OVERTURE

S16–7.

- Though measures 5 through 7 contain faster and more notes than the preceding measures, they continue the pattern of descending seconds (G-F♯ and B-A) in measures 3 and 4.

MOZART: SYMPHONY NO. 36 IN C MAJOR ("LINZ"), K. 425, MVMT. 3

S16–8.

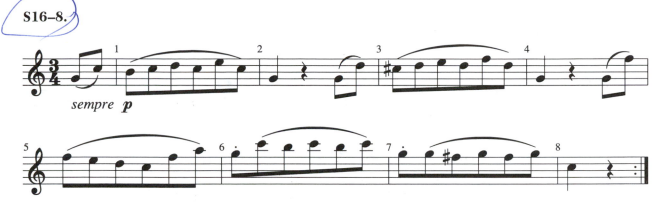

sempre **p**

MOZART: *THE MAGIC FLUTE*, K. 620, ACT 1

S16–9.

Andante

- In measure 1, F♯ (♯$\hat{4}$) embellishes the fifth of the tonic triad. In measure 2, C♯ (♯$\hat{1}$) embellishes the fifth of the dominant triad.

- An ascending arpeggiation of the supertonic (A-D-F) occurs in both measures 3 and 7. In measure 7, the arpeggiation is filled in with passing notes (including the chromatic passing note C♯).

FIELD: NOCTURNE NO. 15 IN C MAJOR

S16–10.

p   **f**   **p**

BRAHMS: PIANO TRIO NO. 3 IN C MINOR, OP. 101, MVMT. 4

S16–11.

- Although C♯ in measure 6 might at first seem to function as ♯$\hat{1}$ in the key of C minor, it would be better to think of it as ♯$\hat{4}$ in the tonicized key of G minor.

BIZET: *CARMEN*, ACT 1

S16–12.

MELODIES IN $\frac{3}{2}$ OR $\frac{4}{2}$ METER

TCHAIKOVSKY: "THE BATTLE OF POLTAVA" FROM *MAZEPPA*, ACT 3

S16–13.

· Breathe after the first E♭ in measure 6.

S16–14.

DUETS

D16–1.

D16–2.

ACCOMPANIED SOLO MELODIES

AFTER SCHUBERT: *SCHWANENGESANG*, D. 957, "AUFENTHALT"

AS16–1.

RHYTHMS

ARPEGGIATION WORKSHOP

A16–1.   Play a pitch that is low in your vocal range at a keyboard. Let this pitch be $\hat{1}$ in a major key. Sing each of the following arpeggiations, either in the order given or in random order.

a. $\hat{1}$ $\hat{3}$ $\hat{5}$ $\hat{1}$ ✿ $\hat{4}$ $\hat{6}$ $\hat{8}$ $\hat{6}$ ✿ $\hat{4}$ $\hat{5}$ $\hat{7}$ $\hat{2}$ ✿ $\hat{3}$ $\hat{5}$ $\hat{8}$ $\hat{3}$

b. $\hat{1}$ $\hat{3}$ $\hat{5}$ $\hat{1}$ ✿ $\hat{4}$ $\hat{6}$ $\hat{2}$ $\hat{6}$ ✿ $\hat{4}$ $\hat{5}$ $\hat{7}$ $\hat{2}$ ✿ $\hat{3}$ $\hat{5}$ $\hat{8}$ $\hat{3}$

c. $\hat{3}$ $\hat{5}$ $\hat{8}$ $\hat{3}$ ✿ $\sharp\hat{4}$ $\hat{6}$ $\hat{2}$ $\hat{6}$ ✿ $\hat{4}$ $\hat{5}$ $\hat{7}$ $\hat{2}$ ✿ $\hat{3}$ $\hat{5}$ $\hat{8}$ $\hat{3}$

d. $\hat{3}$ $\hat{5}$ $\hat{8}$ $\hat{3}$ ✿ $\sharp\hat{4}$ $\hat{6}$ $\hat{8}$ $\hat{2}$ ✿ $\hat{4}$ $\hat{5}$ $\hat{7}$ $\hat{2}$ ✿ $\hat{3}$ $\hat{5}$ $\hat{8}$ $\hat{3}$

e. $\hat{1}$ $\hat{3}$ $\hat{5}$ $\hat{3}$ ✿ $\hat{1}$ $\hat{2}$ $\hat{4}$ $\hat{6}$ ✿ $\hat{7}$ $\hat{2}$ $\hat{4}$ $\hat{5}$ ✿ $\hat{1}$ $\hat{3}$ $\hat{5}$ $\hat{1}$

f. $\hat{1}$ $\hat{3}$ $\hat{5}$ $\hat{3}$ ✿ $\hat{1}$ $\hat{2}$ $\sharp\hat{4}$ $\hat{6}$ ✿ $\hat{7}$ $\hat{2}$ $\hat{4}$ $\hat{5}$ ✿ $\hat{1}$ $\hat{3}$ $\hat{5}$ $\hat{1}$

g. $\hat{1}$ $\hat{3}$ $\hat{5}$ $\hat{8}$ ✿ $\hat{6}$ $\hat{8}$ $\hat{3}$ $\hat{4}$ ✿ $\hat{5}$ $\hat{8}$ $\hat{3}$ $\hat{8}$ ✿

   $\hat{4}$ $\hat{5}$ $\hat{7}$ $\hat{2}$ ✿ $\hat{3}$ $\hat{5}$ $\hat{8}$ $\hat{3}$

h. $\hat{1}$ $\hat{3}$ $\hat{5}$ $\hat{8}$ ✿ $\hat{5}$ $\hat{7}$ $\hat{2}$ $\hat{5}$ ✿ $\hat{2}$ $\hat{5}$ $\hat{7}$ $\hat{2}$ ✿

   $\hat{7}$ $\hat{2}$ $\hat{5}$ $\hat{7}$ ✿ $\hat{1}$ $\hat{3}$ $\hat{5}$ $\hat{1}$

A16–2.   Play a pitch that is low in your vocal range at a keyboard. Let this pitch be $\hat{1}$ in a minor key. Sing each of the following arpeggiations, either in the order given or in random order.

a. $\hat{1}$ $\hat{3}$ $\hat{5}$ $\hat{1}$ ✿ $\hat{4}$ $\hat{6}$ $\hat{8}$ $\hat{6}$ ✿ $\hat{4}$ $\hat{5}$ $\sharp\hat{7}$ $\hat{2}$ ✿ $\hat{3}$ $\hat{5}$ $\hat{8}$ $\hat{3}$

b. $\hat{1}$ $\hat{3}$ $\hat{5}$ $\hat{1}$ ✿ $\hat{4}$ $\hat{6}$ $\hat{2}$ $\hat{6}$ ✿ $\hat{4}$ $\hat{5}$ $\sharp\hat{7}$ $\hat{2}$ ✿ $\hat{3}$ $\hat{5}$ $\hat{8}$ $\hat{3}$

c. $\hat{3}$ $\hat{5}$ $\hat{8}$ $\hat{5}$ ✿ $\sharp\hat{4}$ $\sharp\hat{6}$ $\hat{2}$ $\sharp\hat{6}$ ✿ $\hat{4}$ $\hat{5}$ $\sharp\hat{7}$ $\hat{2}$ ✿ $\hat{3}$ $\hat{5}$ $\hat{8}$ $\hat{3}$

d. $\hat{3}$ $\hat{5}$ $\hat{8}$ $\hat{5}$ ✿ $\sharp\hat{4}$ $\sharp\hat{6}$ $\hat{8}$ $\hat{2}$ ✿ $\hat{4}$ $\hat{5}$ $\sharp\hat{7}$ $\hat{2}$ ✿ $\hat{3}$ $\hat{5}$ $\hat{8}$ $\hat{3}$

e. $\hat{1}$ $\hat{3}$ $\hat{5}$ $\hat{3}$ ✿ $\hat{1}$ $\hat{2}$ $\hat{4}$ $\hat{6}$ ✿ $\sharp\hat{7}$ $\hat{2}$ $\hat{4}$ $\hat{5}$ ✿ $\hat{1}$ $\hat{3}$ $\hat{5}$ $\hat{1}$

f. $\hat{1}$ $\hat{3}$ $\hat{5}$ $\hat{3}$ ✿ $\hat{1}$ $\hat{2}$ $\sharp\hat{4}$ $\sharp\hat{6}$ ✿ $\sharp\hat{7}$ $\hat{2}$ $\hat{4}$ $\hat{5}$ ✿ $\hat{1}$ $\hat{3}$ $\hat{5}$ $\hat{1}$

g. $\hat{1}$ $\hat{3}$ $\hat{5}$ $\hat{8}$ ✿ $\hat{6}$ $\hat{8}$ $\hat{3}$ $\hat{4}$ ✿ $\hat{5}$ $\hat{8}$ $\hat{3}$ $\hat{8}$ ✿

   $\hat{4}$ $\hat{5}$ $\sharp\hat{7}$ $\hat{2}$ ✿ $\hat{3}$ $\hat{5}$ $\hat{8}$ $\hat{3}$

h. $\hat{1}$ $\hat{3}$ $\hat{5}$ $\hat{8}$ ✿ $\hat{5}$ $\sharp\hat{7}$ $\hat{2}$ $\hat{5}$ ✿ $\hat{2}$ $\hat{5}$ $\sharp\hat{7}$ $\hat{2}$ ✿

   $\sharp\hat{7}$ $\hat{2}$ $\hat{5}$ $\sharp\hat{7}$ ✿ $\hat{1}$ $\hat{3}$ $\hat{5}$ $\hat{1}$

QUICK SWITCH

Q16–1.

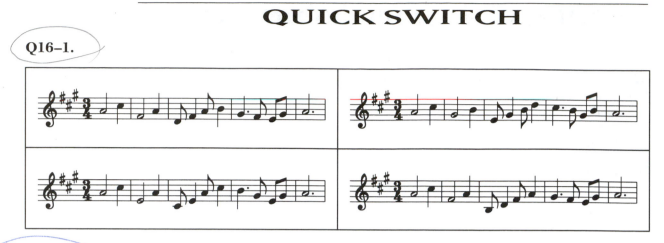

Q16–2.

Q16–3.

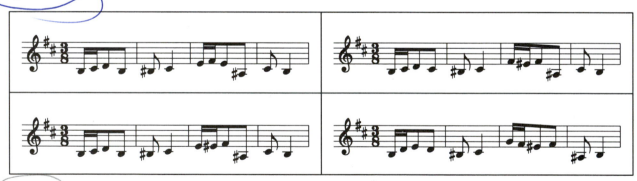

Q16–4.

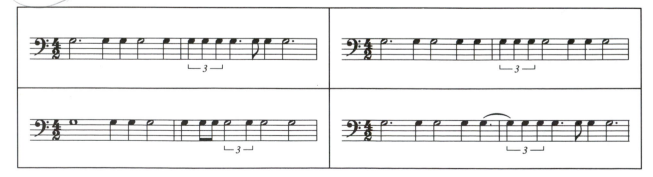

IDENTIFICATIONS

ID16–1.   A chord is performed. Identify its position from among the following choices: $\frac{5}{3}$, $\frac{6}{3}$, $\frac{6}{4}$, 7, $\frac{6}{5}$, or $\frac{4}{2}$.

ID16–2.   What chords occur at **X** and **Y**? Suitable choices are listed below.

C Major:	I	II^6	V	**X**	**Y**
C Major:	I^6	ii^6	V	**X**	**Y**

*Choices for **X**:*

V	V^6	V^7	V$^6_5$	V$^4_2$
V	V^6	V^7	V$^6_5$	V$^4_2$

*Choices for **Y**:*

I	I^6	IV^6	VI
I	I^6	IV^6	vi

ID16–3.   What chord occurs at **Z**? Suitable choices are listed below.

A Minor:	I	**Z**	I^6	II^6	V♯^{7}	I
A Minor:	i	**Z**	i^6	ii°^{6}	V^7	i

Choices:

I$^6_4$	IV^6	V♯$^♯$	V♯$^{4♯}_2$	VI	♯VII$^{6♯}_3$
i$^6_4$	iv^6	V	V$^4_2$	VI	vii°^{6}

ID16–4.   A melody is performed. Identify the correct score notation.

ID16–5. A chord progression in the major mode is performed. Identify a suitable Roman-numeral/figured-bass analysis from among the following choices:

Group 1

a. I VI V$\underset{2}{\overset{4}{\rule{2em}{0.4pt}}}$ I^6 V^7 I   a. I vi V $^4_2$ I^6 V^7 I

b. I VI^6 V$\underset{2}{\overset{4}{\rule{2em}{0.4pt}}}$ I^6 V^7 I   b. I vi V$^6_4$ $^4_2$ I^6 V^7 I

c. I IV^6 V$\underset{2}{\overset{4}{\rule{2em}{0.4pt}}}$ I^6 V^7 I   c. I IV^6 V $^4_2$ I^6 V^7 I

d. I IV V$\underset{2}{\overset{4}{\rule{2em}{0.4pt}}}$ I^6 V^7 I   d. I IV^6 V$^6_4$ $^4_2$ I^6 V^7 I

Group 2

a. I II$^4_2$ V$^6_5$ I IV^6 V$\overset{7}{\sharp}$⌣ V   a. I ii$^4_2$ V$^6_5$ I IV^6 V^7/V V

b. I IV^6 V$^6_5$ I IV^6 V$\overset{7}{\sharp}$⌣ V   b. I IV^6 V$^6_5$ I IV^6 V^7/V V

c. I V$^{4\sharp}_{2}$⌣ V I IV^6 V$\overset{7}{\sharp}$⌣ V   c. I V$^4_2$/V V^6 I IV^6 V^7/V V

d. I V$^{4\sharp}_{2}$⌣ V I IV^6 V$\overset{7}{\sharp}$⌣ V   d. I V$^4_2$/V V$^6_5$ I IV^6 V^7/V V

ID16–6. A chord progression in the minor mode is performed. Identify a suitable Roman-numeral/figured-bass analysis from among the following choices:

Group 1

a. I $\overset{6}{\rule{2em}{0.4pt}}$ IV $\overset{6}{\rule{2em}{0.4pt}}$ V$\sharp\,^{8-7}_{6-5}_{4-\sharp}$ I   a. i^6 iv^6 V$^{8-7}_{6-5}_{4-3}$ i

b. I $\overset{6}{\rule{2em}{0.4pt}}$ IV $\overset{6}{\rule{2em}{0.4pt}}$ V$\sharp\,^{6-5}_{4-\sharp}$ I   b. i^6 iv^6 V$^{6-5}_{4-3}$ i

c. I $\overset{6}{\rule{2em}{0.4pt}}$ IV $\overset{6}{\rule{2em}{0.4pt}}$ V$\sharp\,^{6}_{4}$$^{4\sharp}_{2}$ I   c. i^6 iv^6 V$^6_4$ $^4_2$ i^6

d. I$\overset{6}{\rule{2em}{0.4pt}}$$\overset{6}{\underset{4}{}}$$\overset{5}{\underset{3}{}}$ V$\sharp\,^{6}_{4}$$^{4\sharp}_{2}$ I   d. i^6 $^6_4$ $^5_3$ V$^6_4$ $^4_2$ i^6

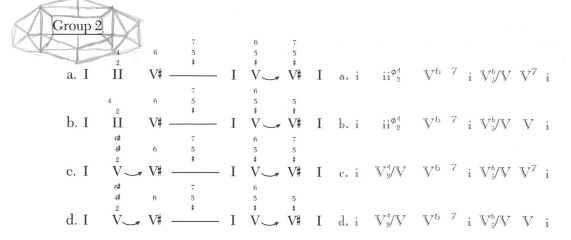

$$
\begin{array}{l}
\text{a. I \quad II \quad } V\sharp \underset{\substack{4\\2}}{\overset{}{\rule{0pt}{0pt}}} \underset{6}{\rule{0pt}{0pt}} \overset{7}{\underset{\substack{5\\\sharp}}{\rule{0pt}{0pt}}} \text{I \quad V} \smile V\sharp \overset{6}{\underset{5}{\rule{0pt}{0pt}}} \overset{7}{\underset{5}{\rule{0pt}{0pt}}} \text{I} \qquad \text{a. i} \quad ii^{\varnothing 4}_{\,2} \quad V^6 \ {}^7 \ \text{i} \ V^6_5/V \ V^7 \ \text{i}
\end{array}
$$

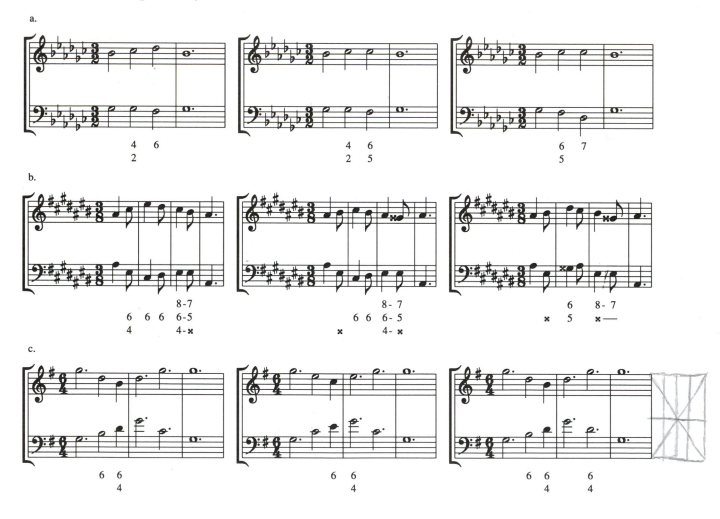

ID16–7.   A chord progression is performed. Identify the correct score notation for the outer voices. Figured-bass symbols have been placed below the bass where appropriate. If you wish, add Roman numerals.

d.

e.

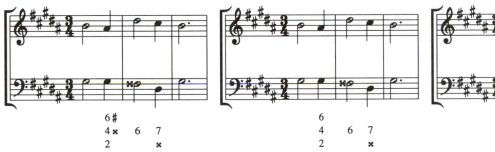

f.

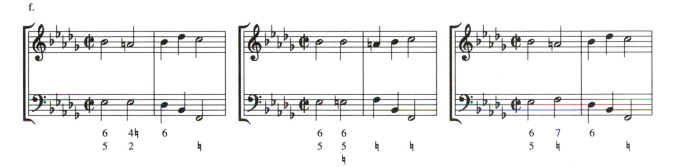

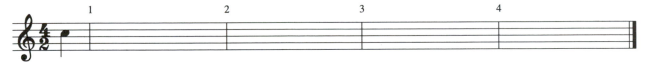

RHYTHMIC DICTATIONS

RD16–1.

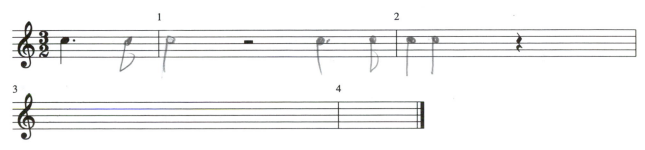

RD16–2.

MELODIC DICTATIONS

SCHUBERT: TRIO NO. 1 IN Bb MAJOR FOR PIANO, VIOLIN, AND CELLO, D. 898, OP. 99, MVMT. 4

MD16–1.

- The melody's structure is shaped by the first pitches of measures 1, 2, 3, 5, 7, and 8 and the second pitches of measures 4 and 6. Write down these eight pitches first, and consider how all the remaining pitches relate to them.

BEETHOVEN: PIANO SONATA NO. 19 IN G MINOR, OP. 49, NO. 1, MVMT. 2

MD16–2.

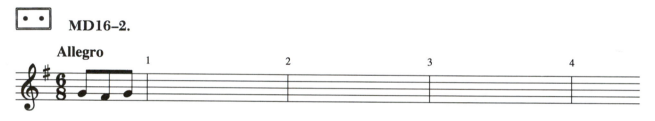

- V of V is outlined in measure 2. The pitch C# thus functions as leading tone to D. Measure 3 does not contain the expected D, however. What melodic advantage did Beethoven achieve by neglecting C#'s upward resolution tendency?

BEETHOVEN: PIANO SONATA NO. 13 IN Eb MAJOR, OP. 27, NO. 1, MVMT. 4

MD16–3.

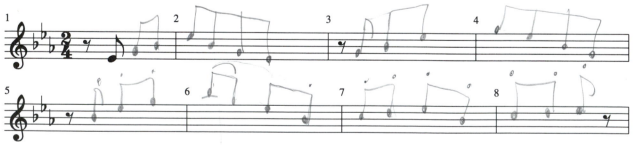

- Does the fourth formed by the first two pitches of measure 5 sound consonant or dissonant? Why?

SCHUBERT: SYMPHONY NO. 6 IN C MAJOR ("LITTLE"), D. 589, MVMT. 1

MD16–4.

Allegro

· Think of the G in measure 1 as $\hat{5}$ in C major, rather than as $\hat{1}$ in G major.

MOZART: PIANO CONCERTO NO. 26 IN D MAJOR ("CORONATION"), K. 537, MVMT. 1

MD16–5.

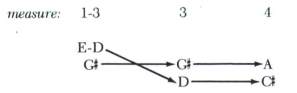

· The dominant harmony is prolonged throughout most of this excerpt. Mozart fills in the diminished fifth G♯ up to D in measures 1 through 3 with diatonic and chromatic passing notes. The diagram below shows how this diminished fifth resolves.

measure:	1-3	3	4

```
            E-D
            G# ──────→ G# ──────→ A
                    ↗
               ↘  D ──────→ C#
```

MENDELSSOHN: VIOLIN CONCERTO IN E MINOR, OP. 64, MVMT. 3

MD16–6.

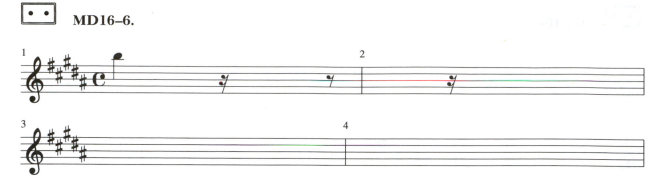

- Mendelssohn embellishes $\hat{2}$ with double neighboring notes in measure 3. Such figures sound best if one of the neighbors is a half step from the embellished note. To accomplish this, Mendelssohn employs a chromatic pitch. Double neighboring notes embellish $\hat{1}$ in measure 4. Because $\hat{7}$ is a half step from $\hat{1}$, chromaticism is unnecessary.

HARMONIC DICTATIONS

BEETHOVEN: SYMPHONY NO. 3 IN E♭ MAJOR ("EROICA"), OP. 55, MVMT. 3

HD16–1.

Allegro vivace

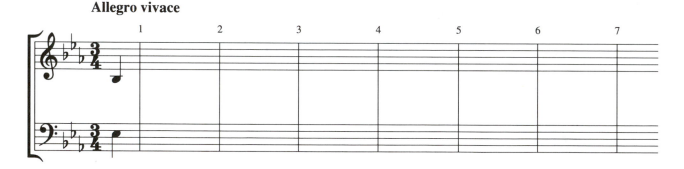

- The bass is very active during this brief excerpt. Movement in the bass does not always imply changes of harmony.

HAYDN: *THE CREATION*, PART 3

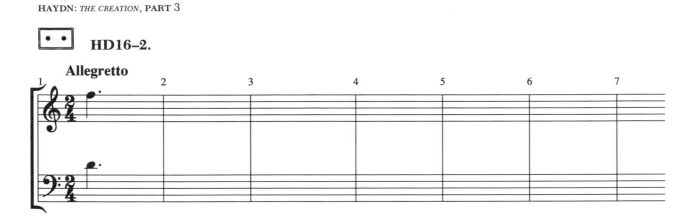

HD16–2.

- The soprano pitch F in measure 1 is consonant. By measure 3, the F (which is retained in the soprano) is dissonant. Its relationship with the bass leads you to expect a downward resolution, which Haydn provides in measure 4.

- Tonic does not appear in this excerpt until measure 4.

SCHUBERT: ÉCOSSAISE, D. 618B, NO. 1

HD16–3.

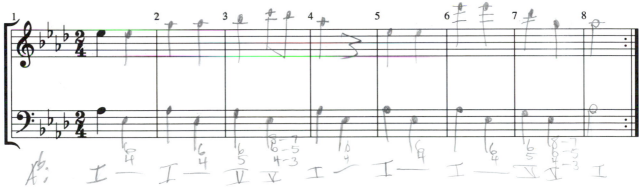

- $\hat{5}$ is the only scale degree shared by the tonic and dominant harmonies. It is often a common tone in the voice leading between the two chords, though rarely in so exposed a position as in dance music, such as this Écossaise by Schubert.

MAHLER: SYMPHONY NO. 9 IN D MAJOR, MVMT. 2

HD16–4.

Etwas täppisch und sehr derb

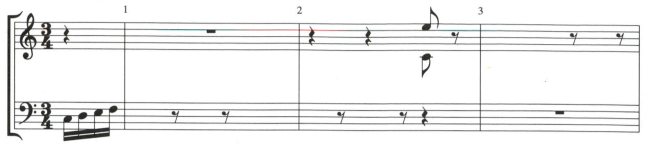

- In the final two measures of the excerpt, Mahler instructs the orchestra to decrescendo from *piano* to *pianissimo*. The decrease in sound is enhanced by his chord construction: the dominant chord in measure 6 lacks the leading tone.

BEETHOVEN: PIANO SONATA NO. 30 IN E MAJOR, OP. 109, MVMT. 2

HD16–5.

- When you write down the soprano pitches of measure 2, try not to let the dissonant bass pitch that sounds with them interfere in your perception. The right-hand part in measures 1 and 2 is straightforward.

BEETHOVEN: PIANO SONATA NO. 14 IN C♯ MINOR ("MOONLIGHT"), OP. 27, NO. 2, MVMT. 2

 ## HD16–6.

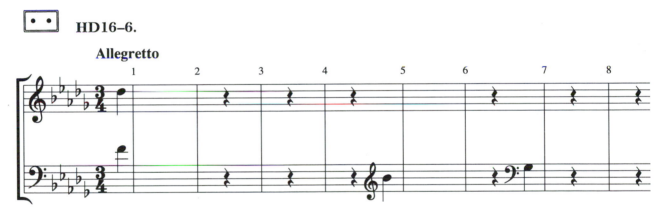

- This excerpt juxtaposes a phrase in the dominant key (A♭ major) and a phrase in the tonic key (D♭ major).

⊡ CASSETTE PROGRAM (TAPE 3, SIDE A)

C16–1. Six melodies are performed, twice each. During the silence after each playing, respond in one of the following ways: (1) Sing the melody, using solmization syllables; (2) Play the melody on the piano or on your primary instrument; (3) Write the melody on staff paper.

C16–2. Six chord progressions are performed, four times each. During the silence after each playing, respond in one of the following ways: (1) Sing the soprano after the first and second playings and the bass after the third and fourth playings, using solmization syllables; (2) Play the soprano on the piano or your primary instrument after the first and second playings and the bass after the third and fourth playings; (3) Play both the soprano and bass on the piano after each playing; (4) Write the soprano and bass on staff paper and provide an analysis.

Chapter 17

PITCH

The ***mediant*** chord often occurs during a progression from tonic to dominant. Its root, $\hat{3}$, falls in the middle (*mediante* in Italian) of the ascending span from $\hat{1}$ to $\hat{5}$. In Example 17–1, the bass ascends from $\hat{1}$ to $\hat{5}$ by way of $\hat{3}$ and $\hat{4}$. The mediant's role in harmonic progression is similar to that of the tonic $\frac{6}{3}$. $\hat{7}$, not $\sharp\hat{7}$, is generally employed as the mediant's fifth in minor keys.

EXAMPLE 17–1

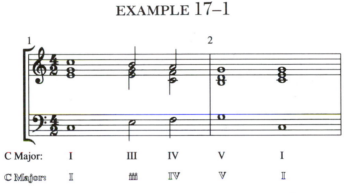

The ***subtonic*** chord occurs only in minor keys. Its root is $\hat{7}$, a whole step below $\hat{1}$. The subtonic chord leads very effectively to the mediant, as shown in Example 17–2. It may also precede the major dominant in minor keys.

EXAMPLE 17–2

A **sequence** is a gradually descending or ascending voice-leading pattern. Chords shed their harmonic implications during a sequence. For example, although the third chord of Example 17–3 may sound like a leading-tone chord, it does not function like one. (If it did, the bass $\hat{7}$ would lead upward by step to $\hat{1}$, and $\hat{7}$ would not be doubled.) The chords of Example 17–3 instead form a **descending fifths sequence**. Each bass pitch is either a descending fifth or ascending fourth (the fifth's inversion) from the preceding bass pitch. All chords are diatonic and in $\frac{5}{3}$ position. The harmonic analysis indicates that this sequence prolongs a single harmony—tonic.

EXAMPLE 17–3

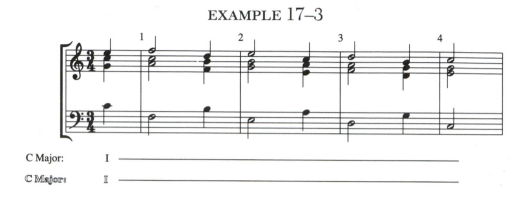

The sequence in Example 17–4 differs from that in Example 17–3 in two respects. First, chords in $\frac{6}{3}$ position substitute for some of the $\frac{5}{3}$-position chords. Consecutive *roots* maintain the descending fifths characteristic, while consecutive *bass* pitches form thirds or seconds. Second, the sequence connects two different harmonies, rather than prolonging a single harmony. Open parentheses in the analysis indicate the sequential region between the tonic and applied dominant harmonies.

EXAMPLE 17–4

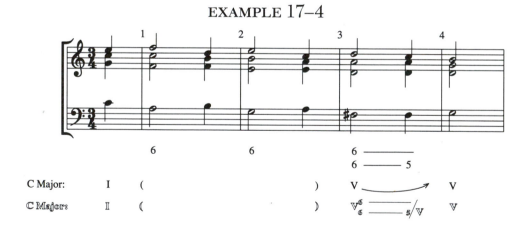

The ***descending 5–6 sequence***, like the descending fifths sequence, follows a characteristic pattern that can be recognized both visually and aurally. In Example 17–5, this sequence prolongs tonic. Example 17–6, a variant of Example 17–5, shows how the sequential $^6_3$ chords can be converted into $^5_3$ chords.

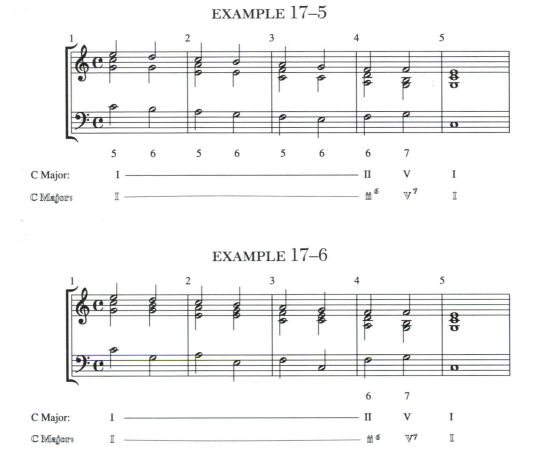

EXAMPLE 17–5

EXAMPLE 17–6

When listening to a sequence, focus first on the bass. Determine which of the descending patterns shown in Examples 17–3 through 17–6 it follows.[1] Then determine the figured bass of each chord. Finally decide whether the sequence prolongs a single harmony or connects two different harmonies.

In major keys, $\hat{5}$ and $\hat{6}$ are separated by a whole step. Chromatic passing and neighboring notes often fill that space, as they do the space between $\hat{1}$ and $\hat{2}$ and between $\hat{4}$ and $\hat{5}$. In minor keys, $\hat{5}$ and $\hat{6}$ are only a half step apart. When $\hat{6}$ is raised (as in the ascending melodic minor scale), chromaticism is possible. Example 17–7 shows $\sharp\hat{5}$ as a chromatic passing note connecting $\hat{5}$ and $\natural\hat{6}$ in C minor.

---

1. Ascending sequences will be explored in chapter 18.

EXAMPLE 17–7

TCHAIKOVSKY: SYMPHONY NO. 1 IN G MINOR ("WINTER REVERIES"), OP. 13, MVMT. 3

METER AND RHYTHM

Just as two sixteenth notes fill the same musical time as an eighth note, two **thirty-second notes** () fill the same musical time as a sixteenth note. Example 17–8 shows two melodies that contain thirty-second notes, along with appropriate counting syllables.

EXAMPLE 17–8

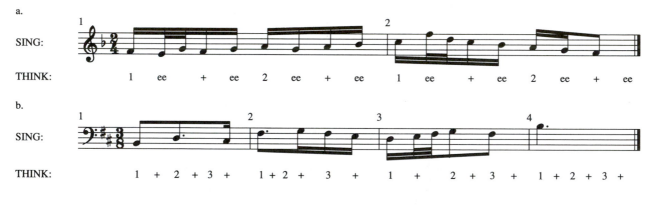

SOLO MELODIES

SCALE DEGREES: *Sing "raised" for ♯5̂ and "low" for ♭6̂.*

MOVABLE DO (DO TONIC IN MINOR): *Sing "si" for ♯5̂ and "le" for ♭6̂.*

MOVABLE DO (LA TONIC IN MINOR): *In any major key, sing "si" for ♯5̂ and "le" for ♭6̂. In any minor key, sing "mis" for ♯5̂.*

FIXED DO: *Sing "misis" for E✗.*

LETTER NAMES: *Sing "Eisis" for E✗.*

MELODIES THAT OUTLINE THE MEDIANT

SAINT-SAËNS: *SAMSON ET DALILA*, ACT 3

S17–1.

· Despite the numerous shifts in direction, this melody's contour is descending. All eight pitches of a descending G minor scale occur in succession from the second pitch to the last pitch of the excerpt.

MENDELSSOHN: SYMPHONY NO. 4 IN A MAJOR ("ITALIAN"), OP. 90, MVMT. 2

S17–2.

BIZET: *CARMEN*, ACT 1

S17–3.

· Think of the leap from C to G in measures 1 and 2 as an ascent from the root to the fifth of a mediant triad.

DVOŘÁK: SYMPHONY NO. 8 IN G MAJOR, OP. 88, MVMT. 4

S17–4.

Allegro ma non troppo

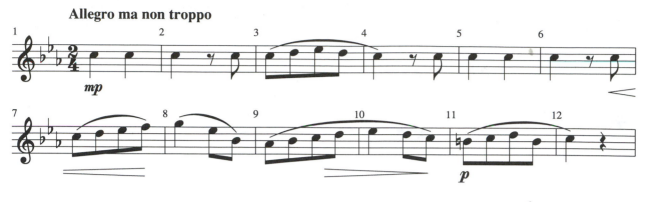

MELODIES THAT EMPLOY ♯5̂

HAYDN: SYMPHONY NO. 99 IN E♭ MAJOR, MVMT. 1

S17–5.

Vivace assai

- Though Haydn retains the contour of measures 1 and 2 in measure 3, he maintains the diatonic pitches for each triad. An exact transposition of the opening four pitches would be F♯-G-E♮-C.

DONIZETTI: *LUCIA DI LAMMERMOOR*, ACT 1

S17–6.

Allegro giusto

SCHUBERT: PIANO SONATA IN D MAJOR, D. 850, OP. 53, MVMT. 4

S17–7.

Allegro moderato

- The basic neighboring motion in measures 1 and 2 is D-C♯-D. (The leading tone, C♯, resolves to D in measure 2.) C♯ is embellished by a neighboring note (C♯-B-C♯). Likewise the basic neighboring motion of measures 3 and 4 is A-B-A. B is embellished by a chromatic neighboring note (B-A♯-B).

SCHUBERT: SYMPHONY NO. 3 IN D MAJOR, D. 200, MVMT. 1

S17–8.

MOZART: SYMPHONY NO. 40 IN G MINOR, K. 550, MVMT. 1

S17–9.

- Measures 5 and 6 are not simply a one-dimensional glide from G to D, but a carefully assembled collection of diatonic and chromatic pitches. (The diatonic pitches F and E♭ are preceded by accidentals to cancel the effect of accidentals inserted for chromatic pitches.) The chromatic pitches (F♯ and E♮) appear on weak beats. They embellish the diatonic descend G-F-E♭-D. Practice this melody by at first singing only the pitches indicated below. Then add the remaining pitches.

measure:	1	2	3	4		5	6		7	8
	F	E♭		D C,		G	F	E♭ D	C	B♭

TCHAIKOVSKY: SYMPHONY NO. 1 IN G MINOR ("WINTER REVERIES"), OP. 13, MVMT. 3

S17–10.

MELODIES THAT EMPLOY THIRTY-SECOND NOTES

TCHAIKOVSKY: 1812 OVERTURE, OP. 49

S17–11.

- The arpeggiation motive of measures 1 and 2 is modified for measures 3 and 4. If measure 3 followed the model of measure 1, the arpeggiation would be an ascending C-F-A♭ (matching measure 1's B♭-E♭-G). The A♭ is a *sixth below* F rather than a *third above* F. Likewise in measure 4, G is a sixth below E♭ rather than a third above it.

HANDEL: *SUSANNA*, ACT 1

S17–12.

BERLIOZ: *LA DAMNATION DE FAUST*, OP. 24, PART 2

S17–13.

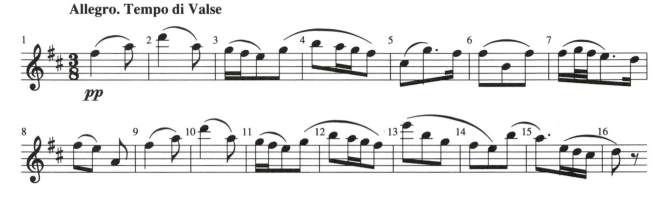

- Solo Melodies #13 and 14 are from the same composition. Their meters and tempos are contrasting, but they are in the same key. What other similarities can you discover?

BERLIOZ: *LA DAMNATION DE FAUST*, OP. 24, PART 2

S17–14.

DUETS

AFTER HAYDN: *THE CREATION*, PART 1

D17–1.

D17–2.

ACCOMPANIED SOLO MELODIES

AFTER DVOŘÁK: *RUSALKA*, OP. 114, ACT 2

AS17–1.

AS17–2.

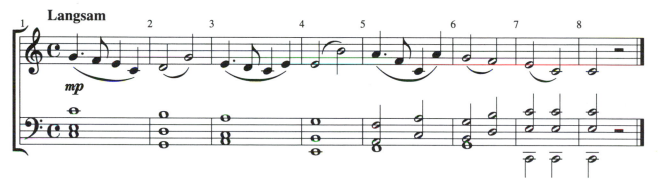

RHYTHMS

R17–1.

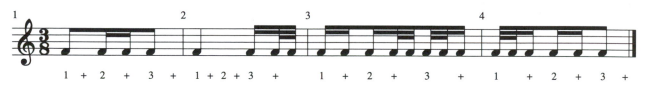

R17–2.

R17–3.

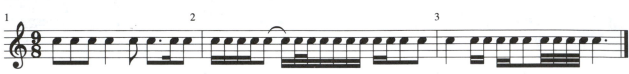

R17–4.

R17–5.

R17–6.

ARPEGGIATION WORKSHOP

A17–1.   Play a pitch that is low in your vocal range at a keyboard. Let this pitch be $\hat{1}$ in a major key. Sing each of the following arpeggiations, either in the order given or in random order.

a. $\hat{1}$ $\hat{3}$ $\hat{5}$ • $\hat{3}$ $\hat{5}$ $\hat{7}$ • $\hat{4}$ $\hat{6}$ $\hat{2}$ • $\hat{5}$ $\hat{7}$ $\hat{2}$ • $\hat{8}$ $\hat{5}$ $\hat{3}$ $\hat{1}$

b. $\hat{1}$ $\hat{3}$ $\hat{5}$ • $\hat{3}$ $\hat{5}$ $\hat{7}$ • $\hat{4}$ $\hat{6}$ $\hat{8}$ • $\hat{5}$ $\hat{7}$ $\hat{2}$ • $\hat{8}$ $\hat{5}$ $\hat{3}$ $\hat{1}$

c. $\hat{1}$ $\hat{3}$ $\hat{5}$ • $\hat{3}$ $\hat{5}$ $\hat{7}$ • $\hat{5}$ $\hat{7}$ $\hat{2}$ • $\hat{8}$ $\hat{5}$ $\hat{1}$

d. $\hat{1}$ $\hat{3}$ $\hat{5}$ • $\hat{3}$ $\hat{5}$ $\hat{7}$ • $\hat{6}$ $\hat{8}$ $\hat{3}$ • $\hat{4}$ $\hat{6}$ $\hat{2}$ • $\hat{5}$ $\hat{7}$ $\hat{2}$

e. $\hat{8}$ $\hat{3}$ $\hat{8}$ • $\hat{6}$ $\hat{8}$ $\hat{6}$ • $\hat{3}$ $\hat{5}$ $\hat{7}$ • $\hat{4}$ $\hat{6}$ $\hat{2}$ • $\hat{5}$ $\hat{7}$ $\hat{2}$

f. $\hat{8}$ $\hat{3}$ $\hat{8}$ • $\hat{4}$ $\hat{6}$ $\hat{4}$ • $\hat{7}$ $\hat{2}$ $\hat{7}$ • $\hat{3}$ $\hat{5}$ $\hat{3}$ • $\hat{6}$ $\hat{8}$ $\hat{6}$ •
    $\hat{2}$ $\hat{4}$ $\hat{2}$ • $\hat{5}$ $\hat{7}$ $\hat{5}$ • $\hat{1}$ $\hat{3}$ $\hat{5}$ $\hat{8}$

g. $\hat{8}$ $\hat{3}$ $\hat{8}$ • $\hat{6}$ $\hat{8}$ $\hat{4}$ • $\hat{7}$ $\hat{2}$ $\hat{7}$ • $\hat{5}$ $\hat{7}$ $\hat{3}$ • $\hat{6}$ $\hat{8}$ $\hat{6}$ •
    $\hat{4}$ $\hat{6}$ $\hat{2}$ • $\hat{5}$ $\hat{7}$ $\hat{5}$ • $\hat{3}$ $\hat{5}$ $\hat{8}$

h. $\hat{8}$ $\hat{3}$ $\hat{8}$ • $\hat{7}$ $\hat{2}$ $\hat{5}$ • $\hat{6}$ $\hat{8}$ $\hat{6}$ • $\hat{5}$ $\hat{7}$ $\hat{3}$ • $\hat{4}$ $\hat{6}$ $\hat{4}$ •
    $\hat{3}$ $\hat{5}$ $\hat{8}$ • $\hat{4}$ $\hat{6}$ $\hat{2}$ • $\hat{5}$ $\hat{7}$ $\hat{2}$ • $\hat{8}$ $\hat{5}$ $\hat{3}$ $\hat{1}$

i. $\hat{8}$ $\hat{3}$ $\hat{5}$ • $\hat{5}$ $\hat{7}$ $\hat{2}$ • $\hat{6}$ $\hat{8}$ $\hat{3}$ • $\hat{3}$ $\hat{5}$ $\hat{7}$ • $\hat{4}$ $\hat{6}$ $\hat{8}$ •
    $\hat{1}$ $\hat{3}$ $\hat{5}$ • $\hat{4}$ $\hat{6}$ $\hat{2}$ • $\hat{5}$ $\hat{7}$ $\hat{2}$ • $\hat{8}$ $\hat{5}$ $\hat{3}$ $\hat{1}$

A17–2.   Play a pitch that is at least a major second above the lowest note of your vocal range at a keyboard. Let this pitch be $\hat{1}$ in a minor key. Sing each of the following arpeggiations, either in the order given or in random order.

a. $\hat{1}$ $\hat{3}$ $\hat{5}$ • $\hat{7}$ $\hat{2}$ $\hat{4}$ • $\hat{3}$ $\hat{5}$ $\hat{7}$ • $\hat{4}$ $\hat{6}$ $\hat{2}$ • $\hat{5}$ $\#\hat{7}$ $\hat{2}$

b. $\hat{1}$ $\hat{3}$ $\hat{5}$ • $\hat{7}$ $\hat{2}$ $\hat{4}$ • $\hat{3}$ $\hat{5}$ $\hat{7}$ • $\hat{4}$ $\hat{6}$ $\hat{8}$ • $\hat{5}$ $\#\hat{7}$ $\hat{2}$

c. $\hat{1}$ $\hat{3}$ $\hat{5}$ • $\hat{2}$ $\hat{4}$ $\hat{7}$ • $\hat{3}$ $\hat{5}$ $\hat{7}$ • $\hat{4}$ $\hat{6}$ $\hat{2}$ • $\hat{5}$ $\#\hat{7}$ $\hat{2}$

d. $\hat{1}$ $\hat{3}$ $\hat{5}$ • $\hat{2}$ $\hat{4}$ $\hat{7}$ • $\hat{3}$ $\hat{5}$ $\hat{7}$ • $\hat{4}$ $\hat{6}$ $\hat{8}$ • $\hat{5}$ $\#\hat{7}$ $\hat{2}$

e. $\hat{1}$ $\hat{3}$ $\hat{5}$ • $\hat{3}$ $\hat{5}$ $\hat{7}$ • $\hat{4}$ $\hat{6}$ $\hat{2}$ • $\hat{5}$ $\#\hat{7}$ $\hat{2}$ • $\hat{8}$ $\hat{5}$ $\hat{1}$

f. $\hat{1}$ $\hat{3}$ $\hat{5}$ • $\hat{3}$ $\hat{5}$ $\hat{7}$ • $\hat{4}$ $\hat{6}$ $\hat{8}$ • $\hat{5}$ $\#\hat{7}$ $\hat{2}$ • $\hat{8}$ $\hat{5}$ $\hat{1}$

g. $\hat{1}$ $\hat{3}$ $\hat{5}$ • $\hat{3}$ $\hat{5}$ $\hat{7}$ • $\hat{6}$ $\hat{8}$ $\hat{3}$ • $\hat{4}$ $\hat{6}$ $\hat{2}$ • $\hat{5}$ $\#\hat{7}$ $\hat{2}$

h. $\hat{8}$ $\hat{3}$ $\hat{8}$ • $\hat{6}$ $\hat{8}$ $\hat{6}$ • $\hat{3}$ $\hat{5}$ $\hat{7}$ • $\hat{4}$ $\hat{6}$ $\hat{2}$ • $\hat{5}$ $\#\hat{7}$ $\hat{2}$

i. $\hat{8}$ $\hat{3}$ $\hat{8}$ • $\hat{4}$ $\hat{6}$ $\hat{4}$ • $\hat{7}$ $\hat{2}$ $\hat{7}$ • $\hat{3}$ $\hat{5}$ $\hat{3}$ • $\hat{6}$ $\hat{8}$ $\hat{6}$ •
    $\hat{2}$ $\hat{4}$ $\hat{2}$ • $\hat{5}$ $\#\hat{7}$ $\hat{5}$ • $\hat{1}$ $\hat{3}$ $\hat{5}$ $\hat{8}$

j. $\hat{8}$ $\hat{3}$ $\hat{8}$ • $\hat{6}$ $\hat{8}$ $\hat{4}$ • $\hat{7}$ $\hat{2}$ $\hat{7}$ • $\hat{5}$ $\hat{7}$ $\hat{3}$ • $\hat{6}$ $\hat{8}$ $\hat{6}$ •
    $\hat{4}$ $\hat{6}$ $\hat{2}$ • $\hat{5}$ $\#\hat{7}$ $\hat{5}$ • $\hat{3}$ $\hat{5}$ $\hat{8}$

k. $\hat{8}$ $\hat{3}$ $\hat{8}$ • $\hat{7}$ $\hat{2}$ $\hat{5}$ • $\hat{6}$ $\hat{8}$ $\hat{6}$ • $\hat{5}$ $\hat{7}$ $\hat{3}$ • $\hat{4}$ $\hat{6}$ $\hat{4}$ •
    $\hat{3}$ $\hat{5}$ $\hat{8}$ • $\hat{4}$ $\hat{6}$ $\hat{2}$ • $\hat{5}$ $\#\hat{7}$ $\hat{2}$ • $\hat{8}$ $\hat{5}$ $\hat{3}$ $\hat{1}$

l. $\hat{8}$ $\hat{3}$ $\hat{5}$ • $\hat{5}$ $\hat{7}$ $\hat{2}$ • $\hat{6}$ $\hat{8}$ $\hat{3}$ • $\hat{3}$ $\hat{5}$ $\hat{7}$ • $\hat{4}$ $\hat{6}$ $\hat{8}$ •
    $\hat{1}$ $\hat{3}$ $\hat{5}$ • $\hat{4}$ $\hat{6}$ $\hat{2}$ • $\hat{5}$ $\#\hat{7}$ $\hat{2}$ • $\hat{8}$ $\hat{5}$ $\hat{3}$ $\hat{1}$

QUICK SWITCH

Q17–1.

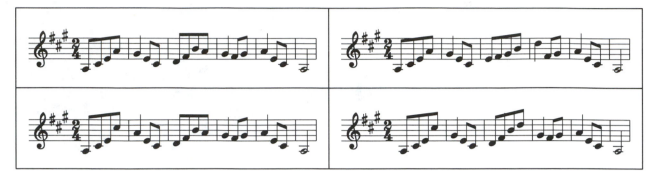

Q17–2.

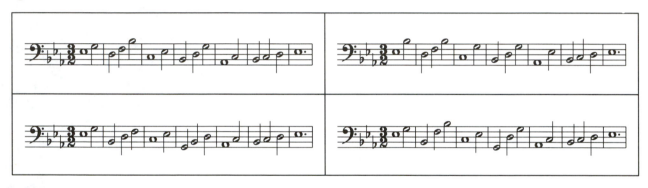

Q17–3.

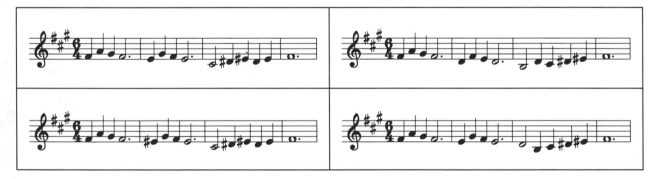

Q17–4.

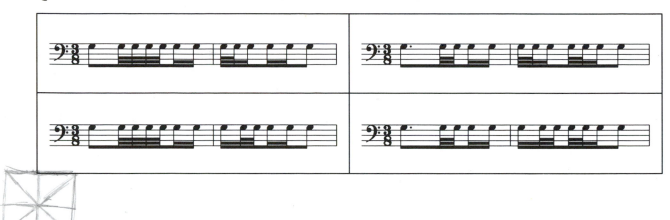

IDENTIFICATIONS

ID17–1.   A descending sequence is performed. Identify it as a descending fifths sequence or a descending 5–6 sequence.

ID17–2.   What chord occurs at **X**? Suitable choices are listed below.

C Major:	I	**X**	II^6	V
C Major:	I	**X**	ii^6	V

Choices:

I^6	II	III	IV
I^6	ii	iii	IV

ID17–3.   What chords occur at **Y** and **Z**? Suitable choices are listed below.

A Minor:	I	**Y**	**Z**	II^6	V$\sharp$^{7}	I
A Minor:	i	**Y**	**Z**	ii^{o6}	V^7	i

Choices for **Y:**

I^6	III	IV	VII	VII^6	$\sharp$VII^6
i^6	III	iv	VII	VII^6	vii^{o6}

Choices for **Z:**

I^6	III	IV
i^6	III	iv

ID17-4.   A melody is performed. Identify the correct score notation.

ID17–5.   A chord progression in the major mode is performed. Identify a suitable Roman-numeral/figured-bass analysis from among the following choices:

Group 1

a. I   III   IV   V^7 I   a. I   iii   IV   V^7 I

b. I   III   V$^6_5$ V^7 I   b. I   iii   V$^6_5$/V   V^7 I

c. I———^{6} II^6 V^7 I   c. I ^{6} ii^{o6} V^7 I

d. I————^{6} V$^6_5$ V^7 I   d. I ^{6} V$^6_5$/V   V^7 I

Group 2

a. I   III   IV   V$^6_5$ I   a. I   iii   IV^6 V$^6_5$ I

b. I   III   VI   V$^6_5$ I   b. I   iii   vi   V$^6_5$ I

c. I———$^6_3$ IV$^6_3$ V$^6_5$ I   c. I ^{6} IV^6 V$^6_5$ I

d. I———$^6_3$ VI$^6_3$ V$^6_5$ I   d. I ^{6} vi   V$^6_5$ I

ID17–6.   A chord progression in the minor mode is performed. Identify a suitable Roman-numeral/figured-bass analysis from among the following choices:

Group 1

a. I   III   IV   I   V$\sharp$ a. i   III   iv   i   V

b. I   III   VI   I   V$\sharp$ b. i   III   VI   i   V

c. I———^{6} IV   I   V$\sharp$ c. i ^{6} iv   i   V

d. I———^{6} VI   I   V$\sharp$ d. i ^{6} VI   i   V

Group 2

a. I   VII   III   II^6 V$^{6-5}_{4-\sharp}$ I   a. i   VII   III   ii^{o6} V$^{6-5}_{4-3}$ i

b. I   VII^6 III   II^6 V$^{6-5}_{4-\sharp}$ I   b. i   VII^6 III   ii^{o6} V$^{6-5}_{4-3}$ i

c. I $\sharp$VII$^{6\sharp}$ I^6 II^6 V$^{6-5}_{4-\sharp}$ I   c. i   vii^{o6} i^6 ii^{o6} V$^{6-5}_{4-3}$ i

d. I   V$\sharp$ I^6 II^6 V$^{6-5}_{4-\sharp}$ I   d. i   V   i^6 ii^{o6} V$^{6-5}_{4-3}$ i

ID17–7.   A chord progression is performed. Identify the correct score notation for the outer voices. Figured-bass symbols have been placed below the bass where appropriate. If you wish, add Roman numerals.

f.

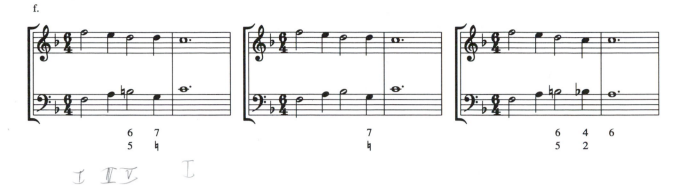

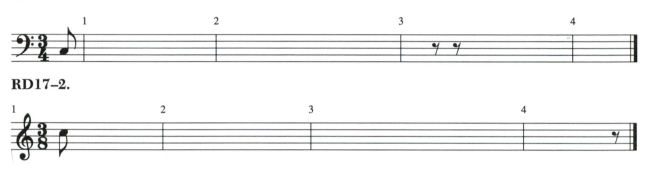

RHYTHMIC DICTATIONS

RD17–1.

RD17–2.

MELODIC DICTATIONS

BEETHOVEN: SYMPHONY NO. 2 IN D MAJOR, OP. 36, MVMT. 2

MD17–1.

· This melody arpeggiates the harmonic progression tonic–supertonic–dominant seventh–tonic. Listen especially for the diminished fifth within the dominant seventh chord and for its resolution.

DVOŘÁK: SYMPHONY NO. 9 IN E MINOR ("FROM THE NEW WORLD"), OP. 95, MVMT. 4

MD17–2.

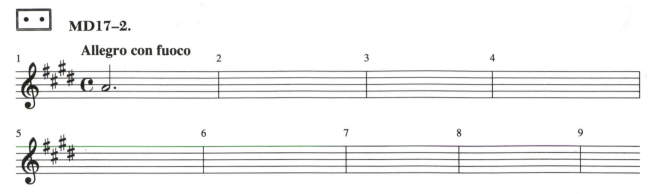

- The interval from beat 1 of measure 1 to beat 1 of measure 2 is a descending half step. The interval from beat 1 of measure 3 to beat 1 of measure 4 is a descending whole step. In which of these situations is chromaticism feasible? How does Dvořák make use of this opportunity?

MENDELSSOHN: SONG WITHOUT WORDS, OP. 102, NO. 1 (BOOK 8)

MD17–3.

- A segment of the ascending melodic minor scale ($\hat{5}$-#$\hat{6}$-#$\hat{7}$-$\hat{8}$) plays a prominent role in measures 1 through 3. In this context $\hat{6}$, which might otherwise play a *diatonic* role, serves as a *chromatic* passing note connecting $\hat{5}$ and #$\hat{6}$.

MOZART: *IDOMENEO, RE DI CRETA*, K. 366, ACT 2

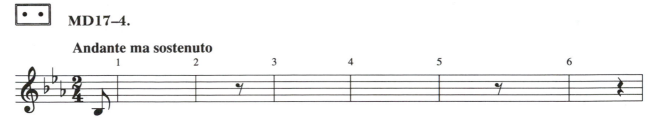

MD17–4.

• Listen for how the *second* pitch of measure 3 relates to the last pitch of measure 2, and for how the *second* pitch of measure 4 relates to the last pitch of measure 3. (While you're at it, consider also how the second pitch of measure 3 relates to the second pitch of measure 4.) When this basic structure is secure, listen for how the initial pitches of measures 3 and 4 embellish the pitches that follow them.

MENDELSSOHN: *THE HEBRIDES* OVERTURE (*FINGAL'S CAVE*), OP. 26

MD17–5.

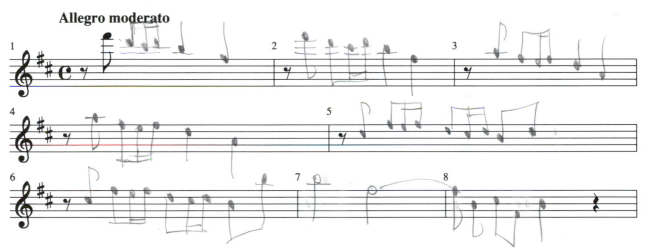

• Though there are many notes in this melody, those in measures 2, 4, and 6 (except for the last pitch of measure 6) are identical to those of measures 1, 3, and 5, respectively.

• In measure 3, listen quickly and carefully to determine which pitch or pitches are common tones with the chord arpeggiated in measure 2. Did the first pitch of measure 3 sound during measure 2? Did the second pitch of measure 3 sound during measure 2? Ask yourself similar questions about the first two pitches of measure 5, in relation to measure 4.

BEETHOVEN: SYMPHONY NO. 8 IN F MAJOR, OP. 68, MVMT. 3

MD17–6.

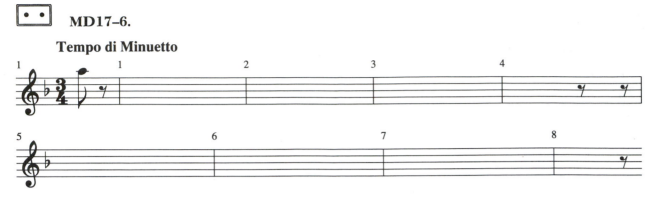

* What is the function of the last pitch in measure 2? What two pitches does it connect? What is the function of the first pitch in measure 3?

HARMONIC DICTATIONS

SCHUMANN: *PHANTASIESTÜCKE*, OP. 12, FABEL

HD17–1.

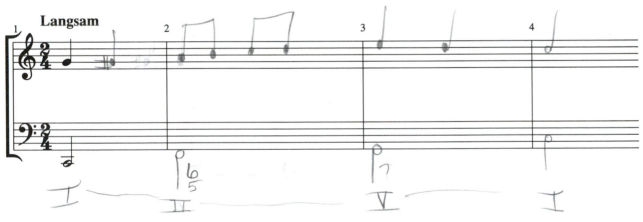

* Some analysts would treat the second chord of measure 1 as an independent harmonic entity: the augmented chord. In Method One analysis, its label might appear as I♯5. In Method Two analysis, its label might appear as I⁺. In this text, such situations will be analyzed as *melodic* rather than *harmonic* in origin. If G♯ is regarded as a chromatic passing note, then no separate analytical symbols are required.

FRANCK: SONATA FOR VIOLIN AND PIANO IN A MAJOR, MVMT. 4

HD17–2.

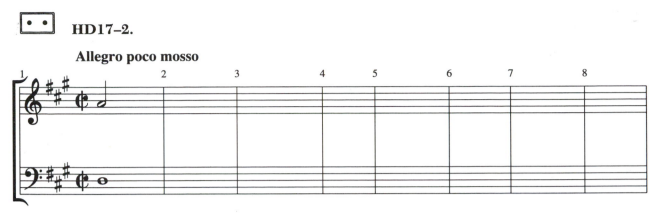

- This interesting progression lacks a strong tonic focus. Analyze it in the key of A major.

MOZART: *DIE ENTFÜHRUNG AUS DEM SERAIL*, K. 384, ACT 2

HD17–3.

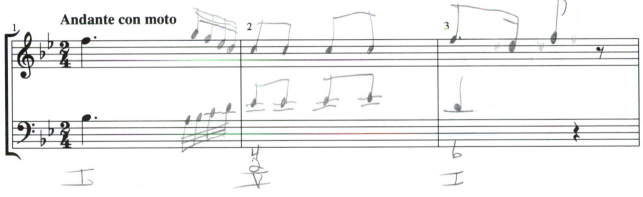

- The chords formed by the thirty-second notes in measure 1 follow one another too quickly to be perceived as a harmonic progression. Your analysis should include only one Roman numeral per measure.

BRAHMS: PIANO TRIO NO. 3 IN C MINOR, OP. 101, MVMT. 1

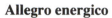 **HD17–4.**

Allegro energico

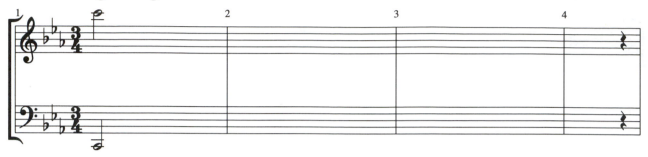

· Your analysis will require only three Roman numerals, coinciding with beat 1 of measures 1 through 3.

CHOPIN: MAZURKA, OP. 68, NO. 3 (POSTHUMOUS)

HD17–5.

Allegro ma non troppo

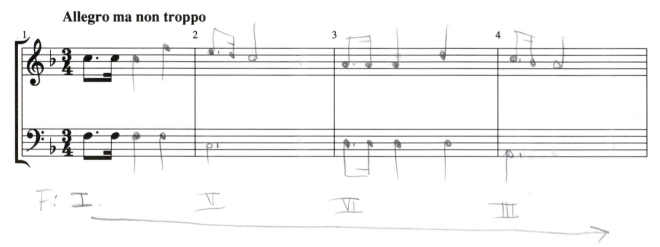

- Before deciding where to place Roman numerals in your analysis, consider the pattern formed by the bass pitches on beat 1 of measures 1 through 6.

- The soprano's contour descends gradually from $\hat{8}$ to $\hat{2}$ (F-E-D-C-B♭-A-G).

MOZART: PIANO SONATA NO. 13 IN B♭ MAJOR, K. 333, MVMT. 2

HD17–6.

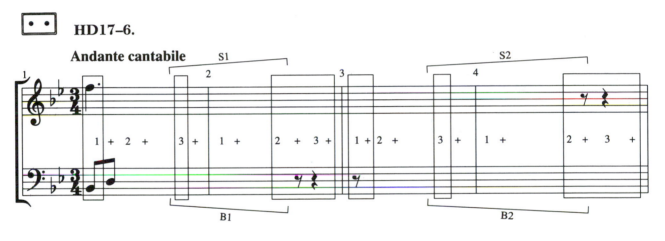

- To best understand the harmonic content of the excerpt, analyze only the chords that are placed within boxes. Then consider the following questions:

  1. How do the bass pitches B1 relate to the soprano pitches S1?
  2. How do the soprano pitches S2 relate to the soprano pitches S1?
  3. How do the bass pitches B2 relate to the bass pitches B1?

[··] CASSETTE PROGRAM (TAPE 3, SIDE A)

C17–1.   Six melodies are performed, twice each. During the silence after each playing, respond in one of the following ways: (1) Sing the melody, using solmization syllables; (2) Play the melody on the piano or on your primary instrument; (3) Write the melody on staff paper.

C17–2.   Six chord progressions are performed, four times each. During the silence after each playing, respond in one of the following ways: (1) Sing the soprano after the first and second playings and the bass after the third and fourth playings, using solmization syllables; (2) Play the soprano on the piano or your primary instrument after the first and second playings and the bass after the third and fourth playings; (3) Play both the soprano and bass on the piano after each playing; (4) Write the soprano and bass on staff paper and provide an analysis.

Chapter 18

PITCH

$^6_4$ **position** (usually abbreviated to $^4_3$) is the second inversion of $^7_5$ position. It occurs when the seventh chord's fifth serves as the bass. It is employed with both ascending and descending bass lines, as shown in Examples 18–1a and 18–1b. Compare its sound with the dominant $^6_5$ in Example 18–1a. The bass of the $^6_5$ has a strong upward tendency because it is the leading tone and forms a diminished fifth with the F above it. Also compare its sound with the dominant $^4_2$ in Example 18–1b. The bass of the $^4_2$ has a strong downward tendency because it is the dominant chord's seventh and forms an augmented fourth with the B above it. The bass of the dominant $^4_3$ has no specific tendency: it could either ascend or descend by step. It could also leap to another chord member, thereby prolonging the dominant.

EXAMPLE 18–1

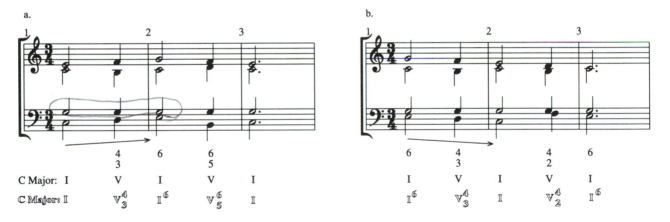

The dominant $^4_3$ and the leading-tone $^6_3$, shown in Example 18–2, are very similar in construction and usage. To distinguish between them, take a careful inventory of the pitches sounding above the bass: a sixth, *a fourth*, and a third; or a sixth and a third. Though the dominant $^4_3$ is by far the most common $^4_3$ chord, seventh chords on other scale degrees may occur in $^4_3$ position if the voice leading is suitably arranged.

EXAMPLE 18–2

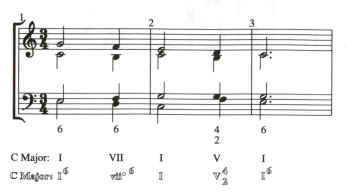

C Major: I   VII   I   V   I

C Major: I⁶   vii°⁶   II   V⁴₂   I⁶

Sequences may ascend as well as descend. The ***ascending 5–6 sequence*** is characterized by an ascending stepwise bass. Each bass pitch supports first a fifth, then a sixth, as shown in Example 18–3. Example 18–4, a variant of Example 18–3, shows how the sequential $^6_3$ chords can be converted into $^5_3$ chords.

EXAMPLE 18–3

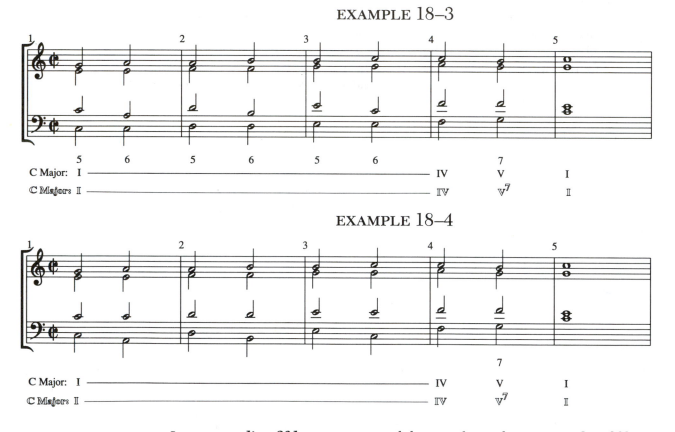

C Major: I ———————————————————————————— IV   V   I

C Major: II ——————————————————————————— IV   V⁷   II

EXAMPLE 18–4

C Major: I ———————————————————————————— IV   V   I

C Major: II ——————————————————————————— IV   V⁷   II

In an ***ascending fifths sequence***, each bass pitch is either an ascending fifth or descending fourth (the fifth's inversion) from the preceding bass pitch. In the ascending direction, fifths do not generate the same momentum as in the descending direction. Example 18–5 shows an ascending fifths sequence that connects tonic and mediant chords.

EXAMPLE 18–5

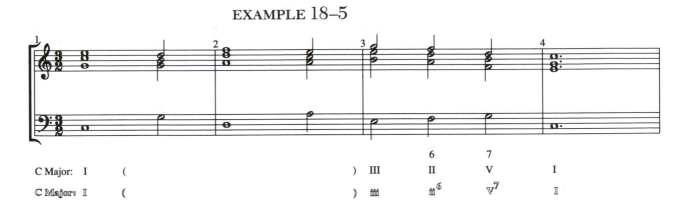

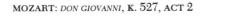

C Major: I   (   )   III   II   V   I

C Major: I   (   )   III   II⁶   V⁷   I

$\hat{2}$ and $\hat{3}$ are separated by a whole step in major keys, but not in minor keys. #$\hat{2}$ and ♭$\hat{3}$ thus occur only in major. Example 18–6 demonstrates the use of #$\hat{2}$ as a chromatic passing note in F major.

EXAMPLE 18–6

MOZART: *DON GIOVANNI*, K. 527, ACT 2

Beginning in this chapter some melodies, such as that in Example 18–7, will be written in ***tenor clef***. Its symbol (𝄡), which is also employed for alto clef, is positioned on the fourth line of the staff to indicate the location of middle C. The tenor clef appears frequently in choral and opera scores published before the twentieth century. It is also employed in cello, trombone, and bassoon parts.

EXAMPLE 18–7

MAHLER: SYMPHONY NO. 4 IN G MAJOR, MVMT. 1

METER AND RHYTHM

Thirty-second notes need not be employed in pairs, as they were in chapter 17. A single thirty-second note (♪) may be preceded or followed by a ***thirty-second rest*** (𝄿) or by a ***dotted sixteenth note*** (♪.). A ***dotted sixteenth rest*** (𝄾.) may occur *before* a thirty-second note to fill the time equivalent of an eighth. (If a thirty-second note is *followed* by silence for the remainder of an eighth, the combination of a thirty-second rest and a sixteenth rest would be used instead.) Example 18–8 demonstrates some of the uses of these new symbols. Whenever possible, beams are used instead of flags to indicate sixteenth, dotted sixteenth, and thirty-second notes.

EXAMPLE 18–8

SING:

THINK: ee   1 ee + ee   2 ee   +   ee   3 ee   +   ee   1 ee + ee   2 ee   +   ee   3 ee   +

SOLO MELODIES

SCALE DEGREES: *Sing "raised" for ♯2̂ and "low" for ♭3̂.*

MOVABLE DO (DO TONIC IN MINOR): *Sing "ri" for ♯2̂ and "me" for ♭3̂.*

MOVABLE DO (LA TONIC IN MINOR): *In any major key, sing "ri" for ♯2̂ and "me" for ♭3̂. ♯2̂ and ♭3̂ do not occur in minor keys.*

MELODIES THAT EMPLOY ♯2̂ OR ♭3̂

MOZART: *DIE ENTFÜHRUNG AUS DEM SERAIL*, K. 384, ACT 2

S18–1.

- Mozart establishes a zigzag pattern using pitches from the tonic chord: C, G, and E in measure 1, C in measure 2. The next pitch in this pattern would be G. Thus the A on beat 3 of measure 2 is a surprise. It is not, however, a "wrong" note. Mozart indeed knows that G comes next, but he embellishes it with a turn (∾), written out as A-G-F♯-G. The ascending zigzag pattern is answered by a descending zigzag pattern in measures 4 through 7.

MOZART: *DON GIOVANNI*, K. 527, ACT 2

S18–2.

TCHAIKOVSKY: SYMPHONY NO. 2 IN C MINOR ("LITTLE RUSSIAN"), OP. 17, MVMT. 2

S18–3.

- Make sure that the first notes of measures 3 through 5 sound like embellishments of the notes that follow them. E (end of measure 2) leads to D (measure 3), which leads to C (measure 4), and finally B (measure 5). This stepwise descent begins with G in measure 1.

SCHUBERT: SYMPHONY NO. 5 IN B♭ MAJOR, D. 485, MVMT. 1

S18–4.

FRANCK: SYMPHONY IN D MINOR, MVMT. 1

S18–5.

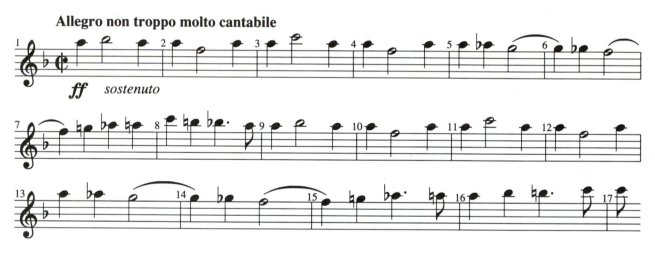

- Some of Franck's accidentals create chromatic pitches, while others restore diatonic pitches. For example, only one of the accidentals in measure 7 creates a chromatic pitch: the flat of A♭. The natural beside G in measure 7 restores G to its diatonic state (redundant here, though a useful reminder). The natural beside A in measure 7 cancels the flat used for A♭.

SCHUBERT: ÉCOSSAISE, D. 781, NO. 1

S18–6.

DONIZETTI: *LUCIA DI LAMMERMOOR*, ACT 3

S18–7.

· The chromatic pitches in measures 5 and 6 should not interfere with the basic structure of the passage. You, as the interpreter, must understand and project how the pitches interrelate. Use the following diagram of the diatonic structure as you practice the melody.

Measure:

Basic shape (thirds):

MOZART: STRING QUARTET NO. 14 IN G MAJOR, K. 387, MVMT. 1

S18–8.

MELODIES WRITTEN IN TENOR CLEF

MAHLER: SYMPHONY NO. 4 IN G MAJOR, MVMT. 1

S18–9.

- Measures 1 and 2 ascend by step: F♯-G-A. Measures 3 and 4 descend by step: F♯-E-D.

ROSSINI: *WILLIAM TELL*, ACT 2

S18–10.

SCHUBERT: STRING QUARTET NO. 15 IN G MAJOR, D. 887, OP. 161, MVMT. 2

S18–11.

· In the second half of measure 3, Schubert embellishes E with a turn (∾), written out as F♯-E-D♯-E. The descending third G-E in measures 1 and 2 is answered by an ascending third D♯-F♯ in measures 3 and 4.

MAHLER: SYMPHONY NO. 4 IN G MAJOR, MVMT. 3

S18–12.

MELODIES THAT EMPLOY DOTTED SIXTEENTH AND INDIVIDUAL THIRTY-SECOND NOTES

BEETHOVEN: SYMPHONY NO. 3 IN E♭ MAJOR ("EROICA"), OP. 55, MVMT. 2

S18–13.

- Solo Melodies are single lines taken from scores that may contain many instruments or voices performing at once. If you studied the full score (as a conductor would), you might more clearly understand the structure of the excerpted part. By learning to sing a melody without consulting those other parts, you develop a skill useful to any orchestral, chamber, or choral musician. In this melody, you must make some assumptions about what else is going on in measures 5 and 7. Because D, F, and A appear prominently near the end of both measures 4 and 6, you should understand that the dominant, not tonic, is likely to follow in measures 5 and 7. In measure 5, C does not represent tonic, but instead leads to the dominant's B. In measure 7, the cadential $^6_4$—not tonic—is being arpeggiated.

SCHUBERT: SYMPHONY NO. 8 IN B MINOR ("UNFINISHED"), D. 759, MVMT. 2

S18–14.

BEETHOVEN: SYMPHONY NO. 3 IN E♭ MAJOR ("EROICA"), OP. 55, MVMT. 2

S18–15.

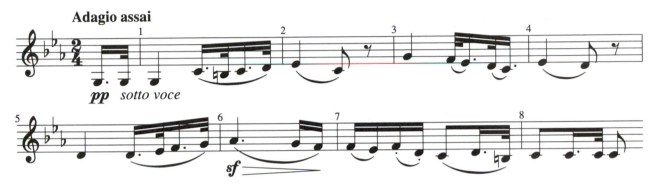

- Isolate the rhythms on beat 2 of measures 1 and 2 for special practice. Maintaining an even and swift clapping (indicated by x below), say "la" at the indicated moments.

measure 1:	la			la	la			la
	x	x	x	x	x	x	x	x
measure 2:	la	la			la	la		
	x	x	x	x	x	x	x	x

BEETHOVEN: STRING QUARTET NO. 7 IN F MAJOR, OP. 59, NO. 1, MVMT. 2

S18–16.

DUETS

AFTER MOZART: *IDOMENEO, RE DI CRETA*, K. 366, ACT 1

D18–1.

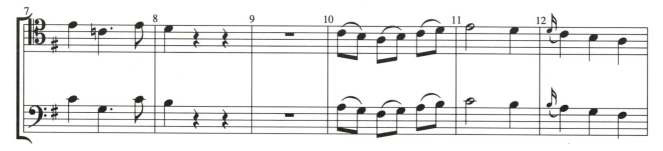

D18–2.

ACCOMPANIED SOLO MELODIES

AFTER MOZART: *COSÌ FAN TUTTE*, K. 588, ACT 2

AS18–1.

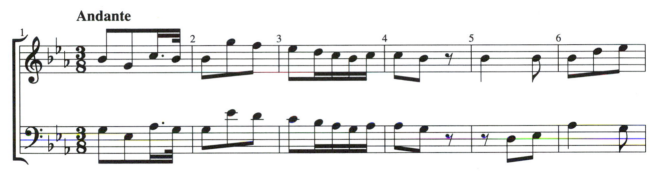

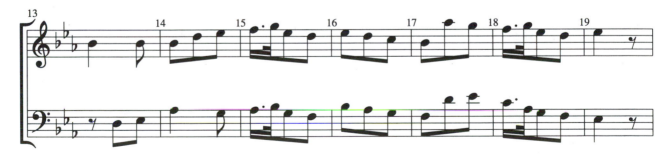

AS18–2.

RHYTHMS

R18–1.

R18–2.

R18–3.

R18–4.

R18–5.

R18–6.

ARPEGGIATION WORKSHOP

A18–1.   Play a pitch that is low in your vocal range at a keyboard. Let this pitch be 1̂ in a major key. Sing each of the following arpeggiations, either in the order given or in random order.

a. $\hat{1}$ $\hat{3}$ $\hat{5}$ $\hat{8}$ ❉ $\hat{2}$ $\hat{4}$ $\hat{5}$ $\hat{7}$ ❉ $\hat{1}$ $\hat{3}$ $\hat{5}$ $\hat{8}$ ❉ $\hat{5}$ $\hat{7}$ $\hat{2}$ $\hat{5}$

b. $\hat{1}$ $\hat{3}$ $\hat{5}$ $\hat{8}$ ❉ $\hat{2}$ $\hat{4}$ $\hat{5}$ $\hat{7}$ ❉ $\hat{3}$ $\hat{5}$ $\hat{8}$ $\hat{3}$ ❉ $\hat{5}$ $\hat{7}$ $\hat{2}$ $\hat{5}$

c. $\hat{3}$ $\hat{5}$ $\hat{8}$ $\hat{3}$ ❉ $\hat{2}$ $\hat{4}$ $\hat{5}$ $\hat{7}$ ❉ $\hat{1}$ $\hat{3}$ $\hat{5}$ $\hat{8}$ ❉ $\hat{5}$ $\hat{7}$ $\hat{2}$ $\hat{5}$

d. $\hat{3}$ $\hat{5}$ $\hat{8}$ $\hat{3}$ ❉ $\hat{2}$ $\hat{4}$ $\hat{5}$ $\hat{7}$ ❉ $\hat{3}$ $\hat{5}$ $\hat{8}$ $\hat{3}$ ❉ $\hat{5}$ $\hat{7}$ $\hat{2}$ $\hat{5}$

e. $\hat{1}$ $\hat{3}$ $\hat{5}$ $\hat{1}$ ❉ $\hat{1}$ $\hat{3}$ $\hat{4}$ $\hat{6}$ ❉ $\hat{7}$ $\hat{2}$ $\hat{4}$ $\hat{5}$ ❉ $\hat{1}$ $\hat{3}$ $\hat{5}$ $\hat{1}$

f. $\hat{3}$ $\hat{5}$ $\hat{8}$ $\hat{3}$ ❉ $\hat{3}$ $\hat{4}$ $\hat{6}$ $\hat{8}$ ❉ $\hat{2}$ $\hat{4}$ $\hat{5}$ $\hat{7}$ ❉ $\hat{3}$ $\hat{5}$ $\hat{8}$ $\hat{3}$

g. $\hat{1}$ $\hat{3}$ $\hat{5}$ $\hat{8}$ ❉ $\hat{6}$ $\hat{8}$ $\hat{3}$ $\hat{4}$ ❉ $\hat{5}$ $\hat{8}$ $\hat{3}$ $\hat{8}$ ❉
　　 $\hat{4}$ $\hat{5}$ $\hat{7}$ $\hat{2}$ ❉ $\hat{3}$ $\hat{5}$ $\hat{8}$ $\hat{3}$

h. $\hat{1}$ $\hat{3}$ $\hat{5}$ $\hat{1}$ ❉ $\hat{2}$ $\hat{4}$ $\hat{5}$ $\hat{7}$ ❉ $\hat{4}$ $\hat{5}$ $\hat{7}$ $\hat{2}$ ❉ $\hat{3}$ $\hat{5}$ $\hat{8}$ $\hat{3}$

i. $\hat{1}$ $\hat{3}$ $\hat{5}$ ❉ $\hat{1}$ $\hat{3}$ $\hat{6}$ ❉ $\hat{2}$ $\hat{4}$ $\hat{6}$ ❉ $\hat{2}$ $\hat{4}$ $\hat{7}$ ❉ $\hat{3}$ $\hat{5}$ $\hat{7}$ ❉
　　 $\hat{3}$ $\hat{5}$ $\hat{8}$ ❉ $\hat{4}$ $\hat{6}$ $\hat{8}$ ❉ $\hat{5}$ $\hat{7}$ $\hat{2}$ ❉ $\hat{8}$ $\hat{5}$ $\hat{3}$ $\hat{1}$

j. $\hat{1}$ $\hat{3}$ $\hat{5}$ ❉ $\hat{5}$ $\hat{7}$ $\hat{2}$ ❉ $\hat{2}$ $\hat{4}$ $\hat{6}$ ❉ $\hat{6}$ $\hat{8}$ $\hat{3}$ ❉ $\hat{3}$ $\hat{5}$ $\hat{7}$ ❉
　　 $\hat{4}$ $\hat{6}$ $\hat{2}$ ❉ $\hat{5}$ $\hat{7}$ $\hat{2}$ ❉ $\hat{8}$ $\hat{5}$ $\hat{3}$ $\hat{1}$

A18–2.   Play a pitch that is at least a perfect fourth above the lowest note of your vocal range at a keyboard. Let this pitch be $\hat{1}$ in a minor key. Sing each of the following arpeggiations, either in the order given or in random order.

a. $\hat{1}$ $\hat{3}$ $\hat{5}$ $\hat{1}$ ❉ $\hat{1}$ $\hat{3}$ $\hat{4}$ $\hat{6}$ ❉ $\sharp\hat{7}$ $\hat{2}$ $\hat{4}$ $\hat{5}$ ❉ $\hat{1}$ $\hat{3}$ $\hat{5}$ $\hat{1}$

b. $\hat{1}$ $\hat{3}$ $\hat{5}$ $\hat{1}$ ❉ $\hat{6}$ $\hat{1}$ $\hat{2}$ $\hat{4}$ ❉ $\hat{5}$ $\hat{1}$ $\hat{3}$ $\hat{5}$ ❉ $\hat{5}$ $\sharp\hat{7}$ $\hat{2}$ $\hat{5}$

c. $\hat{1}$ $\hat{3}$ $\hat{5}$ $\hat{1}$ ❉ $\hat{6}$ $\hat{1}$ $\hat{2}$ $\hat{4}$ ❉ $\hat{5}$ $\sharp\hat{7}$ $\hat{2}$ $\hat{5}$ ❉ $\hat{1}$ $\hat{3}$ $\hat{5}$ $\hat{1}$

d. $\hat{1}$ $\hat{3}$ $\hat{5}$ $\hat{1}$ ❉ $\sharp\hat{6}$ $\hat{1}$ $\hat{2}$ $\sharp\hat{4}$ ❉ $\hat{5}$ $\hat{1}$ $\hat{3}$ $\hat{5}$ ❉ $\hat{5}$ $\sharp\hat{7}$ $\hat{2}$ $\hat{5}$

e. $\hat{1}$ $\hat{3}$ $\hat{5}$ $\hat{1}$ ❉ $\hat{2}$ $\hat{4}$ $\hat{5}$ $\sharp\hat{7}$ ❉ $\sharp\hat{7}$ $\hat{2}$ $\hat{4}$ $\hat{5}$ ❉ $\hat{1}$ $\hat{3}$ $\hat{5}$ $\hat{1}$

f. $\hat{1}$ $\hat{3}$ $\hat{5}$ ❉ $\hat{6}$ $\hat{1}$ $\hat{3}$ ❉ $\hat{2}$ $\hat{4}$ $\hat{6}$ ❉ $\hat{7}$ $\hat{2}$ $\hat{4}$ ❉ $\hat{3}$ $\hat{5}$ $\hat{7}$ ❉
　　 $\hat{1}$ $\hat{3}$ $\hat{5}$ ❉ $\hat{4}$ $\hat{6}$ $\hat{4}$ ❉ $\hat{5}$ $\sharp\hat{7}$ $\hat{5}$ ❉ $\hat{8}$ $\hat{5}$ $\hat{3}$ $\hat{1}$

g. $\hat{1}$ $\hat{3}$ $\hat{5}$ ❉ $\hat{5}$ $\hat{7}$ $\hat{2}$ ❉ $\hat{2}$ $\hat{4}$ $\hat{6}$ ❉ $\hat{6}$ $\hat{1}$ $\hat{3}$ ❉ $\hat{3}$ $\hat{5}$ $\hat{7}$ ❉
　　 $\hat{4}$ $\hat{6}$ $\hat{4}$ ❉ $\hat{5}$ $\sharp\hat{7}$ $\hat{5}$ ❉ $\hat{8}$ $\hat{5}$ $\hat{3}$ $\hat{1}$

QUICK SWITCH

Q18–1.

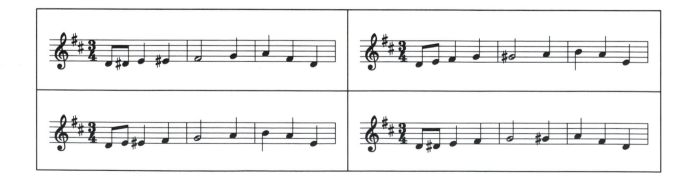

Q18–2.

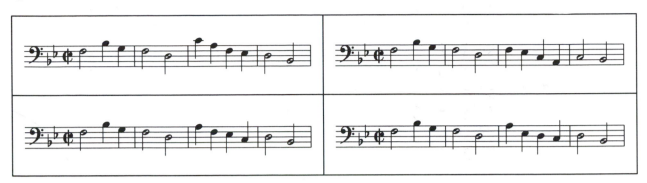

Q18–3.

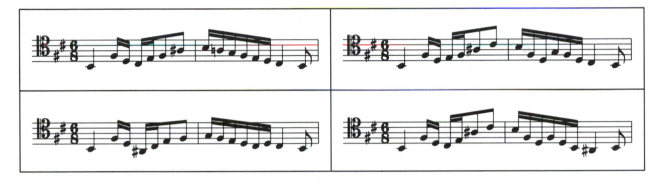

Q18–4.

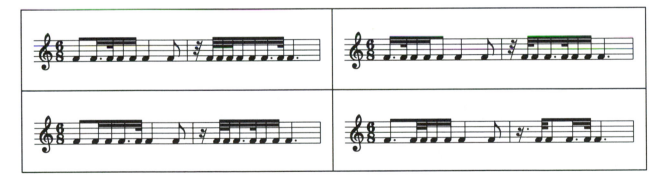

IDENTIFICATIONS

ID18–1. A chord is performed. Identify its position from among the following choices: $^5_3$, $^6_3$, $^6_4$, $^7_5$, $^6_3$, or $^4_2$.

ID18–2. A sequence is performed. Identify it as a descending fifths sequence, a descending 5–6 sequence, an ascending fifths sequence, or an ascending 5–6 sequence.

ID18–3.   What chord occurs at **X**? Suitable choices are listed below.

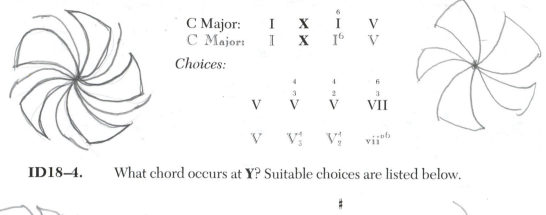

C Major: I   **X**   I   V

C Major: I   **X**   I⁶   V

Choices:

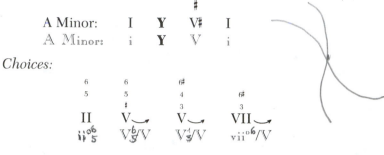

$$V \qquad V_3^4 \qquad V_2^4 \qquad vii^{\circ 6}$$

ID18–4.   What chord occurs at **Y**? Suitable choices are listed below.

A Minor: I   **Y**   V♯   I

A Minor: i   **Y**   V   i

Choices:

$$ii_5^{\circ 6} \qquad V_3^b/V \qquad V_3^4/V \qquad vii^{\circ 6}/V$$

ID18–5.   A melody is performed. Identify the correct score notation.

e.

f.

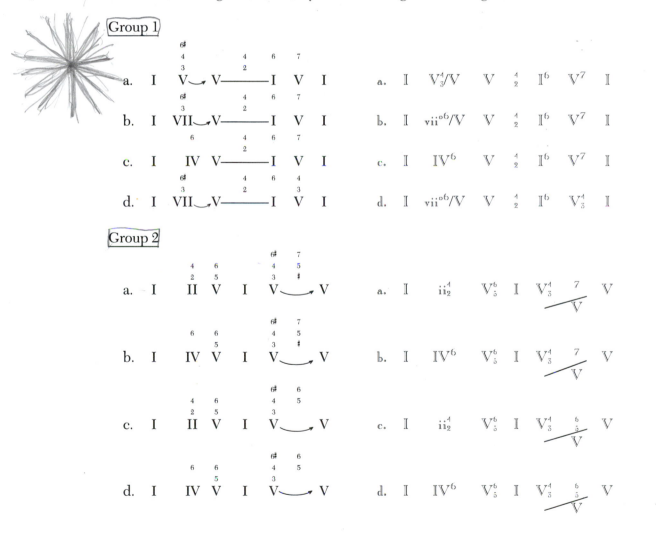

ID18–6.   A chord progression in the major mode is performed. Identify a suitable Roman-numeral/figured-bass analysis from among the following choices:

ID18–7.   A chord progression in the minor mode is performed. Identify a suitable Roman-numeral/figured-bass analysis from among the following choices:

Group 1

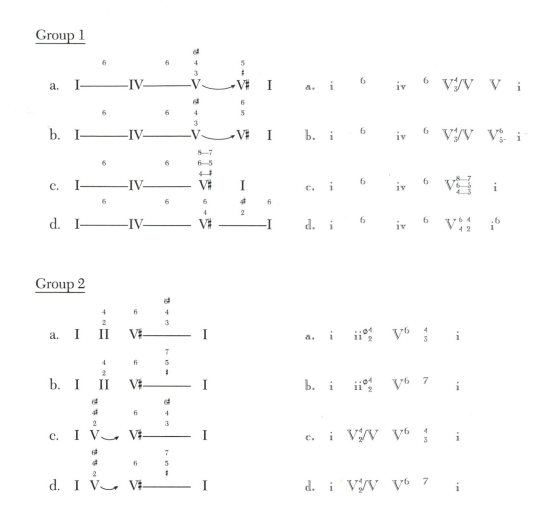

Group 2

ID18–8.   A chord progression is performed. Identify the correct score notation for the outer voices. Figured-bass symbols have been placed below the bass where appropriate. If you wish, add Roman numerals.

a.

b.

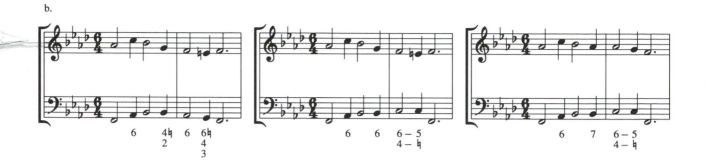

c.

d.

e.

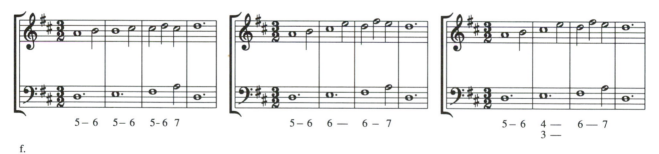

f.

RHYTHMIC DICTATIONS

RD18–1.

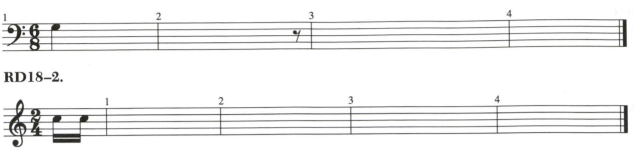

RD18–2.

MELODIC DICTATIONS

HAYDN: SYMPHONY NO. 94 IN G MAJOR ("SURPRISE"), MVMT. 4

MD18–1.

Allegro di molto

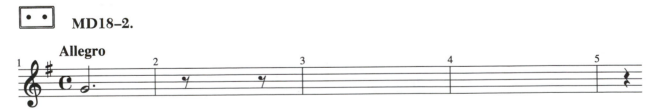

- Leading tones occur in measures 1 and 3. How does Haydn respond in measures 2 and 4?

SCHUBERT: OCTET IN F MAJOR FOR STRINGS AND WINDS, D. 803, OP. 166, MVMT. 1

   MD18–2.

Allegro

- An ascending arpeggiation $\hat{1}$-$\hat{3}$-$\hat{5}$-$\hat{8}$ occurs from beat 1 of measure 1 through beat 1 of measure 3. How are $\hat{1}$, $\hat{3}$, and $\hat{5}$ embellished? Which of these embellishments require a sharp?

DONIZETTI: *LUCIA DI LAMMERMOOR*, ACT 1

MD18–3.

Moderato assai

- What dissonance is outlined in measure 14? How does Donizetti respond in measure 15?

MENDELSSOHN: SONG WITHOUT WORDS, OP. 62, NO. 6 (BOOK 5)

MD18–4.

Allegretto grazioso

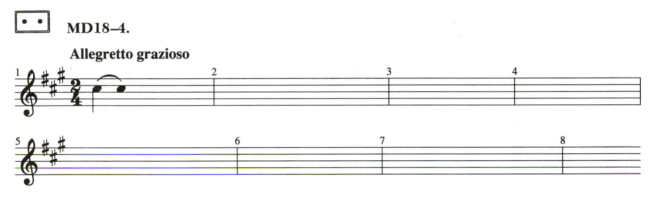

- Measure 2 presents, in the descending direction, a diatonic version of the chromatic ascent of measure 1.

MOZART: *COSÌ FAN TUTTE*, K. 588, ACT 1

MD18–5.

Andante cantabile

- How does the passage from beat 3 of measure 2 through beat 2 of measure 4 relate to the preceding measures? How does the remainder of the excerpt relate to these four measures?

WAGNER: *TANNHÄUSER*, ACT 2

MD18–6.

- Because the dominant key is tonicized at the end of this excerpt, the example of
  $\times\hat{2}$ in measure 6 might also be interpreted as $\times\hat{5}$ in the key of F♯ major. (Reminder: The symbols "$\times\hat{2}$" and "$\times\hat{5}$" are employed because C *double*-sharp [C$\times$] functions as "raised two" in B major and as "raised five" in F♯ major.)

HARMONIC DICTATIONS

SCHUBERT: PIANO SONATA IN A MAJOR, D. 959, MVMT. 1

HD18–1.

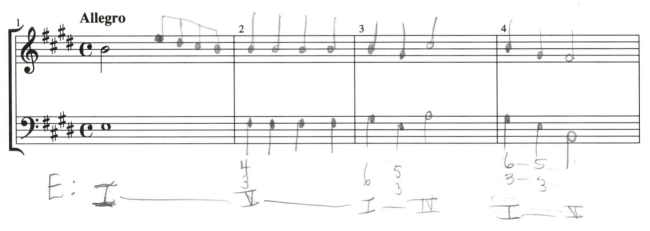

- The bass $\hat{2}$ in measure 2 could support either the dominant $^6_3$ chord or the leading-tone $^6_3$ chord. These two chords sound very similar. The soprano in measure 2 will help you distinguish between these alternatives.

BRAHMS: PIANO TRIO NO. 1 IN B MAJOR, OP. 8, MVMT. 3

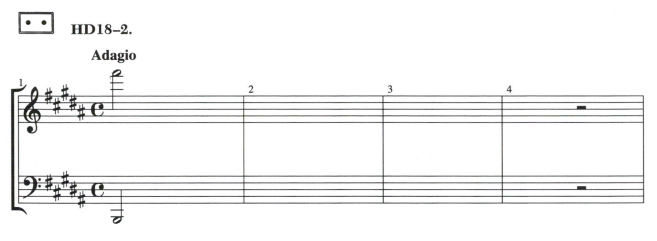

· How do the dissonant pitches in the bass on beat 1 of measure 2 and in the soprano on beat 1 of measure 3 influence the contours of the these lines?

SCHUBERT: MOMENTS MUSICAUX, OP. 94, NO. 2

HD18–3.

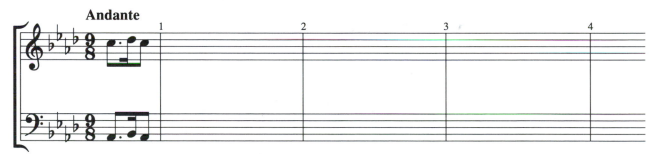

· Sometimes a clearer analytical picture is achieved by omitting details. For this excerpt, restrict your analysis to at most one Roman numeral per beat.

SCHUMANN: TOCCATA, OP. 7

HD18–4.

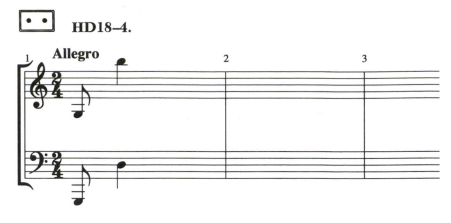

· The *basic* harmonic content of these measures is I-V-I. What precedes the tonic in measure 1? What precedes the dominant in measure 2?

CHOPIN: MAZURKA, OP. 63, NO. 3

HD18–5.

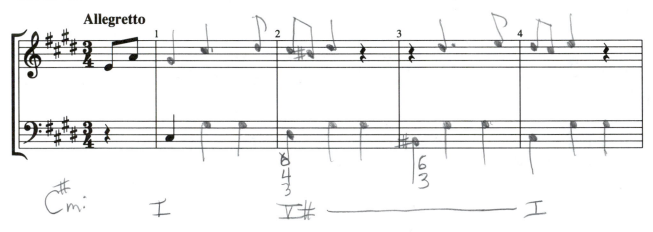

- Chopin instructs the pianist to use pedal to hold the bass pitch that begins each measure through the remainder of the measure. In your analysis, regard the left-hand notes of beats 2 and 3 of each measure as inner voices.

BEETHOVEN: PIANO SONATA IN B♭ MAJOR, OP. 22, MVMT. 4

HD18–6.

Allegretto

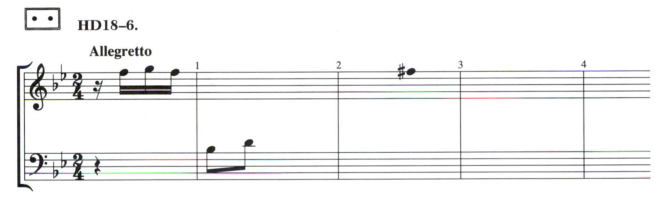

- The sketch below shows the basic structure of this excerpt. Explore how this structure is expanded and embellished through subordinate harmonies (e.g., the expansion of the opening tonic by means of a I–V–I progression in measure 1) and chromaticism.

measure:	1	2	3	4
Soprano:	B♭	C———D		
Bass:	B♭	A———B♭		
Harmony:	I ———V——— I			

💾 CASSETTE PROGRAM (TAPE 3, SIDE B)

C18–1.   Six melodies are performed, twice each. During the silence after each playing, respond in one of the following ways: (1) Sing the melody, using solmization syllables; (2) Play the melody on the piano or on your primary instrument; (3) Write the melody on staff paper.

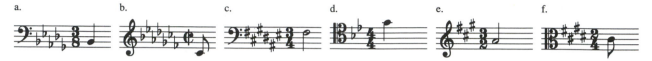

C18–2.   Six chord progressions are performed, four times each. During the silence after each playing, respond in one of the following ways: (1) Sing the soprano after the first and second playings and the bass after the third and fourth playings, using solmization syllables; (2) Play the soprano on the piano or your primary instrument after the first and second playings and the bass after the third and fourth playings; (3) Play both the soprano and bass on the piano after each playing; (4) Write the soprano and bass on staff paper and provide an analysis.

Chapter 19

PITCH

Passing and neighboring notes temporarily displace chord notes. They belong to no chord, but instead embellish or connect pitches that do. On a larger scale, **passing and neighboring chords** temporarily displace chords of harmonic progressions. They play no harmonic role, but instead embellish or connect chords that do.

Methods of labeling passing and neighboring chords in analysis vary widely. Some analysts apply Roman numerals. Others place Roman numerals inside parentheses to indicate that the chords' functions are not what the numerals would normally imply. In this text, *Roman numerals are applied only to chords that play a harmonic role.* Figured bass—but not Roman numerals—will be applied to passing and neighboring chords.

Example 19–1 shows neighboring chords that result when neighboring notes occur in two voices. Although the figured bass $^6_4$ is correctly applied in both measures 1 and 3, in neither case does the chord function as subdominant in second inversion.[1] These $^6_4$ chords are instead melodic embellishments of tonic. The analyses beneath the staff convey that the harmonic progression for these measures is tonic–dominant–tonic.

EXAMPLE 19–1

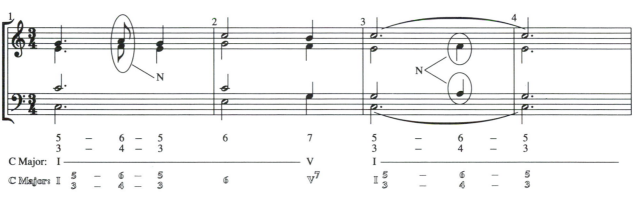

---

1. If the second chord in measure 1 or 3 functioned as subdominant, one would have to regard the bass C as dependent upon the alto F, the alleged "root." Instead, the alto F is dissonant against the stable tonic root C.

In Example 19–2, a $^6_4$ chord is employed during a prolongation of dominant harmony. The soprano E in measure 1 is *not* the resolution of the dominant's seventh, but instead connects its seventh and fifth. At the same time, a passing note in the tenor connects the dominant's fifth and seventh. This situation, shown by arrows in the example, is called a ***voice exchange***. A $^6_4$ chord results from these passing notes and a neighboring note (alto).

EXAMPLE 19–2

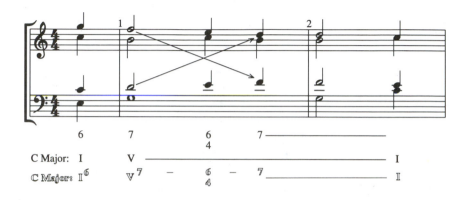

Example 19–3 displays another dominant expansion. In measure 1 the bass and alto move in parallel tenths, connecting the dominant's $^5_3$ and $^6_3$ positions. The $^7_3$ chord between them should not be confused with a submediant seventh chord, whose seventh (G) is a dissonant pitch with a downward tendency for resolution. In Example 19–3, the bass pitch A is dissonant against the dominant root G in the soprano and tenor.

EXAMPLE 19–3

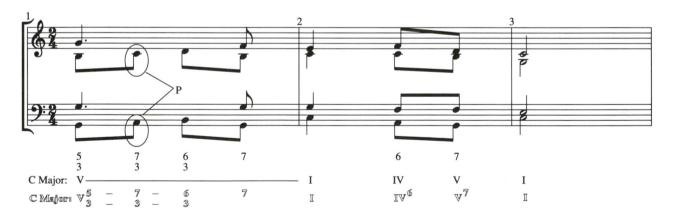

Even a $^5_3$ chord may perform a passing function. In Example 19–4 the dominant $^6_5$ and $^4_3$ are connected by a $^5_3$ chord, in coordination with a voice exchange in the soprano and bass. As a performer, you should convey the prolongation of dominant harmony in measure 3. The $^5_3$ chord is not tonic (which would resolve the dissonance of the dominant $^6_5$) but instead a collection of passing notes (soprano and bass) and a neighboring note (tenor) that form a passing chord. Only in measure 4 should you give the impression of release from the dominant's dissonant tension.

EXAMPLE 19–4

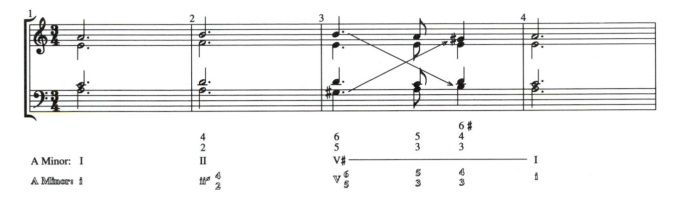

The passing and neighboring chords in Examples 19–1 through 19–4 expand a single harmony that both precedes and follows them. Thus one Roman numeral is employed. Passing chords are also used to connect two *different* harmonies, as shown in Examples 19–5 and 19–6. In Example 19–5, subdominant and supertonic chords are connected by a passing $^6_4$ chord. Parentheses are used to indicate that the $^6_4$ chord functions neither as subdominant nor as supertonic, but instead as a connection between them.[2] In Example 19–6, a succession of $^6_3$ chords connects tonic and supertonic.

EXAMPLE 19–5

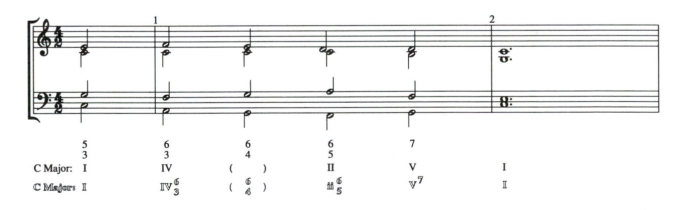

2. In some texts, parentheses surround a Roman numeral, for example "(I)" or "(I$^6_4$)" in this case. That procedure will not be followed in this text.

EXAMPLE 19–6

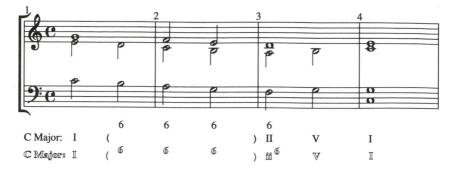

Pedal point is a procedure in which two different harmonies sound at the same time. For example, a composer might expand tonic using the harmonic progression tonic–leading tone–tonic. Pedal point occurs if during the leading-tone chord at least one pitch from the tonic chord is retained. Example 19–7 demonstrates how the A and E of tonic in A minor can coexist with the G♯, B, and D of the leading-tone chord. Two levels of Roman-numeral analysis are supplied. At a basic level, tonic is prolonged through the end of measure 2. On the surface, the progression tonic–leading tone–tonic occurs.

EXAMPLE 19–7

In both major and minor keys, $\hat{6}$ and $\hat{7}$ are separated by a whole step. A whole step also occurs between ♯$\hat{6}$ and ♯$\hat{7}$ in minor. Chromatic passing and neighboring notes often fill these spaces. Example 19–8 demonstrates how ♮$\hat{7}$ may be used as a chromatic upper neighbor to $\hat{6}$ in A major.

EXAMPLE 19–8

BEETHOVEN: SYMPHONY NO. 7 IN A MAJOR, OP. 92, MVMT. 1

METER AND RHYTHM

A single augmentation dot adds 50 percent to the time value of a note or rest. When a second augmentation dot is employed, an additional 25 percent is added to the time value. Thus a **double-dotted note** or **rest** sounds for 75 percent longer than an undotted note or rest of the same type. Example 19–9 employs a double-dotted quarter note and a double-dotted eighth note.

EXAMPLE 19–9

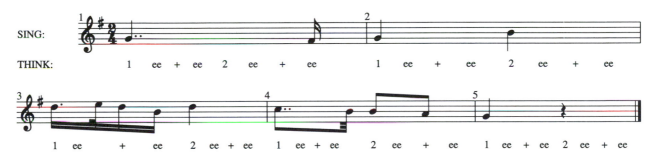

SOLO MELODIES

SCALE DEGREES: *Sing "raised" for ♯6̂ and "low" for ♭7̂. In minor, sing "raised" for the ascending pitch between ♯6̂ and ♯7̂ and "sev" for the descending pitch between ♯7̂ and ♯6̂.*

MOVABLE DO (DO TONIC IN MINOR): *Sing "li" for ♯6̂ and "te" for ♭7̂ in major. Sing "la" for ♯6̂ and "tef" for ♭7̂ in minor. Sing "li" for the ascending pitch between ♯6̂ and ♯7̂ and "te" for the descending pitch between ♯7̂ and ♯6̂ in minor.*

MOVABLE DO (LA TONIC IN MINOR): *In any major key, sing "li" for ♯6̂ and "te" for ♭7̂. In any minor key, sing "fi" for ♯6̂ and "se" for ♭7̂. Sing "fis" for the ascending* pitch between ♯6̂ and ♯7̂ and "sol" for the descending pitch between ♯7̂ and ♯6̂ in minor.

FIXED DO: *Sing "tisis" for B✕ and "sef" for G♭♭.*

LETTER NAMES: *Sing "Bisis" for B✕ and "Geses" for G♭♭.*

SAMPLE SOLMIZATION

Note: *The two examples below demonstrate how to apply solmization syllables in the complicated region between 5̂ and 8̂ in minor keys. The first example follows the model of the melodic minor scale, with diatonic 7̂ and 6̂ during the descent to 5̂ and chromatic ♯6̂ and ♯7̂ in the ascent to 8̂. The second employs chromatic passing notes between 7̂ and 6̂ during the descent and between ♯6̂ and ♯7̂ during the ascent.*

SCALE DEGREES:	1̂	3̂	1̂	7̂	6̂	5̂	raised	raised	8̂
MOVABLE DO (Do = Tonic):	do	me	do	te	le	sol	la	ti	do
MOVABLE DO (La = Tonic):	la	do	la	sol	fa	mi	fi	si	la
FIXED DO:	le	de	le	se	fe	me	fa	sol	le
LETTER NAMES:	As	Ces	As	Ges	Fes	Es	F	G	As

SCALE DEGREES:	1̂	3̂	1̂	7̂	low 6̂	5̂	raised	raised	raised	8̂
MOVABLE DO (Do = Tonic):	do	me	do	te	tef	le	sol	la	li	ti	do
MOVABLE DO (La = Tonic):	la	do	la	sol	se	fa	mi	fi	fis	si	la
FIXED DO:	le	de	le	se	sef	fe	me	fa	fi	sol	le
LETTER NAMES:	As	Ces	As	Ges	Geses	Fes	Es	F	Fis	G	As

MELODIES THAT EMPLOY ♯6̂ OR ♭7̂

CHOPIN: WALTZ, OP. 34, NO. 2

S19–1.

• Practice the following simplified versions of measures 5 through 8 as preparation for singing the actual melody.

ROSSINI: *WILLIAM TELL*, ACT 2

S19–2.

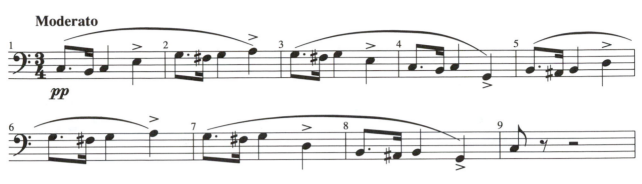

BEETHOVEN: SYMPHONY NO. 5 IN C MINOR, OP. 67, MVMT. 1

S19–3.

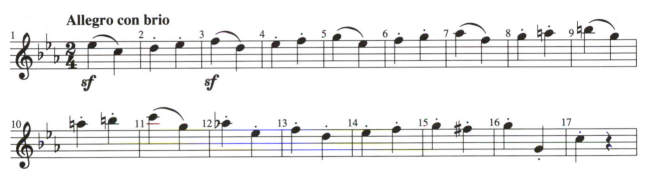

· Beethoven employs a segment of the ascending melodic minor scale to tra-verse the span from $\hat{3}$ to $\hat{8}$ in measures 1 through 11. A♭ in measure 7 connects G in measure 5 and A♮ in measure 8.

TCHAIKOVSKY: SYMPHONY NO. 2 IN C MINOR ("LITTLE RUSSIAN"), OP. 17, MVMT. 1

S19–4.

BEETHOVEN: SYMPHONY NO. 7 IN A MAJOR, OP. 92, MVMT. 1

S19–5.

- The first pitch in each of the first four measures is an upper neighboring note. The line that you (and your listeners) should follow is not F♯ (measure 1), G♮ (measure 2), A (measure 3), B (measure 4), but instead E, F♯, G♯, A ($\hat{5}$-$\hat{6}$-$\hat{7}$-$\hat{8}$ in A major).

VERDI: *FALSTAFF*, ACT 3

S19–6.

TCHAIKOVSKY: SYMPHONY NO. 4 IN F MINOR, OP. 36, MVMT. 1

S19–7.

- The accent mark in measure 3 helps you determine that A♮, G♮, and F (third to root of the major dominant in B♭ minor) are embellished by chromatic passing notes A♭ and G♭.

SCHUMANN: PIANO SONATA NO. 1 IN F♯ MINOR, OP. 11, MVMT. 3

S19–8.

MELODIES THAT EMPLOY DOUBLE-DOTTED NOTES

WAGNER: *LOHENGRIN* PRELUDE

S19–9.

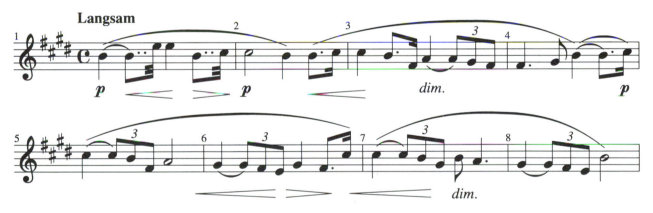

- Isolate the rhythm of measure 1 for special practice. Say the counting syllables out loud while clapping at the points marked by an "x" in the diagram below.

    X   X X   X   X X

  1 ee + ee 2 ee + ee   3 ee + ee 4 ee + ee   1

SCHUBERT: PIANO QUINTET IN A MAJOR ("TROUT"), D. 667, OP. 114, MVMT. 4

S19–10.

BERLIOZ: *LA DAMNATION DE FAUST*, OP. 24, PART 2

S19–11.

- C♯ (measure 3, beat 3) and B (measure 4, beat 3) could but do not continue with A (tonic). Berlioz fulfills this potential later, with C♯-B-A in measures 5-6 and in measures 7-8.

PUCCINI: *LA BOHÈME*, ACT 2

S19–12.

WEBER: CLARINET CONCERTO NO. 1 IN F MINOR, OP. 73, MVMT. 1

S19–13.

· The descending third E♭ to C in measure 2 is answered by an ascending third B♭ to D in measures 3 and 4. This pairing links E♭ and D, two of the steps in the descending seventh traversed by this melody in its opening phrase (outlined below).

measure:	1			2	3	4	
	B♭	A	G	F	E♭	D	C

SCHUBERT: IMPROMPTU, OP. 90, NO. 1

S19–14.

DUETS

AFTER BEETHOVEN: SYMPHONY NO. 6 IN F MAJOR ("PASTORALE"), OP. 68, MVMT. 3

D19–1.

AFTER DVOŘÁK: *RUSALKA*, OP. 114, ACT 1

D19–2.

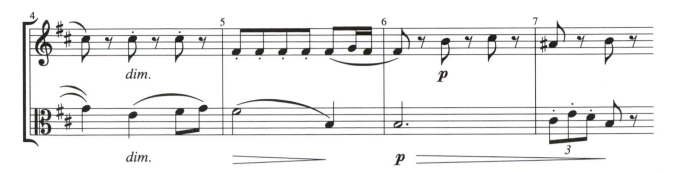

ACCOMPANIED SOLO MELODIES

AFTER SCHUBERT: PIANO SONATA IN A MINOR, D. 784, OP. POST. 143, MVMT. 1

AS19–1.

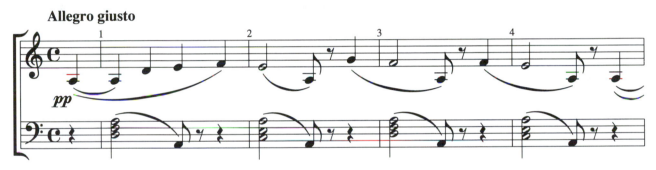

AFTER ROSSINI: *WILLIAM TELL*, ACT 1

AS19–2.

RHYTHMS

R19–1.

1 + 2 + 3 +   1+2+3+   1+2+   3 +   1 + 2 +3 +   1+2+   3   +   1 +   2 +3 +   1 + 2 + 3 +   1+2+3+

R19–2.

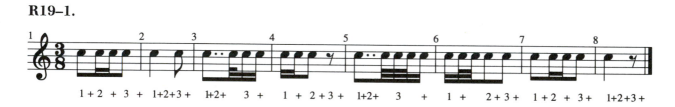

R19–3.

R19–4.

R19–5.

R19–6.

ARPEGGIATION WORKSHOP

A19–1. Play a pitch that is at least a perfect fifth above the lowest note of your vocal range at a keyboard. Let this pitch be $\hat{1}$ in a major key. Sing each of the following arpeggiations, either in the order given or in random order.

a. $\hat{1}$ $\hat{3}$ $\hat{5}$ $\hat{1}$ ❖ $\hat{6}$ $\hat{1}$ $\hat{2}$ $\hat{4}$ ❖ $\hat{5}$ $\hat{7}$ $\hat{2}$ $\hat{4}$ ❖ $\hat{5}$ $\hat{1}$ $\hat{3}$ $\hat{1}$ ❖
   $\hat{5}$ $\hat{7}$ $\hat{2}$ $\hat{5}$ ❖ $\hat{1}$ $\hat{3}$ $\hat{5}$ $\hat{1}$

b. $\hat{1}$ $\hat{3}$ $\hat{5}$ $\hat{1}$ ❖ $\hat{6}$ $\hat{1}$ $\hat{4}$ $\hat{6}$ ❖ $\hat{5}$ $\hat{2}$ $\hat{4}$ $\hat{5}$ ❖ $\hat{5}$ $\hat{1}$ $\hat{3}$ $\hat{5}$ ❖
   $\hat{5}$ $\hat{7}$ $\hat{2}$ $\hat{5}$ ❖ $\hat{1}$ $\hat{3}$ $\hat{5}$ $\hat{1}$

c. $\hat{1}$ $\hat{3}$ $\hat{5}$ $\hat{3}$ ❖ $\hat{1}$ $\hat{4}$ $\hat{6}$ $\hat{4}$ ❖ $\hat{1}$ $\hat{3}$ $\hat{5}$ $\hat{3}$ ❖ $\hat{6}$ $\hat{1}$ $\hat{2}$ $\sharp\hat{4}$ ❖
   $\hat{5}$ $\hat{7}$ $\hat{2}$ $\hat{5}$

d. $\hat{5}$ $\hat{7}$ $\hat{5}$ ❖ $\hat{6}$ $\hat{1}$ $\hat{5}$ ❖ $\hat{7}$ $\hat{2}$ $\hat{5}$ ❖ $\hat{5}$ $\hat{7}$ $\hat{4}$ ❖ $\hat{1}$ $\hat{3}$ $\hat{1}$ ❖
   $\hat{6}$ $\hat{1}$ $\hat{4}$ ❖ $\hat{7}$ $\hat{2}$ $\hat{5}$ ❖ $\hat{1}$ $\hat{3}$ $\hat{1}$

e. $\hat{1}$ $\hat{3}$ $\hat{5}$ $\hat{1}$ ❖ $\hat{2}$ $\hat{4}$ $\hat{6}$ $\hat{2}$ ❖ $\hat{7}$ $\hat{2}$ $\hat{5}$ ❖ $\hat{1}$ $\hat{3}$ $\hat{5}$ ❖
   $\hat{2}$ $\hat{4}$ $\hat{5}$ ❖ $\hat{1}$ $\hat{3}$ $\hat{5}$ $\hat{1}$

f. $\hat{1}$ $\hat{3}$ $\hat{5}$ $\hat{1}$ ❖ $\hat{6}$ $\hat{1}$ $\hat{4}$ $\hat{6}$ ❖ $\hat{5}$ $\hat{1}$ $\hat{3}$ $\hat{5}$ ❖ $\hat{4}$ $\hat{6}$ $\hat{1}$ $\hat{2}$ ❖
   $\hat{5}$ $\hat{7}$ $\hat{2}$ $\hat{5}$ ❖ $\hat{1}$ $\hat{3}$ $\hat{5}$ $\hat{1}$

g. $\hat{1}$ $\hat{3}$ $\hat{1}$ ❖ $\hat{6}$ $\hat{1}$ $\sharp\hat{4}$ ❖ $\hat{5}$ $\hat{7}$ $\hat{5}$ ❖ $\hat{5}$ $\hat{6}$ $\hat{1}$ $\sharp\hat{4}$ ❖
   $\hat{5}$ $\hat{7}$ $\hat{2}$ $\hat{4}$ ❖ $\hat{1}$ $\hat{3}$ $\hat{1}$

A19–2.   Play a pitch that is at least a perfect fifth above the lowest note of your vocal range at a keyboard. Let this pitch be $\hat{1}$ in a minor key. Sing each of the following arpeggiations, either in the order given or in random order.

a. $\hat{1}$ $\hat{3}$ $\hat{5}$ $\hat{1}$ ✽ $\hat{6}$ $\hat{1}$ $\hat{2}$ $\hat{4}$ ✽ $\hat{5}$ $\flat\hat{7}$ $\hat{2}$ $\hat{4}$ ✽ $\hat{5}$ $\hat{1}$ $\hat{3}$ $\hat{1}$ ✽
     $\hat{5}$ $\flat\hat{7}$ $\hat{2}$ $\hat{5}$ ✽ $\hat{1}$ $\hat{3}$ $\hat{5}$ $\hat{1}$

b. $\hat{1}$ $\hat{3}$ $\hat{5}$ $\hat{1}$ ✽ $\hat{6}$ $\hat{1}$ $\hat{4}$ $\hat{6}$ ✽ $\hat{5}$ $\hat{2}$ $\hat{4}$ $\hat{5}$ ✽ $\hat{5}$ $\hat{1}$ $\hat{3}$ $\hat{5}$ ✽
     $\hat{5}$ $\flat\hat{7}$ $\hat{2}$ $\hat{5}$ ✽ $\hat{1}$ $\hat{3}$ $\hat{5}$ $\hat{1}$

c. $\hat{1}$ $\hat{3}$ $\hat{5}$ $\hat{3}$ ✽ $\hat{1}$ $\hat{4}$ $\hat{6}$ $\hat{4}$ ✽ $\hat{1}$ $\hat{3}$ $\hat{5}$ $\hat{3}$ ✽ $\sharp\hat{6}$ $\hat{1}$ $\hat{2}$ $\sharp\hat{4}$ ✽
     $\hat{5}$ $\flat\hat{7}$ $\hat{2}$ $\hat{5}$

d. $\hat{5}$ $\flat\hat{7}$ $\hat{5}$ ✽ $\sharp\hat{6}$ $\hat{1}$ $\hat{5}$ ✽ $\flat\hat{7}$ $\hat{2}$ $\hat{5}$ ✽ $\hat{5}$ $\flat\hat{7}$ $\hat{4}$ ✽ $\hat{1}$ $\hat{3}$ $\hat{1}$ ✽
     $\sharp\hat{6}$ $\hat{1}$ $\hat{4}$ ✽ $\flat\hat{7}$ $\hat{2}$ $\hat{5}$ ✽ $\hat{1}$ $\hat{3}$ $\hat{1}$

e. $\hat{1}$ $\hat{3}$ $\hat{5}$ $\hat{1}$ ✽ $\hat{2}$ $\hat{4}$ $\hat{6}$ $\hat{2}$ ✽ $\flat\hat{7}$ $\hat{2}$ $\hat{5}$ ✽ $\hat{1}$ $\hat{3}$ $\hat{5}$ ✽
     $\hat{2}$ $\hat{4}$ $\hat{5}$ ✽ $\hat{1}$ $\hat{3}$ $\hat{5}$ $\hat{1}$

f. $\hat{1}$ $\hat{3}$ $\hat{5}$ $\hat{1}$ ✽ $\hat{6}$ $\hat{1}$ $\hat{4}$ $\hat{6}$ ✽ $\hat{5}$ $\hat{1}$ $\hat{3}$ $\hat{5}$ ✽ $\hat{4}$ $\hat{6}$ $\hat{1}$ $\hat{2}$ ✽
     $\hat{5}$ $\flat\hat{7}$ $\hat{2}$ $\hat{5}$ ✽ $\hat{1}$ $\hat{3}$ $\hat{5}$ $\hat{1}$

g. $\hat{1}$ $\hat{3}$ $\hat{1}$ ✽ $\sharp\hat{6}$ $\hat{1}$ $\sharp\hat{4}$ ✽ $\hat{5}$ $\flat\hat{7}$ $\hat{5}$ ✽ $\hat{5}$ $\sharp\hat{6}$ $\hat{1}$ $\sharp\hat{4}$ ✽
     $\hat{5}$ $\flat\hat{7}$ $\hat{2}$ $\hat{4}$ ✽ $\hat{1}$ $\hat{3}$ $\hat{1}$

QUICK SWITCH

Q19–1.

Q19–2.

Q19–3.

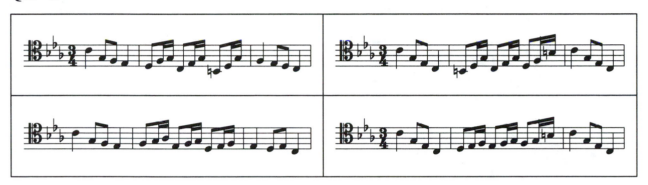

Q19–4.

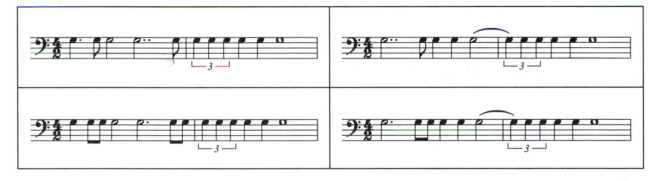

IDENTIFICATIONS

ID19–1.   A melody is performed. Identify the correct score notation.

a.

b.

c.

d.

e.

f.

ID19–2. A chord progression in the major mode is performed. Identify a suitable Roman-numeral/figured-bass analysis from among the following choices:

Group 1

a.   I   V $\begin{smallmatrix}5-6-7\\3-4-3\end{smallmatrix}$ —————   I   a.   I V^{5-6-7}_{3-4-3} I

b.   I   V $\begin{smallmatrix}5-6\\3-4\end{smallmatrix}\ \begin{smallmatrix}6\\5\end{smallmatrix}$ —————   I   b.   I V^{5-6}_{3-4} $^6_5$ I

c.   I   V $\begin{smallmatrix}8-7\\&5\end{smallmatrix}\ \begin{smallmatrix}6\\\end{smallmatrix}$ —————   I   c.   I V^{8-7} $^6_5$ I

d.   I   V $\begin{smallmatrix}5&&6&&7\\3&&5&\end{smallmatrix}$ —————   I   d.   I   V $^6_5$ 7   I

Group 2

a.   I   IV^6 ($^6_4$)   II$^6_5$ V   I   a.   I   IV^6 ($^6_4$)   ii$^6_5$ V   I

b.   I   IV^6 ($^6_4$)   V^6———▸V   I   b.   I   IV^6 ($^6_4$)   V$^6_5$/V   V   I

c.   I   IV^6 ($^6_4$)   II^6 V   I   c.   I   IV^6 ($^6_4$)   ii^6 V   I

d.   I   IV^6 ($^6_4$)   V———▸V   I   d.   I   IV^6 ($^6_4$)   V^6/V   V   I

ID19–3. A chord progression in the minor mode is performed. Identify a suitable Roman-numeral/figured bass analysis from among the following choices:

Group 1

a.   I $\begin{smallmatrix}5-6-5&&6\\3-4-3&&3\end{smallmatrix}$ ————————V$\sharp^7$ I   a. i^{5-6-5}_{3-4-3} 6 V^7 i

b.   I $\begin{smallmatrix}5-6-5\\3-4-3\end{smallmatrix}$ ——— III V$\sharp^7$ I   b. i^{5-6-5}_{3-4-3} III V^7 i

c.   I   IV   I $\begin{smallmatrix}6&&7\\\end{smallmatrix}$———V$\sharp^7$ I   c.   i   iv   i   6 V^7 i

d.   I   IV   I ^{7} III V$\sharp$ I   d.   i   iv   i   III V^7 i

Group 2

a.   I   IV^6 ($^6_4$)   II$^6_5$ V$\sharp$ I   a.   i   iv^6 ($^6_4$)   ii$^{\o6}_5$ V   i

b.   I   IV^6 ($^6_4$)   V$^6_5$—▸V$\sharp$ I   b.   i   iv^6 ($^6_4$)   V$^6_5$/V   V   i

c.   I   II$^{4}_{3}$ ($^6_4$)   IV^6 V$\sharp$ I   c.   i   ii$^{\o4}_3$ ($^6_4$)   iv   V   i

d.   I   II$^{4}_{3}$ ($^6_4$)   V$^6_5$—▸V$\sharp$ I   d.   i   ii$^{\o4}_3$ ($^6_4$)   V$^6_5$/V   V   i

ID19–4.   A chord progression is performed. Identify the correct score notation for the outer voices. Figured-bass symbols have been placed below the bass where appropriate. If you wish, add Roman numerals.

a.

b.

c.

d.

e.

f.

RHYTHMIC DICTATIONS

RD19–1.

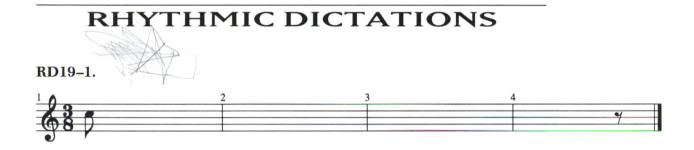

RD19–2.

MELODIC DICTATIONS

VERDI: *FALSTAFF*, ACT 3

MD19–1.

- At a basic level, this melody arpeggiates tonic: $\hat{5}$-$\hat{1}$-$\hat{3}$-$\hat{5}$-$\hat{8}$. At an intermediate level, the intervals $\hat{3}$-$\hat{5}$ and $\hat{5}$-$\hat{8}$ are filled in with diatonic passing notes. At a local level, some of the diatonic whole steps are filled in with chromatic passing notes.

BRAHMS: STRING QUARTET NO. 3 IN B♭ MAJOR, OP. 67, MVMT. 1

MD19–2.

- Where do passing or neighboring chords occur in this excerpt? Do they fall on metrically strong or metrically weak beats?

BRAHMS: SYMPHONY NO. 2 IN D MAJOR, OP. 73, MVMT. 2

MD19–3.

- Write down the first pitch of each measure before considering the embellishing pitches.

HAYDN: SYMPHONY NO. 99 IN E♭ MAJOR, MVMT. 3

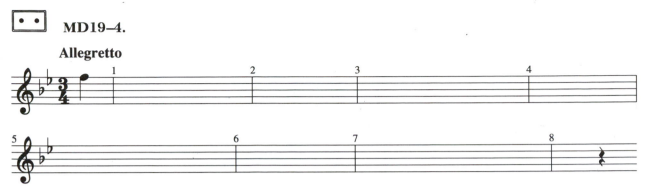

MD19–4.

Allegretto

- Some of the relationships between the two phrases of this excerpt are straight-forward. For example, measure 5 is an exact repetition of measure 1. Other relationships are less obvious. Consider, for example, how measures 7 and 8 relate to measures 3 and 4. *Hint*: What three diatonic pitches occur in measure 3? Do they recur (perhaps in a different register) in measure 7?

LISZT: PIANO CONCERTO NO. 2 IN A MINOR

MD19–5.

Adagio sostenuto assai

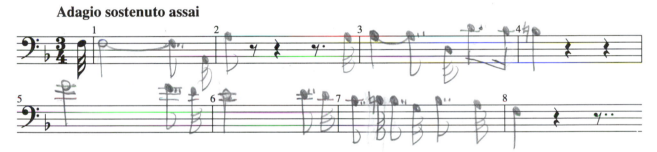

- Although the excerpt begins and ends on the pitch F, it is in the key of D minor.

- The first pitch in measure 1 must be written using two noteheads connected by a tie because no single notehead represents two and seven-eighths beats. Write a half note to fill the first two beats, and tie it to a note that represents seven-eighths of a beat.

DVOŘÁK: SYMPHONY NO. 1 IN C MINOR ("THE BELLS OF ZLONICE"), MVMT. 3

MD19–6.

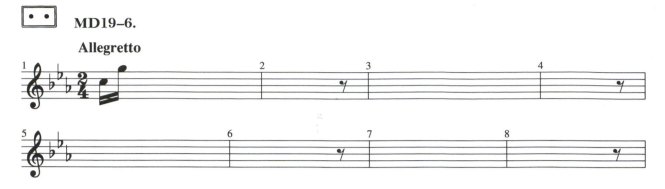

- The underlying figured bass for measures 5 and 6 (and for measures 7 and 8) is as follows:

HARMONIC DICTATIONS

WAGNER: *LOHENGRIN*, ACT 2

HD19–1.

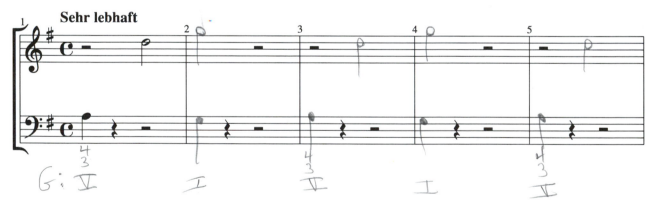

- The bass pitch A should be understood for all of measures 1, 3, and 5. The bass pitch G should be understood for all of measures 6 through 9.

MOZART: SYMPHONY NO. 41 IN C MAJOR ("JUPITER"), K. 553, MVMT. 2

HD19–2.

Andante cantabile

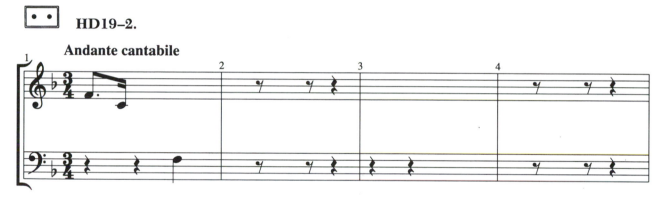

- One of the inner-voice pitches on beat 1 of measure 2 is B♭. How is this pitch prolonged? When and where does it resolve?

HAYDN: SYMPHONY NO. 95 IN C MINOR, MVMT. 3

HD19–3.

- One must hear all of measure 3 before its harmonic meaning becomes clear. A tonic pedal point is employed in the bass, while the pitches above (including the leading tone, which is delayed until the last eighth note of the measure) form a dominant chord.

BEETHOVEN: MISSA SOLEMNIS IN D MAJOR, OP. 123, CREDO

HD19–4.

Allegro ma non troppo

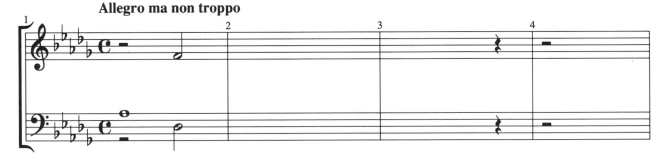

· The chord on beat 3 of measure 5 would normally resolve to an A♭ major chord. It does not, however, resolve to the A♭ major chord on beat 3 of measure 6. When *does* it resolve?

WAGNER: *LOHENGRIN*, ACT 3

HD19–5.

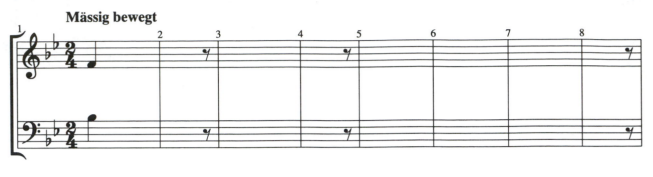

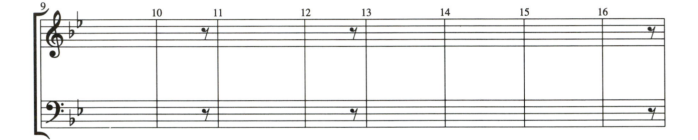

· The dominant seventh chord on beat 2 of measure 15 is followed by melodic embellishment in the upper voices that could be regarded either as upper neighbors of dominant pitches or as anticipations of the tonic chord in measure 16.

MOZART: *THE MAGIC FLUTE*, K. 620, ACT 2

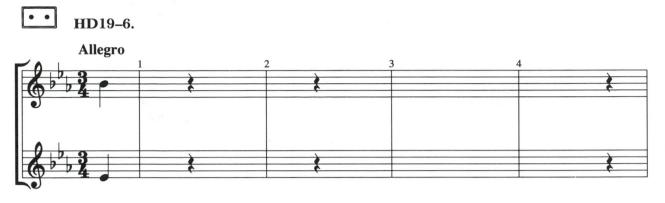

HD19–6.

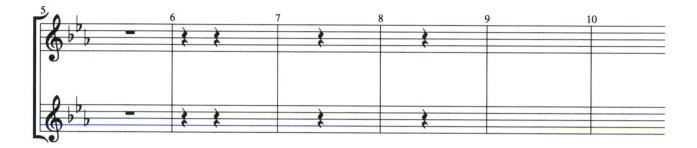

· The passing chord in measure 9 occurs in the middle of a voice exchange. The dissonant A♭ that appears in the soprano on beat 1 of that measure is transferred to an inner voice, where it resolves in measure 10.

⊡ CASSETTE PROGRAM (TAPE 3, SIDE B)

C19–1.   Six melodies are performed, twice each. During the silence after each playing, respond in one of the following ways: (1) Sing the melody, using solmization syllables; (2) Play the melody on the piano or on your primary instrument; (3) Write the melody on staff paper.

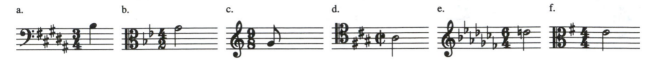

C19–2.   Six chord progressions are performed, four times each. During the silence after each playing, respond in one of the following ways: (1) Sing the soprano after the first and second playings and the bass after the third and fourth playings, using solmization syllables; (2) Play the soprano on the piano or your primary instrument after the first and second playings and the bass after the third and fourth playings; (3) Play both the soprano and bass on the piano after each playing; (4) Write the soprano and bass on staff paper and provide an analysis.

Chapter 20

PITCH

The accidentals found in almost all scores of the eighteenth and nineteenth centuries have three principal causes: (1) melodic embellishment (chromatic passing and neighboring notes); (2) applied chords, tonicization, or modulation; and (3) ***modal mixture***, the borrowing of chords from the parallel key. Major subdominant, major dominant, and diminished leading-tone chords that occur in the context of minor keys are common examples of modal mixture.

In Example 20–1, A♭ and D♭ (diatonic pitches of F minor) are employed in the context of F major. The root of the submediant chord is lowered by a half step, and its quality is major. The quality of the supertonic seventh chord is half-diminished. In the Method One analysis, both the figured bass and the Roman numerals are affected. Because the *fifth* above the root is lowered in both of these chords, "♭5" appears to the right of their Roman numerals. (When the root is altered, an accidental appears to the left of the numeral; when the third is altered, an accidental appears to the right of the numeral; when the fifth or seventh is altered, an accidental and that number appear to the right of

EXAMPLE 20–1

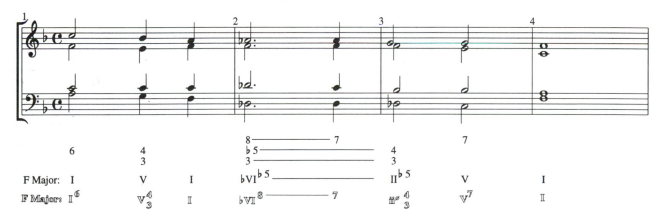

the numeral.) In the Method Two analysis, chord quality is indicated in the usual manner. Because the submediant's root is D♭ rather than D, a flat appears to the left of "VI" in both methods of analysis.[1]

In major keys modal mixture occurs most often when ♭$\hat{6}$ replaces $\hat{6}$, creating a diminished supertonic chord (II♭5 or ii°), a minor subdominant chord (IV♭ or iv), or (when ♭$\hat{3}$ is employed as well) a major submediant chord (♭VI♭5 or ♭VI). When ♭$\hat{3}$ replaces $\hat{3}$, a minor tonic chord is formed (I♭ or i).

Occasionally ♯$\hat{5}$ replaces $\hat{5}$ to form a major mediant chord (III♯ or III) in major keys. Although not a borrowing from the parallel minor key, this alteration is usually classified as mixture anyway.

Example 20–2 shows a common type of mixture in the minor mode—that in which the cadential tonic's third is raised to form a major chord. This third, called a ***Picardy third***, requires a natural, sharp, or double sharp, depending on the key signature of the given minor key.

EXAMPLE 20–2

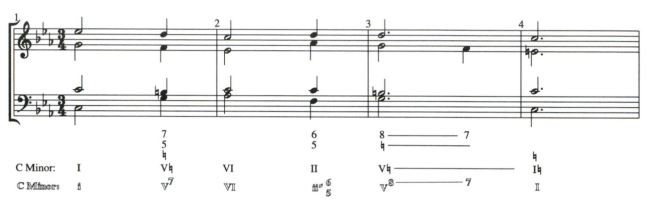

One of the most dissonant chords of music—the ***diminished seventh chord***—owes its existence to modal mixture. It occurs when a diminished seventh (an interval that is diatonic neither in major nor in natural minor) is added to a diminished chord. The ***leading-tone diminished seventh chord*** employs the $\hat{7}$ of major and the $\hat{6}$ of natural minor. Example 20–3 demonstrates its use in minor, where ✗$\hat{7}$ is borrowed from G♯ major.[2] Example 20–4 demonstrates its use in major, where ♭$\hat{6}$ is borrowed from B♭ minor. Example 20–4 also contrasts it with the diatonic ***leading-tone half-diminished seventh chord*** and shows how it may occur as an applied diminished seventh chord.

---

1. To be consistent, the leading-tone chord in minor should be analyzed as "♯vii°" rather than as "vii°" in Method Two analysis. That alternative is not common in American harmony texts, however, and will not be employed here.

2. The key of G♯ major is not one of the standard fifteen major keys. Its scale is G♯-A♯-B♯-C♯-D♯-E♯-F✗-G♯. D♯ minor and A♯ minor also have uncommon parallel major keys.

EXAMPLE 20–3

EXAMPLE 20–4

Great precision is required in listening to compositions that employ modal mixture. Knowing the bass and the figured bass, which was often sufficient for determining the exact label for a chord in earlier chapters, must now be complemented by a full awareness of which pitches, if any, are altered.

In minor keys, $\hat{3}$ to $\hat{4}$ and $\hat{7}$ to $\hat{8}$ are separated by a whole step. Chromatic passing and neighboring notes may fill these spaces. Example 20–5 demonstrates how $\sharp\hat{7}$ may be used as a chromatic passing note connecting $\hat{7}$ and $\hat{8}$ in A minor.

EXAMPLE 20–5

MOZART: *DIE ENTFÜHRUNG AUS DEM SERAIL*, K. 384, ACT 1

METER AND RHYTHM

Partial-beat triplets are employed when a segment of the beat that would normally divide into two parts is instead divided into three parts. Example 20–6 provides two examples of partial-beat triplets. In Example 20–6a, sixteenth-note triplets occur where two sixteenth notes would normally occur. In Example 20–6b, eighth-note triplets occur where two eighth notes would normally occur.

EXAMPLE 20–6

a.

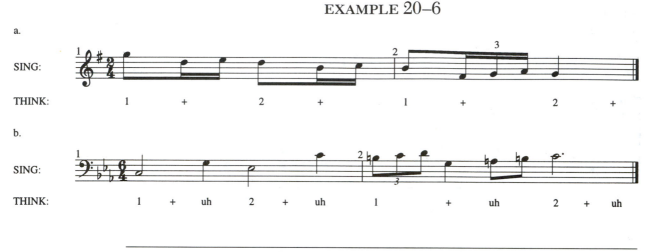

b.

SOLO MELODIES

MELODIES THAT EMPLOY MODAL MIXTURE

WAGNER: *LOHENGRIN*, ACT 1

S20–1.

· The key may change numerous times during an opera. Sometimes a composer will add accidentals within the score rather than change key signatures. Here Wagner writes in the key of A♭ minor, though the key signature of A♭ major is retained. Visually the natural sign in measure 8 affirms the key signature, but aurally it is perceived as a Picardy third.

SCHUBERT: STRING QUARTET NO. 15 IN G MAJOR, D. 887, OP. 161, MVMT. 1

S20–2.

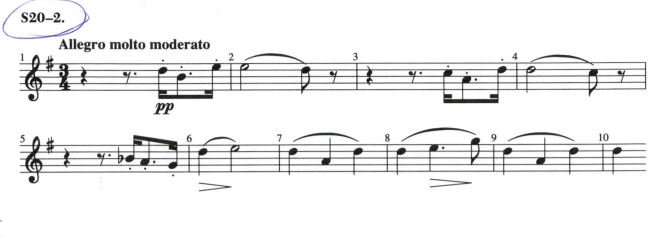

LISZT: PIANO CONCERTO NO. 2 IN A MAJOR

S20–3.

- Measure 2 is based on the dominant harmony's perfect fifth D–G. Both of these pitches are embellished by chromatic upper neighbors. Practice measure 4, a variant of measure 2, by gradually adding layers of embellishment, as follows:

D				G	(perfect fifth)
D	B			G	(triadic arpeggiation)
D	B	A		G	(with passing note)
E♭	D	B	A	A♭	G	(with chromatic pitches)

BEETHOVEN: PIANO SONATA NO. 29 IN B♭ MAJOR ("HAMMERCLAVIER"), OP. 106, MVMT. 1

S20–4.

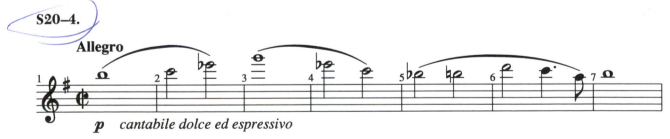

MELODIES THAT OUTLINE DIMINISHED OR HALF-DIMINISHED SEVENTH CHORDS

MOZART: *IDOMENEO, RE DI CRETA*, K. 366, ACT 3

S20–5.

- C♯ in measure 1 forms a diminished seventh with the B♭ that begins measure 2. Among the notes in between, E and G are members of the harmony while D, F, and A are passing notes.

MOZART: STRING QUARTET NO. 16 IN E♭ MAJOR, K. 428, MVMT. 3

S20–6.

HAYDN: *THE CREATION*, PART 2

S20–7.

- Your performance should emphasize the melodic connections among the pitches that fall on the beats. Measures 1 and 2, for example, contain a smooth melodic ascent, F-G-A-B♭.

CHOPIN: PIANO SONATA NO. 2 IN B♭ MINOR, OP. 35, MVMT. 1

S20–8.

MOZART: STRING QUARTET NO. 17 IN B♭ MAJOR ("HUNTING"), K. 458, MVMT. 4

S20–9.

· Interpret this melody in the key of F minor. The excerpt ends with a half cadence on the dominant.

MOZART: *DON GIOVANNI*, K. 527, ACT 2

S20–10.

MELODIES THAT EMPLOY #$\hat{3}$ OR #$\hat{7}$

MOZART: *DIE ENTFÜHRUNG AUS DEM SERAIL*, K. 384, ACT 1

S20–11.

- Although all the pitches between $\hat{5}$ and $\hat{8}$ occur in the first three measures, those of the natural minor scale are the most prominently positioned within the meter. Your performance should convey a sense that F# connects F and G and that G# connects G and A.

VIVALDI: CONCERTO IN E MAJOR ("THE FOUR SEASONS: SPRING"), RV 269, OP. 8, NO. 1, MVMT. 1

S20–12.

MELODIES THAT EMPLOY PARTIAL-BEAT
TRIPLETS

MOZART: SYMPHONY NO. 35 IN D MAJOR ("HAFFNER"), K. 385, MVMT. 2

S20–13.

· In measure 4, Mozart connects A and B using A♯. In measures 11 and 12, he connects B and A using B♭.

ROSSINI: *THE BARBER OF SEVILLE*, ACT 1

S20–14.

BIZET: *CARMEN*, ACT 1

S20–15.

- The descending natural (or melodic) minor scale forms the foundation for this excerpt. Compare Bizet's score with the following model to determine which pitches embellish other pitches.

measure:	1		2		3	4		5		6			7	8
	D	C	B♭	A	G	F	E,	D	C	B♭	A	G	F E	D

MOZART: *IDOMENEO, RE DI CRETA*, K. 366, ACT 3

S20–16.

DUETS

AFTER WAGNER: *TANNHAUSER*, ACT 3

D20–1.

Moderato

AFTER TCHAIKOVSKY: SYMPHONY NO. 2 IN C MINOR ("LITTLE RUSSIAN"), OP. 17, MVMT. 4

D20–2.

Allegro vivo

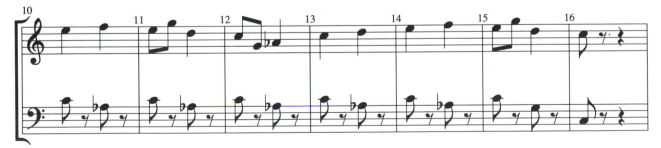

ACCOMPANIED SOLO MELODIES

AFTER MOZART: *DIE ENTFÜHRUNG AUS DEM SERAIL*, K. 384, ACT 1

AS20–1.

AFTER SCHUBERT: *FIERRABRAS*, D. 796, ACT 2

AS20–2.

RHYTHMS

R20–1.

1 + uh 2 + uh   1 + uh 2 + uh   1 + uh 2 + uh   1 + uh 2 + uh

R20–2.

R20–3.

R20–4.

R20–5.

R20–6.

INTERVAL WORKSHOP

I20–1.   Practice singing the interval of a diminished seventh higher than a sounding pitch. The sounding pitch should be at or beyond the lower limit of your vocal range, and could be sung by a classmate or your instructor or performed on the piano or another instrument such as the cello. Also practice singing compound versions of this interval.

I20–2.   Practice singing the interval of a diminished seventh lower than a sounding pitch. The sounding pitch should be at or beyond the upper limit of your vocal range, and could be sung by a classmate or your instructor or performed on the piano or another instrument such as the flute. Also practice singing compound versions of this interval.

I20–3.   Play a pitch that is low in your vocal range at a keyboard. Sing it. Then sing the pitch a diminished seventh higher (e.g., sing B-A♭.) Then sing an ascending arpeggiation of a diminished seventh chord based upon the diminished seventh that you sang (e.g., sing B-D-F-A♭.) Use the keyboard to confirm your performance. Then sing ascending diminished sevenths and diminished seventh chords on other pitches.

I20–4.　Play a pitch that is high in your vocal range at a keyboard. Sing it. Then sing the pitch a diminished seventh lower (e.g., sing A♭-B.) Then sing a descending arpeggiation of a diminished seventh chord based upon the diminished seventh that you sang (e.g., sing A♭-F-D-B.) Use the keyboard to confirm your performance. Then sing descending diminished sevenths and diminished seventh chords on other pitches.

I20–5.　Choose a classmate with a similar vocal range as a partner. Then perform the following exercises, using each of the following six pairs of intervals.

X	Inv(X)
Minor second	Major seventh
Major second	Minor seventh
Augmented second	Diminished seventh
Diminished seventh	Augmented second
Minor seventh	Major second
Major seventh	Minor second

　a.　Your partner sings a pitch that is low in your vocal range. Then your partner sings the pitch a second time, while you sing the pitch that is **X** higher than your partner's. Then you sing the pitch you just sang a second time, while your partner sings the pitch that is **Inv(X)** higher than yours.

　b.　Your partner sings a pitch that is high in your vocal range. Then your partner sings the pitch a second time, while you sing the pitch that is **X** lower than your partner's. Then you sing the pitch you just sang a second time, while your partner sings the pitch that is **Inv(X)** lower than yours.

ARPEGGIATION WORKSHOP

A20–1.　Play a pitch that is at least a perfect fifth above the lowest note of your vocal range at a keyboard. Let this pitch be $\hat{1}$ in a major key. Sing each of the following arpeggiations, either in the order given or in random order.

a.　$\hat{1}$　$\hat{3}$　$\hat{5}$　✿　$\hat{4}$　$♭\hat{6}$　$\hat{2}$　✿　$\hat{5}$　$\hat{7}$　$\hat{2}$　✿　$\hat{8}$　$\hat{5}$　$\hat{1}$

b.　$\hat{1}$　$\hat{3}$　$\hat{5}$　✿　$\hat{4}$　$♭\hat{6}$　$\hat{8}$　✿　$\hat{5}$　$\hat{7}$　$\hat{2}$　✿　$\hat{8}$　$\hat{5}$　$\hat{1}$

c.　$\hat{1}$　$\hat{3}$　$\hat{5}$　$\hat{3}$　✿　$\hat{4}$　$♭\hat{6}$　$\hat{8}$　$\hat{2}$　✿　$\hat{5}$　$\hat{7}$　$\hat{2}$　$\hat{7}$　✿　$\hat{8}$　$\hat{5}$　$\hat{3}$　$\hat{1}$

d.　$\hat{1}$　$\hat{3}$　$\hat{5}$　✿　$\hat{3}$　$♯\hat{5}$　$\hat{7}$　✿　$\hat{4}$　$\hat{6}$　$\hat{2}$　✿　$\hat{5}$　$\hat{7}$　$\hat{2}$　✿　$\hat{8}$　$\hat{5}$　$\hat{1}$

e.　$\hat{1}$　$\hat{3}$　$\hat{5}$　✿　$\hat{3}$　$♯\hat{5}$　$\hat{7}$　✿　$\hat{4}$　$\hat{6}$　$\hat{8}$　$\hat{2}$　✿　$\hat{5}$　$\hat{7}$　$\hat{2}$　✿　$\hat{8}$　$\hat{5}$　$\hat{1}$

f.　$\hat{1}$　$\hat{3}$　$\hat{1}$　✿　$\hat{♭6}$　$\hat{1}$　$♭\hat{3}$　✿　$\hat{4}$　$\hat{♭6}$　$\hat{1}$　✿　$\hat{5}$　$\hat{7}$　$\hat{2}$　✿　$\hat{1}$　$\hat{3}$　$\hat{1}$

g.　$\hat{1}$　$\hat{3}$　$\hat{1}$　✿　$\hat{♭6}$　$\hat{1}$　$\hat{4}$　✿　$\hat{4}$　$\hat{♭6}$　$\hat{1}$　✿　$\hat{5}$　$\hat{7}$　$\hat{2}$　✿　$\hat{1}$　$\hat{3}$　$\hat{1}$

h.　$\hat{1}$　$\hat{3}$　$\hat{1}$　✿　$\hat{♭6}$　$\hat{1}$　$♭\hat{3}$　✿　$\hat{4}$　$\hat{♭6}$　$\hat{2}$　✿　$\hat{5}$　$\hat{7}$　$\hat{2}$　✿　$\hat{1}$　$\hat{3}$　$\hat{1}$

i.　$\hat{1}$　$\hat{3}$　$\hat{1}$　✿　$\hat{♭6}$　$\hat{1}$　$\hat{4}$　✿　$\hat{4}$　$\hat{♭6}$　$\hat{2}$　✿　$\hat{5}$　$\hat{7}$　$\hat{2}$　✿　$\hat{1}$　$\hat{3}$　$\hat{1}$

j. $\hat{1}$ $\hat{3}$ $\hat{5}$ $\hat{1}$ ° $\hat{7}$ $\hat{2}$ $\hat{4}$ $\hat{6}$ ° $\hat{5}$ $\hat{3}$ $\hat{1}$ $\hat{3}$ ° $\hat{2}$ $\hat{5}$ $\hat{7}$ $\hat{5}$

k. $\hat{1}$ $\hat{3}$ $\hat{5}$ $\hat{1}$ ° $\hat{7}$ $\hat{2}$ $\hat{4}$ $\flat\hat{6}$ ° $\hat{5}$ $\hat{3}$ $\hat{1}$ $\hat{3}$ ° $\hat{2}$ $\hat{5}$ $\hat{7}$ $\hat{5}$

l. $\hat{1}$ $\hat{3}$ $\hat{5}$ $\hat{1}$ ° $\hat{5}$ $\hat{7}$ $\hat{2}$ $\hat{4}$ ° $\hat{7}$ $\hat{2}$ $\hat{4}$ $\flat\hat{6}$ ° $\hat{5}$ $\hat{3}$ $\hat{5}$ $\hat{1}$

m. $\hat{1}$ $\hat{3}$ $\hat{5}$ $\hat{1}$ ° $\hat{7}$ $\hat{2}$ $\hat{4}$ $\hat{5}$ ° $\hat{7}$ $\hat{2}$ $\hat{4}$ $\flat\hat{6}$ ° $\hat{5}$ $\hat{3}$ $\hat{5}$ $\hat{1}$

n. $\hat{1}$ $\hat{3}$ $\hat{5}$ $\hat{1}$ ° $\hat{6}$ $\hat{1}$ $\hat{3}$ $\sharp\hat{4}$ ° $\hat{7}$ $\hat{2}$ $\hat{5}$ $\hat{7}$ ° $\hat{1}$ $\hat{3}$ $\hat{5}$ $\hat{1}$

o. $\hat{1}$ $\hat{3}$ $\hat{5}$ $\hat{1}$ ° $\hat{6}$ $\hat{1}$ $\flat\hat{3}$ $\sharp\hat{4}$ ° $\hat{7}$ $\hat{2}$ $\hat{5}$ $\hat{7}$ ° $\hat{1}$ $\hat{3}$ $\hat{5}$ $\hat{1}$

p. $\hat{1}$ $\hat{3}$ $\hat{5}$ $\hat{1}$ ° $\hat{1}$ $\hat{3}$ $\sharp\hat{4}$ $\hat{6}$ ° $\hat{7}$ $\hat{2}$ $\hat{5}$ $\hat{7}$ ° $\hat{1}$ $\hat{3}$ $\hat{5}$ $\hat{1}$

q. $\hat{1}$ $\hat{3}$ $\hat{5}$ $\hat{1}$ ° $\hat{1}$ $\flat\hat{3}$ $\sharp\hat{4}$ $\hat{6}$ ° $\hat{7}$ $\hat{2}$ $\hat{5}$ $\hat{7}$ ° $\hat{1}$ $\hat{3}$ $\hat{5}$ $\hat{1}$

A20–2.   Play a pitch that is at least a minor second above the lowest note of your vocal range at a keyboard. Let this pitch be $\hat{1}$ in a minor key. Sing each of the following arpeggiations, either in the order given or in random order.

a. $\hat{1}$ $\hat{3}$ $\hat{5}$ $\hat{3}$ ° $\hat{4}$ $\hat{6}$ $\hat{8}$ $\hat{2}$ ° $\hat{5}$ $\sharp\hat{7}$ $\hat{2}$ $\sharp\hat{7}$ ° $\hat{8}$ $\hat{5}$ $\sharp\hat{3}$ $\hat{1}$

b. $\hat{1}$ $\hat{3}$ $\hat{5}$ $\hat{1}$ ° $\sharp\hat{7}$ $\hat{2}$ $\hat{4}$ $\hat{6}$ ° $\hat{5}$ $\hat{3}$ $\hat{1}$ $\hat{3}$ ° $\hat{2}$ $\hat{5}$ $\sharp\hat{7}$ $\hat{2}$

c. $\hat{1}$ $\hat{3}$ $\hat{5}$ $\hat{1}$ ° $\sharp\hat{7}$ $\hat{2}$ $\hat{4}$ $\hat{5}$ ° $\sharp\hat{7}$ $\hat{2}$ $\hat{4}$ $\hat{6}$ ° $\hat{5}$ $\hat{3}$ $\hat{5}$ $\hat{1}$

d. $\hat{3}$ $\hat{5}$ $\hat{8}$ $\hat{3}$ ° $\hat{2}$ $\hat{4}$ $\hat{6}$ $\sharp\hat{7}$ ° $\hat{3}$ $\hat{5}$ $\hat{8}$ $\hat{3}$ ° $\hat{2}$ $\hat{5}$ $\sharp\hat{7}$ $\hat{2}$

e. $\hat{3}$ $\hat{5}$ $\hat{8}$ $\hat{3}$ ° $\hat{2}$ $\hat{4}$ $\hat{6}$ $\sharp\hat{7}$ ° $\hat{4}$ $\hat{6}$ $\sharp\hat{7}$ $\hat{2}$ ° $\hat{3}$ $\hat{5}$ $\hat{8}$ $\hat{3}$

f. $\hat{3}$ $\hat{5}$ $\hat{8}$ $\hat{3}$ ° $\hat{4}$ $\hat{6}$ $\sharp\hat{7}$ $\hat{2}$ ° $\hat{2}$ $\hat{4}$ $\hat{6}$ $\sharp\hat{7}$ ° $\hat{3}$ $\hat{5}$ $\hat{8}$ $\hat{3}$

g. $\hat{1}$ $\hat{3}$ $\hat{5}$ $\hat{8}$ ° $\sharp\hat{4}$ $\sharp\hat{6}$ $\hat{8}$ $\hat{3}$ ° $\hat{5}$ $\sharp\hat{7}$ $\hat{2}$ $\sharp\hat{7}$ ° $\hat{8}$ $\hat{5}$ $\hat{3}$ $\hat{1}$

h. $\hat{1}$ $\hat{3}$ $\hat{5}$ $\hat{8}$ ° $\sharp\hat{4}$ $\sharp\hat{6}$ $\hat{8}$ $\hat{3}$ ° $\hat{5}$ $\hat{8}$ $\hat{3}$ $\hat{8}$ ° $\hat{5}$ $\sharp\hat{7}$ $\hat{2}$ $\sharp\hat{7}$

i. $\hat{1}$ $\hat{3}$ $\hat{5}$ $\hat{1}$ ° $\hat{1}$ $\hat{3}$ $\sharp\hat{4}$ $\sharp\hat{6}$ ° $\sharp\hat{7}$ $\hat{2}$ $\hat{5}$ $\sharp\hat{7}$ ° $\hat{1}$ $\hat{3}$ $\hat{5}$ $\hat{1}$

j. $\hat{1}$ $\hat{5}$ $\hat{3}$ $\hat{1}$ ° $\hat{4}$ $\hat{8}$ $\hat{6}$ $\hat{2}$ ° $\hat{5}$ $\hat{2}$ $\sharp\hat{7}$ $\hat{5}$ ° $\hat{8}$ $\sharp\hat{3}$ $\hat{5}$ $\hat{1}$

k. $\hat{1}$ $\hat{5}$ $\hat{3}$ $\hat{1}$ ° $\sharp\hat{7}$ $\hat{4}$ $\hat{2}$ $\hat{6}$ ° $\hat{5}$ $\hat{1}$ $\hat{3}$ $\hat{1}$ ° $\hat{2}$ $\sharp\hat{7}$ $\hat{5}$ $\hat{2}$

l. $\hat{1}$ $\hat{5}$ $\hat{3}$ $\hat{1}$ ° $\sharp\hat{7}$ $\hat{4}$ $\hat{2}$ $\hat{5}$ ° $\sharp\hat{7}$ $\hat{4}$ $\hat{2}$ $\hat{6}$ ° $\hat{5}$ $\hat{3}$ $\hat{5}$ $\hat{1}$

m. $\hat{3}$ $\hat{8}$ $\hat{5}$ $\hat{3}$ ° $\hat{2}$ $\hat{6}$ $\hat{4}$ $\sharp\hat{7}$ ° $\hat{3}$ $\hat{8}$ $\hat{5}$ $\hat{3}$ ° $\hat{2}$ $\sharp\hat{7}$ $\hat{5}$ $\hat{2}$

n. $\hat{3}$ $\hat{8}$ $\hat{5}$ $\hat{3}$ ° $\hat{2}$ $\hat{6}$ $\hat{4}$ $\sharp\hat{7}$ ° $\hat{4}$ $\sharp\hat{7}$ $\hat{6}$ $\hat{2}$ ° $\hat{3}$ $\hat{8}$ $\hat{5}$ $\hat{3}$

o. $\hat{3}$ $\hat{8}$ $\hat{5}$ $\hat{3}$ ° $\hat{4}$ $\sharp\hat{7}$ $\hat{6}$ $\hat{2}$ ° $\hat{2}$ $\hat{6}$ $\hat{4}$ $\sharp\hat{7}$ ° $\hat{3}$ $\hat{8}$ $\hat{5}$ $\hat{3}$

p. $\hat{1}$ $\hat{5}$ $\hat{3}$ $\hat{8}$ ° $\sharp\hat{4}$ $\hat{8}$ $\sharp\hat{6}$ $\hat{3}$ ° $\hat{5}$ $\hat{2}$ $\sharp\hat{7}$ $\hat{5}$ ° $\hat{8}$ $\hat{3}$ $\hat{5}$ $\hat{1}$

q. $\hat{1}$ $\hat{5}$ $\hat{3}$ $\hat{8}$ ° $\sharp\hat{4}$ $\hat{8}$ $\sharp\hat{6}$ $\hat{3}$ ° $\hat{5}$ $\hat{3}$ $\hat{8}$ $\hat{5}$ ° $\hat{5}$ $\hat{2}$ $\sharp\hat{7}$ $\hat{5}$

r. $\hat{1}$ $\hat{5}$ $\hat{3}$ $\hat{1}$ ° $\hat{1}$ $\sharp\hat{4}$ $\hat{3}$ $\sharp\hat{6}$ ° $\sharp\hat{7}$ $\hat{5}$ $\hat{2}$ $\sharp\hat{7}$ ° $\hat{1}$ $\hat{5}$ $\hat{3}$ $\hat{1}$

QUICK SWITCH

Q20–1.

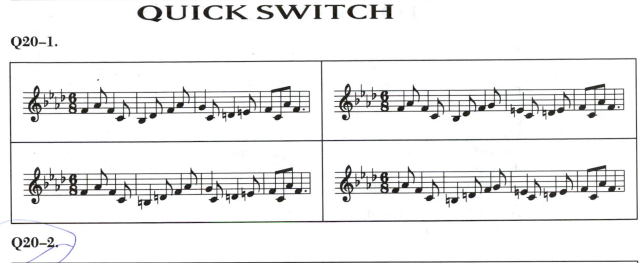

Q20–2.

Q20–3.

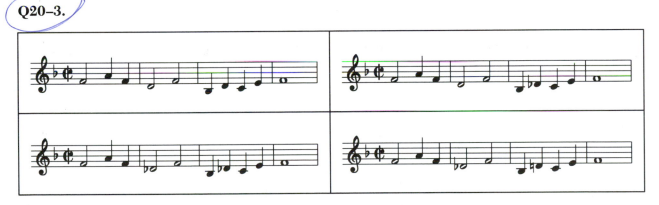

Q20–4.

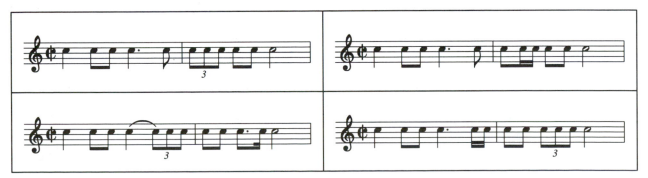

IDENTIFICATIONS

ID20–1.   An interval is performed melodically (ascending or descending) or as a simultaneity. Identify it as a diminished seventh, minor seventh, or major seventh.

ID20–2.   A seventh chord in ^{7}, $^6_5$, $^4_3$, or $^4_2$ position is performed. Is its quality major-minor (dominant), major, minor, half-diminished, or diminished?

ID20–3.   A diminished seventh chord is performed. Then two of its four pitches are performed melodically: root-third, root-fifth, root-seventh, third-root, third-fifth, third-seventh, fifth-root, fifth-third, fifth-seventh, seventh-root, seventh-third, or seventh-fifth. Identify which of these choices is performed.

ID20–4. $\hat{7}$, $\hat{2}$, $\hat{4}$, and $\hat{6}$ in a minor key are performed simultaneously. Then two of these four scale degrees are performed simultaneously. Identify the two scale degrees performed, from among the following choices: $\hat{7}$-2, $\hat{7}$-4, $\hat{7}$-6, $\hat{2}$-4, $\hat{2}$-6, $\hat{4}$-6.

ID20–5.   What chord occurs at **X**? Suitable choices are listed below.

$$\begin{array}{cccc} & & & ^7 \\ \text{C Major} & \text{I} & \textbf{X} & \text{V} & \text{I} \\ \text{C Major:} & \text{I} & \textbf{X} & \text{V}^7 & \text{I} \end{array}$$

Choices:

$$\begin{array}{cccccccc} ^6_3 & ^6_5 & ^6_\flat & ^6_5{}^\flat & ^6_3 & ^6_5 & 7 & 7\flat \\ \text{II} & \text{II} & \text{II}^{\flat5} & \text{II}^{\flat5} & \text{V}\smallsmile & \text{V}\smallfrown & \text{VII}\smallsmile & \text{VII}^{\flat7}\smallsmile \\ \text{ii}^6 & \text{ii}^6_5 & \text{ii}^{\emptyset6} & \text{ii}^{\emptyset6}_5 & \text{V}^6/\text{V} & \text{V}^6_5/\text{V} & \text{vii}^{\emptyset7}/\text{V} & \text{vii}^{\circ7}/\text{V} \end{array}$$

ID20–6.   What chord occurs at **Y**? Suitable choices are listed below.

$$\begin{array}{cccc} & ^6 & & \\ \text{F Major:} & \text{I} & \textbf{Y} & \text{I} & \text{V} \\ \text{F Major:} & \text{I}^6 & \textbf{Y} & \text{I} & \text{V} \end{array}$$

Choices:

$$\begin{array}{cccccccc} ^6 & ^6_5 & ^4_3 & ^6 & 7 & ^{\flat7} & ^6_5 & ^6_{\flat5} \\ \text{V} & \text{V} & \text{V} & \text{VII} & \text{VII} & \text{VII}^{\flat7} & \text{VII} & \text{VII}^{\flat7} \\ \text{V}^6 & \text{V}^6_5 & \text{V}^4_3 & \text{vii}^{\circ6} & \text{vii}^{\emptyset7} & \text{vii}^{\circ7} & \text{vii}^{\emptyset6}_5 & \text{vii}^{\circ6}_5 \end{array}$$

ID20–7.   A melody is performed. Identify the correct score notation.

ID20–8.   A chord progression in the major mode is performed. Identify a suitable Roman-numeral/figured-bass analysis from among the following choices:

Group 1

a.	I	♭VI$^{♭5}_{\substack{5♭\\3}}$	II$^{♭5}_{\substack{6\\5\\♭}}$	V^{7}	I	a.	I	♭VI	ii$^{ø6}_{5}$	V^{7}	I
b.	I	♭VI$^{♭5}_{\substack{5♭\\3}}$	IV♭$^{\substack{♭}}$	V^{7}	I	b.	I	♭VI	iv	V^{7}	I
c.	I	VI	II$^{♭5}_{\substack{6\\5\\♭}}$	V^{7}	I	c.	I	vi	ii$^{ø6}_{5}$	V^{7}	I
d.	I	VI	IV♭$^{\substack{♭}}$	V^{7}	I	d.	I	vi	iv	V^{7}	I

Group 2

a.	I	III♯$^{\substack{♯}}$	II^{6}	V^{7}	I	a.	I	III	ii^{6}	V^{7}	I
b.	I	III♯$^{\substack{♯}}$	IV	V^{7}	I	b.	I	III	IV	V^{7}	I
c.	I	III	II^{6}	V^{7}	I	c.	I	iii	ii^{6}	V^{7}	I
d.	I	III	IV	V^{7}	I	d.	I	iii	IV	V^{7}	I

ID20–9.   A chord progression in the minor mode is performed. Identify a suitable Roman-numeral/figured-bass analysis from among the following choices:

Group 1

a.	I	IV	VII$^{♭7}_{\substack{7\\♯}}$↘	V♯$^{\substack{♯}}$	I	a.	i	iv^{7}	vii^{o7}/V	V	i
b.	I	II$^{\substack{6\\5}}$	VII$^{♭7}_{\substack{7\\♯}}$↘	V♯$^{\substack{♯}}$	I♯$^{\substack{♯}}$	b.	i	ii$^{ø6}_{5}$	vii^{o7}/V	V	I
c.	I	IV	V↘$^{\substack{7\\♯}}$	V♯$^{\substack{♯}}$	I	c.	i	iv^{7}	V$^{6}_{5}$/V	V	i
d.	I	II$^{\substack{6\\5}}$	V↘$^{\substack{6\\5\\♯}}$	V♯$^{\substack{♯}}$	I♯$^{\substack{♯}}$	d.	i	ii$^{ø6}_{5}$	V$^{6}_{5}$/V	V	I

Group 2

a.	I	♯VII^{7}	I	II$^{\substack{6\\5}}$	V↘$^{\substack{6\\5\\♯}}$	V♯$^{\substack{♯}}$	I	a.	i	vii^{o7}	i	ii$^{ø6}_{5}$	V$^{6}_{5}$/V	V	i
b.	I	♯VII^{7}	I	II$^{\substack{6\\5}}$	VII↘$^{\substack{7\\♯}}$	V♯$^{\substack{♯}}$	I	b.	i	vii^{o7}	i	ii$^{ø6}_{5}$	vii^{o7}/V	V	i
c.	I	V♯$^{\substack{♯}}$	I	II$^{\substack{6\\5}}$	V↘$^{\substack{6\\5\\♯}}$	V♯$^{\substack{♯}}$	I	c.	i	V$^{6}_{5}$	i	ii$^{ø6}_{5}$	V$^{6}_{5}$/V	V	i
d.	I	V♯$^{\substack{♯}}$	I	II$^{\substack{6\\5}}$	VII↘$^{\substack{7\\♯}}$	V♯$^{\substack{♯}}$	I♯$^{\substack{♯}}$	d.	i	V$^{6}_{5}$	i	ii$^{ø6}_{5}$	vii^{o7}/V	V	I

ID20–10.   A chord progression is performed. Identify the correct score notation for the outer voices. Figured-bass symbols have been placed below the bass where appropriate. If you wish, add Roman numerals.

a.

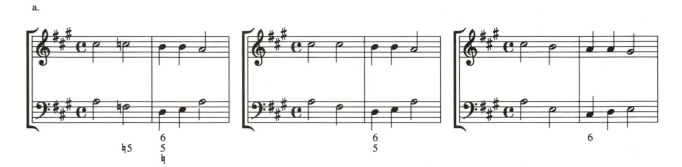

b.

c.

d.

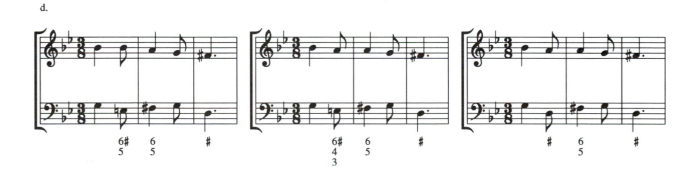

e.

f.

RHYTHMIC DICTATIONS

RD20–1.

RD20–2.

MELODIC DICTATIONS

WAGNER: *LOHENGRIN*, ACT 1

MD20–1.

Etwas weniger schnell

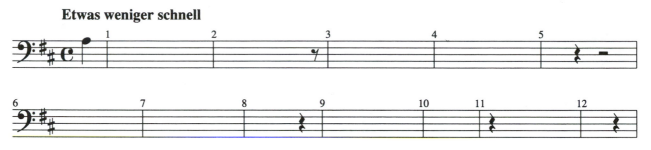

· This melody begins in the key of D minor and ends in the key of D major.

CHOPIN: TARANTELLE, OP. 43

MD20–2.

Presto

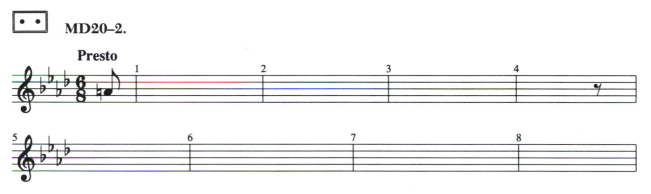

· Music theory textbooks codify a minor scale—the melodic minor—that employs ♯6̂. A major scale that employs ♭6̂ would be equally feasible. This excerpt might serve as an example of its use.

BEETHOVEN: *FIDELIO*, OP. 72, ACT 1

MD20–3.

- Keep the three pitches of the tonic triad in mind as you listen to this melody. Does the descent in the opening measures lead to $\hat{1}$ or even lower than $\hat{1}$? Does the descent in measures 2 through 4 lead to $\hat{1}$ or even lower than $\hat{1}$? Does the ascent in measures 4 through 6 lead to $\hat{3}$ or even higher than $\hat{3}$?

J.S. BACH: WELL-TEMPERED CLAVIER, VOL. 1, PRELUDE 20, BWV 865

MD20–4.

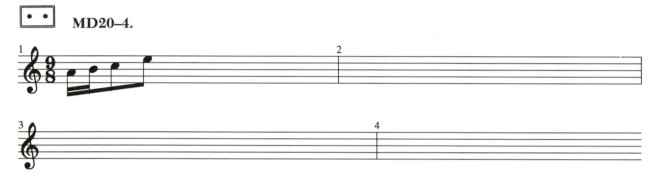

- The leading tone (G♯) occurs in measure 2. It is transferred up an octave in measure 3 and resolves to A in that register in measure 4.

MAHLER: SYMPHONY NO. 4 IN G MAJOR, MVMT. 2

MD20–5.

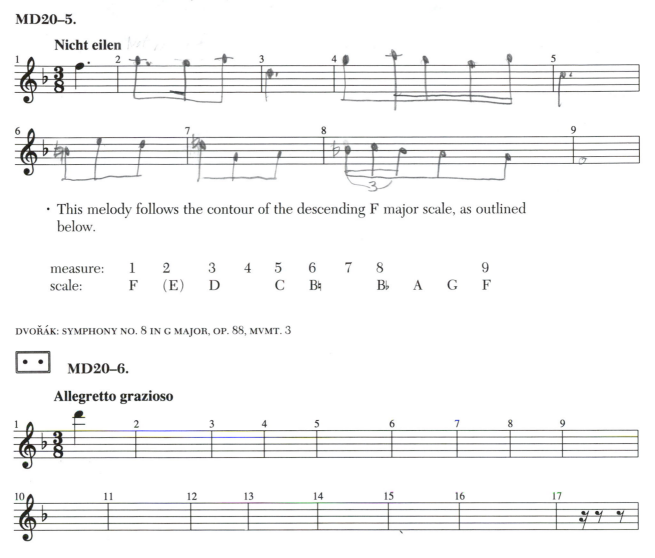

· This melody follows the contour of the descending F major scale, as outlined below.

measure:	1	2	3	4	5	6	7	8		9
scale:	F	(E)	D		C	B♮		B♭	A	G	F

DVOŘÁK: SYMPHONY NO. 8 IN G MAJOR, OP. 88, MVMT. 3

MD20–6.

Allegretto grazioso

· The numerous half steps of this melody fill in intervals of an underlying tonic arpeggiation.

HARMONIC DICTATIONS

DVOŘÁK: *RUSALKA*, OP. 114, ACT 2

HD20–1.

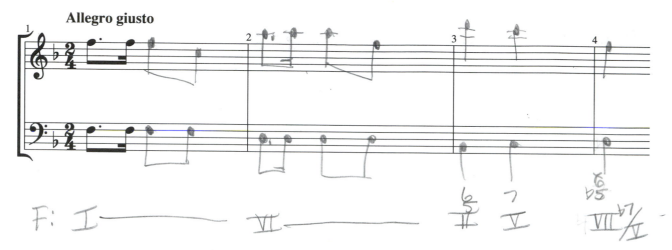

- A deceptive cadence is characterized by a stepwise ascent from $\hat{5}$ to $\hat{6}$ in the bass. This excerpt demonstrates a new choice for the chord built upon $\hat{6}$.

MOZART: PIANO SONATA NO. 14 IN C MINOR, K. 457, MVMT. 3

HD20–2.

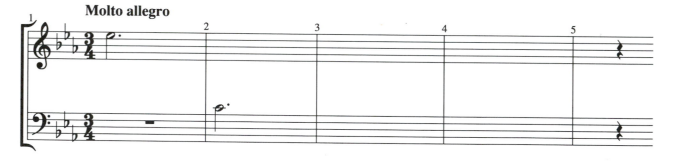

- The chord in the second measure is incomplete. What other pitch belongs to the chord? The chord on beat 1 of measure 4 is incomplete. What other pitch belongs to the chord?

SCHUBERT: MENUET, D. 41, NO. 7

HD20–3.

• Though the chord on beat 3 of measure 3 is incomplete, the bass arpeggiation leading to that beat clarifies Schubert's intent.

BEETHOVEN: STRING QUARTET NO. 10 IN E♭ MAJOR ("HARP"), OP. 74, MVMT. 2

HD20–4.

Adagio ma non troppo

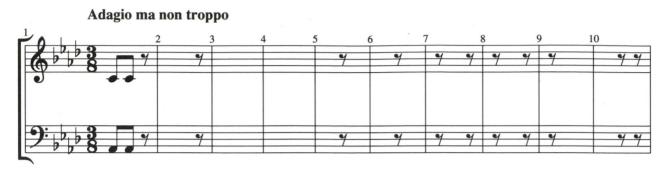

· What is the relationship between measures 1 and 2? What *melodic* role is played
  by the soprano in measure 2? Has there been a change of *harmony*?

MOZART: SYMPHONY NO. 39 IN E♭ MAJOR, K. 543, MVMT. 2

HD20–5.

- Modal mixture is not restricted to harmonies. Measure 3 contains a neighboring note borrowed from A♭ minor. Measure 5 contains a passing note borrowed from A♭ minor.

MOZART: *THE MAGIC FLUTE*, K. 620, ACT 2

HD20–6.

- Dominant and leading-tone harmonies often follow one another. The leading-tone harmony in measure 5 does not resolve the dominant tendencies of measure 4, but intensifies them.

- Beat 2 of measure 5 should be analyzed as a passing chord, not as a resolution of the leading-tone chord.

📼 CASSETTE PROGRAM (TAPE 3, SIDE B)

C20–1.   Six melodies are performed, twice each. During the silence after each playing, respond in one of the following ways: (1) Sing the melody, using solmization syllables; (2) Play the melody on the piano or on your primary instrument; (3) Write the melody on staff paper.

a.   b.   c.   d.   e.   f.

C20–2.   Six chord progressions are performed, four times each. During the silence after each playing, respond in one of the following ways: (1) Sing the soprano after the first and second playings and the bass after the third and fourth playings, using solmization syllables; (2) Play the soprano on the piano or your primary instrument after the first and second playings and the bass after the third and fourth playings; (3) Play both the soprano and bass on the piano after each playing; (4) Write the soprano and bass on staff paper and provide an analysis.

a.   b.   c.   d.   e.   f.

Chapter 21

PITCH

Just as $\hat{\sharp 4}$ is used in applied chords that resolve to the dominant, $\hat{\sharp 1}$ is used in applied chords that resolve to the supertonic. Tonicization of and modulation to the supertonic also occur. The diminished supertonic of natural minor is not a suitable goal of applied chords—and certainly not appropriate for a tonicization or modulation. Only the minor supertonic in major keys or the minor supertonic with raised fifth in minor keys may function in these ways. Because the goal chord is minor, an applied leading-tone seventh chord will be of diminished quality, as demonstrated in Example 21–1.

EXAMPLE 21–1

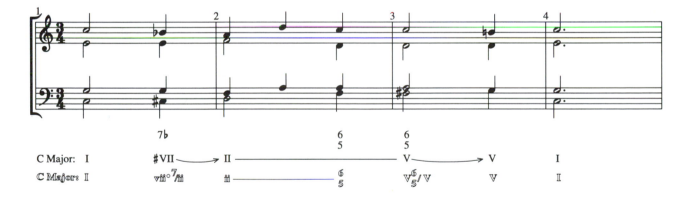

In Method One analysis, the applied chord's Roman numeral appears as $\sharp$VII⌐. A sharp is placed to the left of the numeral because, in the context of D *minor* (the chord to which this chord is applied), the leading-tone chord is analyzed as $\sharp$VII to distinguish it from the subtonic chord of minor keys. Because the pitch B♭ is diatonic in D minor but not in C major, it is acknowledged only in the figured-bass analysis. The $_3^5$-position applied dominant of the supertonic will be analyzed with Roman numeral V$\sharp$⌐ and figured bass $\sharp$, because C$\sharp$ is diatonic in neither C major nor D minor.

Suspension is a procedure in which a pitch from one chord lingers even after the other voices have moved to the next chord, against which the suspended pitch clashes. The suspended pitch occurs typically on a strong beat and resolves on a weaker beat. Example 21–2 displays a **9–8 suspension**, the focus of this chapter. The three phases of the suspension are marked: preparation, suspension, and resolution. The ninth (G against bass pitch F) resolves downward by step to an octave on beat 4 of measure 2. Although only one of the four beats of the measure contains only pitches of the sub-dominant chord, the entire measure is analyzed as subdominant. The suspended pitch may be rearticulated when the new bass pitch arrives, as in Example 21–2. Or it may be connected to the note that prepares it with a tie (♩‿♩ ♩) or, when the suspension occurs in the middle of a measure, through the use of a longer rhythmic value (♩. ♩ ♩).

EXAMPLE 21–2

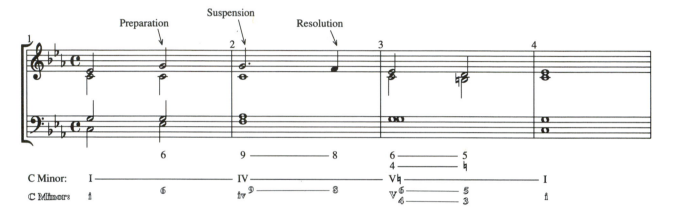

Although compound intervals have been used in constructing chords throughout the text, they have not yet appeared in Solo Melodies and Melodic Dictations. These larger intervals will be introduced over the next five chapters. In chapter 21, the **minor ninth** and the **major ninth** are emphasized, in coordination with the introduction of the 9–8 suspension. These intervals are one octave larger than the minor second and major second, respectively. The *size* of a compound interval is seven larger than that of its simple counterpart for every octave that is added (e.g., 2 + 7 = 9). Its *quality* is the same as that of its simple counterpart.

METER AND RHYTHM

Triplets that fill a beat or part of a beat have been introduced in earlier chapters. **Multiple-beat triplets** are also possible, although less common. Such triplets clash against the prevailing metrical pulse, as Example 21–3 displays.

EXAMPLE 21–3

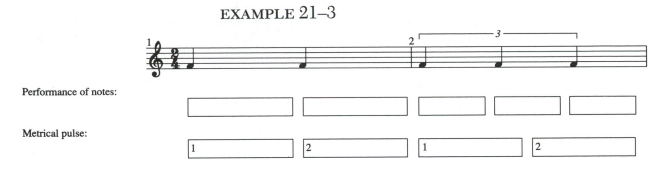

Performance of notes:

Metrical pulse:

Counting syllables will help you perform multiple-beat triplets accurately. The strategy suggested below corresponds to the notation shown in Example 21–3.

1. Start by counting just the beats to establish a solid metrical pulse:

   1   2   1   2   . . .

2. Retaining the same pulse, add duple subdivisions:

   1   +   2   +   1   +   2   +   . . .

3. Alternate measures of duple and triple subdivision:

   1   +   2   +   1   +   uh   2   +   uh   . . .

4. Clap at the spots marked with an X:

   X   X   X   X   X
   1   +   2   +   1   +   uh   2   +   uh   . . .

Example 21–4 demonstrates multiple-beat triplets.

EXAMPLE 21–4

SING:

THINK: 1 + 2 + 3 + 4 +   1 + uh 2 + uh 3 + 4 + 1   +   2   +   3 + 4 +

SOLO MELODIES

MELODIES IN WHICH THE SUPERTONIC IS PRECEDED BY ITS LEADING TONE

SCHUBERT: SYMPHONY NO. 8 IN B MINOR ("UNFINISHED"), D. 759, MVMT. 1

S21–1.

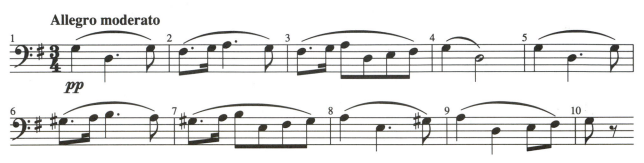

- Measures 6 and 7 relate to the A of measure 8 in exactly the same way that measures 2 and 3 relate to the G of measure 4.

SCHUBERT: PIANO SONATA IN B♭ MAJOR, D. 960, MVMT. 4

S21–2.

MENDELSSOHN: SONG WITHOUT WORDS, OP. 53, NO. 4 (BOOK 4)

S21–3.

· Measure 5 contains a descending arpeggiation of the supertonic's applied leading-tone chord (with passing notes B♭ and G filling in the diminished triad's two thirds).

BEETHOVEN: *FIDELIO*, OP. 72, ACT 1

S21–4.

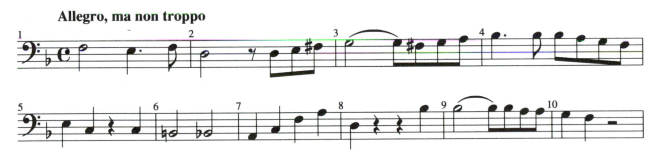

GRIEG: "THE LAST SPRING," FROM TWO ELEGAIC MELODIES FOR STRING ORCHESTRA, OP. 34

S21–5.

- Tonic G major's fifth D is embellished by a written-out turn (∾) in measures 1 and 2. Likewise supertonic A minor's fifth E is embellished by a written-out turn in measures 5 and 6.

- Grieg emphasizes the supertonic without employing its leading tone, G♯, in the melody. His accompaniment in measure 6 would include a G♯, however. (The E, B, and D along with the "missing" G♯ form the dominant seventh chord of A minor.)

MENDELSSOHN: VIOLIN CONCERTO IN E MINOR, OP. 64, MVMT. 2

S21–6.

MELODIES THAT EMPLOY A MINOR NINTH
OR A MAJOR NINTH

CHOPIN: MAZURKA, OP. 24, NO. 4

S21–7.

- C in measure 2 is an upper neighbor of the following pitch, B♭. When B♭ is lowered a half step to B♭♭ in measure 6 (an instance of modal mixture), so is its neighbor.

SCHUBERT: *SCHWANENGESANG*, D. 957, "AUFENTHALT"

S21–8.

VERDI: *OTELLO*, ACT 2

S21–9.

· Sing the following two melodies as preparation for singing measures 7 through 11.

BERLIOZ: *LA DAMNATION DE FAUST*, OP. 24, PART 4

S21–10.

MELODIES THAT EMPLOY MULTIPLE-BEAT TRIPLETS

DVOŘÁK: SYMPHONY NO. 8 IN G MAJOR, OP. 88, MVMT. 1

S21–11.

- Practice by tapping the beats with your hand or foot. The fourth tap of measure 5 should come midway between the G♭ and F of the two-beat triplet.

S21–12.

DUETS

AFTER HAYDN: SYMPHONY NO. 94 IN G MAJOR ("SURPRISE"), MVMT. 1

D21–1.

AFTER MOZART: *IDOMENEO, RE DI CRETA*, K. 366, ACT 3

D21–2.

ACCOMPANIED SOLO MELODIES

AFTER MOZART: PIANO CONCERTO NO. 25 IN C MAJOR, K. 503, MVMT. 2

AS21–1.

AS21–2.

RHYTHMS

R21–1.

R21–2.

R21–3.

R21–4.

R21–5.

R21–6.

INTERVAL WORKSHOP

I21–1.   Practice singing the intervals of a minor ninth and a major ninth higher than a sounding pitch. The sounding pitch should be at or beyond the lower limit of your vocal range, and could be sung by a classmate or your instructor or performed on the piano or another instrument such as the cello. Also practice minor and major sixteenths and twenty-thirds, using very low sounding pitches.

I21–2.   Practice singing the intervals of a minor ninth and a major ninth lower than a sounding pitch. The sounding pitch should be at or beyond the upper limit of your vocal range, and could be sung by a classmate or your instructor or performed on the piano or another instrument such as the flute. Also practice singing minor and major sixteenths and twenty-thirds, using very high sounding pitches.

I21–3.   Play a pitch low in your vocal range at a keyboard. Sing it. Then sing the pitch a minor ninth higher. Use the keyboard to confirm your performance. Then sing ascending minor ninths starting on other pitches. Repeat this exercise for the major ninth.

I21–4.   Play a pitch high in your vocal range at a keyboard. Sing it. Then sing the pitch a minor ninth lower. Use the keyboard to confirm your performance. Then sing descending minor ninths starting on other pitches. Repeat this exercise for the major ninth.

ARPEGGIATION WORKSHOP

A21–1.   Play a pitch that is low in your vocal range at a keyboard. Let this pitch be $\hat{1}$ in a major key. Sing each of the following arpeggiations, either in the order given or in random order.

a. $\hat{1}\ \hat{5}\ \hat{8}\ \hat{3}$ • $\hat{2}\ \hat{4}\ \hat{6}\ \hat{3}$ • $\hat{2}\ \hat{4}\ \hat{6}\ \hat{2}$ • $\hat{5}\ \hat{7}\ \hat{2}\ \hat{5}$

b. $\hat{1}\ \hat{3}\ \hat{5}\ \hat{8}$ • $\hat{5}\ \hat{7}\ \hat{2}\ \hat{5}$ • $\hat{1}\ \hat{3}\ \hat{5}\ \hat{2}$ • $\hat{1}\ \hat{3}\ \hat{5}\ \hat{8}$

c. $\hat{1}\ \hat{5}\ \hat{8}\ \hat{3}$ • $\hat{2}\ \hat{4}\ \hat{7}\ \hat{3}$ • $\hat{2}\ \hat{4}\ \hat{7}\ \hat{2}$ • $\hat{3}\ \hat{5}\ \hat{8}\ \hat{3}$

d. $\hat{1}\ \hat{5}\ \hat{3}\ \hat{5}$ • $\hat{4}\ \hat{6}\ \hat{8}\ \hat{5}$ • $\hat{4}\ \hat{6}\ \hat{8}\ \hat{4}$ • $\hat{5}\ \hat{7}\ \hat{2}\ \hat{4}$ •
     $\hat{1}\ \hat{5}\ \hat{8}\ \hat{3}$

e. $\hat{1}\ \hat{3}\ \hat{5}\ \hat{3}$ • $\sharp\hat{1}\ \hat{3}\ \hat{5}\ \hat{6}$ • $\hat{2}\ \hat{4}\ \hat{6}\ \hat{4}$ • $\hat{5}\ \hat{7}\ \hat{2}\ \hat{5}$

f. $\hat{1}\ \hat{3}\ \hat{5}\ \hat{3}$ • $\sharp\hat{1}\ \hat{3}\ \hat{5}\ \flat\hat{7}$ • $\hat{2}\ \hat{4}\ \hat{6}\ \hat{4}$ • $\hat{5}\ \hat{7}\ \hat{2}\ \hat{5}$

g. $\hat{3}\ \hat{5}\ \hat{8}\ \hat{3}$ • $\hat{3}\ \hat{5}\ \hat{6}\ \sharp\hat{8}$ • $\hat{4}\ \hat{6}\ \hat{2}\ \hat{4}$ • $\hat{5}\ \hat{7}\ \hat{2}\ \hat{5}$

h. $\hat{3}\ \hat{5}\ \hat{8}\ \hat{3}$ • $\hat{3}\ \hat{5}\ \flat\hat{7}\ \sharp\hat{8}$ • $\hat{4}\ \hat{6}\ \hat{2}\ \hat{4}$ • $\hat{5}\ \hat{7}\ \hat{2}\ \hat{5}$

A21–2.   Play a pitch that is low in your vocal range at a keyboard. Let this pitch be $\hat{1}$ in a minor key. Sing each of the following arpeggiations, either in the order given or in random order.

a. $\hat{1}\ \hat{5}\ \hat{8}\ \hat{3}$ • $\hat{2}\ \hat{4}\ \hat{6}\ \hat{3}$ • $\hat{2}\ \hat{4}\ \hat{6}\ \hat{2}$ • $\hat{5}\ \sharp\hat{7}\ \hat{2}\ \hat{5}$

b. $\hat{1}\ \hat{3}\ \hat{5}\ \hat{8}$ • $\hat{5}\ \sharp\hat{7}\ \hat{2}\ \hat{5}$ • $\hat{1}\ \hat{3}\ \hat{5}\ \hat{2}$ • $\hat{1}\ \hat{3}\ \hat{5}\ \hat{8}$

c. $\hat{1}\ \hat{5}\ \hat{8}\ \hat{3}$ • $\hat{2}\ \hat{4}\ \sharp\hat{7}\ \hat{3}$ • $\hat{2}\ \hat{4}\ \sharp\hat{7}\ \hat{2}$ • $\hat{3}\ \hat{5}\ \hat{8}\ \hat{3}$

d. $\hat{1}\ \hat{5}\ \hat{3}\ \hat{5}$ • $\hat{4}\ \hat{6}\ \hat{8}\ \hat{5}$ • $\hat{4}\ \hat{6}\ \hat{8}\ \hat{4}$ • $\hat{5}\ \sharp\hat{7}\ \hat{2}\ \hat{4}$ •
     $\hat{1}\ \hat{5}\ \hat{8}\ \hat{3}$

e. $\hat{1}\ \hat{3}\ \hat{5}\ \hat{1}$ • $\sharp\hat{3}\ \hat{5}\ \sharp\hat{8}\ \sharp\hat{3}$ • $\hat{4}\ \sharp\hat{6}\ \hat{2}\ \hat{4}$ • $\hat{5}\ \sharp\hat{7}\ \hat{2}\ \sharp\hat{7}$ •
     $\hat{8}\ \hat{5}\ \hat{3}\ \hat{1}$

QUICK SWITCH

Q21–1.

Q21–2.

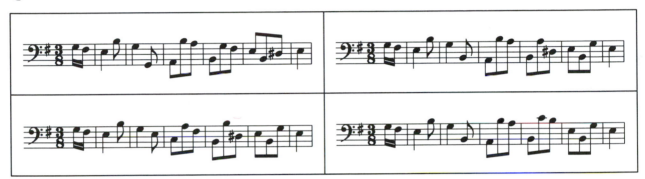

Q21–3.

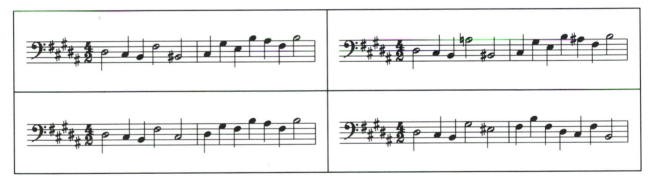

Q21–4.

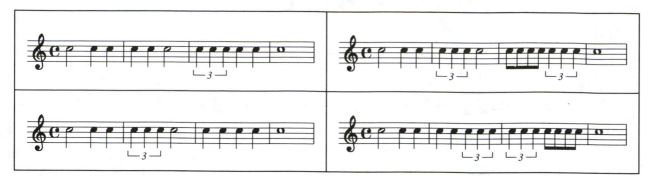

IDENTIFICATIONS

ID21–1.   An interval not larger than a major ninth is performed melodically or as a simultaneity. Identify it.

ID21–2.   What chord occurs at **X**? Suitable choices are listed below.

C Major: I   **X**   II $\overset{7}{V}$ I
C Major: I   **X**   ii V^7 I

Choices:

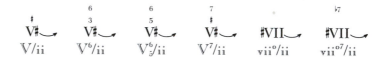

$\overset{}{V\sharp}$ $\overset{6}{\underset{3}{V\sharp}}$ $\overset{6}{\underset{5}{V\sharp}}$ $\overset{7}{\underset{\sharp}{V\sharp}}$ $\overset{}{\sharp VII}$ $\overset{\flat 7}{\sharp VII}$
V/ii V^6/ii V^6_5/ii V^7/ii   vii°/ii   vii°7/ii

ID21–3.   What chord occurs at **Y**? Suitable choices are listed below.

F Major: I $\overset{6}{V}$ VI   **Y** $\overset{6}{II}$ V   I
F Major: I V^6 vi   **Y** ii^6 V   I

Choices:

$\overset{6}{\underset{3}{I}}$ $\overset{6}{\underset{\overset{4\sharp}{2}}{V\sharp}}$ $\overset{6}{\underset{\overset{4}{2}}{VI}}$ $\overset{6}{\underset{\overset{4\sharp}{3\flat}}{\sharp VII}}$
I^6 V^4_2/ii vi^4_2 $vii°^4_3$/ii

ID21–4.   A melody is performed. Identify the correct score notation.

a.

b.

c.

d.

e.

f.

ID21–5.   A chord progression in the major mode is performed. Identify a suitable Roman-numeral/figured-bass analysis from among the following choices:

Group 1

a. I   V♯($^{6♯}_{4}$)(^{3})↷II   V(^{6})↷V(^{6})   a. I^6 V$^4_3$/ii   ii^6 V$^6_5$/V   V

b. I   ♯VII(^{6})($^{5♭}_{3}$)↷II   VII$^{♭7}$($^{♭7}$)↷V   b. I^6 vii$^{o6}_5$/ii   ii^6 vii^{o7}/V   V

c. I   V♯($^{6♯}_{4}$)(^{3})↷II   VII$^{♭7}$($^{♭7}$)↷V   c. I^6 V$^4_3$/ii   ii^6 vii^{o7}/V   V

d. I   ♯VII(^{6})($^{5♭}_{3}$)↷II   V(^{6})↷V(^{5})   d. I^6 vii$^{o6}_5$/ii   ii^6 V$^6_5$/V   V

Group 2

a. I   V   VI   ♯VII($^{6♯}_{5}$)(^{3})↷II   V(^{6})   I($^{4}_{2}$)   a. I   V^7 vi   vii$^{o6}_5$/ii   ii^6 V$^4_2$ I^6

b. I   V   VI   V♯($^{6♯}_{4}$)(^{3})↷II   V(^{6})   I($^{4}_{2}$)   b. I   V^7 vi   V$^4_3$/ii   ii^6 V$^4_2$ I^6

c. I   V   VI   VII$^{♭7}$($^{♭7}$)($^{5}_{3}$)↷V————($^{4}_{2}$)I   c. I   V^7 vi   vii^{o7}/V   V   ($^4_2$)   I^6

d. I   V   VI   V($^{6}_{5}$)↷V($^{5}_{3}$)————($^{4}_{2}$)I   d. I   V^7 vi   V$^6_5$/V   V   ($^4_2$)   I^6

ID21–6.   A chord progression in the minor mode is performed. Identify a suitable Roman-numeral/figured-bass analysis from among the following choices:

Group 1

a.   I   IV $\text{V}\sharp\substack{9-8\\7-\\\sharp-}$ I   a.   i   iv V_7^{9-8} i

b.   I   IV $\text{V}\sharp\substack{6-5\\4-\sharp}$ I   b.   i   iv V_{4-3}^{6-5} i

c.   I $\text{II}\substack{6\\5}$ $\text{V}\sharp\substack{9-8\\\sharp-}$ I   c.   i $\text{ii}^{\o 6}_{5}$ V^{9-8} i

d.   I $\text{II}\substack{6\\5}$ $\text{V}\sharp\substack{6-5\\4-\sharp}$ I   d.   i $\text{ii}^{\o 6}_{5}$ V_{4-3}^{6-5} i

Group 2

a.   I $\sharp\text{VII}\substack{9-8\\6\sharp-}$ I $\text{V}\sharp\substack{6\\ \ }$ $\substack{7\\\sharp}$ I   a.   i $\text{vii}^{\circ}_{6}{}^{9-8}$ i^6 V^7 i

b.   I $\sharp\text{VII}^{6\sharp}$———I $\text{V}\sharp\substack{6\\4\sharp\\3}$ $\substack{6\\ \ }$ $\substack{7\\\sharp}$ I   b.   i $\text{vii}^{\circ 6}$ $\substack{4\\3}$ i^6 V^7 i

c.   I $\sharp\text{VII}^{6\sharp}$ $\text{V}\sharp\substack{6\\4\sharp\\2}$ I $\substack{6\\ \ }$ $\substack{7\\\sharp}$ I   c.   i $\text{vii}^{\circ 6}$ V_2^4 i^6 V^7 i

d. $\text{I}\substack{5\\3}$———$\substack{6\\3}$ $\text{V}\sharp\substack{6\\4\sharp\\2}$ I $\substack{6\\ \ }$ $\substack{7\\\sharp}$ I   d.   i $\substack{6\\ \ }$ V_2^4 i^6 V^7 i

ID21–7.   A chord progression is performed. Identify the correct score notation for the outer voices. Figured-bass symbols have been placed below the bass where appropriate. If you wish, add Roman numerals.

a.

b.

c.

d.

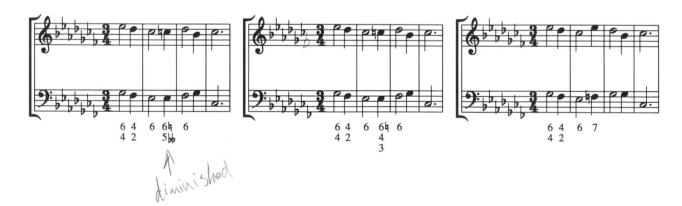

e.

f.

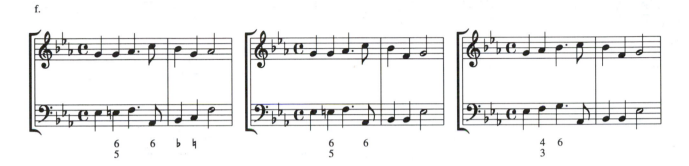

RHYTHMIC DICTATIONS

RD21–1.

RD21–2.

MELODIC DICTATIONS

HAYDN: SYMPHONY NO. 93 IN D MAJOR, MVMT. 1

MD21–1.

      · Complete measure 5 before writing down the pitches of measure 4, beat 3. Does measure 5 sound familiar? What is the structure of these eight measures?

FIELD: PIANO CONCERTO NO. 2 IN A♭ MAJOR, MVMT. 3

MD21–2.

      · Determine the first pitch of measure 4 by relating it to the first pitch of measure 1 and the pitch of measure 5.

MOZART: SYMPHONY NO. 35 IN D MAJOR ("HAFFNER"), K. 385, MVMT. 4

MD21–3.

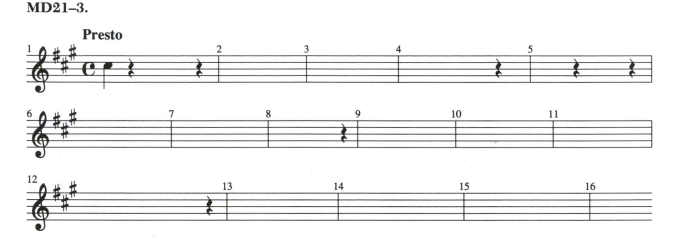

• Determine the first pitch of measure 5 by relating it to the first pitch of measure 2.

HAYDN: SYMPHONY NO. 98 IN B♭ MAJOR, MVMT. 4

MD21–4.

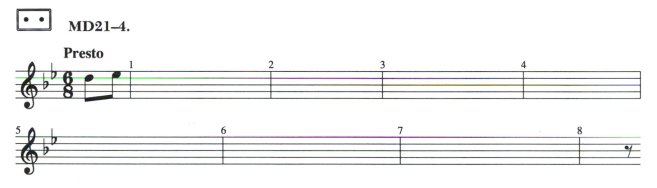

• Listening to measure 5 and the first three pitches of measure 6, what do you expect as the fourth pitch of measure 6? Does Haydn fulfill your expectation, or instead surprise you? Listening to measure 6 and the first two pitches of measure 7, what do you expect as the third pitch of measure 7? What does Haydn do this time?

HAYDN: SYMPHONY NO. 102 IN B♭ MAJOR, MVMT. 3

MD21–5.

Allegro

• What descending interval is filled in from beat 3 of measure 5 through beat 1 of measure 8? Compare that passage with measures 14 and 15.

WAGNER: *LOHENGRIN*, ACT 3

MD21–6.

Sehr leidenshaftlich

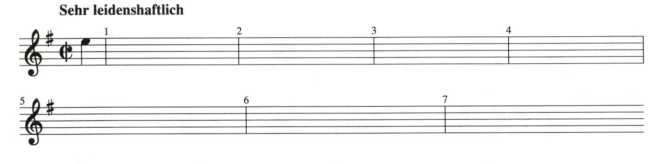

• A single harmony is prolonged during these measures.

HARMONIC DICTATIONS

BEETHOVEN: SYMPHONY NO. 1 IN C MAJOR, OP. 21, MVMT. 2

HD21–1.

Andante cantabile con moto

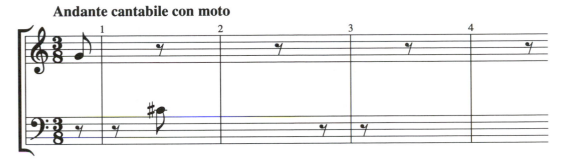

- From the material that precedes this excerpt, a listener would understand that the first two soprano pitches represent tonic, C major. When C♯ enters in the bass, these pitches take on a new meaning.

SCHUBERT: SONATA FOR ARPEGGIONE AND PIANO IN A MINOR, D. 821, MVMT. 2

HD21–2.

Adagio

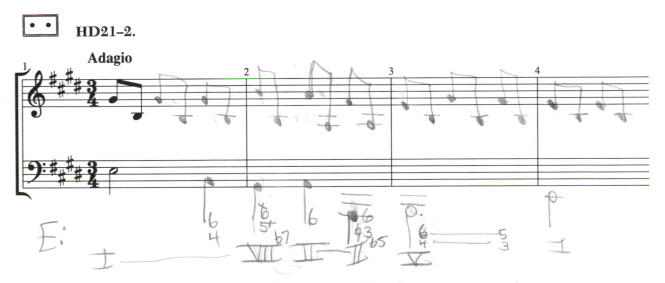

- In its context, the first bass pitch of measure 2 could easily support tonic in first inversion. Schubert's chord is dissonant, however. What chords other than tonic employ both G♯ and B (the two outer voices)? Which one occurs here?

MOZART: PIANO SONATA NO. 13 IN B♭ MAJOR, K. 333, MVMT. 1

HD21–3.

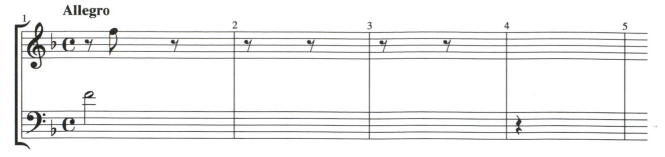

· Why is an accidental employed in the soprano during measure 1?

BRAHMS: PIANO TRIO NO. 1 IN B MAJOR, OP. 8, MVMT. 3

HD21–4.

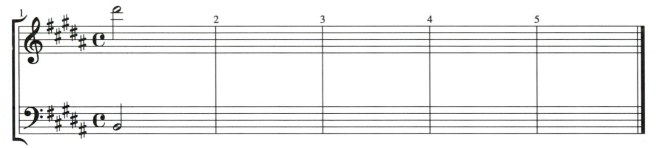

· Twice during this excerpt, a compound diminished fifth occurs in the outer voices (measure 1, beat 3, and measure 3, beat 1). Do the two chords that contain this interval function in a similar way? Does the diminished fifth resolve in the same way in both instances?

SCHUBERT: *FIERRABRAS*, D. 796, ACT 1

HD21–5.

Allegro vivace

- The twenty-two chords of this excerpt expand the basic progression shown below.

measure:	1	2	3	4	5		6	7		8
C Major:	I		II			V	I	V		I
C Major:	I		ii			V	I	V		I

BEETHOVEN: PIANO SONATA NO. 13 IN E♭ MAJOR, OP. 27, NO. 1, MVMT. 1

HD21–6.

- The descending line 5̂-4̂-3̂-2̂-1̂ in the soprano of measures 3 and 4 is embellished between 2̂ and 1̂. 1̂ arrives in the bass before it arrives in the soprano.

⊡ CASSETTE PROGRAM
(TAPE 4, SIDE A)

C21–1.　　Six melodies are performed, twice each. During the silence after each playing, respond in one of the following ways: (1) Sing the melody, using solmization syllables; (2) Play the melody on the piano or on your primary instrument; (3) Write the melody on staff paper.

C21–2.　　Six chord progressions are performed, four times each. During the silence after each playing, respond in one of the following ways: (1) Sing the soprano after the first and second playings and the bass after the third and fourth playings, using solmization syllables; (2) Play the soprano on the piano or your primary instrument after the first and second playings and the bass after the third and fourth playings; (3) Play both the soprano and bass on the piano after each playing; (4) Write the soprano and bass on staff paper and provide an analysis.

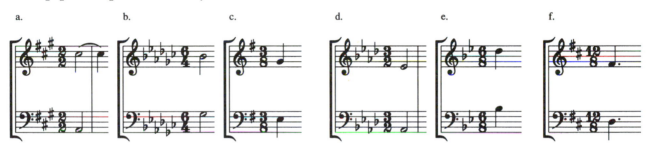

Chapter 22

PITCH

The subdominant, like the supertonic and the dominant, may serve as the goal of an applied chord, tonicization, or modulation. In the major mode, tonic $\frac{5}{3}$ is indistinguishable from V of IV and is usually better analyzed as "I." Only if $\flat\hat{7}$ is added is its role as an applied dominant confirmed. In the minor mode, an accidental is required to convert the minor tonic into the major applied dominant of the subdominant. The subdominant's applied leading-tone seventh chord, shown in Example 22–1, is usually of diminished quality.

EXAMPLE 22–1

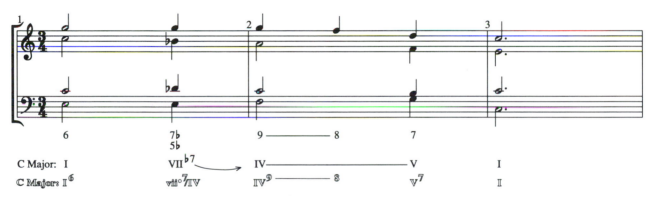

The *minor tenth*, **major tenth**, **perfect eleventh**, and *augmented eleventh* are emphasized in this chapter. Compound thirds and fourths may be used in a ***4-3 suspension***, which works like a 9-8 suspension. Measure 2 of Example 22–2 contains a 4-3 suspension. Compound seconds and thirds may be used in a ***2-3 bass suspension***, in which the suspended pitch is the lowest voice. In Example 22–2, the bass pitch A on beat 3 of measure 1 is a suspension, forming a compound second against the soprano pitch B. The upper voices are pitches of the dominant harmony, while the bass lingers on a pitch from the preceding tonic chord and belatedly resolves downward by step to the leading tone. Example 22–2 shows two distinct styles of figured bass for Method One analysis: (1) the figured bass $^{5\ 6}_{2\ 3}$, which indicates the interval content of both chords in the conventional manner; or (2) the figured bass $^{5-}_{2-}$, which indicates that the pitches a second and fifth above the bass suspension are retained even after the suspension resolves.

EXAMPLE 22–2

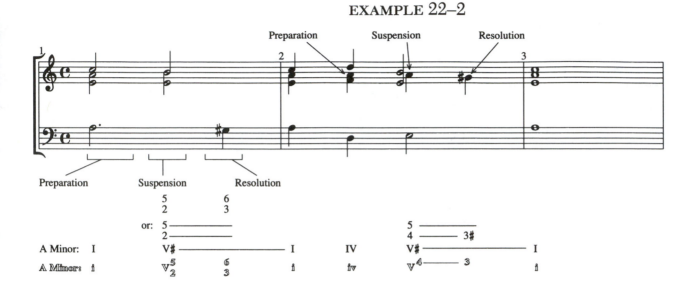

METER AND RHYTHM

Triplets not only *substitute for* two notes; but also may *coexist with* two notes—**three against two**. Once you get the hang of it, it is probably easier not to count subdivisions of the beat at all. Just make sure that the beats (e.g., "1 2 1 2") are evenly spaced in time. Until you attain that proficiency, divide the beat into six parts. The duple subdivisions of the beat will each fill three of those parts, while the triplets will each fill two of those parts. Practice Example 22–3 using your right hand for the upper part and your left hand for the lower part. Make sure that the tempo does not waver, perhaps by using a metronome set at forty beats per minute. A similar procedure could be developed for partial-beat and multiple-beat triplets as well.

EXAMPLE 22–3

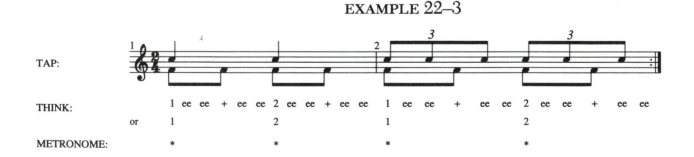

SOLO MELODIES

MELODIES THAT OUTLINE A CHORD
APPLIED TO THE SUBDOMINANT

VERDI: *FALSTAFF*, ACT 1

S22–1.

- What chord is arpeggiated from beat 4 of measure 4 through beat 1 of measure 6? (The D in measure 5 is an upper neighbor to the following C.)

BEETHOVEN: STRING QUARTET NO. 10 IN E♭ MAJOR ("HARP"), OP. 74, MVMT. 1

S22–2.

ROSSINI: *WILLIAM TELL*, ACT 1

S22–3.

- What chord is arpeggiated by the pitches of measures 2 and 3?

MENDELSSOHN: ORGAN SONATA NO. 2 IN C MINOR, MVMT. 3

S22–4.

WAGNER: *THE FLYING DUTCHMAN*, ACT 1

S22–5.

· After an extended arpeggiation of the subdominant's applied diminished-seventh leading-tone chord (measures 9 through 12), the single pitch F (= $\hat{4}$) in measure 13 must suffice as a resolution. F is immediately called into service for yet another diminished-seventh chord.

MOZART: PIANO CONCERTO NO. 24 IN C MINOR, K. 491, MVMT. 1

S22–6.

MELODIES THAT EMPLOY A MAJOR TENTH

CHOPIN: NOCTURNE, OP. 9, NO. 2

S22–7.

- Sing the following melody as preparation for singing the ascending major tenth in measure 3.

MOZART: SYMPHONY NO. 36 IN C MAJOR ("LINZ"), K. 425, MVMT. 3

S22–8.

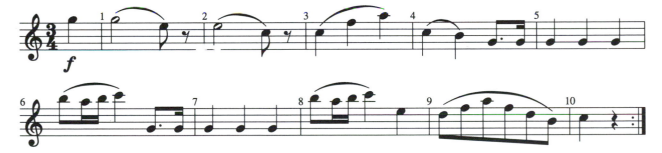

DUETS

AFTER SCHUBERT: PIANO SONATA IN A MINOR, D. 537, OP. POST. 164, MVMT. 2

D22–1.

AFTER BEETHOVEN: VARIATIONS IN C MINOR, WOO 80, VARIATION 14

D22–2.

AFTER HAYDN: SYMPHONY NO. 94 IN G MAJOR ("SURPRISE"), MVMT. 2

D22–3.

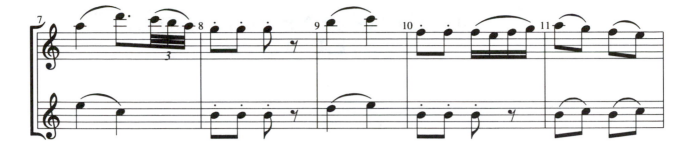

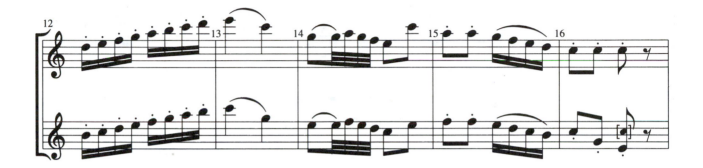

ACCOMPANIED SOLO MELODIES

AFTER BRAHMS: STRING QUARTET NO. 2 IN A MINOR, OP. 51, NO. 2, MVMT. 2

AS22–1.

AFTER J. S. BACH: TRIO SONATA FOR ORGAN NO. 4 IN E MINOR, BWV 528, MVMT. 3

AS22–2.

AFTER SCHUBERT: PIANO SONATA IN A MAJOR, D. 959, MVMT. 2

AS22–3.

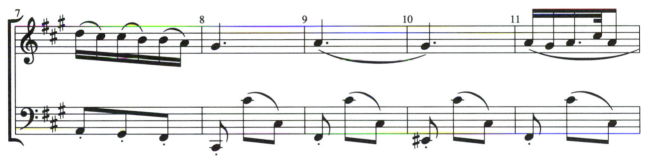

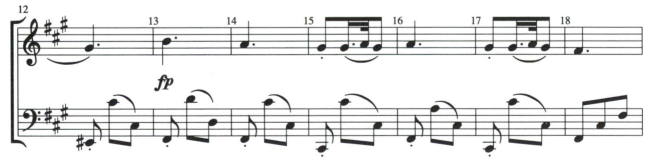

RHYTHMS

R22–1.

R22–2.

R22–3.

R22–4.

R22–5.

R22–6.

INTERVAL WORKSHOP

I22–1. Practice singing the intervals of a minor tenth, major tenth, perfect eleventh, and augmented eleventh higher than a sounding pitch. The sounding pitch should be at or beyond the lower limit of your vocal range, and could be sung by a classmate or your instructor or performed on the piano or another instrument such as the cello. Also practice singing seventeenths, eighteenths, twenty-fourths, and twenty-fifths, using very low sounding pitches.

I22–2. Practice singing the intervals of a minor tenth, major tenth, perfect eleventh, and augmented eleventh lower than a sounding pitch. The sounding pitch should be at or beyond the upper limit of your vocal range, and could be sung by a classmate or your instructor or performed on the piano or another instrument such as the flute. Also practice singing seventeenths, eighteenths, twenty-fourths, and twenty-fifths, using very high sounding pitches.

I22–3. Play a pitch low in your vocal range at a keyboard. Sing it. Then sing the pitch a minor tenth higher. Use the keyboard to confirm your performance. Then sing ascending minor tenths starting on other pitches. Repeat this exercise for the major tenth, perfect eleventh, and augmented eleventh.

I22–4. Play a pitch high in your vocal range at a keyboard. Sing it. Then sing the pitch a minor tenth lower. Use the keyboard to confirm your performance. Then sing descending minor tenths starting on other pitches. Repeat this exercise for the major tenth, perfect eleventh, and augmented eleventh.

ARPEGGIATION WORKSHOP

A22–1.   Play a pitch that is at least a minor second above the lowest note of your vocal range at a keyboard. Let this pitch be 1̂ in a major key. Sing each of the following arpeggiations, either in the order given or in random order.

a. 1̂ 5̂ 8̂ 3̂ ❂ 4̂ 6̂ 8̂ 2̂ ❂ 5̂ 8̂ 2̂ 8̂ ❂ 5̂ 7̂ 2̂ 7̂ ❂
       8̂ 5̂ 3̂ 1̂

b. 1̂ 3̂ 5̂ 8̂ ❂ 2̂ 5̂ 6̂ 8̂ ❂ 2̂ 4̂ 6̂ 8̂ ❂ 4̂ 5̂ 7̂ 2̂ ❂
       3̂ 5̂ 8̂ 3̂

c. 1̂ 3̂ 5̂ 3̂ ❂ 5̂ 8̂ 3̂ 8̂ ❂ 5̂ 6̂ 2̂ 6̂ ❂ 4̂ 6̂ 2̂ 6̂ ❂
       5̂ 7̂ 2̂ 7̂ ❂ 8̂ 5̂ 3̂ 1̂

d. 1̂ 3̂ 5̂ 1̂ ❂ 1̂ 2̂ 4̂ 5̂ ❂ 7̂ 2̂ 4̂ 5̂ ❂ 1̂ 3̂ 5̂ 1̂

e. 1̂ 3̂ 5̂ 8̂ ❂ 1̂ 3̂ 5̂ ♭7̂ ❂ 6̂ 4̂ 6̂ 8̂ ❂ 7̂ 5̂ 7̂ 2̂ ❂
       8̂ 5̂ 3̂ 1̂

f. 1̂ 3̂ 5̂ 8̂ ❂ 3̂ 5̂ ♭7̂ 8̂ ❂ 4̂ 6̂ 8̂ 4̂ ❂ 5̂ 7̂ 2̂ 5̂ ❂
       8̂ 5̂ 3̂ 1̂

g. 1̂ 3̂ 5̂ 8̂ ❂ 3̂ 5̂ ♭7̂ ♭2̂ ❂ 4̂ 6̂ 8̂ 4̂ ❂ 5̂ 7̂ 2̂ 5̂ ❂
       8̂ 5̂ 3̂ 1̂

A22–2.   Play a pitch that is at least a perfect fourth above the lowest note of your vocal range at a keyboard. Let this pitch be 1̂ in a minor key. Sing each of the following arpeggiations, either in the order given or in random order.

a. 1̂ 3̂ 5̂ 3̂ ❂ 1̂ 2̂ 5̂ 2̂ ❂ ♯7̂ 2̂ 5̂ 2̂ ❂ 1̂ 3̂ 5̂ 1̂

b. 1̂ 3̂ 5̂ 1̂ ❂ 6̂ 1̂ 4̂ 6̂ ❂ 5̂ 1̂ 2̂ 1̂ ❂ 5̂ ♯7̂ 2̂ ♯7̂ ❂
       1̂ 3̂ 5̂ 1̂

c. 1̂ 3̂ 5̂ 8̂ ❂ 1̂ ♯3̂ 5̂ 7̂ ❂ 6̂ 4̂ 6̂ 8̂ ❂ ♯7̂ 5̂ ♯7̂ 2̂ ❂
       8̂ 5̂ 3̂ 1̂

d. 1̂ 3̂ 5̂ 8̂ ❂ ♯3̂ 5̂ 7̂ 8̂ ❂ 4̂ 6̂ 8̂ 4̂ ❂ 5̂ ♯7̂ 2̂ 5̂ ❂
       8̂ 5̂ 3̂ 1̂

e. 1̂ 3̂ 5̂ 8̂ ❂ ♯3̂ 5̂ 7̂ ♭2̂ ❂ 4̂ 6̂ 8̂ 4̂ ❂ 5̂ ♯7̂ 2̂ 5̂ ❂
       8̂ 5̂ 3̂ 1̂

f. 3̂ 5̂ 8̂ 3̂ ❂ ♯3̂ 5̂ 7̂ 8̂ ❂ 4̂ 7̂ 8̂ 7̂ ❂ 4̂ 6̂ 8̂ 6̂ ❂
       5̂ ♯7̂ 2̂ 5̂

QUICK SWITCH

Q22–1.

Q22–2.

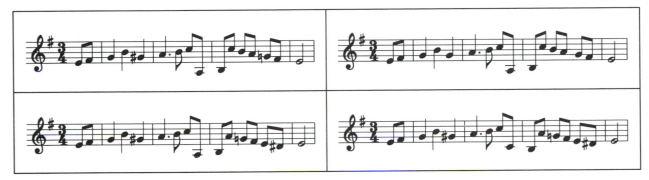

Q22–3.

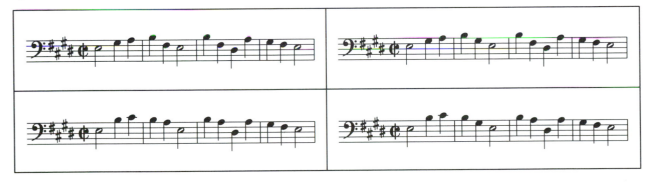

Q22–4.

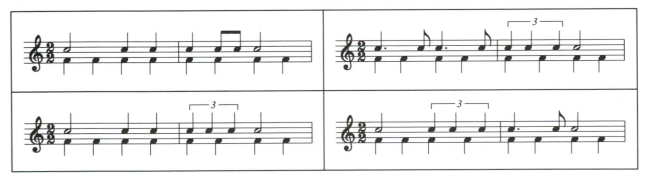

IDENTIFICATIONS

ID22–1.   An interval not larger than an augmented eleventh is performed melodically or as a simultaneity. Identify it.

ID22–2.   What chord occurs at **X**? Suitable choices are listed below.

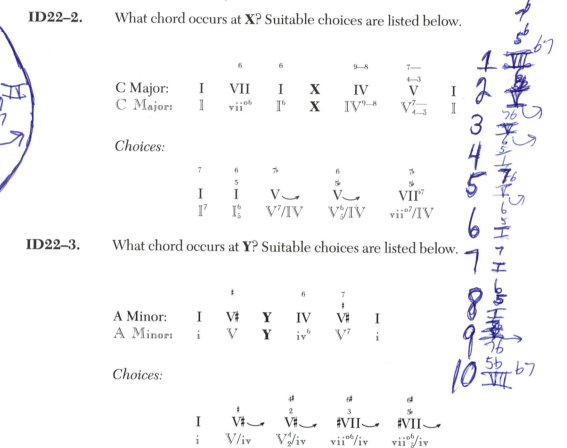

			6	6		9—8	7—	
C Major:	I	VII	I	**X**	IV		V	I
C Major:	I	vii°⁶	I⁶	**X**	IV⁹⁻⁸		V⁷₄₋₃	I

Choices:

7	6/5	7♭/5	6/5♭	7♭/5
I	I	V⤵	V⤵	VII⁷
I⁷	I⁶₅	V⁷/IV	V⁶₅/IV	vii°⁷/IV

ID22–3.   What chord occurs at **Y**? Suitable choices are listed below.

		♯		6	7♯	
A Minor:	I	V♯	**Y**	IV	V♯	I
A Minor:	i	V	**Y**	iv⁶	V⁷	i

Choices:

	♯	4♯/2	6♯/3	6♯/5♭
I	V♯⤵	V♯⤵	♯VII⤵	♯VII⤵
i	V/iv	V⁴₂/iv	vii°⁶/iv	vii°⁶₅/iv

ID22–4.   A melody is performed. Identify the correct score notation.

a.

b.

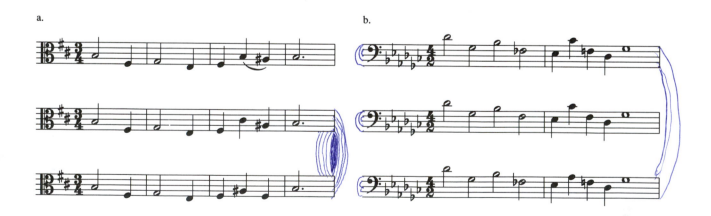

c.

d.

e.

f.

ID22–5.   A chord progression in the major mode is performed. Identify a suitable Roman-numeral/figured-bass analysis from among the following choices:

Group 1

a. I   V   V↷IV   V   I   a. I   V⁶₅   V⁴₂/IV   IV⁶   V⁷   I

b. I   V   VII♭⁷↷IV   V   I   b. I   V⁶₅   vii°⁴₃/IV   IV⁶   V⁷   I

c. I   V   V↷IV   V   I   c. I   V⁶   V⁴₂/IV   IV⁶   V⁷   I

d. I   V   VII♭⁷↷IV   V   I   d. I   V⁶   vii°⁴₃/IV   IV⁶   V⁷   I

F#ACE
F#ADC

1 c
2 b

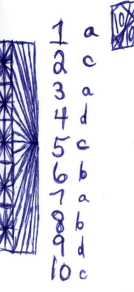

Group 2

a.   I   IV   V$^{4—3}$ I   a.   I   IV   V$^{4—3}$ I

b.   I   IV   V$^{9—8}_{7—}$ I   b.   I   IV   V$^{9—8}_{7—}$ I

c.   I   IV   V$^{7—}_{4—3}$ I   c.   I   IV   V$^{7—}_{4—3}$ I

d.   I   IV   V$^{6—5}_{4—3}$ I   d.   I   IV   V$^{6—5}_{4—3}$ I

ID22–6.   A chord progression in the minor mode is performed. Identify a suitable Roman-numeral/figured-bass analysis from among the following choices:

Group 1

a.   I   V$^{4—3}$ VI$^{9—8}$ II^6 V$^{6—5}_{4—\#}$♯   I♯   a.   i   v$^{4—3}$ VI$^{9—8}$ ii^{o6} V$^{6—5}_{4—3}$

b.   I   V$^{4—3}$ VI$^{4—3}$ II^6 V$^{6—5}_{4—\#}$♯   I♯   b.   i   v$^{4—3}$ VI$^{4—3}$ ii^{o6} V$^{6—5}_{4—3}$ I

c.   I   V$^{4—3}$ VI$^{9—8}$ IV   V$^{5—}_{4—\#}$♯   I♯   c.   i   v$^{4—3}$ VI$^{9—8}$ iv   V$^{5—}_{4—3}$ I

d.   I   V$^{4—3}$ VI$^{4—3}$ IV   V$^{5—}_{4—\#}$♯   I♯   d.   i   v$^{4—3}$ VI$^{4—3}$ iv   V$^{5—}_{4—3}$ I

Group 2

a.   I   IV^6 ♯VII$^{♭7}$ ⟶ IV   V$^{4—\#}_{\#}$♯   I   a.   i^6 iv   vii^{o7}/iv   iv   V$^{4—3}$ i

b.   I   IV^6 V$^{6}_{5}$♯ ⟶ IV   V$^{4—\#}_{\#}$♯   I   b.   i^6 iv   V$^6_5$/iv   iv   V$^{4—3}$ i

c.   I   IV^6 ♯VII$^{♭7}$ ⟶ IV   V$^{9—8}_{7—}$♯   I   c.   i^6 iv   vii^{o7}/iv   iv   V$^{9—8}_{7—}$ i

d.   I   IV^6 V$^{6}_{5}$♯ ⟶ IV   V$^{9—8}_{7—}$♯   I   d.   i^6 iv   V$^6_5$/iv   iv   V$^{9—8}_{7—}$ i

IB22–7. A chord progression is performed. Identify the correct score notation for the outer voices. Figured-bass symbols have been placed below the bass where appropriate. If you wish, add Roman numerals.

a.

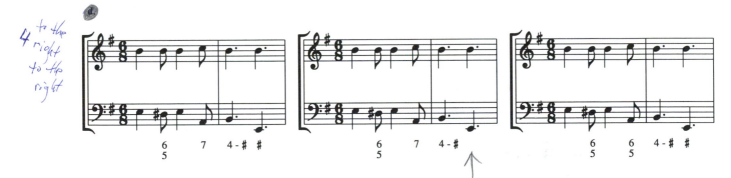

e.

6	6	4♭ – 3	6	
5	5♭		5	

6	7♭♭	4♭ – 3	6
5	5♭		5

6	6	9 – 8	6
5	5		5

f.

V IV

| 4# | 5 — | 6 | 6–5 |
| 2 | 2— | | 4–# |

V   no chord change

| ⑥ | 4#6 | 6 | 6–5 |
| | 2 | | 4–# |

II

| 4# — | 6 | 6 | 6–5 |
| 2 — | | | 4–# |

V

RHYTHMIC DICTATIONS

RD22–1.

RD22–2.

1 middle
2 left
3 middle
4 right
5 left

1 middle
2 right
3 middle
4 left
5 right

MELODIC DICTATIONS

VERDI: *OTELLO*, ACT 1

MD22–1.

- The compound interval that occurs in measure 2 is merely a side effect of a more important structural relationship. Consider instead the interval that is formed by the first pitch of the excerpt and the pitch on beat 3 of measure 2.

MOZART: *DON GIOVANNI*, **K.** 527, ACT 2

MD22–2.

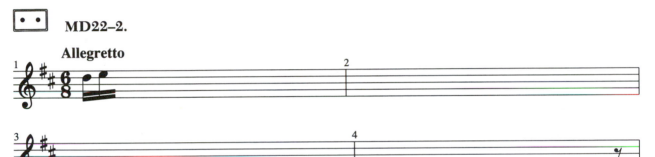

- Before writing down any other pitches, write down the first pitch of each measure.

FIELD: PIANO CONCERTO NO. 1 IN E♭ MAJOR, MVMT. 3

MD22–3.

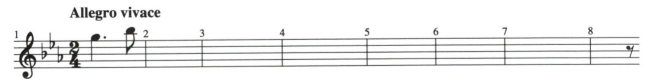

- The last pitch of measure 4 should be determined through reference to measure 1, not through reference to the preceding pitch in measure 4.

J. S. BACH: SUITE FOR ORCHESTRA NO. 2 IN B MINOR, BWV 1067, BADINERIE

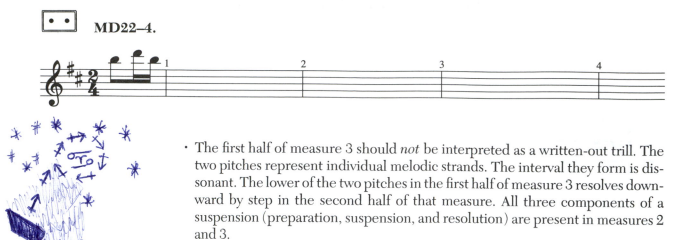

MD22–4.

- The first half of measure 3 should *not* be interpreted as a written-out trill. The two pitches represent individual melodic strands. The interval they form is dissonant. The lower of the two pitches in the first half of measure 3 resolves downward by step in the second half of that measure. All three components of a suspension (preparation, suspension, and resolution) are present in measures 2 and 3.

J. S. BACH: MASS IN B MINOR, BWV 232, CREDO

MD22–5.

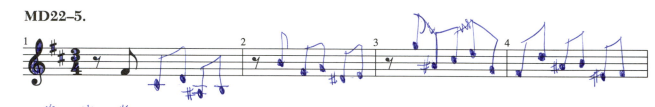

- In measures 1, 2, and 4, the pitches that form the harmonies occur on the second half of each beat. The pitches that occur on the beats are lower neighbors to these structural pitches. The intervals (including some diminished fourths and a diminished fifth) formed by adjacent pitches from the second half of one beat to the first half of the next have no structural importance.

BERLIOZ: *BENVENUTO CELLINI*, ACT 3

MD22–6.

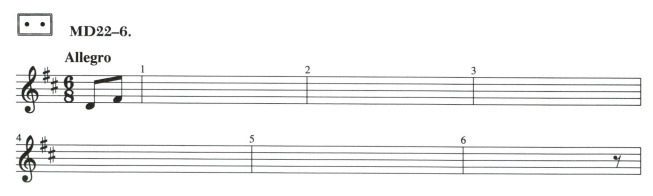

Allegro

- Berlioz accents the pitches that occur on beat 1 of measures 2 and 4. Both pitches belong to the harmony that precedes the bar line, and both resolve downward by step to a pitch from the new harmony.

HARMONIC DICTATIONS

BEETHOVEN: SYMPHONY NO. 1 IN C MAJOR, OP. 21, MVMT. 1

HD22–1.

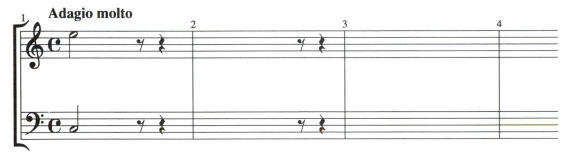

- The first chord of Beethoven's first symphony is a daring application of one of the applied chords introduced in this chapter. Although tonic does not appear within this excerpt, the first chord is a modification of tonic and the second chord of measure 2 is a substitute for tonic.

SCHUMANN: *KINDERSCENEN*, OP. 15, NO. 1

HD22–2.

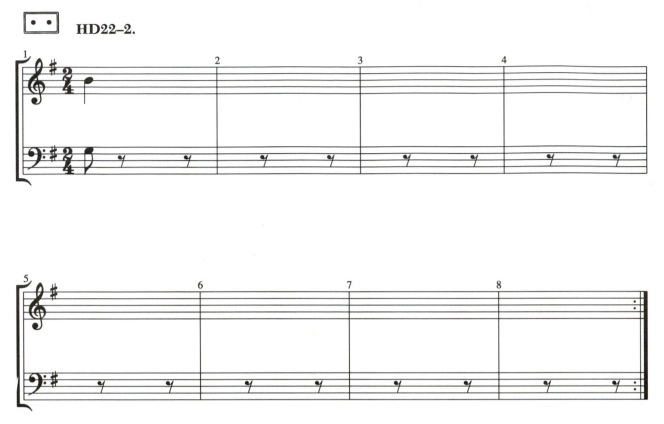

· When there are more than four voices, composers double pitches with considerable freedom. For example, two of the three inner voices in the first half of measure 7 double the same pitch, which functions as a suspension. That would not happen in four-part chorale writing.

SCHUBERT: *SCHWANENGESANG*, D. 957, "AUFENTHALT"

HD22–3.

Nicht zu geschwind, doch kräftig

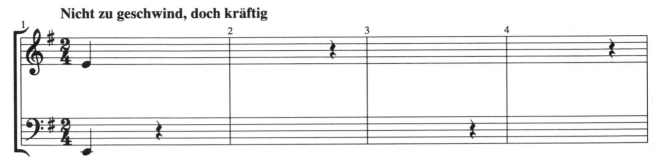

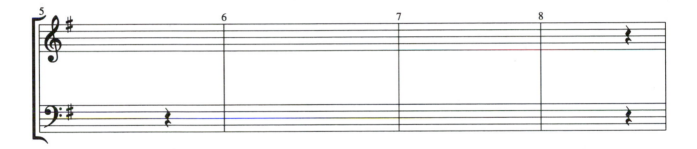

· The vocal melody and the bass employ standard subdivisions of the beat in $\frac{2}{4}$ meter (eighth notes, dotted eighth notes, sixteenth notes). Inner voices in triplets are juxtaposed with those lines.

CHOPIN: FANTAISIE, OP. 49

  HD22–4.

Tempo di marcia.

- Analyze this excerpt in the key of F minor.

- What changes during measure 1? How many different harmonies occur during that measure? What changes during the first half of measure 2? How many different harmonies occur during those beats?

SCHUMANN: *BUNTE BLÄTTER*, OP. 99, "ABENDMUSIK"

HD22–5.

Im Menuetttempo.

- A challenging application of "three against two" rhythm is employed in this excerpt. It might better be described as "four against three" because the "two" is subdivided into four sixteenths and written as a dotted eighth plus a sixteenth (♪♪) against triplets (♪♪♪).

SCHUMANN: *ARABESQUE*, OP. 18

HD22–6.

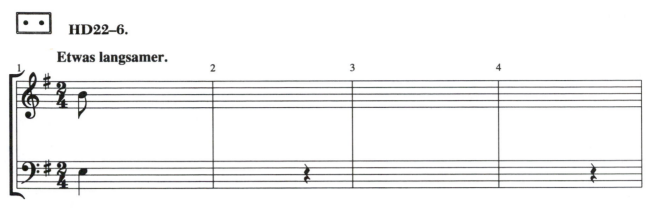

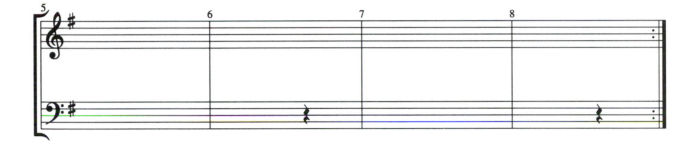

- Measures 3 and 4 are identical to measures 1 and 2. How does measure 5 differ from measure 1?

⊡ CASSETTE PROGRAM
(TAPE 4, SIDE A)

C22–1.   Six melodies are performed, twice each. During the silence after each playing, respond in one of the following ways: (1) Sing the melody, using solmization syllables; (2) Play the melody on the piano or on your primary instrument; (3) Write the melody on staff paper.

C22–2.   Six chord progressions are performed, four times each. During the silence after each playing, respond in one of the following ways: (1) Sing the soprano after the first and second playings and the bass after the third and fourth playings, using solmization syllables; (2) Play the soprano on the piano or your primary instrument after the first and second playings and the bass after the third and fourth playings; (3) Play both the soprano and bass on the piano after each playing; (4) Write the soprano and bass on staff paper and provide an analysis.

Chapter 23

PITCH

The seven diatonic pitches of any pair of relative keys can form only one major-minor seventh chord. For example, G-B-D-F is the only diatonic major-minor seventh chord in C major or A natural minor. In major, that chord is the dominant. In minor, it is the *applied* dominant of the mediant. Because the chord is diatonic, the analytical symbols

$$\overset{7}{V} \longrightarrow III \quad \text{and} \quad \overset{7}{VII} \quad III$$
$$V^7/III \qquad III \quad \text{and} \quad VII^7 \qquad III$$

are interchangeable in minor keys. Example 23–1 shows G-B-D-F as an applied dominant of A minor's mediant, C major. In Example 23–2, it participates in the mediant's tonicization. A diminished leading-tone chord may also be applied to the mediant in minor keys. In major keys, the mediant's applied dominant seventh chord requires two accidentals (e.g., B-D♯-F♯-A in C major), as does its applied diminished seventh (e.g., D♯-F♯-A-C).

EXAMPLE 23–1

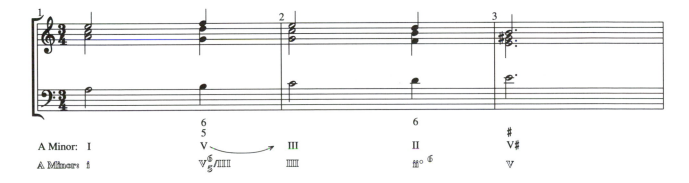

A Minor: I   V⁶₅ ⟶ III   II   V♯

A Minor: i   V⁶₅/III   III   iii°⁶   V

EXAMPLE 23–2

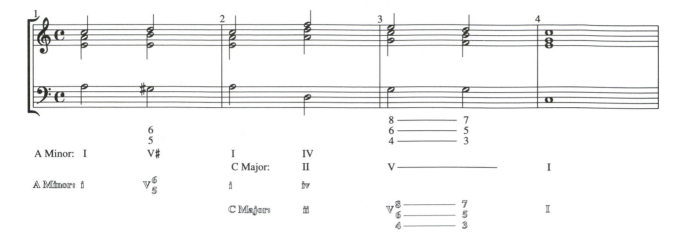

The ***diminished twelfth***, ***perfect twelfth***, ***minor thirteenth***, and ***major thirteenth*** are emphasized in this chapter. These intervals may be used in forming a **5-4 suspension** or a **6-5 suspension**, both of which occur in Example 23–3.

EXAMPLE 23–3

The sequences introduced in chapters 17 and 18 were constructed from chords in $^5_3$ and $^6_3$ positions. Dissonant seventh chords and their inversions may substitute for those consonant chords, thereby intensifying the forward momentum of the sequence. Example 23–4 shows a variant of the descending fifths sequence. Chords in $^6_5$ and $^5_3$ positions alternate. When you hear a sequence, ask yourself the following questions: (1) Is the contour of the sequence ascending or descending? (2) Which basic pattern does the sequence follow? (3) Are any of the chords in the sequence dissonant? (4) What is the figured bass of each chord? (5) At what point does the sequence end? (6) Does the sequence prolong a single harmony, or does it connect two different harmonies?

EXAMPLE 23–4

METER AND RHYTHM

A *hemiola*, like other forms of syncopation, involves a temporary departure from a meter's pattern of strong and weak beats or subdivisions of beats. Two groups of three beats or subdivisions of beats

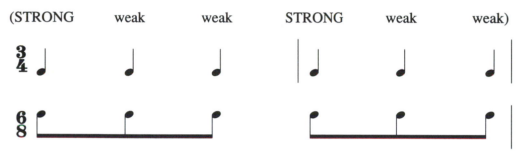

are replaced by three groups of two beats or subdivisions of beats

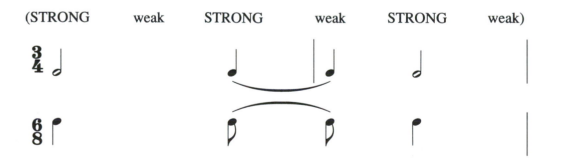

A hemiola can occur only when the prevailing meter supplies two groups of three: for example, the beats of two consecutive measures in $\frac{3}{4}$, $\frac{3}{2}$, or $\frac{3}{8}$ meter; or the subdivisions of the beat within a single measure in $\frac{6}{8}$, $\frac{12}{8}$, or $\frac{6}{4}$ meter. Example 23–5 shows two samples of hemiola, along with appropriate counting syllables.

EXAMPLE 23–5

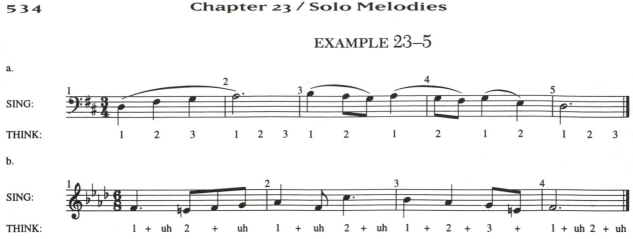

a.

b.

Although most compositions establish and maintain a single meter, composers sometimes employ ***shifts of meter***. Such shifts are usually indicated at the appropriate points in the score, although occasionally, when such shifts occur repeatedly, a composer may indicate two alternative meters at the beginning and leave it to the performer to decide which pertains to each measure. Example 23–6 demonstrates the latter procedure.

EXAMPLE 23–6

SOLO MELODIES

MELODIES THAT OUTLINE A CHORD APPLIED TO THE MEDIANT OR THAT TONICIZE THE MEDIANT KEY

J. S. BACH: SUITE FOR UNACCOMPANIED CELLO NO. 2 IN D MINOR, BWV 1008, GIGUE

S23–1.

• The key of D minor is established in part through the C♯–G diminished fifth of measure 2, which resolves to the D–F minor third outlined by the motive of

measures 3 and 4. When Bach establishes the mediant key, F major, in measures 5 through 8, he follows the same strategy. The diminished fifth E-B♭ in measure 5 resolves to the F-A major third outlined by the motive of measures 7 and 8.

SCHUBERT: SYMPHONY NO. 8 IN B MINOR ("UNFINISHED"), D. 759, MVMT. 1

S23–2.

WAGNER: *TANNHÄUSER*, ACT 3

S23–3.

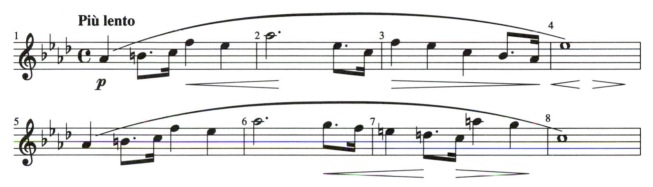

· The key tonicized at the end of this excerpt is the *major* mediant, C major, not the diatonic mediant, C minor.

ROSSINI: *WILLIAM TELL*, ACT 2

S23–4.

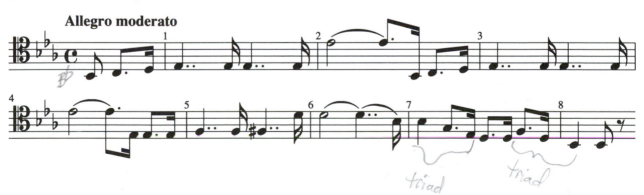

HANDEL: *SUSANNA*, ACT 2

S23–5.

· Handel's treatment of dissonance in this excerpt is exemplary. A♯, the leading tone in the opening tonic key of B minor, is stated prominently at the beginning of measure 2 and is repeated in measure 3. Later in measure 3, the dominant chord's seventh (E) sounds, forming an augmented fourth against A♯. The resolution pitches (B and D) occur in measure 4. Similarly, B and C♯ in measure 9 form a minor seventh (a component of the leading-tone seventh chord in the tonicized key of D major), whose resolution pitches (A and D) occur in measure 10.

BIZET: *CARMEN*, ACT 3

S23–6.

MELODIES THAT EMPLOY HEMIOLA

HANDEL: *WATER MUSIC*

S23–7.

- Consecutive downbeats in measures 6 through 8 emphasize the pitches B♮, G and D. Consecutive downbeats during the hemiola of measures 14 and 15 emphasize the same three pitches.

BRAHMS: STRING QUARTET NO. 3 IN B♭ MAJOR, OP. 67, MVMT. 3

S23–8.

SCHUMANN: SYMPHONY NO. 3 IN E♭ MAJOR ("RHENISH"), OP. 97, MVMT. 1

S23–9.

- These are the first measures of the symphony. Schumann employs hemiola even before establishing the meter indicated by the time signature, to which hemiola would typically serve as a contrast. A listener could not be criticized for processing the opening measures as 𝄴 ♩ ♩ ♩. ♪|♩ ♩ ♩. ♪|♩ ♩ ♩. ♪|.

J. S. BACH: MASS IN B MINOR, BWV 232, SANCTUS

S23–10.

MELODIES THAT EMPLOY SHIFTS OF METER

VERDI: *FALSTAFF*, ACT 2

S23–11.

- This melody shifts both meters and tempi. To better understand the relationship between the sections, use a metronome set for the eighth-note subdivisions of the beat: 184 eighth notes per minute (92 beats times 2 eighth notes per beat) during the Allegro moderato sections; 168 eighth notes per minute (56 beats times 3 eighth notes per beat) during the Largo section.

DVOŘÁK: *RUSALKA*, OP. 114, ACT 2

S23–12.

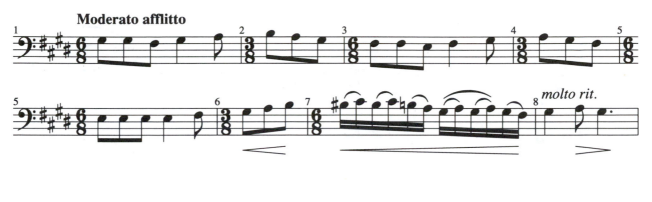

DUETS

AFTER SCHUBERT: TRIO NO. 1 IN B♭ MAJOR FOR PIANO, VIOLIN, AND CELLO, D. 898, OP. 99, MVMT. 3

D23–1.

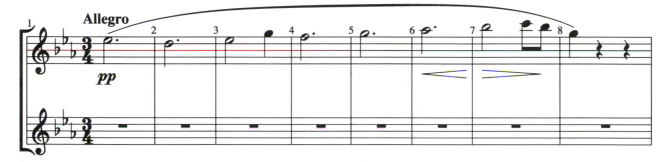

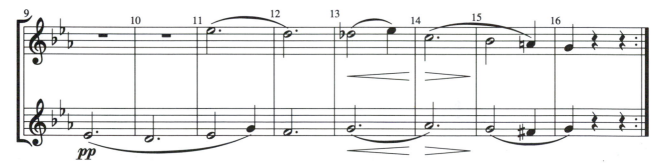

AFTER BRAHMS: SYMPHONY NO. 2 IN D MAJOR, OP. 73, MVMT. 1

D23–2.

AFTER SCHUBERT: STRING QUINTET IN C MAJOR, D. 956, OP. 163, MVMT. 1

D23–3.

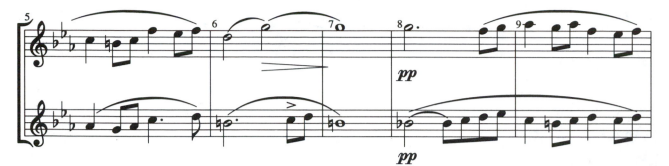

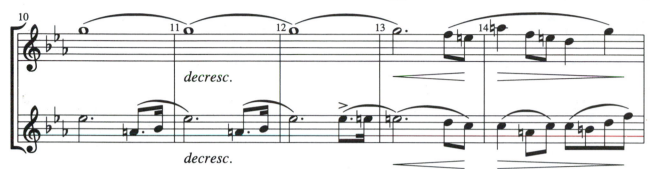

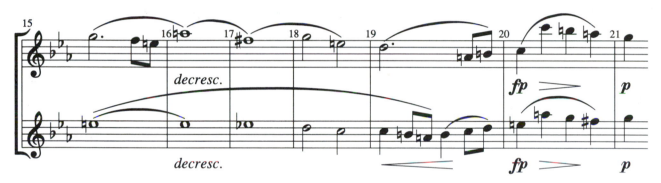

ACCOMPANIED SOLO MELODIES

AFTER SCHUBERT: *FIERRABRAS*, D. 796, ACT 1

AS23–1.

AFTER WAGNER: *LOHENGRIN*, ACT 3

AS23–2.

AFTER DVOŘÁK: SYMPHONY NO. 9 IN E MINOR ("FROM THE NEW WORLD"), OP. 95, MVMT. 2

AS23–3.

RHYTHMS

R23–1.

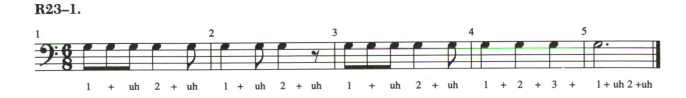

R23–2.

R23–3.

R23–4.

R23–5.

R23–6.

INTERVAL WORKSHOP

I23–1.　　Practice singing the intervals of a diminished twelfth, perfect twelfth, minor thirteenth, and major thirteenth higher than a sounding pitch. The sounding pitch should be beyond the lower limit of your vocal range, and could be sung by a classmate or your instructor or performed on the piano or another instrument such as the cello. Also practice singing nineteenths, twentieths, twenty-sixths, and twenty-sevenths, using very low sounding pitches.

I23–2.　　Practice singing the intervals of a diminished twelfth, perfect twelfth, minor thirteenth, and major thirteenth lower than a sounding pitch. The sounding pitch should be beyond the upper limit of your vocal range, and could be sung by a classmate or your instructor or performed on the piano or another instrument such as the flute. Also practice singing nineteenths, twentieths, twenty-sixths, and twenty-sevenths, using very high sounding pitches.

I23–3.   If the size of your vocal range permits, practice the following exercise. Play a pitch low in your vocal range at a keyboard. Sing it. Then sing the pitch a diminished twelfth higher. Use the keyboard to confirm your performance. Then sing ascending diminished twelfths starting on other pitches. Repeat this exercise for the perfect twelfth, minor thirteenth, and major thirteenth.

I23–4.   If the size of your vocal range permits, practice the following exercise. Play a pitch high in your vocal range at a keyboard. Sing it. Then sing the pitch a diminished twelfth lower. Use the keyboard to confirm your performance. Then sing descending diminished twelfths starting on other pitches. Repeat this exercise for the perfect twelfth, minor thirteenth, and major thirteenth.

ARPEGGIATION WORKSHOP

A23–1.   Play a pitch that is at least a perfect fifth above the lowest note of your vocal range at a keyboard. Let this pitch be $\hat{1}$ in a major key. Sing each of the following arpeggiations, either in the order given or in random order.

a.	$\hat{1}$	$\hat{3}$	$\hat{5}$	$\hat{1}$	✦	$\flat\hat{7}$	$\sharp\hat{2}$	$\sharp\hat{4}$	$\hat{7}$	✦	$\hat{3}$	$\hat{5}$	$\hat{7}$	$\hat{3}$	✦	$\hat{4}$	$\hat{6}$	$\hat{8}$	$\hat{4}$	✦
			$\hat{5}$	$\hat{7}$	$\hat{5}$														
b.	$\hat{1}$	$\hat{3}$	$\hat{5}$	$\hat{1}$	✦	$\flat\hat{7}$	$\sharp\hat{2}$	$\sharp\hat{4}$	$\hat{6}$	✦	$\hat{3}$	$\hat{5}$	$\hat{7}$	$\hat{3}$	✦	$\hat{4}$	$\hat{6}$	$\hat{8}$	$\hat{4}$	✦
			$\hat{5}$	$\hat{7}$	$\hat{5}$														
c.	$\hat{1}$	$\hat{3}$	$\hat{5}$	$\hat{3}$	✦	$\sharp\hat{2}$	$\sharp\hat{4}$	$\hat{6}$	$\hat{7}$	✦	$\hat{3}$	$\hat{5}$	$\hat{7}$	$\hat{3}$	✦	$\hat{4}$	$\hat{6}$	$\hat{8}$	$\hat{4}$	✦
			$\hat{5}$	$\hat{7}$	$\hat{5}$														
d.	$\hat{1}$	$\hat{3}$	$\hat{5}$	$\hat{3}$	✦	$\sharp\hat{2}$	$\sharp\hat{4}$	$\hat{6}$	$\hat{8}$	✦	$\hat{3}$	$\hat{5}$	$\hat{7}$	$\hat{3}$	✦	$\hat{4}$	$\hat{6}$	$\hat{8}$	$\hat{4}$	✦
			$\hat{5}$	$\hat{7}$	$\hat{5}$														
e.	$\hat{1}$	$\hat{3}$	$\hat{5}$	$\hat{8}$	✦	$\hat{5}$	$\hat{3}$	$\hat{4}$	$\hat{7}$	✦	$\hat{5}$	$\hat{2}$	$\hat{4}$	$\hat{7}$	✦	$\hat{1}$	$\hat{3}$	$\hat{5}$	$\hat{8}$	
f.	$\hat{1}$	$\hat{3}$	$\hat{5}$	$\hat{1}$	✦	$\hat{4}$	$\hat{2}$	$\hat{4}$	$\hat{6}$	✦	$\hat{5}$	$\hat{2}$	$\hat{3}$	$\hat{5}$	✦	$\hat{5}$	$\hat{1}$	$\hat{3}$	$\hat{5}$	✦
			$\hat{5}$	$\hat{1}$	$\hat{2}$	$\hat{4}$	✦	$\hat{5}$	$\hat{7}$	$\hat{2}$	$\hat{4}$	✦	$\hat{1}$	$\hat{3}$	$\hat{1}$				
g.	$\hat{1}$	$\hat{3}$	$\hat{5}$	✦	$\hat{6}$	$\hat{1}$	$\hat{3}$	$\hat{4}$	✦	$\hat{7}$	$\hat{2}$	$\hat{4}$	✦	$\hat{5}$	$\hat{7}$	$\hat{2}$	$\hat{3}$	✦		
			$\hat{6}$	$\hat{1}$	$\hat{3}$	✦	$\hat{4}$	$\hat{6}$	$\hat{1}$	$\hat{2}$	✦	$\hat{5}$	$\hat{7}$	$\hat{2}$	✦	$\hat{1}$	$\hat{3}$	$\hat{1}$	
h.	$\hat{1}$	$\hat{3}$	$\hat{5}$	✦	$\hat{1}$	$\hat{3}$	$\hat{4}$	$\hat{6}$	✦	$\hat{7}$	$\hat{2}$	$\hat{4}$	✦	$\hat{7}$	$\hat{2}$	$\hat{3}$	$\hat{5}$	✦		
			$\hat{6}$	$\hat{1}$	$\hat{3}$	✦	$\hat{6}$	$\hat{1}$	$\hat{2}$	$\hat{4}$	✦	$\hat{5}$	$\hat{7}$	$\hat{2}$	✦	$\hat{1}$	$\hat{3}$	$\hat{1}$	

A23–2.   Play a pitch that is at least a perfect fifth above the lowest note of your vocal range at a keyboard. Let this pitch be $\hat{1}$ in a minor key. Sing each of the following arpeggiations, either in the order given or in random order.

a.	$\hat{1}$	$\hat{3}$	$\hat{5}$	$\hat{1}$	✦	$\flat\hat{7}$	$\hat{2}$	$\hat{4}$	$\hat{7}$	✦	$\hat{3}$	$\hat{5}$	$\hat{7}$	$\hat{3}$	✦	$\hat{4}$	$\hat{6}$	$\hat{8}$	$\hat{4}$	✦
			$\hat{5}$	$\sharp\hat{7}$	$\hat{5}$														
b.	$\hat{1}$	$\hat{3}$	$\hat{5}$	$\hat{1}$	✦	$\flat\hat{7}$	$\hat{2}$	$\hat{4}$	$\hat{6}$	✦	$\hat{3}$	$\hat{5}$	$\hat{7}$	$\hat{3}$	✦	$\hat{4}$	$\hat{6}$	$\hat{8}$	$\hat{4}$	✦
			$\hat{5}$	$\sharp\hat{7}$	$\hat{5}$														

c. $\hat{1}$ $\hat{3}$ $\hat{5}$ $\hat{3}$ ❖ $\hat{2}$ $\hat{4}$ $\hat{6}$ $\hat{7}$ ❖ $\hat{3}$ $\hat{5}$ $\hat{7}$ $\hat{3}$ ❖ $\hat{4}$ $\hat{6}$ $\hat{8}$ $\hat{4}$ ❖
        $\hat{5}$ $\sharp\hat{7}$ $\hat{5}$

d. $\hat{1}$ $\hat{3}$ $\hat{5}$ $\hat{3}$ ❖ $\hat{2}$ $\hat{4}$ $\hat{6}$ $\flat\hat{8}$ ❖ $\hat{3}$ $\hat{5}$ $\hat{7}$ $\hat{3}$ ❖ $\hat{4}$ $\hat{6}$ $\hat{8}$ $\hat{4}$ ❖
        $\hat{5}$ $\sharp\hat{7}$ $\hat{5}$

e. $\hat{1}$ $\hat{3}$ $\hat{5}$ $\hat{8}$ ❖ $\hat{}_5$ $\hat{3}$ $\hat{4}$ $\sharp\hat{7}$ ❖ $\hat{}_5$ $\hat{2}$ $\hat{4}$ $\sharp\hat{7}$ ❖ $\hat{1}$ $\hat{3}$ $\hat{5}$ $\hat{8}$

f. $\hat{1}$ $\hat{3}$ $\hat{5}$ $\hat{1}$ ❖ $\hat{}_4$ $\hat{2}$ $\hat{4}$ $\hat{6}$ ❖ $\hat{}_5$ $\hat{2}$ $\hat{3}$ $\hat{5}$ ❖ $\hat{}_5$ $\hat{1}$ $\hat{3}$ $\hat{5}$ ❖
        $\hat{}_5$ $\hat{1}$ $\hat{2}$ $\hat{4}$ ❖ $\hat{}_5$ $\hat{}_7$ $\hat{2}$ $\hat{4}$ ❖ $\hat{1}$ $\hat{3}$ $\hat{1}$

g. $\hat{1}$ $\hat{3}$ $\hat{5}$ ❖ $\hat{}_6$ $\hat{1}$ $\hat{3}$ $\hat{4}$ ❖ $\hat{}_7$ $\hat{2}$ $\hat{4}$ ❖ $\hat{}_5$ $\hat{}_7$ $\hat{2}$ $\hat{3}$ ❖
        $\hat{}_6$ $\hat{1}$ $\hat{3}$ ❖ $\hat{}_4$ $\hat{}_6$ $\hat{1}$ $\hat{2}$ ❖ $\hat{}_5$ $\hat{}_7$ $\hat{2}$ ❖ $\hat{1}$ $\hat{3}$ $\hat{1}$

h. $\hat{1}$ $\hat{3}$ $\hat{5}$ ❖ $\hat{1}$ $\hat{3}$ $\hat{4}$ $\hat{6}$ ❖ $\hat{}_7$ $\hat{2}$ $\hat{4}$ ❖ $\hat{}_7$ $\hat{2}$ $\hat{3}$ $\hat{5}$ ❖
        $\hat{}_6$ $\hat{1}$ $\hat{3}$ ❖ $\hat{}_6$ $\hat{1}$ $\hat{2}$ $\hat{4}$ ❖ $\hat{}_5$ $\sharp\hat{7}$ $\hat{2}$ ❖ $\hat{1}$ $\hat{3}$ $\hat{1}$

QUICK SWITCH

Q23–1.

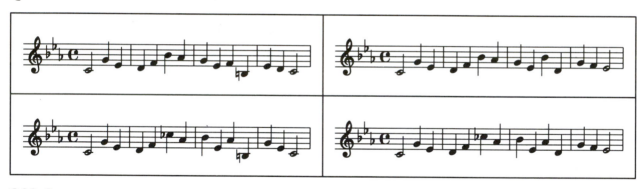

Q23–2.

Q23–3.

Q23–4.

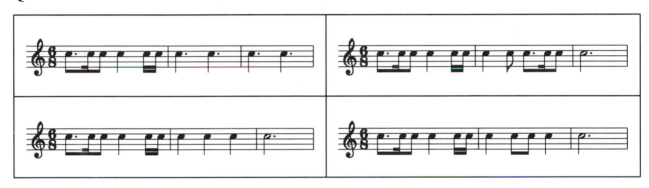

IDENTIFICATIONS

ID23–1. An interval not larger than a major thirteenth is performed melodically or as a simultaneity. Identify it.

ID23–2. What chord occurs at **X**? Suitable choices are listed below.

				6	8—7	
					6—5	
					4—3	
C Major:	I	**X**	III	II	V	I
C Major:	I	**X**	iii	ii·⁶	V$^{8—7}_{6—5}_{4—3}$	I

Choices:

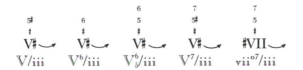

ID23–3.   What chord occurs at **Y**? Suitable choices are listed below.

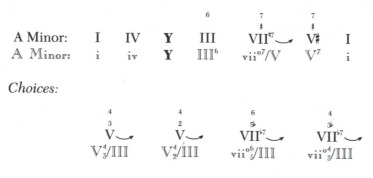

Choices:

ID23–4.   A melody is performed. Identify the correct score notation.

f.

g.

ID23–5.   A chord progression in the major mode is performed. Identify a suitable Roman-numeral/figured-bass analysis from among the following choices:

Group 1

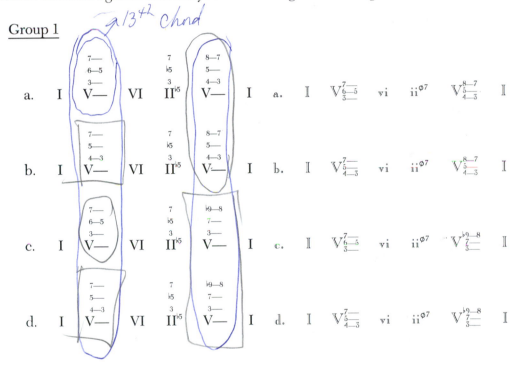

a13th chord

a. I   V—   VI   II♭5   V—   I   a.   I   V⁷₆₋₅₃   vi   ii°⁷   V⁸₅₋₇₄₋₃   I

b. I   V—   VI   II♭5   V—   I   b.   I   V⁷₅₋₄₋₃   vi   ii°⁷   V⁸₅₋₇₄₋₃   I

c. I   V—   VI   II♭5   V—   I   c.   I   V⁷₆₋₅₃   vi   ii°⁷   V♭⁹₇₋₈₃   I

d. I   V—   VI   II♭5   V—   I   d.   I   V⁷₅₋₄₋₃   vi   ii°⁷   V♭⁹₇₋₈₃   I

1 a
2 c
3 a
4 d
5 c
6 b
7 c
8 d
9 a
10 d

10/10

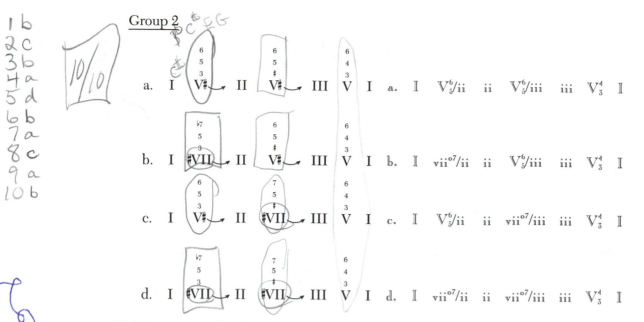

Group 2

a. I V# II V# III V I   a. I V$_5^6$/ii ii V$_5^6$/iii iii V$_3^4$ I

b. I #VII II V# III V I   b. I vii°⁷/ii ii V$_5^6$/iii iii V$_3^4$ I

c. I V# II #VII III V I   c. I V$_5^6$/ii ii vii°⁷/iii iii V$_3^4$ I

d. I #VII II #VII III V I d. I vii°⁷/ii ii vii°⁷/iii iii V$_3^4$ I

ID23–6.　A chord progression in the minor mode is performed. Identify a suitable Roman-numeral/figured-bass analysis from among the following choices:

Group 1

a. I VI V III IV# #VII I   a. i VI V⁷/III III IV$_2^4$ vii°⁶ i

b. I IV V III IV# #VII I   b. i iv⁶ V⁷/III III IV$_2^4$ vii°⁶ i

c. I VI V III IV# #VII I   c. i VI⁶ V⁶/III III IV$_2^4$ vii°⁶ i

d. I VI V III IV# #VII I   d. i VI⁶ V$_5^6$/III III IV$_2^4$ vii°⁶ i

Group 2

a. Tonic Key: I   V♯   I   V⌣   III
     Mediant Key: V   I   ♭VI♭5   II♭5   V   I

a. Tonic Key: i   V6   i   V6/III   III
     Mediant Key: V6   I   ♭VI   ii∅65   V   I

b. Tonic Key: I   V♯   I   V⌣   III
     Mediant Key: V   I   ♭VI♭5   II♭5   V   I

b. Tonic Key: i   V6   i   V65/III   III
     Mediant Key: V65   I   ♭VI   ii∅65   V   I

c. I   V♯   I   V⌣   III   I   II   V♯   I♯

c. i   V6   i   V6/III   III   i   ii∅65   V   I

d. I   V♯   I   V⌣   III   I   II   V♯   I♯

d. i   V6   i   V65/III   III   i   ii∅65   V   I

ID23–7.   A chord progression is performed. Identify the correct score notation for the outer voices. Figured-bass symbols have been placed below the bass where appropriate. If you wish, add Roman numerals.

b.

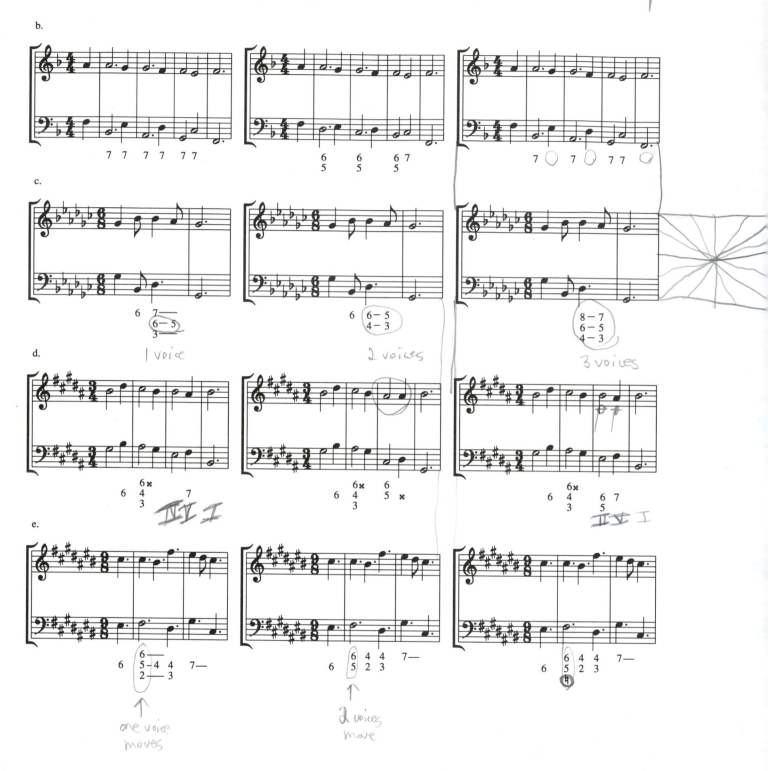

c.

d.

e.

f.

RHYTHMIC DICTATIONS

RD23–1.

RD23–2.

MELODIC DICTATIONS

HAYDN: SYMPHONY NO. 94 IN G MAJOR ("SURPRISE"), MVMT. 3

MD23–1.

- The C of measure 3, which forms an augmented fourth against the F# earlier in the measure, does not resolve to B until measure 7. How and when does the F# of measure 3 resolve?

BEETHOVEN: *MISSA SOLEMNIS* IN D MAJOR, OP. 123, GLORIA

MD23–2.

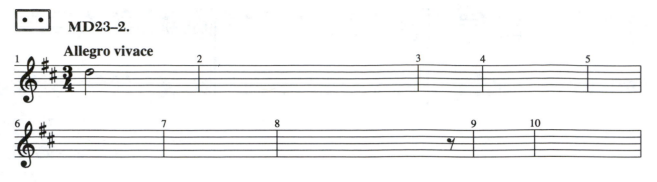

- The first few measures sound as if they are in $\frac{2}{4}$ meter. Do not add or subtract any bar lines from the given staff.

FRANCK: SYMPHONY IN D MINOR, MVMT. 1

MD23–3.

- At first, consider only the first and third pitches of measures 1 and 2. The second pitch is in both cases an incomplete lower neighbor of the first pitch.

J. S. BACH: SUITE FOR UNACCOMPANIED CELLO NO. 1 IN G MAJOR, BWV 1007, COURANTE

MD23–4.

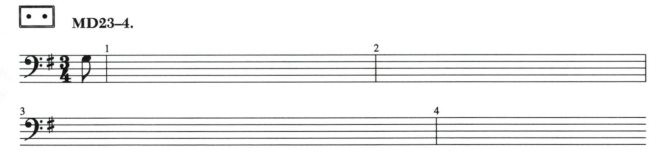

- Compare the fourth through sixth pitches of each measure.

BEETHOVEN: SYMPHONY NO. 9 IN D MINOR ("CHORAL"), OP. 125, MVMT. 1

MD23–5.

Allegro, ma non troppo, un poco maestoso.

- Both the dominant and leading-tone chords applied to the mediant in major keys require two accidentals. You will need these accidentals in measures 7 and 8.

BEETHOVEN: SYMPHONY NO. 2 IN D MAJOR, OP. 36, MVMT. 4

MD23–6.

Allegro molto

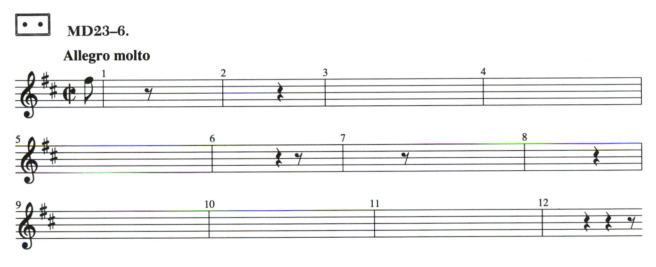

- What dissonant interval is formed by the first two pitches of measure 1? When and how does it resolve?

HARMONIC DICTATIONS

WEBER: CLARINET CONCERTO NO. 1 IN F MINOR, OP. 73, MVMT. 2

HD23–1.

Adagio, ma non troppo

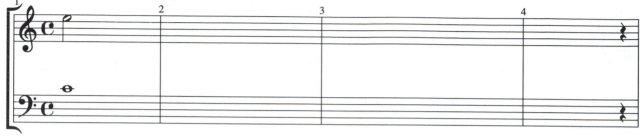

- Weber employs only three pitches to form each chord. Some rarely omitted chord members are omitted. Your internal ear should add a B during the first two beats of measure 2, a D during beat 1 of measure 3, and a G during beats 3 and 4 of measure 3.

SCHUBERT: PIANO SONATA IN A MINOR, D. 845, OP. 42, MVMT. 1

HD23–2.

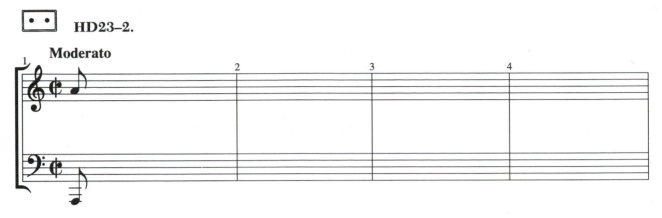

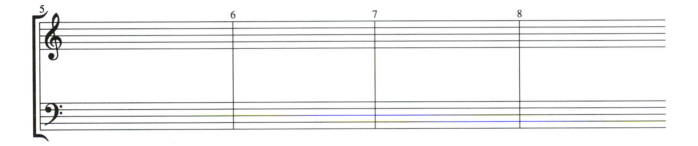

· Schubert employs an extraordinarily small number of different chords in this excerpt. How do the chords of measures 5 through 8 relate to those of measures 1 through 4?

GLUCK: *IPHIGENIA IN TAURIS*, ACT 2

HD23–3.

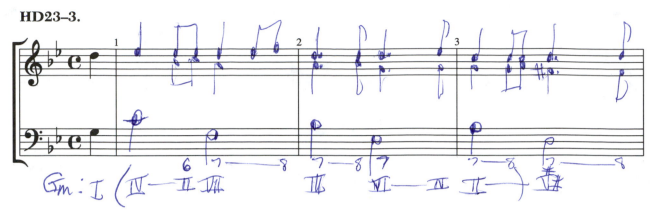

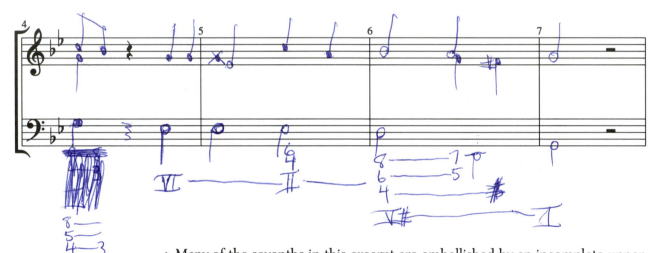

- Many of the sevenths in this excerpt are embellished by an incomplete upper neighbor before their resolution, as shown below.

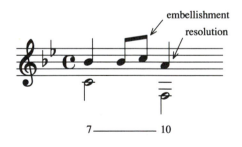

SCHUMANN: *DAVIDSBÜNDLERTÄNZE*, OP. 6, NO. 11

HD23–4.

Einfach.

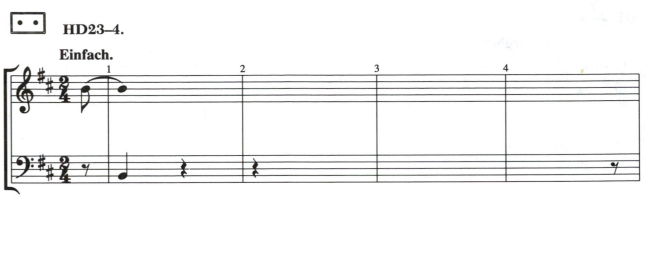

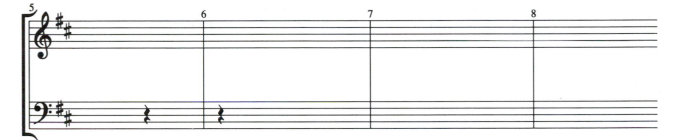

· Both of the phrases of this excerpt begin with a progression from tonic to mediant (via the mediant's dominant). In one of the phrases, the mediant remains for only one beat. In the other, it is tonicized.

HANDEL: *SUSANNA*, ACT 2

HD23–5.

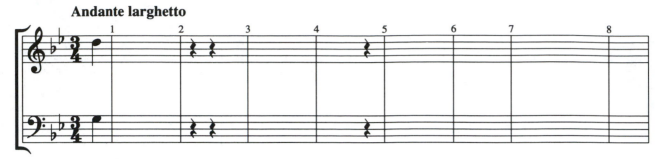

· An unusual combination of pitches occurs at the end of measure 3. The soprano
  pitch is an anticipation; the alto pitch is a passing note.

SCHUBERT: PIANO SONATA IN E♭ MAJOR, D. 568, OP. POST. 122, MVMT. 2

HD23–6.

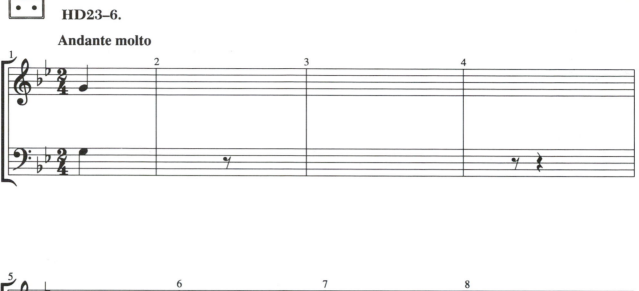

- The first chord of measure 7 has a startling impact, for several reasons. First, it becomes apparent at that point that the mediant will be tonicized. Second, the chord employs modal mixture. Third, its bass (G♭) clashes against the soprano (G) of measure 6, beat 1—an example of a "cross relation."

▣ CASSETTE PROGRAM (TAPE 4, SIDE A)

C23–1.   Six melodies are performed, twice each. During the silence after each playing, respond in one of the following ways: (1) Sing the melody, using solmization syllables; (2) Play the melody on the piano or on your primary instrument; (3) Write the melody on staff paper.

C23–2.   Six chord progressions are performed, four times each. During the silence after each playing, respond in one of the following ways: (1) Sing the soprano after the first and second playings and the bass after the third and fourth playings, using solmization syllables; (2) Play the soprano on the piano or your primary instrument after the first and second playings and the bass after the third and fourth playings; (3) Play both the soprano and bass on the piano after each playing; (4) Write the soprano and bass on staff paper and provide an analysis.

Chapter 24

PITCH

The submediant's applied chords, tonicization, and modulation are introduced in this chapter. In major keys, the chromatic bass ascent $\hat{5}$-$\sharp\hat{5}$-$\hat{6}$ is an ideal context for the submediant's applied dominant or leading-tone chord, as in Example 24–1.

EXAMPLE 24–1

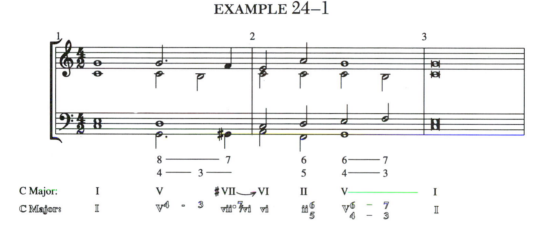

A $^5_3$-position chord may be modified not only to form a seventh chord, but also to form **ninth**, **eleventh**, and **thirteenth chords**. Each of these sonorities occurs also in the context of a suspension: a ninth chord resembles the suspension phase of a 9-8 suspension; an eleventh chord resembles the suspension phase of a 4-3 suspension; and a thirteenth chord resembles the suspension phase of a 6-5 suspension. Of course, the *behavior* of these chords will not be the same as that of chords with suspensions. A ninth, eleventh, or thirteenth that functions as a chord member will resolve only when the harmony changes.

In the nineteenth century composers began to build "stacked thirds" chords that contain a ninth, eleventh, and thirteenth all at once. Perhaps more common, though, are less complex chords such as those in the sample progressions of Example 24–2. Dominants, applied dominants, and all other harmonies that support a major or minor seventh may be constructed using these new members. Inversions of these chords are possible as well. The ninth is figured using the number "9." The eleventh and thirteenth may be figured using either "11" and "13" or "4" and "6."

EXAMPLE 24–2

The ***diminished fourteenth***, ***minor fourteenth***, and ***major fourteenth*** are emphasized in this chapter. These intervals may be used in forming a ***7-6 suspension***. Two 7-6 suspensions occur in Example 24–3. The one in measure 3 embellishes the 6 of the cadential $^6_4$. In this context the sixth, C, is a passing note connecting the D of measure 2 and the B at the end of measure 3.

EXAMPLE 24–3

METER AND RHYTHM

When triplets are employed in a simple meter, three notes are performed in the time normally required for two notes. They provide a moment of compound meter in the context of a simple meter. When **duplets** are employed in a compound meter, two notes are performed in the time normally required for three notes. They provide a moment of simple meter in the context of a compound meter.

In $\frac{12}{8}$ meter, for example, a beat that would typically be filled by three eighth notes (♫) might instead be filled by two eighth notes designated as duplets (♫). Example 24–4 demonstrates their use. Although usually written in the manner presented here, duplets are occasionally written with longer note values, for example ♩♩ instead of ♫ to fill a beat in $\frac{12}{8}$ meter.

EXAMPLE 24–4

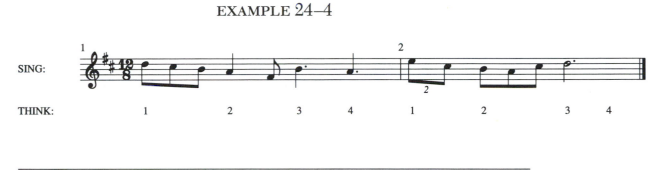

SOLO MELODIES

MELODIES THAT OUTLINE A CHORD APPLIED TO THE SUBMEDIANT

SCHUBERT: STRING QUINTET IN C MAJOR, D. 956, OP. 163, MVMT. 1

S24–1.

- Measure 8's A connects the G♯ of measure 7 and the B of measure 9. It does not resolve the leading tone's tendency.

BERLIOZ: *BENVENUTO CELLINI*, ACT 2

S24–2.

MELODIES THAT OUTLINE A NINTH CHORD

SCHUBERT: PIANO SONATA IN A MINOR, D. 845, OP. 42, MVMT. 1

S24–3.

- Many times during preceding chapters, you have been asked to decide when and where a dissonant pitch resolves and to shape your musical interpretation accordingly. In the case of the dominant ninth, an explicit resolution is often lacking. The A♭ of measures 5 forms a minor ninth with the G of measure 6, but its resolution pitch (G) does not occur in measure 8, where tonic is implied. (G occurs in a lower register among the accompanying voices.)

SCHUBERT: SYMPHONY NO. 5 IN Bb MAJOR, D. 485, MVMT. 3

S24–4.

CHOPIN: PIANO SONATA NO. 2 IN Bb MINOR, OP. 35, MVMT. 2

S24–5.

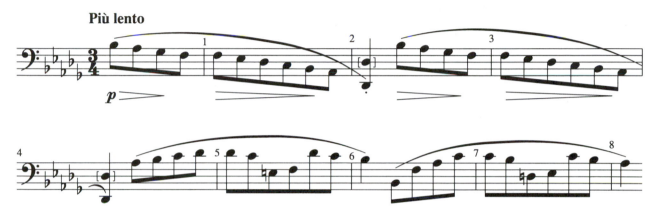

- The lowest structural pitches of measures 5 through 8 form a pattern of descending fifths (ascending fourths): F-Bb-Eb-Ab.

PUCCINI: *LA BOHÈME*, ACT 4

S24–6.

MELODIES THAT IMPLY A 7-6 SUSPENSION

GOUNOD: *FAUST*, ACT 1

S24–7.

 · Divide the six pitches of measure 6 into two groups of three. Though the first
four pitches may appear to outline a submediant seventh chord, a more appropriate reading of the measure is shown below.

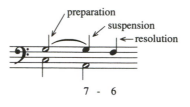

BEETHOVEN: STRING QUARTET NO. 14 IN C♯ MINOR, OP. 131, MVMT. 7

S24–8.

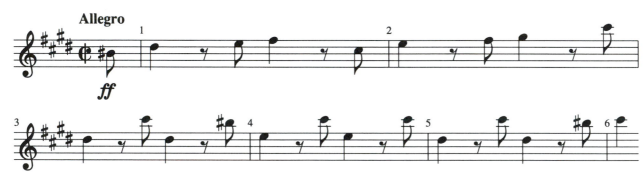

BRAHMS: PIANO TRIO NO. 3 IN C MINOR, OP. 101, MVMT. 1

S24–9.

- When you perform this melody, think of measure 9's G stretching across measure 10 and resolving to F at the beginning of measure 11 (as a 7-6 suspension above bass A). Likewise, measure 11's A stretches across measure 12.

ROSSINI: *THE BARBER OF SEVILLE*, ACT 1

S24–10.

MELODIES THAT EMPLOY DUPLETS

GOUNOD: *FAUST*, ACT 1

S24–11.

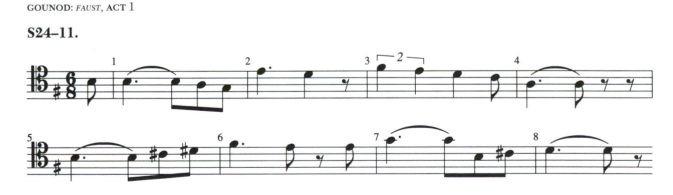

- This melody outlines two applied chords. In measures 5 and 6, B-D♯-F♯ functions as an applied dominant of the submediant. E-G-C♯ in measures 6 and 7 suggests either the dominant's applied dominant or its applied leading-tone chord.

TCHAIKOVSKY: SYMPHONY NO. 5 IN E MINOR, OP. 64, MVMT. 2

S24–12.

DUETS

AFTER DONIZETTI: *LUCIA DI LAMMERMOOR*, ACT 1

D24–1.

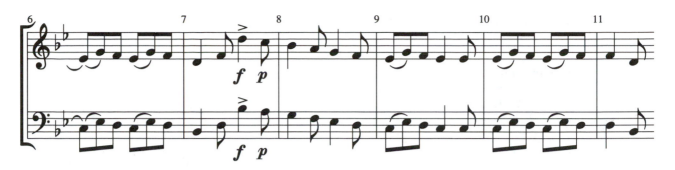

AFTER SCHUBERT: *FIERRABRAS*, D. 796, ACT 2

D24–2.

Andantino

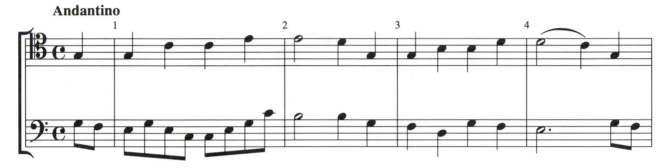

AFTER TCHAIKOVSKY: INCIDENTAL MUSIC TO *HAMLET*, OP. 67 BIS, ACT 2

D24–3.

ACCOMPANIED SOLO MELODIES

AFTER BRAHMS: PIANO TRIO NO. 3 IN C MINOR, OP. 101, MVMT. 3

AS24–1.

AFTER VIVALDI: CONCERTO IN F MINOR ("THE FOUR SEASONS: WINTER"), RV 297, OP. 8, NO. 4, MVMT. 2

AS24–2.

AFTER MOZART: *DIE ENTFÜHRUNG AUS DEM SERAIL*, K. 384, ACT 1

AS24–3.

AFTER WAGNER: *LOHENGRIN*, ACT 3

AS24–4.

RHYTHMS

R24–1.

R24–2.

R24–3.

R24–4.

R24–5.

R24–6.

INTERVAL WORKSHOP

I24–1.   Practice singing the intervals of a diminished fourteenth, minor fourteenth, and major fourteenth higher than a sounding pitch. The sounding pitch should be beyond the lower limit of your vocal range, and could be sung by a classmate or your instructor or performed on the piano or another instrument such as the cello. Also practice singing twenty-firsts and twenty-eighths, using very low sounding pitches.

I24–2.   Practice singing the intervals of a diminished fourteenth, minor fourteenth, and major fourteenth lower than a sounding pitch. The sounding pitch should be beyond the upper limit of your vocal range, and could be sung by a classmate or your instructor or performed on the piano or another instrument such as the flute. Also practice singing twenty-firsts and twenty-eighths, using very high sounding pitches.

I24–3.   If the size of your vocal range permits, practice the following exercise. Play a pitch low in your vocal range at a keyboard. Sing it. Then sing the pitch a diminished fourteenth higher. Use the keyboard to confirm your performance. Then sing ascending fourteenths starting on other pitches. Repeat this exercise for the minor fourteenth and major fourteenth.

I24–4.   If the size of your vocal range permits, practice the following exercise. Play a pitch high in your vocal range at a keyboard. Sing it. Then sing the pitch a diminished fourteenth lower. Use the keyboard to confirm your performance. Then sing descending fourteenths starting on other pitches. Repeat this exercise for the minor fourteenth and major fourteenth.

ARPEGGIATION WORKSHOP

A24–1.   Play a pitch that is at least a minor second above the lowest note of your vocal range at a keyboard. Let this pitch be $\hat{1}$ in a major key. Sing each of the following arpeggiations, either in the order given or in random order.

a. $\hat{1}$ $\hat{3}$ $\hat{5}$ $\hat{8}$ ✻ $\hat{3}$ $\sharp\hat{5}$ $\hat{7}$ $\hat{2}$ ✻ $\hat{6}$ $\hat{8}$ $\hat{3}$ $\hat{6}$ ✻ $\hat{5}$ $\hat{7}$ $\hat{4}$ $\hat{7}$ ✻
         $\hat{8}$ $^{\hat{3}}$ $\hat{8}$ $\hat{1}$

b. $\hat{1}$ $\hat{3}$ $\hat{5}$ $\hat{8}$ ✻ $\sharp\hat{5}$ $\hat{7}$ $\hat{2}$ $\hat{3}$ ✻ $\hat{6}$ $\hat{8}$ $\hat{3}$ $\hat{6}$ ✻ $\hat{5}$ $\hat{7}$ $\hat{4}$ $\hat{7}$ ✻
         $\hat{8}$ $^{\hat{3}}$ $\hat{8}$ $\hat{1}$

c. $\hat{1}$ $\hat{3}$ $\hat{5}$ $\hat{8}$ ✻ $\sharp\hat{5}$ $\hat{7}$ $\hat{2}$ $\hat{4}$ ✻ $\hat{6}$ $\hat{8}$ $\hat{3}$ $\hat{6}$ ✻ $\hat{5}$ $\hat{7}$ $\hat{4}$ $\hat{7}$ ✻
         $\hat{8}$ $^{\hat{3}}$ $\hat{8}$ $\hat{1}$

d. $\hat{1}$ $\hat{3}$ $\hat{5}$ $\hat{8}$ ✻ $\hat{5}$ $\hat{7}$ $\hat{2}$ $\hat{5}$ ✻ $\sharp\hat{5}$ $\hat{7}$ $\hat{2}$ $\hat{4}$ ✻ $\hat{6}$ $\hat{8}$ $\hat{3}$ $\hat{6}$ ✻
         $\hat{7}$ $^{\hat{2}}$ $^{\hat{4}}$ $\hat{5}$ ✻ $\hat{8}$ $\hat{5}$ $\hat{3}$ $\hat{1}$

e. $\hat{1}$ $\hat{3}$ $\hat{5}$ $\hat{8}$ ✻ $\hat{2}$ $\sharp\hat{4}$ $\hat{8}$ $\hat{3}$ ✻ $\hat{5}$ $\hat{7}$ $\hat{2}$ $\hat{7}$ ✻ $\hat{8}$ $\hat{5}$ $\hat{3}$ $\hat{1}$ ✻

f. $\hat{1}$ $\hat{5}$ $\hat{8}$ ✻ $\hat{2}$ $\hat{4}$ $\hat{8}$ ✻ $\hat{2}$ $\hat{4}$ $\hat{7}$ ✻ $\hat{3}$ $\hat{5}$ $\hat{8}$

g. $\hat{1}$ $\hat{3}$ $\hat{5}$ $\hat{8}$ ✻ $\hat{2}$ $\hat{4}$ $\hat{5}$ $\hat{8}$ ✻ $\hat{2}$ $\hat{4}$ $\hat{5}$ $\hat{7}$ ✻ $\hat{1}$ $\hat{3}$ $\hat{5}$ $\hat{8}$

h. $\hat{1}$ $\hat{5}$ $\hat{8}$ $\hat{3}$ ✻ $\hat{4}$ $\hat{6}$ $\hat{3}$ $\hat{6}$ ✻ $\hat{4}$ $\hat{6}$ $\hat{2}$ $\hat{6}$ ✻ $\hat{5}$ $\hat{7}$ $\hat{2}$ $\hat{5}$

i. $\hat{1}$ $\hat{3}$ $\hat{5}$ $\hat{1}$ ❖ $\hat{7}$ $\hat{2}$ $\hat{4}$ $\hat{6}$ ❖ $\hat{7}$ $\hat{2}$ $\hat{4}$ $\hat{5}$ ❖ $\hat{1}$ $\hat{3}$ $\hat{5}$ $\hat{1}$

j. $\hat{1}$ $\hat{3}$ $\hat{5}$ $\hat{8}$ ❖ $\hat{4}$ $\hat{6}$ $\hat{8}$ $^{\hat{4}}$ ❖ $\hat{5}$ $\hat{8}$ $^{\hat{4}}$ ❖ $\hat{5}$ $\hat{8}$ $^{\hat{3}}$ ❖

   $\hat{5}$ $\hat{7}$ $^{\hat{3}}$ ❖ $\hat{5}$ $\hat{7}$ $^{\hat{2}}$ ❖ $\hat{8}$ $\hat{5}$ $\hat{3}$ $\hat{1}$

A24–2.   Play a pitch that is at least a minor second above the lowest note of your vocal range at a keyboard. Let this pitch be $\hat{1}$ in a minor key. Sing each of the following arpeggiations, either in the order given or in random order.

a. $\hat{1}$ $\hat{3}$ $\hat{5}$ $\hat{8}$ ❖ $\hat{3}$ $\hat{5}$ $\hat{7}$ $^{\flat\hat{2}}$ ❖ $\hat{6}$ $\hat{8}$ $^{\hat{3}}$ $\hat{6}$ ❖ $\hat{5}$ $\sharp\hat{7}$ $^{\hat{4}}$ $\sharp\hat{7}$ ❖
   $\hat{8}$ $^{\hat{3}}$ $\hat{8}$ $\hat{1}$

b. $\hat{1}$ $\hat{3}$ $\hat{5}$ $\hat{8}$ ❖ $\hat{5}$ $\hat{7}$ $^{\flat\hat{2}}$ $^{\hat{3}}$ ❖ $\hat{6}$ $\hat{8}$ $^{\hat{3}}$ $\hat{6}$ ❖ $\hat{5}$ $\sharp\hat{7}$ $^{\hat{4}}$ $\sharp\hat{7}$ ❖
   $\hat{8}$ $^{\hat{3}}$ $\hat{8}$ $\hat{1}$

c. $\hat{1}$ $\hat{3}$ $\hat{5}$ $\hat{8}$ ❖ $\hat{5}$ $\hat{7}$ $^{\flat\hat{2}}$ $^{\hat{4}}$ ❖ $\hat{6}$ $\hat{8}$ $^{\hat{3}}$ $\hat{6}$ ❖ $\hat{5}$ $\sharp\hat{7}$ $^{\hat{4}}$ $\sharp\hat{7}$ ❖
   $\hat{8}$ $^{\hat{3}}$ $\hat{8}$ $\hat{1}$

d. $\hat{1}$ $\hat{3}$ $\hat{5}$ $\hat{8}$ ❖ $\hat{5}$ $\hat{7}$ $^{\flat\hat{2}}$ $^{\flat\hat{4}}$ ❖ $\hat{6}$ $\hat{8}$ $^{\hat{3}}$ $\hat{6}$ ❖ $\hat{5}$ $\sharp\hat{7}$ $^{\hat{4}}$ $\sharp\hat{7}$ ❖
   $\hat{8}$ $^{\hat{3}}$ $\hat{8}$ $\hat{1}$

e. $\hat{1}$ $\hat{3}$ $\hat{5}$ $\hat{8}$ ❖ $\hat{5}$ $\sharp\hat{7}$ $^{\hat{2}}$ $\hat{5}$ ❖ $\hat{5}$ $\hat{7}$ $^{\flat\hat{2}}$ $^{\hat{4}}$ ❖ $\hat{6}$ $\hat{8}$ $^{\hat{3}}$ $\hat{6}$ ❖
   $\hat{5}$ $\sharp\hat{7}$ $^{\hat{2}}$ $^{\hat{4}}$ ❖ $\hat{8}$ $\hat{5}$ $\hat{3}$ $\hat{1}$

f. $\hat{1}$ $\hat{3}$ $\hat{5}$ $\hat{8}$ ❖ $\hat{5}$ $\sharp\hat{7}$ $^{\hat{2}}$ $\hat{5}$ ❖ $\hat{5}$ $\hat{7}$ $^{\flat\hat{2}}$ $^{\flat\hat{4}}$ ❖ $\hat{6}$ $\hat{8}$ $^{\hat{3}}$ $\hat{6}$ ❖
   $\hat{5}$ $\sharp\hat{7}$ $^{\hat{2}}$ $^{\hat{4}}$ ❖ $\hat{8}$ $\hat{5}$ $\hat{3}$ $\hat{1}$

g. $\hat{1}$ $\hat{3}$ $\hat{5}$ $\hat{8}$ ❖ $\hat{2}$ $\sharp\hat{4}$ $\hat{8}$ $^{\hat{3}}$ ❖ $\hat{5}$ $\sharp\hat{7}$ $^{\hat{2}}$ $\sharp\hat{7}$ ❖ $\hat{8}$ $\hat{5}$ $\hat{3}$ $\hat{1}$

h. $\hat{1}$ $\hat{5}$ $\hat{8}$ ❖ $\hat{2}$ $\hat{4}$ $\hat{8}$ ❖ $\hat{2}$ $\hat{4}$ $\sharp\hat{7}$ ❖ $\hat{3}$ $\hat{5}$ $\hat{8}$

i. $\hat{1}$ $\hat{3}$ $\hat{5}$ $\hat{8}$ ❖ $\hat{2}$ $\hat{4}$ $\hat{5}$ $\hat{8}$ ❖ $\hat{2}$ $\hat{4}$ $\hat{5}$ $\sharp\hat{7}$ ❖ $\hat{1}$ $\hat{3}$ $\hat{5}$ $\hat{8}$

j. $\hat{1}$ $\hat{5}$ $\hat{8}$ $^{\hat{3}}$ ❖ $\hat{4}$ $\hat{6}$ $^{\hat{3}}$ $\hat{6}$ ❖ $\hat{4}$ $\hat{6}$ $^{\hat{2}}$ $\hat{6}$ ❖ $\hat{5}$ $\sharp\hat{7}$ $^{\hat{2}}$ $\hat{5}$

k. $\hat{1}$ $\hat{3}$ $\hat{5}$ $\hat{1}$ ❖ $\sharp\hat{7}$ $\hat{2}$ $\hat{4}$ $\hat{6}$ ❖ $\sharp\hat{7}$ $\hat{2}$ $\hat{4}$ $\hat{5}$ ❖ $\hat{1}$ $\hat{3}$ $\hat{5}$ $\hat{1}$

l. $\hat{1}$ $\hat{3}$ $\hat{5}$ $\hat{8}$ ❖ $\hat{4}$ $\hat{6}$ $\hat{8}$ $^{\hat{4}}$ ❖ $\hat{5}$ $\hat{8}$ $^{\hat{4}}$ ❖ $\hat{5}$ $\hat{8}$ $^{\hat{3}}$ ❖
   $\hat{5}$ $\sharp\hat{7}$ $^{\hat{3}}$ ❖ $\hat{5}$ $\sharp\hat{7}$ $^{\hat{2}}$ ❖ $\hat{8}$ $\hat{5}$ $\hat{3}$ $\hat{1}$

QUICK SWITCH

Q24–1.

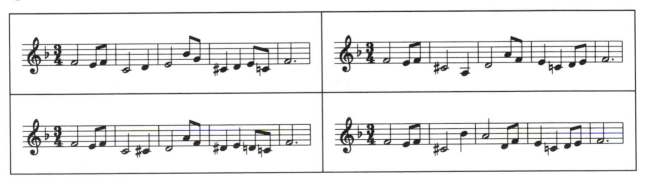

Q24–2.

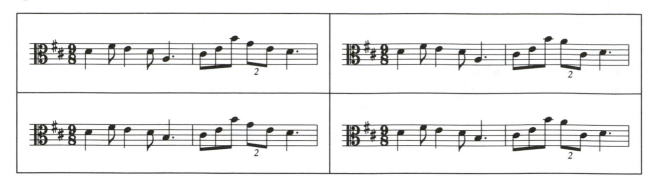

Q24–3.

Q24–4.

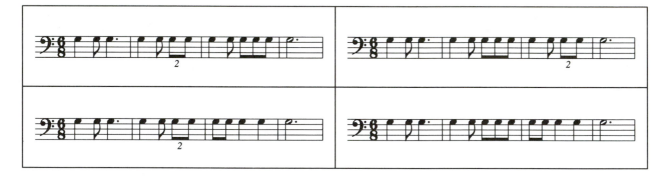

IDENTIFICATIONS

ID24–1.   An interval not larger than a major fourteenth is performed melodically or as a simultaneity. Identify it.

ID24–2.   What chord occurs at **X**? Suitable choices are listed below.

C Major:	I	V	**X**	VI	II^6	V^7	I
C Major:	I	V	**X**	vi	ii$^{\flat 6}$	V^7	I

Choices:

III   V♯   V♯   V♯   V♯   ♯VII
iii   V/vi   V$^6_5$/vi   V^7/vi   V$^9_7$/vi   vii^{o7}/vi

ID24–3.   What chord occurs at **Y**? Suitable choices are listed below.

A Minor: I   V♯   I   **Y**   VI   V♯   V♯
A Minor: i^6 V$^6_5$ i   **Y**   VI   V$^6_5$/V   V

Choices:

V♯   V   ♮VII$^{♭7}$
V^7 V$^6_5$/VI   ♮vii^{o7}/VI

ID24–4.   A melody is performed. Identify the correct score notation.

ID24–5. A chord progression in the major mode is performed. Identify a suitable Roman-numeral/figured-bass analysis from among the following choices:

Group 1

a. I   VI   IV   V$^{\frac{7}{6}}$ I   a. I   vi   IV   V$_7^{13}$ I

b. I   VI   IV   V^7 I   b. I   vi   IV   V^7 I

c. I   VI   IV   V$^{\frac{9}{7}}$ I   c. I   vi   IV·   V$_7^9$ I

d. I   VI   IV   V$^{\frac{7}{4}}$ I   d. I   vi   IV   V$_7^{11}$ I

Group 2

a. I   V$^{\frac{6\sharp}{4}}_{3}$↷   VI   V$^{\frac{4}{3\flat}}$↷   IV   V$^{\frac{4}{2}}$ I   a. I   V$^4_3$/vi   vi   V$^4_3$/IV   IV   V$^4_2$ I^6

b. I   ♯VII↷   VI   V$^{\frac{4}{3\flat}}$↷   IV   V$^{\frac{4}{2}}$ I   b. I   vii^{o6}/vi   vi   V$^4_3$/IV   IV   V$^4_2$ I^6

c. I   V$^{\frac{6\sharp}{4}}_{3}$↷   VI   V$^{\frac{6\sharp}{4}}_{3}$↷   V–   I   c. I   V$^4_3$/vi   vi   V$^4_3$/V   V$^{6\;4}_{4\;2}$ I^6

d. I   ♯VII↷   VI   V$^{\frac{6\sharp}{4}}_{3}$↷   V–   I   d. I   vii^{o6}/vi   vi   V$^4_3$/V   V$^{6\;4}_{4\;2}$ I^6

ID24–6.   A chord progression in the minor mode is performed. Identify a suitable Roman-numeral/figured-bass analysis from among the following choices:

Group 1

a. V^6_5 I $V^7_\sharp$ VI II $V^{6-5}_{4-\sharp}$ I   a. V^6_5 i V^7 VI ii^{o6} V^{6-5}_{4-3} i

b. V^6_5 I $V\!\!\smile\!\!VI$ II $V^{6-5}_{4-\sharp}$ I   b. V^6_5 i V^6_5/VI VI ii^{o6} V^{6-5}_{4-3} i

c. V^6_5 I $V^7_\sharp$ VI $V\!\!\smile\!\!V^{6-5}_{\sharp\,4-\sharp}$ I   c. V^6_5 i V^7 VI V^6_5/V V^{6-5}_{4-3} i

d. V^6_5 I $V\!\!\smile\!\!VI$ $V\!\!\smile\!\!V^{6-5}_{\sharp\,4-\sharp}$ I   d. V^6_5 i V^6_5/VI VI V^6_5/V V^{6-5}_{4-3} i

Group 2

a. I $V^{7-6\sharp}_{4-\,3}$ I $VII^{\flat7}\!\!\smile\!\!V^{6\sharp}_{4\sharp\,3}$ a. i $V^{7-6}_{4\,3}$ i^6 vii^{o4}_3/V V^6

b. I $V^{6-}_{5-4\sharp\,2-}$ I $VII^{\flat7}\!\!\smile\!\!V^{6\sharp}_{4\sharp\,3}$ b. i $V^6_{5-4\,2}$ i^6 vii^{o4}_3/V V^6

c. I $V^{7-6\sharp}_{4-\,3}$ I $V\!\!\smile\!\!V^{6\sharp}_{4\sharp\,2}$ c. i $V^{7-6}_{4\,3}$ i^6 V^4_2/V V^6

d. I $V^{6-}_{5-4\sharp\,2-}$ I $V\!\!\smile\!\!V^{6\sharp}_{4\sharp\,2}$ d. i $V^6_{5-4\,2}$ i^6 V^4_2/V V^6

ID24–7.   A chord progression is performed. Identify the correct score notation for the outer voices. Figured-bass symbols have been placed below the bass where appropriate. If you wish, add Roman numerals.

a.

b.

c.

d.

RHYTHMIC DICTATIONS

RD24–1.

RD24–2.

MELODIC DICTATIONS

MD24–1.

Allegro non troppo e molto maestoso

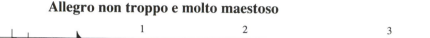

- The second pitch of measure 1 sounds extraordinarily dissonant both because the interval it forms with the preceding pitch is a dissonance and because it is not diatonic in D♭ major. Write down the remaining notes through the end of measure 2 before considering this dissonant pitch. It is closely related to the second pitch of measure 2.

MD24–2.

Allegro

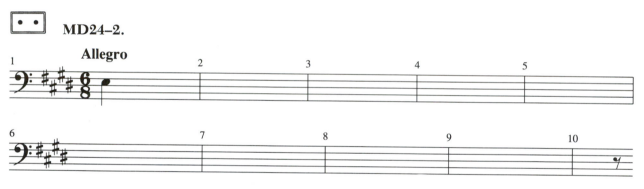

- Before considering measure 9, study the pattern that emerges beginning in measure 6. The last pitch of measure 6 resolves to the second pitch of measure 7, the last pitch of measure 7 resolves to the second pitch of measure 8, and so on. If that pattern were to continue into measure 9, what pitches would you hear? Now listen to measure 9. There is a surprise, but it is not quite so surprising as you might at first think.

MOZART: *DIE ENTFÜHRUNG AUS DEM SERAIL*, K. 384, ACT 2

MD24–3.

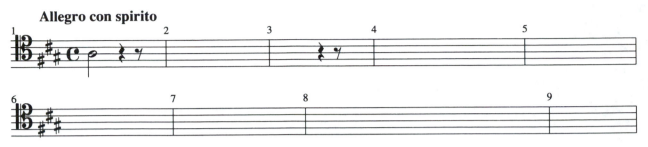

- Mozart employs G♯, the leading tone, within a chromatic descent: A-G♯-G♮-F♯ in measures 1 through 7. The dissonance formed by G♮ and C♯ in measure 6 is appropriately resolved in measure 7.

BRAHMS: PIANO TRIO NO. 3 IN C MINOR, OP. 101, MVMT. 3

MD24–4.

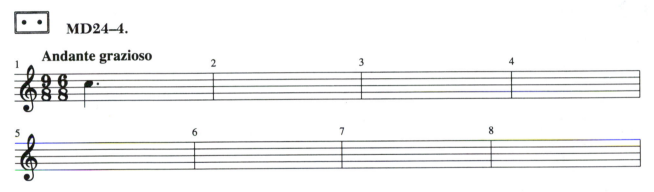

- Measure 3 is not exactly like measure 1. Why not?

BEETHOVEN: *FIDELIO*, OP. 72, ACT 1

MD24–5.

Allegro con brio

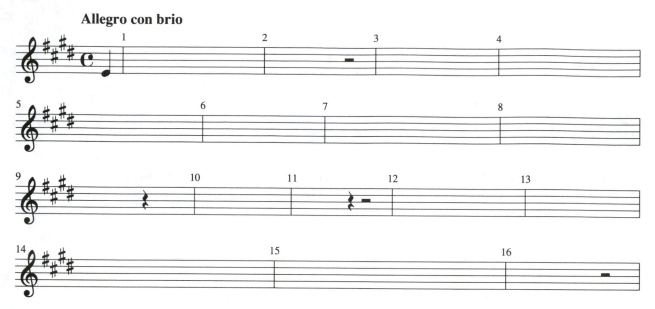

- After you have completed measures 1 through 9, circle the following pitches, which define the structure of the first phrase: measure 1, beat 1; measure 6, beat 1; measure 6, beat 3; measure 7, beat 1; measure 8, beat 3; and measure 9, beat 2. Now listen carefully to measures 14 and 15. How do they relate to the structure of measures 1 through 9? What role does measure 16 play?

HANDEL: *GIULIO CESARE*, ACT 2

MD24–6.

Andante, e staccato

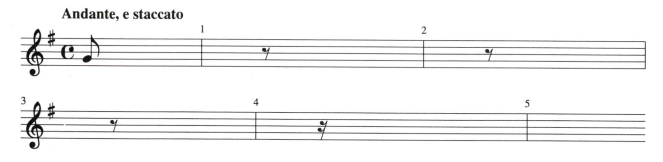

- 7-6 suspensions are outlined during measures 2 through 4.

HARMONIC DICTATIONS

SCHUMANN: *KINDERSCENEN*, OP. 15, NO. 6

HD24–1.

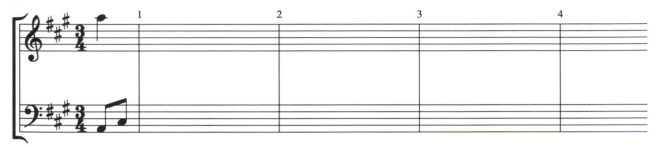

- This excerpt contains two applied chords directed toward the submediant. The first, in measure 1, is directed toward the submediant C♯ minor in the tonicized dominant key, E major. The second, in measure 3, is directed toward the submediant F♯ minor in the tonic key, A major.

SCHUBERT: PIANO SONATA IN B MAJOR, D. 575, OP. POST. 147, MVMT. 2

HD24–2.

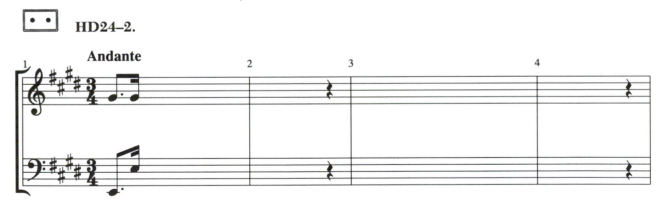

- In major, tonic *is* V of IV. At the beginning of measure 1, the E major chord establishes the tonic key. By the end of the measure (with the help of an added dissonant pitch), it directs the progression toward the subdominant.

FIELD: PIANO CONCERTO NO. 2 IN A♭ MAJOR, MVMT. 1

HD24–3.

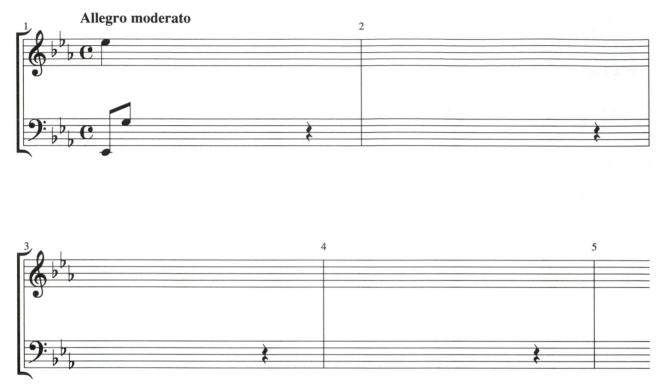

- The pianist's left hand is responsible for the bass pitches (beat 1 of each measure) and for inner-voice pitches (all the other left-hand pitches of each measure). Field indicates that the piano's sustaining pedal should be used, so that the bass sounds through each measure. Your analysis should treat the first pitch of each measure as if it were a dotted half note. For example, all of measure 1 *sounds* like tonic in $^5_3$ position even though part of the measure may *appear* to be in $^6_3$ position.

DVOŘÁK: SYMPHONY NO. 8 IN G MAJOR, OP. 88, MVMT. 2

HD24–4.

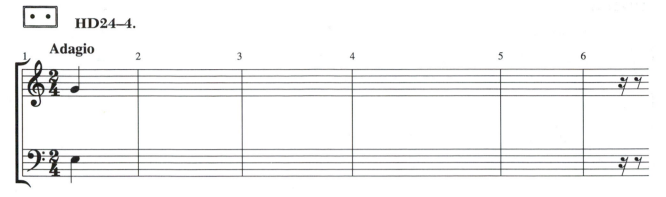

· The bass pitch of measure 5, beat 1, is a chromatic passing note. Dvořák connects the root position and first inversion of dominant with the ascending bass line G-A-B♭-B♭-B♮.

MOZART: PIANO CONCERTO NO. 23 IN A MAJOR, K. 488, MVMT. 1

HD24–5.

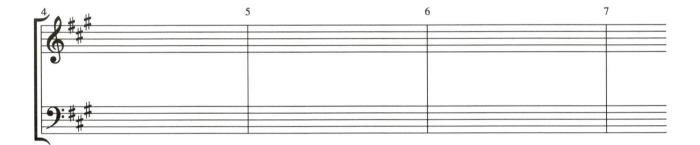

· A descending fifths sequence connects the subdominant $^6_3$ chord in measure 4 and the supertonic $^6_3$ chord in measure 5.

SCHUBERT: *FIERRABRAS*, D. 796, ACT 2

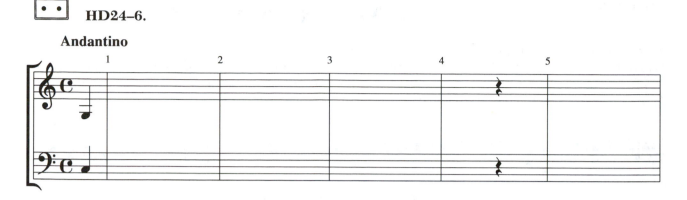

HD24–6.

Andantino

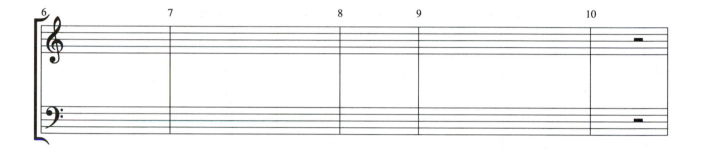

· The soprano pitch G in measure 6 is a passing note connecting A and F, the ninth and seventh of a dominant ninth chord. The figured bass for measure 6 is as follows:

9 - 8 - 7
7 - 6 - 5
3————

⟦··⟧ CASSETTE PROGRAM
(TAPE 4, SIDE B)

C24–1.   Six melodies are performed, twice each. During the silence after each playing, respond in one of the following ways: (1) Sing the melody, using solmization syllables; (2) Play the melody on the piano or on your primary instrument; (3) Write the melody on staff paper.

C24–2.   Six chord progressions are performed, four times each. During the silence after each playing, respond in one of the following ways: (1) Sing the soprano after the first and second playings and the bass after the third and fourth playings, using solmization syllables; (2) Play the soprano on the piano or your primary instrument after the first and second playings and the bass after the third and fourth playings; (3) Play both the soprano and bass on the piano after each playing; (4) Write the soprano and bass on staff paper and provide an analysis.

Chapter 25

PITCH

Heard in isolation, a **Neapolitan chord** sounds like any other major chord. Heard in context, it draws attention to itself because ♭$\hat{2}$—a pitch foreign to both major and minor keys—serves as its root. The Neapolitan chord functions much like a diatonic supertonic chord. Because its quality is major, an applied chord or tonicization may reinforce it in both major and minor keys. The preference for first inversion (the "Neapolitan sixth") stems from the linear bass line ($\hat{4}$-$\hat{5}$) that results when its $^6_3$ position leads to the dominant, as it often does. Root position would result in the awkward bass line ♭$\hat{2}$-$\hat{5}$.

Example 25–1 shows the Neapolitan as a dominant preparation. The cadential $^6_4$ supports $\hat{1}$, an accented passing note that fills in the difficult, dissonant melodic interval ♭$\hat{2}$-♯$\hat{7}$ in the soprano. The label "♭II" is used for the Neapolitan in Method One analysis.[1] The abbreviation "N" is used for the Neapolitan in Method Two analysis.

EXAMPLE 25–1

The **perfect fifteenth** is emphasized in this chapter. It may be used in forming a **7-8 suspension**. Unlike other suspensions, the 7-8 suspension resolves *upward* by step. The normative downward resolution is overruled because the pitch that is suspended functions as the leading tone. A 7-8 suspension will rarely occur alone. It is almost always part of a **multiple suspension**, in which two or three pitches are suspended at

---

1. As usual, Method One labels employ the accidentals of the given key. In A minor, the Neapolitan (B♭-D-F) is ♭II. In B major, the Neapolitan (C♮-E-G♮) is ♮II$^{♭5}$. In A♭ major, the Neapolitan (B♭♭-D♭-F♭) is ♭II$^{♭5}$.

once. Multiple suspensions that resolve to tonic are emphasized in this chapter. Measures 4 and 5 of Example 25–2 contain a multiple suspension: 7-8 (G♯ to A); 4-3 (D to C); and 9-8 (B to A).

EXAMPLE 25–2

Suspensions usually resolve during the prolongation of a single chord. Occasionally, however, a change of chord may occur *at the very moment the suspension resolves*. In Example 25–3a, the soprano of measure 2 begins with F, the "4" of a 4-3 suspension. By the time E (the "3") arrives on beat 2, the bass pitch C, against which E would form a third, is gone. The chord on beat 2 is tonic, to be sure, but in $^6_3$ rather than in $^5_3$ position.[2] In Example 25–3b, the alto C of measure 1, beat 3, is the "4" of a 4-3 suspension. The bass moves to G♯ at the same time that the suspension resolves. The alto B at the end of measure 1 is a third above G♯, but not a *major* third, as was expected. The analysis indicates that a dominant harmony occurs in measure 1 even though there is no point in the measure where all of the dominant pitches sound at the same time.

EXAMPLE 25–3

a.

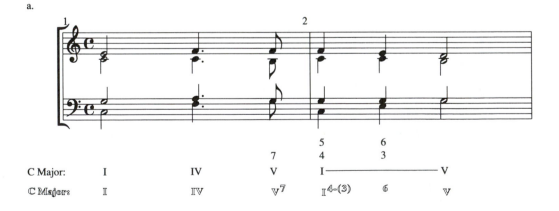

2. The "3" of the figured bass $^6_3$ here refers to G, and not to E, the "3" of the 4-3 suspension.

b.

METER AND RHYTHM

Just as two thirty-second notes fill the same musical time as a sixteenth note, two *sixty-fourth notes* (♬) fill the same musical time as a thirty-second note. A *dotted thirty-second note* (♪) may either precede or follow a single sixty-fourth note. Example 25–4 demonstrates their use.

EXAMPLE 25–4

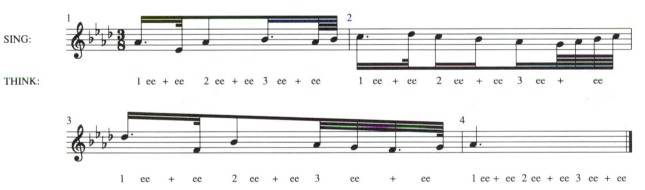

SOLO MELODIES

MELODIES THAT OUTLINE THE NEAPOLITAN CHORD

SCHUMANN: *DICHTERLIEBE*, OP. 48, NO. 8

S25–1.

· What interval is formed by the first pitch of measure 4 and the first pitch of measure 5? Compare it with the interval formed by the pitches of measure 7.

MOZART: STRING QUARTET NO. 15 IN D MINOR, K. 421, MVMT. 1

S25–2.

BERLIOZ: *BENVENUTO CELLINI*, ACT 2

S25–3.

- Observe the similarity between the two phrases. After measures 1 through 4, the first phrase proceeds to the Neapolitan in measure 6. After measures 9 through 12, the second phrase proceeds to the mediant (also a major chord, a whole step higher than the Neapolitan) in measure 14.

SCHUBERT: SYMPHONY NO. 4 IN C MINOR ("TRAGIC"), D. 417, MVMT. 4

S25–4.

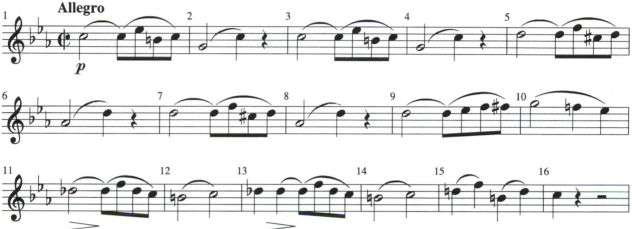

MOZART: *THE MAGIC FLUTE*, K. 620, ACT 1

S25–5.

- Underlying all the leaps that occur in measures 1 through 10 is a stepwise line: measures 0 through 2, C; measures 3 through 5, D; measure 6, E♭; measures 6 through 8, repeat of the C-E♭ phase of the ascent; measure 9, F and F♯; measure 10, G.

BERLIOZ: *LA DAMNATION DE FAUST*, OP. 24, PART 3

S25–6.

MELODIES THAT EMPLOY ♭2̂

MOZART: *THE MAGIC FLUTE*, K. 620, ACT 2

S25–7.

- The first pitch of measure 8 should sound like a surprise. G was expected instead. The melody could work well without measures 8 and 9, though with less interest. The inclusion of these measures expands an eight-measure phrase to ten measures.

BRAHMS: STRING QUARTET NO. 1 IN C MINOR, OP. 51, NO. 1, MVMT. 4

S25–8.

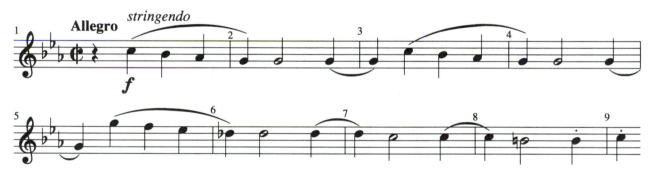

SAINT-SAËNS: *SAMSON ET DALILA*, ACT 3

S25–9.

- The occurrences of ♭2̂ in this melody have nothing to do with the Neapolitan. They do, however, show how composers of the nineteenth century composed "exotic" music.

CHOPIN: NOCTURNE, OP. 27, NO. 1

S25–10.

MELODIES THAT EMPLOY SIXTY-FOURTH NOTES

SCHUBERT: *SCHWANENGESANG*, D. 957, "AM MEER"

S25–11.

- The C on beat 1 of measure 4 is a passing note connecting D and B. It does not imply the arrival of tonic.

HANDEL: *GIULIO CESARE*, ACT 2

S25–12.

DUETS

AFTER SCHUBERT: *FIERRABRAS*, D. 796, ACT 1

D25–1.

Un poco più mosso

AFTER J. S. BACH: MASS IN B MINOR, BWV 232, AGNUS DEI

D25–2.

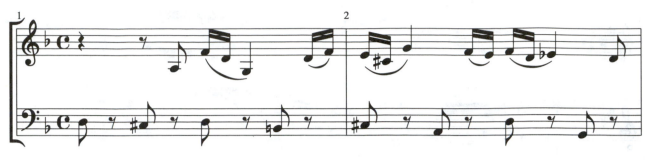

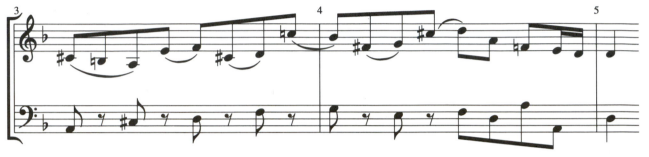

AFTER DVOŘÁK: SYMPHONY NO. 8 IN G MAJOR, OP. 88, MVMT. 2

D25–3.

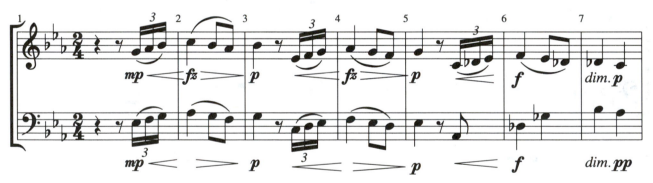

ACCOMPANIED SOLO MELODIES

AFTER SCHUBERT: PIANO SONATA IN A MINOR, D. 537, OP. POST. 164, MVMT. 1

AS25–1.

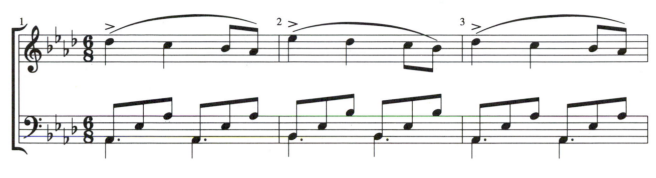

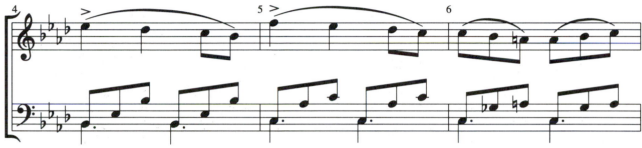

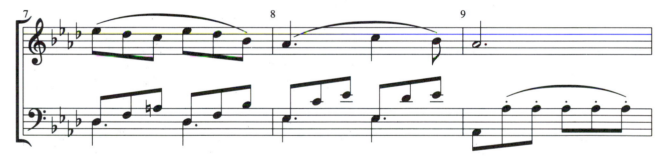

AFTER J. S. BACH: TRIO SONATA FOR ORGAN NO. 4 IN E MINOR, BWV 528, MVMT. 2

AS25–2.

RHYTHMS

R25–1.

R25–2.

R25–3.

R25–4.

R25–5.

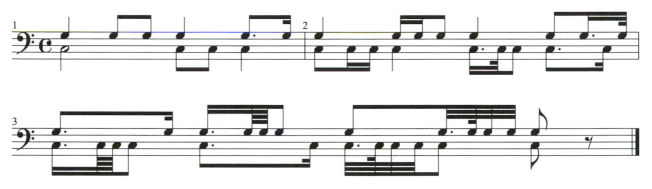

R25–6.

INTERVAL WORKSHOP

I25–1. Practice singing the interval of a perfect fifteenth higher than a sounding pitch. The sounding pitch should be beyond the lower limit of your vocal range, and could be sung by a classmate or your instructor or performed on the piano or another instrument such as the cello. Also practice singing twenty-seconds and twenty-ninths, using very low sounding pitches.

I25–2. Practice singing the interval of a perfect fifteenth lower than a sounding pitch. The sounding pitch should be beyond the upper limit of your vocal range, and could be sung by a classmate or your instructor or performed on the piano or another instrument such as the flute. Also practice singing twenty-seconds and twenty-ninths, using very high sounding pitches.

ARPEGGIATION WORKSHOP

A25–1. Play a pitch that is low in your vocal range at a keyboard. Let this pitch be $\hat{1}$ in a major key. Sing each of the following arpeggiations, either in the order given or in random order.

a. $\hat{1}$ $\hat{3}$ $\hat{5}$ $\hat{8}$ ❋ $\hat{4}$ $\flat\hat{6}$ $\flat\hat{2}$ $\flat\hat{6}$ ❋ $\hat{5}$ $\hat{7}$ $\hat{5}$ $\hat{2}$ ❋ $\hat{8}$ $\hat{5}$ $\hat{3}$ $\hat{1}$

b. $\hat{1}$ $\hat{3}$ $\hat{5}$ $\hat{8}$ ❋ $\hat{3}$ $\hat{5}$ $\hat{8}$ $\hat{3}$ ❋ $\hat{4}$ $\flat\hat{6}$ $\flat\hat{2}$ $\hat{4}$ ❋ $\hat{5}$ $\hat{7}$ $\hat{5}$ $\hat{4}$ ❋
    $\hat{3}$ $\hat{8}$ $\hat{5}$ $\hat{1}$

c. $\hat{1}$ $\hat{3}$ $\hat{5}$ $\hat{8}$ ❋ $\hat{4}$ $\flat\hat{6}$ $\flat\hat{2}$ $\hat{4}$ ❋ $\#\hat{4}$ $\hat{6}$ $\hat{8}$ $\hat{2}$ ❋ $\hat{5}$ $\hat{7}$ $\hat{2}$ $\hat{5}$ ❋
    $\hat{8}$ $\hat{5}$ $\hat{3}$ $\hat{1}$

d. $\hat{1}$ $\hat{3}$ $\hat{5}$ $\hat{8}$ ❋ $\hat{4}$ $\flat\hat{6}$ $\flat\hat{2}$ $\hat{4}$ ❋ $\#\hat{4}$ $\hat{6}$ $\hat{8}$ $\flat\hat{3}$ ❋ $\hat{5}$ $\hat{7}$ $\hat{2}$ $\hat{5}$ ❋
    $\hat{8}$ $\hat{5}$ $\hat{3}$ $\hat{1}$

e. $\hat{1}$ $\hat{3}$ $\hat{5}$ $\hat{8}$ ❋ $\hat{4}$ $\flat\hat{6}$ $\flat\hat{2}$ $\hat{4}$ ❋ $\hat{5}$ $\hat{8}$ $\hat{3}$ $\hat{8}$ ❋ $\hat{5}$ $\hat{7}$ $\hat{2}$ $\hat{7}$

f. $\hat{1}$ $\hat{5}$ $\hat{8}$ $\hat{3}$ ❋ $\hat{2}$ $\hat{4}$ $\hat{7}$ $\hat{2}$ ❋ $\hat{1}$ $\hat{4}$ $\hat{7}$ $\hat{2}$ ❋ $\hat{1}$ $\hat{3}$ $\hat{8}$ $\hat{1}$

g. $\hat{1}$ $\hat{5}$ $\hat{8}$ $\hat{3}$ ❋ $\hat{5}$ $\hat{7}$ $\hat{2}$ $\hat{4}$ ❋ $\hat{1}$ $\hat{5}$ $\hat{2}$ $\hat{4}$ ❋ $\hat{1}$ $\hat{5}$ $\hat{8}$ $\hat{3}$

A25–2.   Play a pitch that is low in your vocal range at a keyboard. Let this pitch be $\hat{1}$ in a minor key. Sing each of the following arpeggiations, either in the order given or in random order.

a. $\hat{1}$ $\hat{3}$ $\hat{5}$ $\hat{8}$ ❋ $\hat{4}$ $\hat{6}$ $\flat\hat{2}$ $\hat{6}$ ❋ $\hat{5}$ $\#\hat{7}$ $\hat{5}$ $\hat{2}$ ❋ $\hat{8}$ $\hat{5}$ $\hat{3}$ $\hat{1}$

b. $\hat{1}$ $\hat{3}$ $\hat{5}$ $\hat{8}$ ❋ $\hat{3}$ $\hat{5}$ $\hat{8}$ $\hat{3}$ ❋ $\hat{4}$ $\hat{6}$ $\flat\hat{2}$ $\hat{4}$ ❋ $\hat{5}$ $\#\hat{7}$ $\hat{5}$ $\hat{4}$ ❋
    $\hat{3}$ $\hat{8}$ $\hat{5}$ $\hat{1}$

c. $\hat{1}$ $\hat{3}$ $\hat{5}$ $\hat{8}$ ❋ $\hat{4}$ $\hat{6}$ $\flat\hat{2}$ $\hat{4}$ ❋ $\#\hat{4}$ $\#\hat{6}$ $\hat{8}$ $\hat{2}$ ❋ $\hat{5}$ $\#\hat{7}$ $\hat{2}$ $\hat{5}$ ❋
    $\hat{8}$ $\hat{5}$ $\hat{3}$ $\hat{1}$

d. $\hat{1}$ $\hat{3}$ $\hat{5}$ $\hat{8}$ ❋ $\hat{4}$ $\hat{6}$ $\flat\hat{2}$ $\hat{4}$ ❋ $\#\hat{4}$ $\#\hat{6}$ $\hat{8}$ $\flat\hat{3}$ ❋ $\hat{5}$ $\#\hat{7}$ $\hat{2}$ $\hat{5}$ ❋
    $\hat{8}$ $\hat{5}$ $\hat{3}$ $\hat{1}$

e. $\hat{1}$ $\hat{3}$ $\hat{5}$ $\hat{8}$ ❋ $\hat{4}$ $\hat{6}$ $\flat\hat{2}$ $\hat{4}$ ❋ $\hat{5}$ $\hat{8}$ $\hat{3}$ $\hat{8}$ ❋ $\hat{5}$ $\#\hat{7}$ $\hat{2}$ $\#\hat{7}$

f. $\hat{1}$ $\hat{5}$ $\hat{8}$ $\hat{3}$ ❋ $\hat{2}$ $\hat{4}$ $\#\hat{7}$ $\hat{2}$ ❋ $\hat{1}$ $\hat{4}$ $\#\hat{7}$ $\hat{2}$ ❋ $\hat{1}$ $\hat{3}$ $\hat{8}$ $\hat{1}$

g. $\hat{1}$ $\hat{5}$ $\hat{8}$ $\hat{3}$ ❋ $\hat{5}$ $\#\hat{7}$ $\hat{2}$ $\hat{4}$ ❋ $\hat{1}$ $\hat{5}$ $\hat{2}$ $\hat{4}$ ❋ $\hat{1}$ $\hat{5}$ $\hat{8}$ $\hat{3}$

QUICK SWITCH

Q25–1.

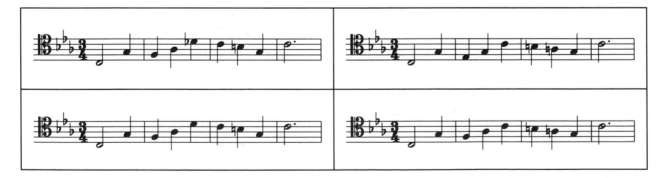

Q25–2.

Q25–3.

Q25–4.

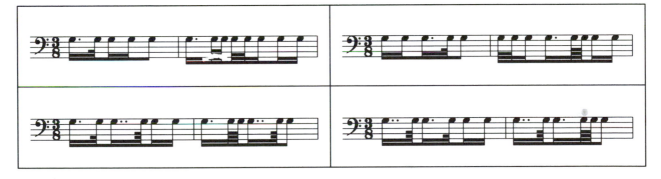

IDENTIFICATIONS

ID25–1.   An interval not larger than a perfect fifteenth is performed melodically or as a simultaneity. Identify it.

ID25–2. What chord occurs at **X**? Suitable choices are listed below.

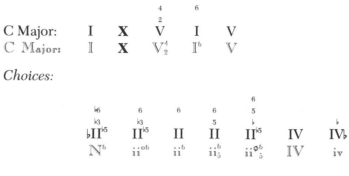

Choices:

ID25–3. What chord occurs at **Y**? Suitable choices are listed below.

Choices:

ID25–4. A melody is performed. Identify the correct score notation.

a.

b.

c.

d.

e.

f.

ID25–5.   A chord progression in the major mode is performed. Identify a suitable Roman-numeral/figured-bass analysis from among the following choices:

<u>Group 1</u>

a.   I   VI   II^6 V^7 I   a.   I   vi   ii^6 V^7 I

b.   I   VI   II$^6_{\flat5}$ V^7 I   b.   I   vi   ii$^{\circ6}$ V^7 I

c.   I $\flat$VI$^{\flat5}$ $\flat$II$^{\flat6}_{\flat5}$ V^7 I   c.   I $\flat$VI   N^6 V^7 I

d.   I $\flat$VI$^{\flat5}$ II$^6_{\flat5}$ V^7 I   d.   I $\flat$VI   ii$^{\circ6}$ V^7 I

<u>Group 2</u>

a.   I   V $\curvearrowright$ $\flat$II$^{\flat6\;\flat5}_{\flat5\;4\;\flat2}$ —— $^{6\;7}_{5\;6}$ V —— I   a.   I   V^7/N   N $^4_2$ V$^6_5$ $^{13}_7$ I

b.   I   V$^7_{5\sharp}$ $\curvearrowright$ II —— $^6_4\,^7_5\,_2$ V —— I   b.   I   V^7/ii   ii $^4_2$ V$^6_5$ $^{13}_7$ I

c.   I   V $\curvearrowright$ $\flat$II$^{\flat6\;\flat5}_{\flat5\;4\;\flat2}$ —— $^{6\;9}_{5\;7}$ V —— I   c.   I   V^7/N   N $^4_2$ V$^6_5$ $^9_7$ I

d.   I   V$^7_{5\sharp}$ $\curvearrowright$ II —— $^6_4\,^9_5\,_2$ V —— I   d.   I   V^7/ii   ii $^4_2$ V$^6_5$ $^9_7$ I

ID25–6.   A chord progression in the minor mode is performed. Identify a suitable Roman-numeral/figured-bass analysis from among the following choices:

Group 1

a.   I   V$\smile$ $\flat$II———   V$\sharp$—   I   a.   i   V$^6_5$/N   N ^{6} V$^{6-5}_{4-3}$ i

b.   I   VII$^{\flat7}\smile$ $\flat$II———   V$\sharp$—   I   b.   i   vii^{o7}/N   N ^{6} V$^{6-5}_{4-3}$ i

c.   I   V$\smile$ $\flat$II———   V$\sharp$—   I   c.   i   V^6/N   N ^{6} V$^{6-5}_{4-3}$ i

d.   I   V$\smile$ $\flat$II———   V$\sharp$—   I$\sharp$ d.   i   V$^6_5$/N   N ^{6} V$^{6-4}_{4-3}$ I

Group 2

a.   I   II   V$\sharp$ I—   a.   i   ii$^{\o6}_5$ V^7 i$^{9-8}_{4-3}$

b.   I   II   V$\sharp$ I—   b.   i   ii$^{\o6}_5$ V^7 i$^{9-8}_{7-8}_{4-3}$

c.   I   II   V$\sharp$ I—   c.   i   ii$^{\o6}_5$ V^7 i$^{7-8}_{4-3}$

d.   I   II   V$\sharp$ I—   d.   i   ii$^{\o6}_5$ V^7 i$^{4-3}$

ID25-7. A chord progression is performed. Identify the correct score notation for the outer voices. Figured-bass symbols have been placed below the bass where appropriate. If you wish, add Roman numerals.

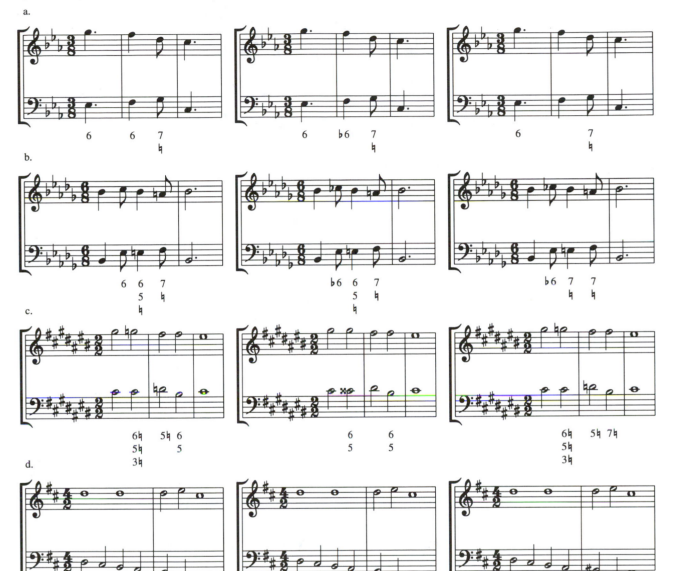

e.

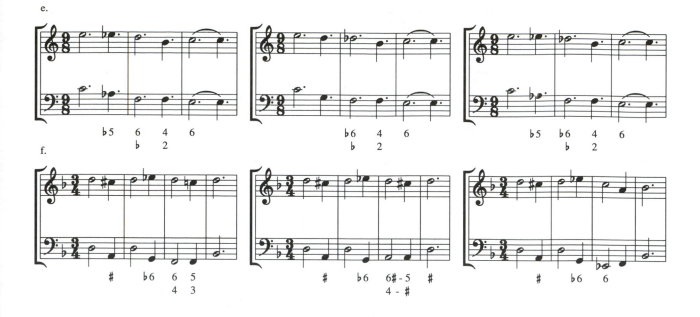

f.

RHYTHMIC DICTATIONS

RD25–1.

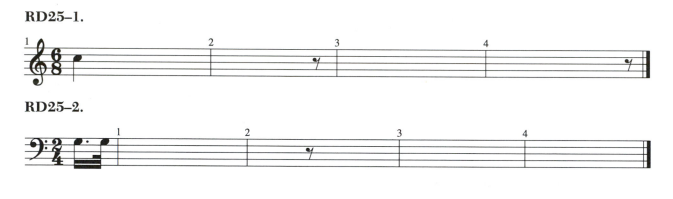

RD25–2.

MELODIC DICTATIONS

ROSSINI: *WILLIAM TELL*, ACT 3

MD25–1.

Allegretto

- What scale degree is the first pitch of measure 3? What scale degree is the first pitch of measure 4? Use this information to decide what pitch occurs on beat 2 of measure 3.

SCHUBERT: PIANO SONATA IN B♭ MAJOR, D. 960, MVMT. 4

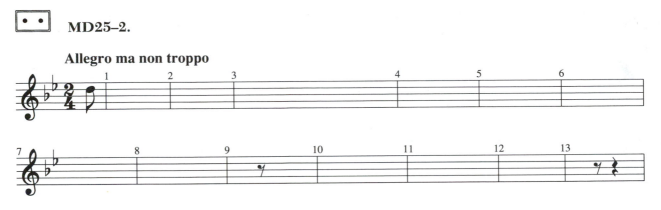

MD25–2.

- What interval is formed by the pitches of measure 12? Compare those pitches with the second and fourth pitches of measure 8.

CHOPIN: MAZURKA, OP. 41, NO. 2

MD25–3.

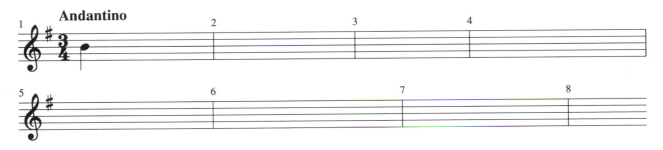

- How do measures 3 and 4 relate to measures 1 and 2? How do measures 5 and 6 relate to measures 1 and 2? Which measure serves as a model for measure 7?

BEETHOVEN: PIANO SONATA NO. 28 IN A MAJOR, OP. 101, MVMT. 3

MD25–4.

- The G♯ that begins measure 2 resolves to A. The G♯ that begins measure 4 passes through A to B (the last pitch of measure 4).

SCHUBERT: SONATA FOR ARPEGGIONE AND PIANO IN A MINOR, D. 821, MVMT. 1

MD25–5.

Allegro moderato

· Follow the descending line E (measures 3 and 4), D (measure 5), C (measure 6; an octave higher in measure 7), B♭ (measure 7), A (measure 8).

SCHUMANN: SYMPHONY NO. 4 IN D MINOR, OP. 120, MVMT. 3

MD25–6.

Lebhaft

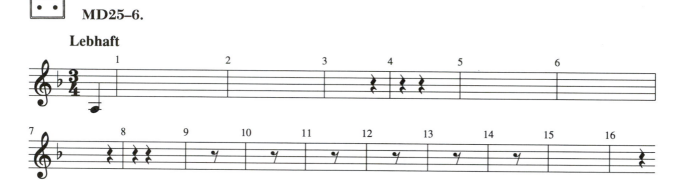

· The numerous leaps in measures 9 through 16 will be less problematic if you consider which intervals are dissonant and which are consonant. The interval of measure 9 resolves to the interval of measure 10; the interval of measure 11 resolves to the interval of measure 12; the interval of measure 14 resolves to the interval implied in measure 15. (A B♮ is understood in measure 15. Why?)

HARMONIC DICTATIONS

SCHUBERT: PIANO SONATA IN A MINOR, D. 845, OP. 42, MVMT. 2

HD25–1.

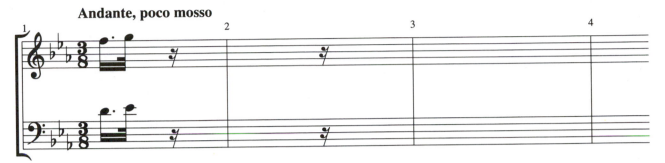

- The pitches F, G, and A♭ are juxtaposed on beat 2 of measure 1. Analyze the sonority as the third inversion of a dominant ninth chord.

- Measure 3 begins with a 7-6 suspension (in the alto) that embellishes the Neapolitan chord in $^6_4$ position.

BEETHOVEN: PIANO SONATA NO. 14 IN C♯ MINOR, OP. 27, NO. 2, MVMT. 1

HD25–2.

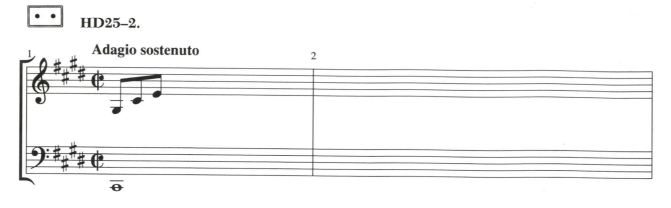

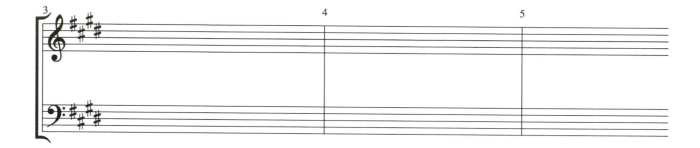

- A $^6_4$ chord often precedes the cadential dominant. In measure 4, a $^6_4$ chord comes between two dominant chords. The sixth and the fourth do not lead downward to the fifth and third at the same time.

SCHUBERT: PIANO SONATA IN G MAJOR, D. 894, OP. 78, MVMT. 2

HD25–3.

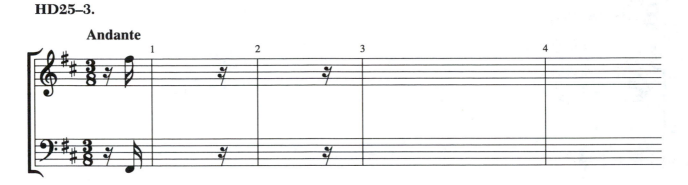

· Regard beat 2 of measure 3 as a passing chord, connecting two dominant harmonies.

BEETHOVEN: PIANO SONATA NO. 6 IN F MAJOR, OP. 10, NO. 2, MVMT. 2

HD25–4.

Allegretto

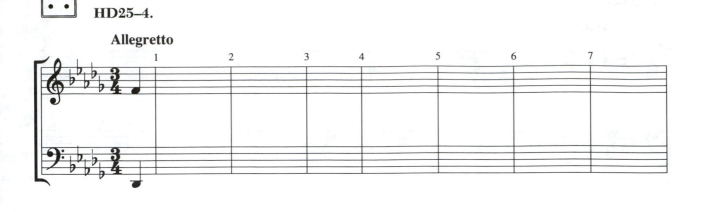

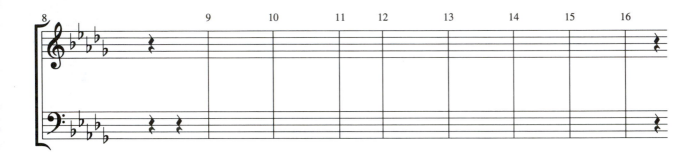

· The natural required for the last pitch of measure 8 is a subtle hint that a modulation is about to occur.

· Regard measure 10 as a passing chord, connecting the dominant preparation chord of measure 9 and the inverted dominant seventh chord of measures 11 and 12.

GLUCK: *IPHIGENIA IN TAURIS*, ACT 3

HD25–5.

Andante poco lento

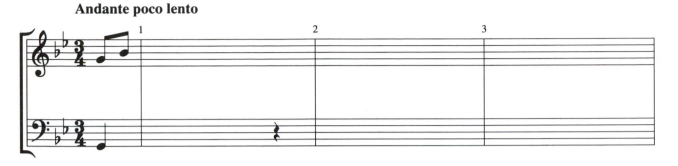

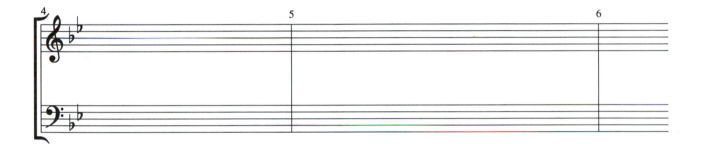

· Both a seventh (raised) and a ninth are suspended on beat 1 of measure 4. Does the upward resolution of the 7-8 suspension affect the resolution of the ninth?

SCHUBERT: *FIERRABRAS*, D. 796, ACT 1

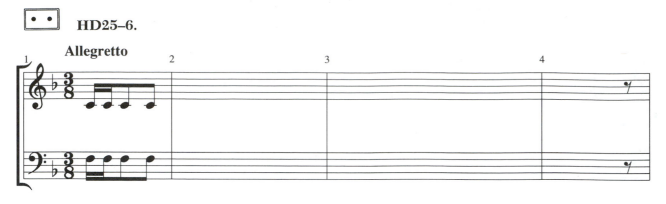

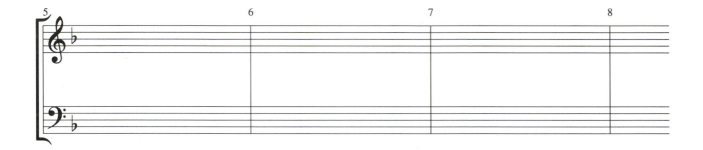

· Measure 6 contains an applied chord that would typically resolve to G minor in $^6_3$ position (supertonic). Measure 7, beat 1, supplies the expected bass pitch, B♭. However, the chord that resides there is in $^5_3$ position (subdominant).

⊡ CASSETTE PROGRAM
(TAPE 4, SIDE B)

C25–1. Six melodies are performed, twice each. During the silence after each playing, respond in one of the following ways: (1) Sing the melody, using solmization syllables; (2) Play the melody on the piano or on your primary instrument; (3) Write the melody on staff paper.

C25–2. Six chord progressions are performed, four times each. During the silence after each playing, respond in one of the following ways: (1) Sing the soprano after the first and second playings and the bass after the third and fourth playings, using solmization syllables; (2) Play the soprano on the piano or your primary instrument after the first and second playings and the bass after the third and fourth playings; (3) Play both the soprano and bass on the piano after each playing; (4) Write the soprano and bass on staff paper and provide an analysis.

Chapter 26

PITCH

The ***Italian***, ***French***, and ***German augmented sixth chords*** are similar in structure and function to the dominant's applied dominant and leading-tone chords. Their sound is distinctive because an augmented sixth cannot be formed from the diatonic pitches of either major or minor keys. In minor keys, augmented sixth chords share the applied chords' ♯$\hat{4}$, but with diatonic $\hat{6}$ rather than ♯$\hat{6}$. Example 26–1 demonstrates that each augmented sixth chord requires only one accidental, whereas the dominant's applied chords require two. In Method One analysis, the abbreviations "It.," "Fr.," and "Ger." are employed. In Method Two analysis, the symbols It⁺⁶, Fr⁺⁶, and Ger⁺⁶ are employed.

EXAMPLE 26–1

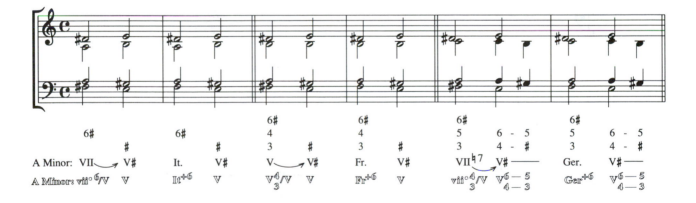

In major keys, at least two accidentals are required for each augmented sixth chord, as shown in Example 26–2. The German augmented sixth chord typically resolves to a dominant embellished by a cadential $^6_4$, to avoid parallel fifths. In major, it is usually spelled using ♯$\hat{2}$ rather than ♭$\hat{3}$ (D♯ rather than E♭ in Ex. 26–2), because ♯$\hat{2}$-$\hat{3}$ coordinates better with ♯$\hat{4}$-$\hat{5}$ than does ♭$\hat{3}$-♮$\hat{3}$.

EXAMPLE 26–2

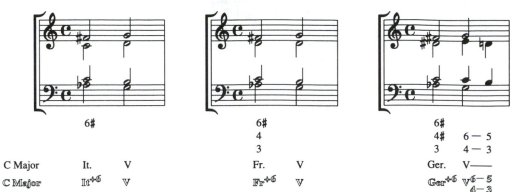

Chromaticized sequences

C Major: It+6   V   Fr+6   V   Ger+6   V6—5
                                                        4—3

Chromaticized sequences make use of the same techniques that convert the supertonic into the dominant's applied dominant or the mediant into the submediant's applied dominant. The tendency for forward motion, already strong in a sequence, becomes even stronger. Example 26–3 shows diatonic and chromaticized models for the descending fifths, descending 5-6, and ascending 5-6 sequences. The ascending fifths sequence does not readily accommodate chromatic alteration.

EXAMPLE 26–3

Descending fifths: Diatonic

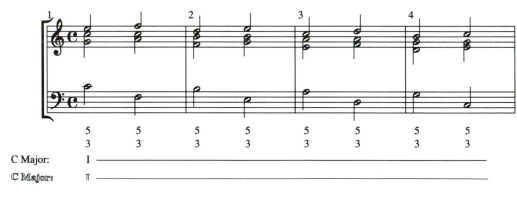

Descending fifths: Chromatic

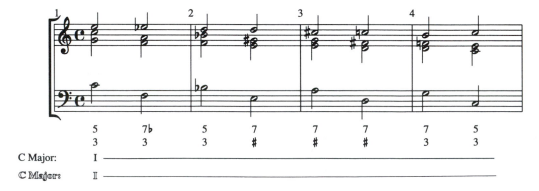

Descending 5-6: Diatonic

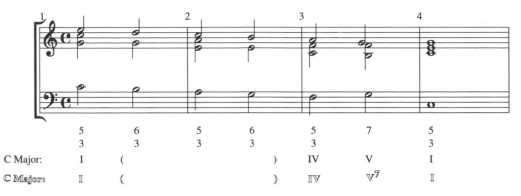

Descending 5-6: Chromatic

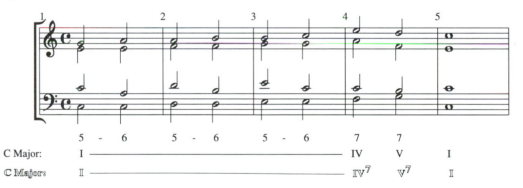

Ascending 5-6: Diatonic

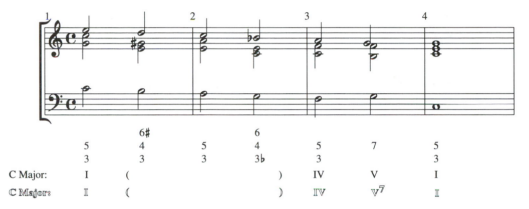

Ascending 5-6: Chromatic

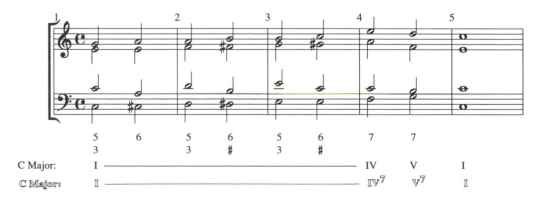

Multiple suspensions that embellish non-tonic chords are emphasized in this chapter. Example 26–4 shows a context in which the pitches C, D, E, and F sound at the same time. In isolation this sonority hardly belongs within the domain of tonal music, but in this specific context, with the careful preparation and resolution that the C and E receive, the sonority is very beautiful. Throughout this text you have been encouraged to listen not only for the *factual description* of a sonority, but also for its *contextual meaning*. "Listening" without awareness is like hearing a poem in a language you do not understand. The words may have a sonorous beauty, and the interpreter may spark emotions in you, but you have not begun to understand the poem. Listening *with* awareness, and performing with awareness, lead you closer to the feeling, inspiration, and joy that for centuries have been the delight of those who know music.

EXAMPLE 26–4

METER AND RHYTHM

Most music of the eighteenth and nineteenth centuries is written in one of the eleven meters that have been employed throughout this text. **Less common meters** contrast these meters either in the number of beats per measure or in the note value that represents the beat. Use your understanding of the eleven common meters to determine how to perform and listen to any less common meter that you encounter. For example, $\frac{5}{4}$ meter resembles $\frac{4}{4}$ meter, but with five rather than four beats per measure; $\frac{2}{8}$ meter resembles $\frac{3}{8}$ meter, but with two rather than three beats per measure; and $\frac{6}{16}$ and $\frac{12}{16}$ meters are similar to $\frac{6}{8}$ and $\frac{12}{8}$ meters, except that a dotted eighth note, rather than a dotted quarter note, fills one beat.

A simple-meter beat is often divided into two (♫), three (♪♪♪), or four (♬♬) parts. **Quintuplets** (♬♬♬) occur when the beat is divided into five parts. Just as triplets use the same note value as the division into two parts (e.g., eighth notes in $\frac{4}{4}$ meter or quarter notes in $\frac{2}{2}$ meter), quintuplets use the same note value as the division into four parts (e.g., sixteenth notes in $\frac{4}{4}$ meter or eighth notes in $\frac{2}{2}$ meter). Example 26–5 demonstrates their use.

EXAMPLE 26–5

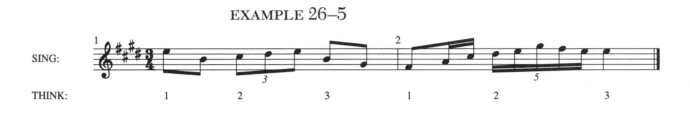

SOLO MELODIES

MELODIES THAT FOLLOW THE CONTOUR OF A CHROMATICIZED SEQUENCE

MOZART: STRING QUARTET NO. 17 IN B♭ MAJOR ("HUNTING"), K. 458, MVMT. 3

S26–1.

- The third note of measure 1, the third note of measure 2, and the sixth note of measure 3 all function as leading tones. Which one leads to the excerpt's tonic pitch?

BIZET: *CARMEN*, ACT 2

S26–2.

MELODIES THAT EMPLOY A LESS COMMON METER

MENDELSSOHN: SONG WITHOUT WORDS, OP. 67, NO. 2 (BOOK 6)

S26–3.

- Compare the first five pitches of the excerpt (A-A-B-C♯-D) with the passage starting in the middle of measure 2 (F♯-F♯-G♯-A-?). The C♯ on beat 1 of measure 3 is accented, and it is slurred to the following B. Which of those two pitches embellishes the other one?

BEETHOVEN: PIANO SONATA NO. 31 IN A♭ MAJOR, OP. 110, MVMT. 3

S26–4.

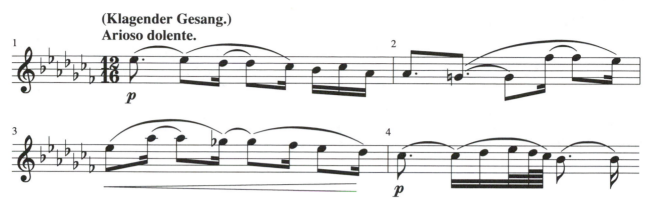

BRAHMS: SYMPHONY NO. 3 IN F MAJOR, OP. 90, MVMT. 1

S26–5.

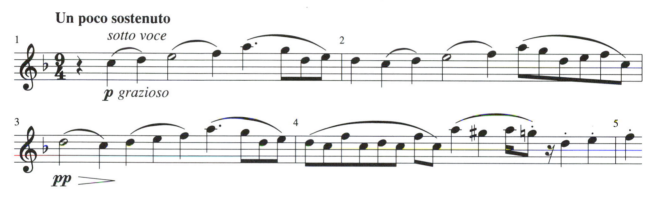

- Why does F sometimes follow immediately after the leading tone, E, and sometimes not?

BERLIOZ: *LA DAMNATION DE FAUST*, OP. 24, PART 2

S26–6.

MELODIES THAT EMPLOY QUINTUPLETS

CHOPIN: PIANO SONATA NO. 3 IN B MINOR, OP. 58, MVMT. 3

S26–7.

- In this excerpt, quintuplets fill two beats. Five eighth notes occur in the time that would normally be filled by four eighth notes.

DVOŘÁK: SYMPHONY NO. 9 IN E MINOR ("FROM THE NEW WORLD"), OP. 95, MVMT. 2

S26–8.

CHOPIN: PRELUDE, OP. 28, NO. 13

S26–9.

- Quintuplets may occur in compound as well as in simple meters. In this excerpt, five quarter notes occur in the time that would normally be filled by three quarter notes.

BRAHMS: SYMPHONY NO. 3 IN F MAJOR, OP. 90, MVMT. 3

S26–10.

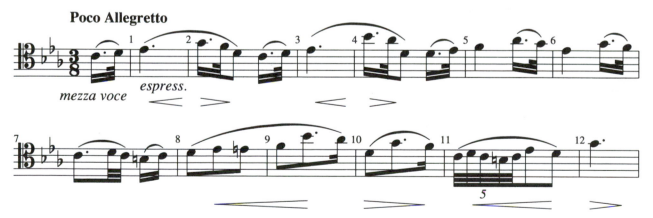

DUETS

AFTER VIVALDI: CONCERTO IN F MAJOR (“THE FOUR SEASONS: AUTUMN”), RV 293, OP. 8, NO. 3 MVMT. 1

D26–1.

AFTER SCHUBERT: SYMPHONY NO. 9 IN C MAJOR (“THE GREAT”), D. 944, MVMT. 4

D26–2.

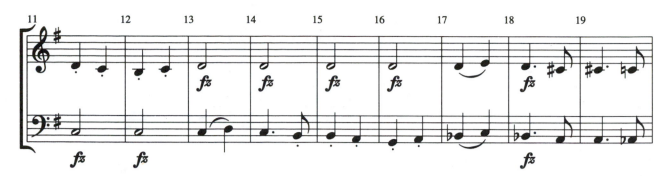

AFTER TCHAIKOVSKY: SYMPHONY NO. 1 IN G MINOR ("WINTER REVERIES"), OP. 13, MVMT. 4

D26–3.

ACCOMPANIED SOLO MELODIES

AFTER HAYDN: SYMPHONY NO. 94 IN G MAJOR ("SURPRISE"), MVMT. 3

AS26–1.

AFTER HAYDN: *THE CREATION*, PART 3

AS26–2.

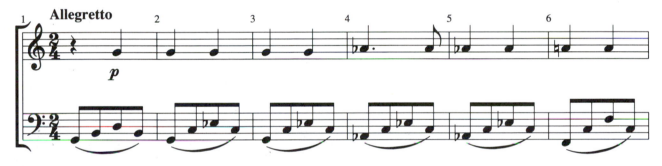

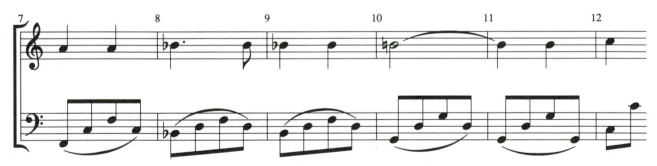

AFTER BRAHMS: STRING QUARTET NO. 3 IN B♭ MAJOR, OP. 67, MVMT. 1

AS26–3.

RHYTHMS

R26–1.

R26–2.

R26–3.

R26–4.

R26–6.

ARPEGGIATION WORKSHOP

A26–1.   Play a pitch that is at least a perfect fifth above the lowest note of your vocal range at a keyboard. Let this pitch be $\hat{1}$ in a major key. Sing each of the following arpeggiations, either in the order given or in random order.

a. $\hat{1}$ $\hat{3}$ $\hat{5}$ $\hat{1}$. ❀ $\hat{4}$ $\hat{6}$ $\hat{3}$ $\hat{5}$ ❀ $\hat{4}$ $\hat{6}$ $\hat{2}$ $\hat{4}$ ❀ $\hat{5}$ $\hat{7}$ $\hat{2}$ $\hat{4}$ ❀
          $\hat{1}$ $\hat{3}$ $\hat{1}$

b. $\hat{1}$ $\hat{3}$ $\hat{5}$ $\hat{1}$ ❀ $\hat{5}$ $\hat{7}$ $\hat{2}$ $\hat{4}$ ❀ $\hat{6}$ $\hat{2}$ $\hat{4}$ ❀ $\hat{6}$ $\hat{1}$ $\hat{3}$ ❀
          $\hat{4}$ $\hat{6}$ $\hat{1}$ $\hat{2}$ ❀ $\hat{5}$ $\hat{7}$ $\hat{2}$ ❀ $\hat{1}$ $\hat{5}$ $\hat{3}$ $\hat{1}$

c. 1̂ 3̂ 5̂ 1̂ ✤ ₇2̂ 3̂ ♯5̂ ✤ ₆1̂ 3̂ 6̂ ✤ ₅5̂ ♭₇7̂ 1̂ 3̂ ✤
     ₄4̂ ₆6̂ 1̂ ₄4̂ ✤ ₅5̂ ₇7̂ 2̂ ₅5̂ ✤ 1̂ ₅5̂ 3̂ 1̂

d. 1̂ 3̂ 5̂ 1̂ ✤ ₆6̂ 1̂ 4̂ ₆6̂ ✤ ♭₆6̂ 1̂ ♯4̂ 1̂ ✤ ₅5̂ ₇7̂ 2̂ 5̂ ✤
     1̂ 3̂ 5̂ 1̂

e. 1̂ 3̂ 5̂ 1̂ ✤ ₆6̂ 1̂ 4̂ ₆6̂ ✤ ♭₆6̂ 1̂ 2̂ ♯4̂ ✤ ₅5̂ ₇7̂ 2̂ 5̂ ✤
     1̂ 3̂ 5̂ 1̂

f. 1̂ 3̂ 5̂ 1̂ ✤ ₆6̂ 1̂ 2̂ 4̂ ✤ ♭₆6̂ 1̂ ♯2̂ ♯4̂ ✤ ₅5̂ 1̂ 3̂ 5̂ ✤
     ₅5̂ ₇7̂ 2̂ 4̂ ✤ 3̂ 5̂ 3̂ 1̂

A26–2.   Play a pitch that is at least a perfect fifth above the lowest note of your vocal range at a keyboard. Let this pitch be 1̂ in a minor key. Sing each of the following arpeggiations, either in the order given or in random order.

a. 1̂ 3̂ 5̂ 1̂ ✤ ₄4̂ ₆6̂ 3̂ 5̂ ✤ ₄4̂ ₆6̂ 2̂ 4̂ ✤ ₅5̂ ♯₇7̂ 2̂ 4̂ ✤
     1̂ 3̂ 1̂

b. 1̂ 3̂ 5̂ 1̂ ✤ ₅5̂ ♯₇7̂ 2̂ 4̂ ✤ ₆6̂ 2̂ 4̂ ✤ ₆6̂ 1̂ 3̂ ✤
     ♯₄4̂ ♯₆6̂ 1̂ 2̂ ✤ ₅5̂ ♯₇7̂ 2̂ ✤ 1̂ ₅5̂ 3̂ 1̂

c. 1̂ 3̂ 5̂ 1̂ ✤ ₇7̂ ♭2̂ 3̂ 5̂ ✤ ₆6̂ 1̂ 3̂ 6̂ ✤ ₅5̂ ₇7̂ 1̂ ♯3̂ ✤
     ₄4̂ ₆6̂ 1̂ ₄4̂ ✤ ₅5̂ ♯₇7̂ 2̂ ₅5̂ ✤ 1̂ ₅5̂ 3̂ 1̂

d. 1̂ 3̂ 5̂ 1̂ ✤ ₆6̂ 1̂ 4̂ ₆6̂ ✤ ₆6̂ 1̂ ♯4̂ 1̂ ✤ ₅5̂ ♯₇7̂ 2̂ 5̂ ✤
     1̂ 3̂ 5̂ 1̂

e. 1̂ 3̂ 5̂ 1̂ ✤ ₆6̂ 1̂ 4̂ ₆6̂ ✤ ₆6̂ 1̂ 2̂ ♯4̂ ✤ ₅5̂ ♯₇7̂ 2̂ 5̂ ✤
     1̂ 3̂ 5̂ 1̂

f. 1̂ 3̂ 5̂ 1̂ ✤ ₆6̂ 1̂ 2̂ 4̂ ✤ ₆6̂ 1̂ 3̂ ♯4̂ ✤ ₅5̂ 1̂ 3̂ 5̂ ✤
     ₅5̂ ♯₇7̂ 2̂ 4̂ ✤ 3̂ 5̂ 3̂ 1̂

QUICK SWITCH

Q26–1.

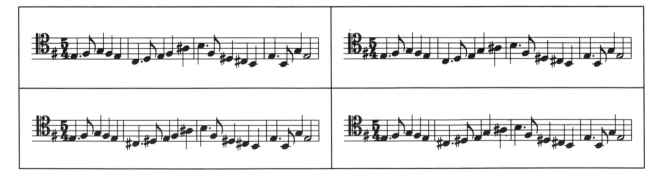

Q26–2.

Q26–3.

Q26–4.

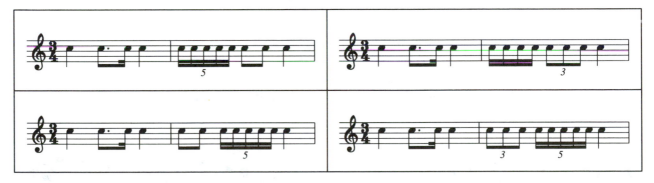

IDENTIFICATIONS

ID26–1.   An augmented sixth chord is performed. Indicate whether it is a French, German, or Italian augmented sixth chord.

ID26–2.   What chord occurs at **X**? Suitable choices are listed below.

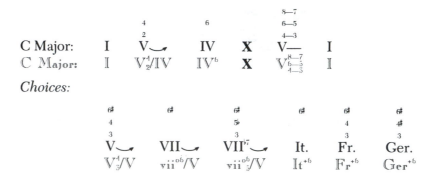

Choices:

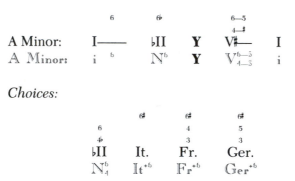

ID26–3.   What chord occurs at **Y**? Suitable choices are listed below.

Choices:

ID26–4.   A melody is performed. Identify the correct score notation.

a.   b.

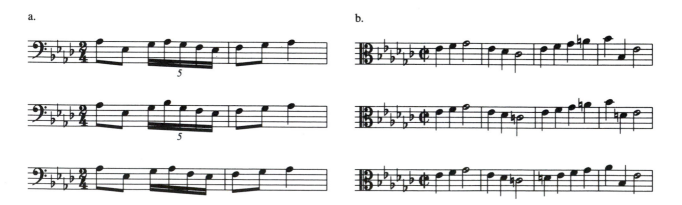

ID26–5. A chord progression in the major mode is performed. Identify a suitable Roman-numeral/figured-bass analysis from among the following choices:

Group 1

a. $\quad$ I $\quad$ V$\overset{6}{\underset{5\flat}{}}\searrow$ IV $\quad$ It. $\overset{6\sharp}{}$ $\quad$ V $\qquad$ a. $\quad$ I $\quad$ V$^{6}_{3}$/IV $\quad$ IV $\quad$ It^{+6} $\quad$ V

b. $\quad$ I $\quad$ V$\overset{6}{\underset{5\flat}{}}\searrow$ IV $\quad$ Fr. $\overset{6\sharp}{\underset{4}{3}}$ $\quad$ V $\qquad$ b. $\quad$ I $\quad$ V$^{6}_{3}$/IV $\quad$ IV $\quad$ Fr^{+6} $\quad$ V

c. $\quad$ I $\quad$ V$\overset{6}{\underset{5\flat}{}}\searrow$ IV $\quad$ V$\overset{6\sharp}{\underset{4}{3}}\searrow$ V $\qquad$ c. $\quad$ I $\quad$ V$^{6}_{3}$/IV $\quad$ IV $\quad$ V$^{4}_{3}$/V $\quad$ V

d. $\quad$ I $\quad$ V$\overset{6}{\underset{5\flat}{}}\searrow$ IV $\quad$ VII $\overset{6\sharp}{}$ $\quad$ V $\qquad$ d. $\quad$ I $\quad$ V$^{6}_{3}$/IV $\quad$ IV $\quad$ vii$^{\circ6}$/V $\quad$ V

Group 2

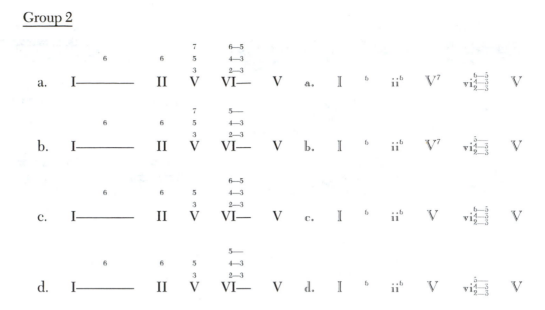

ID26–6.　　A chord progression in the minor mode is performed. Identify a suitable Roman-numeral/figured-bass analysis from among the following choices:

Group 1

a. I V#↘IV— V#— I—　a. i^6 V^6_5/iv iv^{9-8}_{4-5} V^6_5 $^9_7$ i^{6-5}_{4-5}

b. I V#↘IV— V#— I—　b. i^6 V^6_5/iv iv^{4-5} V^6_5 $^9_7$ i^{6-5}_{4-5}

c. I V#↘IV— V#— I—　c. i^6 V^6_5/iv iv^{9-8} V^6_5 $^9_7$ i^{6-5}_{4-5}

d. I V#↘IV— V#— I—　d. i^6 V^6_5/iv iv^{9-8}_{4-5} V^6_5 $^9_7$ i^{5-}_{4-5}

Group 2

ID26–7.   A chord progression is performed. Identify the correct score notation for the outer voices. Figured-bass symbols have been placed below the bass where appropriate. If you wish, add Roman numerals.

d.

e.

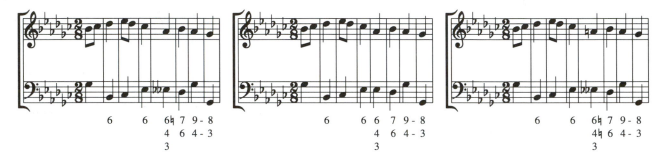

f.

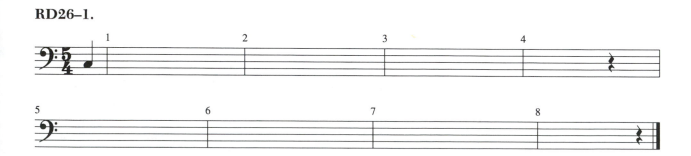

RHYTHMIC DICTATIONS

RD26–1.

RD26–2.

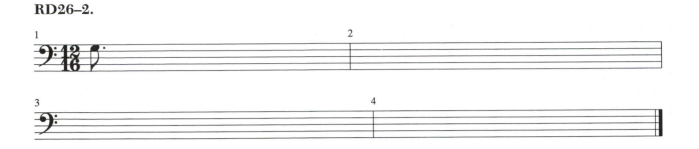

MELODIC DICTATIONS

BEETHOVEN: PIANO SONATA NO. 32 IN C MINOR, OP. 111, MVMT. 2

MD26–1.

Adagio molto semplice e cantabile.

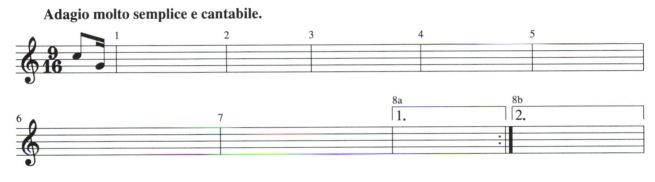

· What do the first pitch of measure 4 and the first pitch of measure 6 have in common?

PUCCINI: *LA BOHÈME*, ACT 1

MD26–2.

Allegretto mosso

· Though this melody is structured symmetrically around the pitch C, it is in the key of F major.

TCHAIKOVSKY: SYMPHONY NO. 6 IN B MINOR ("PATHÉTIQUE"), OP. 74, MVMT. 2

MD26–3.

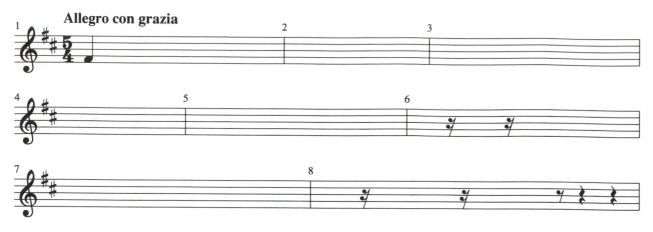

· The third beats of measures 1, 3, 5, and 7 contain a neighboring-note motive. Some of the neighbors are lower neighbors, while others are upper neighbors. In measures 6 and 8, both upper and lower neighbors are employed.

GRIEG: PIANO CONCERTO IN A MINOR, OP. 16, MVMT. 1

 **MD26–4.**

· Grieg descends using diatonic pitches C-B-A-G in measures 1 and 2. In measure 3 he employs B♭ and A♭. What interval is outlined during beat 2 of measure 4? What is the relationship between the first pitch of measure 4, beat 2, and the pitch of measure 4, beat 3?

VIVALDI: CONCERTO IN F MAJOR ("THE FOUR SEASONS: AUTUMN"), RV 293, OP. 8, NO. 3, MVMT. 3

MD26–5.

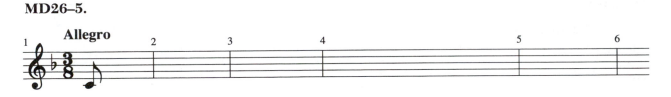

- Augmented sixth chords sometimes resolve to tonic. In this melody, Vivaldi outlines a German augmented sixth chord whose augmented sixth G♭-E♮ resolves to an F-F octave on tonic.

VIVALDI: CONCERTO IN E MAJOR ("THE FOUR SEASONS: SPRING"), RV 269, OP. 8, NO. 1, MVMT. 3

MD26–6.

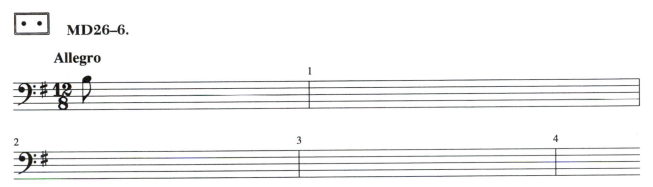

- The sequence outlined in this melody is not uniformly chromaticized. Listen especially for pitches that function as leading tones. For example, the third pitch before the first bar line is the leading tone of the chord outlined in the first half of measure 1. Yet the fourth pitch of measure 1 is not the leading tone of the chord outlined in the second half of measure 1.

HARMONIC DICTATIONS

GOUNOD: *FAUST*, ACT 2

HD26–1.

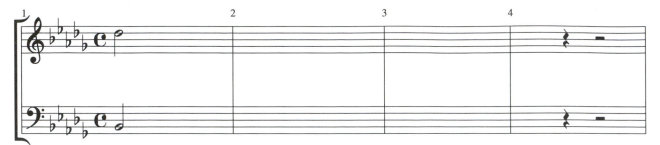

· The second chord of measure 2 would be a likely spot for the descending fifths sequence to end. How does Gounod prevent that from happening?

SCHUBERT: PIANO SONATA IN G MAJOR, D. 894, OP. 78, MVMT. 3

HD26–2.

Allegro moderato

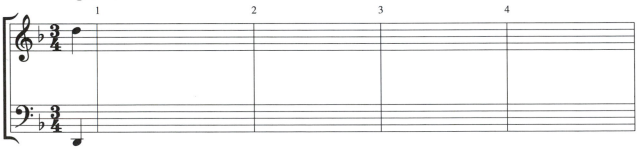

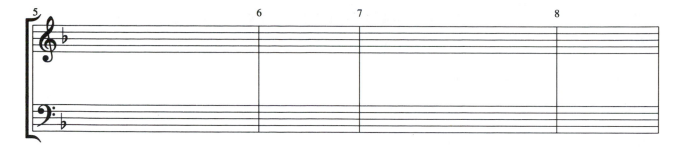

- One of the two augmented sixth chords of this excerpt is of the German type. The dominant harmony that follows is not embellished by a cadential $^6_4$ chord. Schubert prevents parallel fifths by leaping from $\hat{3}$ down to $\sharp\hat{7}$ ($\hat{3}$–$\sharp\hat{7}$ instead of $\hat{3}$–$\hat{2}$).

J. S. BACH: SUITE FOR UNACCOMPANIED CELLO NO. 4 IN E♭ MAJOR, BWV 1010, SARABANDE

HD26–3.

- Double suspensions occur twice within this excerpt: measure 2, beat 1, and measure 4, beat 1.

BRAHMS: SONATA FOR VIOLIN AND PIANO NO. 3 IN D MINOR, OP. 108, MVMT. 3

HD26–4.

Un poco presto e con sentimento

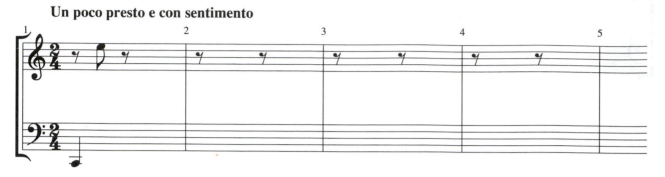

- The sequence of this excerpt leads downward from mediant to tonic.

- During a chromaticized descending fifths sequence, the position of the diminished-fifth or augmented-fourth leap may not coincide with the diatonic norm. (In A minor, it would typically occur between F and B.) In measure 2 Brahms lowers B to B♭, avoiding the diminished B-D-F chord altogether.

BEETHOVEN: PIANO SONATA NO. 10 IN G MAJOR, OP. 14, NO. 2, MVMT. 2

HD26–5.

Andante

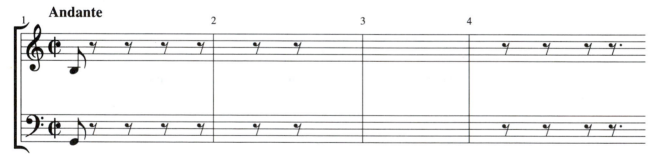

- Among the seven chords of measures 1 and 2, only the second, sixth and seventh should be analyzed using a Roman numeral.

FIELD: NOCTURNE NO. 14 IN C MAJOR

 **HD26–6.**

Molto moderato

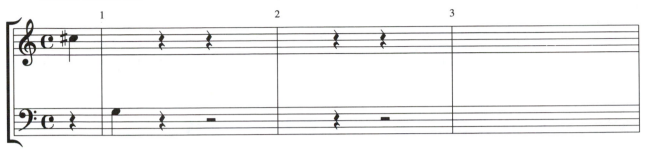

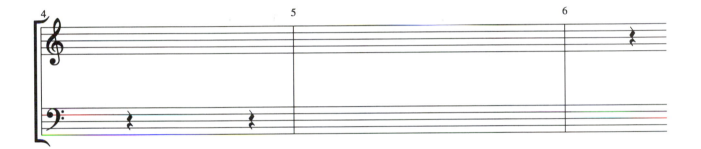

- On beat 2 of measure 4, tonic is converted into the subdominant's applied dominant. The seventh (B♭) is added, and the fifth is raised (G♯ replaces G). Both of these pitches are suspended when the subdominant root arrives on beat 3. What interval is formed by G♯ above B♭? How does this interval resolve?

- In Method Two analysis, show that the applied dominant of measure 4 is augmented by placing a plus (⁺) after the numeral V.

⟨··⟩ CASSETTE PROGRAM
(TAPE 4, SIDE B)

C26–1.   Six melodies are performed, twice each. During the silence after each playing, respond in one of the following ways: (1) Sing the melody, using solmization syllables; (2) Play the melody on the piano or on your primary instrument; (3) Write the melody on staff paper.

C26–2.   Six chord progressions are performed, four times each. During the silence after each playing, respond in one of the following ways: (1) Sing the soprano after the first and second playings and the bass after the third and fourth playings, using solmization syllables; (2) Play the soprano on the piano or your primary instrument after the first and second playings and the bass after the third and fourth playings; (3) Play both the soprano and bass on the piano after each playing; (4) Write the soprano and bass on staff paper and provide an analysis.

Appendix: Solmization Systems

SCALE DEGREES

Inflected

Major

♭	♮	#	
	one	raised	1̂
low	two	raised	2̂
low	three		3̂
	four	raised	4̂
low	five	raised	5̂
low	six	raised	6̂
low	sev		7̂
	eight (one)	raised	8̂

Minor

♭	♮	#	×	
low	one	raised		1̂
low	two			2̂
	three	raised		3̂
low	four	raised		4̂
low	five	raised		5̂
	six	raised	raised	6̂
low	sev	raised		7̂
low	eight (one)	raised		8̂

Uninflected

Major or Minor

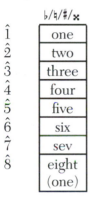

♭/♮/#/×	
one	1̂
two	2̂
three	3̂
four	4̂
five	5̂
six	6̂
sev	7̂
eight (one)	8̂

MOVABLE DO

Major

♭	♮	#	
	do	di	1̂
ra	re	ri	2̂
me	mi		3̂
	fa	fi	4̂
se	sol	si	5̂
le	la	li	6̂
te	ti		7̂
	do	di	8̂

Minor (Do = Tonic)

♭	♮	#	×	
de	do	di		1̂
ra	re			2̂
	me	mi		3̂
fe	fa	fi		4̂
se	sol	si		5̂
	le	la	li	6̂
tef	te	ti		7̂
de	do	di		8̂

Minor (La = Tonic)

♭	♮	#	×	
le	la	li		1̂
te	ti			2̂
	do	di		3̂
ra	re	ri		4̂
me	mi	mis		5̂
	fa	fi	fis	6̂
se	sol	si		7̂
le	la	li		8̂

FIXED DO

Inflected   *Uninflected*

♭♭	♭	♮	♯	𝄪		♭♭/♭/♮/♯/𝄪
def	de	do	di	dis	C	do
raf	ra	re	ri	ris	D	re
mef	me	mi	mis	misis	E	mi
fef	fe	fa	fi	fis	F	fa
sef	se	sol	si	sis	G	sol
lef	le	la	li	lis	A	la
tef	te	ti	tis	tisis	B	ti
def	de	do	di	dis	C	do

LETTER NAMES

Inflected   *Uninflected*

♭♭	♭	♮	♯	𝄪	♭♭/♭/♮/♯/𝄪
Ceses	Ces	C	Cis	Cisis	C
Deses	Des	D	Dis	Disis	D
Eses	Es	E	Eis	Eisis	E
Feses	Fes	F	Fis	Fisis	F
Geses	Ges	G	Gis	Gisis	G
Ases	As	A	Ais	Aisis	A
Beses	Bes	B	Bis	Bisis	B
Ceses	Ces	C	Cis	Cisis	C

Glossary

Adagio: Slow, leisurely.

Afflitto: Melancholy, sad.

Agitato: Agitated.

Alla: In the style of, like.

Allargate: Growing slower.

Allegrissimo: Very rapidly.

Allegretto: Quite lively; moderately fast (faster than *Andante*, slower than *Allegro*).

Allegro: Lively, brisk, rapid.

> *Allegro giusto:* A movement the rapidity of which is suited to its subject.

> *Allegro ma non troppo:* Rapidly, but not too fast.

> *Allegro moderato:* Moderately fast.

Andante: "Going," "moving"; a tempo mark indicating a moderately slow, easily flowing movement between *Adagio* and *Allegretto*.

> *Andante cantabile:* Flowingly, in a singing style.

> *Andante con moto:* A flowing and rather more animated movement.

Andantino: This word is a diminutive of *Andante*, and means, properly, a little slower than *Andante*; but it is often used as if meaning a little faster.

Anima or **Animato:** With spirit, spiritedly, vivaciously.

Appassionato: Impassioned, with passion.

Appena: Hardly, very little.

Assai: Very.

A tempo: In time; at the preceding rate of speed.

Bewegt: Moved, agitated.

Breit: Broadly.

Cantabile: "Singable"; in a singing or vocal style.

Cantando: Singing; smooth and flowing.

Con: With.

    Con alcuna licenza: "With a certain freedom" (as regards tempo).

    Con brio: "With noise" and gusto; spiritedly.

    Con fuoco: With fire, fiery, spirited.

Crescendo: Swelling, increasing in loudness.

Cupo: Dark, deep, obscure; reserved.

Decrescendo or *Diminuendo:* Diminishing in loudness.

Dolente: Doleful, plaintive, sad.

Doppio movimento: Twice as fast.

Dolce: Sweet, soft, suave.

E or *ed:* And.

Eilen: To hasten, accelerate, go faster.

Einfach: Simple; simply.

Espressivo: With expression, expressively.

Etwas: Rather, somewhat.

Fieramente: Wildly, boldly.

Geschwindt: Swift(ly), rapid(ly).

Giocoso: Playfully, sportively, merrily.

Grazioso: Gracefully, elegantly.

Kräftig: Forceful, vigorous, energetic.

Lamentoso: Lamentingly, plaintively, mournfully.

Langsam: Slow.

Larghetto: The diminutive of *Largo,* and demands a somewhat more rapid tempo, nearly *Andantino.*

Largo: Large, broad; the slowest tempo-mark, calling for a slow and stately movement with ample breadth of style.

Lebhaft: Lively, animated.

Legato: Bound, slurred; a direction to perform the passage in a smooth and connected manner, with no break between the tones.

Leggiero: Light, airy.

Lento: Slow; calls for a tempo between *Andante* and *Largo*.

Lo stesso movimento: The same movement.

Lugubre: Mournful.

Ma: But.

Maestoso: Majestic, dignified; in a style characterized by lofty breadth.

Marcato: With distinctness and emphasis.

Marziale: Martial, warlike.

Mässig: Measured; moderate.

Meno mosso: Not so fast.

Mezzo voce: "With half the power of the voice."

Moderato: Moderate; that is, at a moderate tempo, or rate of speed.

Molto: Very, much.

Mosso: Moved.

Non: Not.

Più: More.

Poco: Little.

Portando: "Carrying"; i.e., a smooth gliding from one tone to another, differing from the legato in its more deliberate execution.

Prestissimo: Very rapidly.

Presto: Fast, rapid; faster than *Allegro*.

Quasi: As if; as it were; nearly; approaching.

Rallentando: Growing slower and slower.

Ritardando: Growing slower and slower.

Ritenuto: Held back; at a slower rate of speed.

Rubato: "Robbed"; meaning "dwell on, and (often almost insensibly) prolong prominent melody tones or chords." This requires an equivalent acceleration of less prominent tones, which are thus "robbed" of a portion of their time value.

Ruhig: Quiet, calm, tranquil.

Scherzando: In a playful, sportive, toying manner; lightly, jestingly.

Schnell: Fast, quick, rapid.

Sehr: Very.

Semplice: In a simple, natural, unaffected style.

Sempre: Always, continually; throughout.

Sentimento: Feelingly.

Sostenuto: Sustained, prolonged. Standing alone, as a tempo-mark, it is much the same as *Andante cantabile.*

Sotto voce: In an undertone, aside, under the breath.

Staccato: Detached, separated; a style in which the notes played or sung are more or less abruptly disconnected.

Stringendo: Hastening, accelerating the movement, usually suddenly and rapidly, with a *Crescendo.*

Tranquillo: Tranquilly, quietly, calmly.

Troppo: Too, too much.

Vif: Lively.

Vivace: Lively, animated, brisk.

Vivo: Lively, spirited, briskly.

Voce: Voice; part.

Wenig: Little.

Zu: Too.

Excerpts from the *Schirmer Pronouncing Pocket Manual of Musical Terms,* edited by Theodore Baker, revised by Nicolas Slonimsky (Schirmer Books, 1978)

Index